Individual and Team Sports

for Girls and Women

Maryhelen Vannier, Ed.D.

PROFESSOR AND DIRECTOR OF THE WOMEN'S DIVISION,
DEPARTMENT OF HEALTH AND PHYSICAL EDUCATION,
SOUTHERN METHODIST UNIVERSITY, DALLAS, TEXAS.

Hally Beth Poindexter, Ed.D.

ASSISTANT PROFESSOR, DEPARTMENT OF HEALTH, PHYSICAL
EDUCATION, AND RECREATION, TEACHERS COLLEGE, COLUMBIA
UNIVERSITY, NEW YORK CITY, NEW YORK.

Illustrated by William Osburn

W. B. Saunders Company

1960   PHILADELPHIA   AND   LONDON

Reprinted March, 1962

This book is dedicated to

Marjorie Hillas

*who through her inspired leadership and masterful
teaching has made such a significant and lasting contribution to the development of individual and team sports
for the girls and women of America.*

Preface

This book is first of all a presentation of individual and team sports, and the role they can play in helping others live a fuller, more joyous life. Secondly, it is a book of methods for teaching these activities successfully.

It has been written largely for four groups: (1) the physical education major student in training to be a teacher; (2) the beginning and experienced teacher searching for productive ways to teach others to play games and sports more expertly and to enjoy doing so; (3) the individual player desirous of mastering the many refined and unique skills of her favorite games, and (4) the playground, community center, and other recreational leaders in camps or clubs seeking fresh methods and materials for conducting activities in a recreational setting.

The authors, both of whom have had a wide experience as secondary and college teachers, directors of teacher training programs in universities, and recreational leaders, believe that superior sports teaching methods can be mastered by those determined to develop them. They contend that instructors must be ever cognizant of *"teachable moments"* for character development which are inherent in most game situations; that they must be the skillful leader in the right place at the right time in these situations, in order to lead and inspire others to fulfill and carry out their present and future life goals and responsibilities as an individual and a democratic citizen.

The authors recognize that there are many ways of presenting an activity, and that real educators will find their own teaching method by the slow process of carefully blending the ingredients of theory, the techniques used by former admired instructors, and their own trial and error attempts. They can profit immeasurably by the many learning short cuts presented in this book and tailoring them to fit their own needs and teaching situations.

In the chapters for each sport the reader will find a description of the nature and purpose of the game, needed facilities and equipment, teaching units for beginning and advanced players and for rainy days, an analysis of the basic skills of each activity, plans for organizing large classes, a large variety of sample lesson plans showing clearly the steps of good teaching progression, a unique analysis of skill learning difficulties and their correction (which is presented both verbally and visually through unique illustrations unavailable in any other book of this kind), game strategy, the duties and specific responsibilities of each player, lead-up games and novelty events, officiating techniques for each sport, suggested skill and knowledge tests, game terminology, class discussion questions, as well as carefully screened and highly recommended audio-visual aids and suggested readings.

The techniques of teaching all skills described herein have been slanted to right-handed players. In general, left-handed students should perform them in the opposite way, and usually will automatically do so when they see a demonstration of correct form they are to copy.

The sports guides of The Division for Girls and Women's Sports of the American Association of Health, Physical Education, and Recreation are essential supplements of this text. All teachers and coaches using this text should receive locally, and preferably nationally, DGWS ratings as trained and approved game officials.

Dallas, Texas   MARYHELEN VANNIER
New York City   HALLY BETH POINDEXTER

Acknowledgements

The authors are indebted to many persons who have made this book possible. To Lloyd Messersmith, Steve Brown, and all the women staff members of the Deparment of Health and Physical Education of Southern Methodist University; John Hutchinson of Teachers College, Columbia University; Sue Garrison of The University of Houston and numerous other professional colleagues and students, we wish to express our appreciation for their inspiration, suggestions and reactions to the material in this book. Mrs. Wanda Joyner and Mrs. Mabel Montgomery typed the manuscript. Carl Troester, Rachael Bryant, and Jane Mott of the AAHPER and DGWS gave permission to reprint materials from *Standards in Sports for Girls and Women.*

We are also grateful to the staff of the W. B. Saunders Company and to William Osburn who did the marvelous illustrations. Mr. Osburn was aided in the preparation of illustrations by Ellen Cole and Barbara Fennison. Our special thanks go also to our families and friends for their encouragement during the preparation of the manuscript, and especially to Mrs. Yvonne Cessna and Miss Mildred Alford.

Contents

Orientation

THERE IS ONE LESSON AT ALL TIMES AND PLACES—
ONE CHANGELESS TRUTH ON ALL THINGS WRIT,
FOR BOYS AND GIRLS, WOMEN, MEN, NATIONS, RACES,
BE FIT—BE FIT! AND ONCE AGAIN, BE FIT! . . . . .
RUDYARD KIPLING

"I BELIEVE THAT WE LEARN BY PRACTICE. WHETHER IT MEANS TO LEARN TO DANCE BY PRACTICING DANCING OR TO LEARN TO LIVE BY PRACTICING LIVING, THE PRINCIPLES ARE THE SAME. IN EACH IT IS THE PERFORMANCE OF A DEDICATED PRECISE SET OF ACTS, PHYSICAL OR INTELLECTUAL, FROM WHICH COMES SHAPE OF ACHIEVEMENT, A SENSE OF ONE'S BEING, A SATISFACTION OF SPIRIT. ONE BECOMES IN SOME AREA AN ATHLETE OF GOD" . . . . . MARTHA GRAHAM

The Unique Contributions
of Sports to Life

Individual and team sports have a valuable contribution to make to all who discover the fun, challenge, and adventure in playing them. Such riches are equally available to women and girls as well as men and boys, to youth as well as adults. These endowments are for all who engage in rugged play, whether they do so under instructor guidance at a school, park, church, or private club or on their own in a city street, backyard, or corner vacant lot. For each individual these contributions are found in (1) developing physical fitness, (2) increasing movement skills, (3) socializing the person, (4) creating better mental and emotional health, (5) increasing knowledges and appreciations, and (6) fostering better use of leisure time. As each one benefits from play so does society, for a vigorous nation can only be composed of strong, joyous, and productive people. Little drops of water and little grains of sand do, indeed, make a mighty ocean and a mighty land. Likewise, the health and well-being of one determines the health and well-being for all.

DEVELOPING PHYSICAL FITNESS

Buoyant health does not come naturally or without effort. It must be carefully built and determinedly maintained, for fitness is the product of habit and a strong desire to possess it. Such well-being results from taking part in active play, following positive health practices, and maintaining emotional and spiritual balance. Like the two sides of a coin, a sound mind and body are inseparable and the health of one, or lack of it, greatly affects the other. The body increases in strength, efficiency, endurance, and beauty through just the *right* amount and kind of activity, for too little or too much can be equally detrimental. Total fitness cannot be stored away for future use or an emergency, like food or money, but must be maintained when once acquired, replaced when used.

One is physically fit when (1) she is free from disease, (2) does not have significant deviations from normal body structure or function, (3) has sufficient strength, speed, agility, endurance, and skill to do the maximum tasks of daily life, (4) is mentally and emotionally adjusted, and (5) has high morale and spiritual concepts. Such a person can do her daily tasks effectively and efficiently without undue fatigue, strain, or boredom. She is buoyant, happy, and contributes to her close primary family group as well as to her more remote secondary community one. Exercise, sports, and games regularly played are the foundation upon which such fitness rests.

INCREASING MOVEMENT SKILLS

Good body coordination results from trying, failing, catching on *how* to do it, and repeated practice so that success comes automatically and seemingly without effort. Mistakes play a vital role in such mastery, for success is built upon failure, from evaluating past performances and finding improved ways to try again until one succeeds. The drive to do it is the spur or dynamic plunger to keep on until one succeeds. Such motivating seed often comes from the teacher, who by some magical process, sows it into the desires of each student so that it takes root, is carefully nurtured and finally bursts into full bloom. A real teacher is one who can get her students to try, try, and try again until they *do* succeed!

Skills develop from movements which range from simple to complex. Basic foundational experiences in body control are found in running, jumping, landing, pushing, pulling, climbing, carrying, lifting, throwing, hitting, and catching. For mastery, all require body balance, control, and rhythm. Peaked movement skills are those which combine any locomotor or axial movement with speed, accuracy, agility, rhythm, power, timing, and beauty. Kinesiologists believe that such perfection can be reached through (1) gaining a true working understanding of how to control all body movements, and (2) playing sports and games with above average skill as well as mastering dance skills. Certainly how the body is used in the everyday activities of work and play has a great effect upon one's figure. High school girls and college women who have been physically educated well realize that sports and games can do more to help them gain or keep a good figure than they can obtain by going to a masseur to have him pound or roll away bulging hip fat, or by signing up for a slenderizing experience with a jiggling machine.

Activity as the key to well-being need not be only for those of high school or college age. Women past the age of 25 should continue to play games or take part in the following activities, modifying them according to their own needs and interests:

Apparatus and Gymnastics
Archery
Badminton
Bait Casting
Basketball
Bicycling
Billiards
Boating
Bowling
Canoeing
Croquet
Curling
Dart Ball
Diving
Deck Tennis
Duckpins
Fencing
Field Hockey
Fly and Bait Casting
Golf
Hiking
Horseshoes
Ice Skating
La Bocce
Lacrosse
Lawn Bowling

Paddle Tennis
Pistol Shooting
Quoits
Riding
Rifle Shooting
Roller and Ice Skating
Roque
Sailing
Shuffleboard
Skeet Shooting
Skiing
Skiish
Softball
Squash Rackets
Swimming and Water Sports
Synchronized Swimming
Table Tennis
Tennis
Tetherball
Track and Field
Trap Shooting
Trampoline
Tumbling
Volleyball
Wiskit

SOCIALIZING THE PERSON

The greatest value in team sports is in socializing the individual, who, as a group member engaged in a united effort, both contributes and cooperates by substituting selfish "I" drives for the finer "We" drives. Through such endeavor one learns the lessons of give and take, of failure as well as success, which have a direct carry over value into life. Consequently, during adolescence when the desire to belong to a gang, club, or team is intensified, such group activities gain special importance. It is while playing on a team that many of the techniques for successful group life, both for the present as well as later life, are best learned. It is here that leaders as well as good followers are often developed. Likewise, it is then that our American way of life, our cultural values of "all for one and one for all," and "where there is unity there is strength," or "unite or perish" gain fuller understanding and appreciation. Just as our forefathers, whether they were the signers of the Declaration of Independence, members of a wagon train group rolling out to new glory and adventure on the way West, or soldiers on the side of the Blue or the Gray, learned that in numbers there was safety, and that only through united group effort could dreams become realities and desired goals be possessed. We of today are aware of the importance of the individual in relationship to, and as part of a group.

This great socializing value inherent in sports and games is not found only in team activities, however; it also abides in games for the single player, as well as in those for two. Even when playing alone on the golf course or archery range, one is filled with the desire to do her best so she can improve and give a challenger a highly competitive game or gain a real victory. In all dual activities such common courtesies as consideration for the other player or taking turns, rotating courts so one does not always face into the sun or play under a disadvantage, do much to develop our valued social concepts of respect and consideration for the rights of others. Refereeless play, wherein one calls her own games honestly according to the rules, helps a person to gain self-respect and to develop habits of truthfulness, and a wise teacher, parent, or leader becomes progressively unnecessary. Consequently, what one does when *away* from watchful adults, policemen, game officials, or one's family is of vital importance. The best discipline is, of course, self-discipline rooted in self-control. It is, among other things, the desire to do or be what our society considers good, fair, or right. Since today, more than ever before, we need fewer prisons and law officers and far more upright citizens in every age group, all methods and activities which produce such individuals must be used to their utmost.

INCREASING KNOWLEDGES AND APPRECIATIONS

It has been often said that self-understanding is the key to understanding others. Socrates' challenge to "know yourself" has lived throughout the ages because self-understanding is basic to gaining insight into why all people behave as they do. Through sports and games numerous opportunities are found for gaining such self-discovery. One soon senses or learns how she is regarded by her teammates or opponents—as a dub who cheats, or one who plays according to the rules. Coupled with this self detection is the development of new interests, challenges, and hobbies enduring enough, with or without some slight modification, for later life. Learning game rules and the strategy, the best kind of equipment to buy in order to play skillfully, or numerous other types of marginal or associated learnings helps one gain deeper appreciations for these once-played games. Those fortunate enough to gain superior sport skills receive the utmost as game spectators, for only they fully appreciate the beauty of the movements they watch, or know of the hard, long hours of practice that go into the making of such a finished product.

FOSTERING BETTER USE OF LEISURE TIME

Although more people have more free time than ever before, this is only the beginning of a glorious new age of leisure. In this rapidly approaching new era brought about basically by the discovery of the wheel, the machine, and the following Industrial Revolution with its resulting labor-saving devices and mechanical push-button servants, millions have benefited from shortened work hours. Although there are many assets in this new age of increased freedom, liabilities are numerous, too. Many seers warn us that too many among us are living at too fast a pace both in work and play, and too few are finding the release, refreshment, or recreation inherent in this newly found leisure. Others scoffingly say "What leisure?" and then relate that they, since taking over the chauffeur's, gardner's, or maid's job, are constantly either picking children up or taking them to school, dashing to the grocery store, or a meeting every whipstitch, or working themselves into an exhausted state with do-it-yourself projects. Certainly there is evidence that Americans are as frenzied in their leisure time as their work time pursuits. We are all aware that in our country greater and greater numbers are becoming increasingly content to watch fewer and fewer play, and that we are becoming a nation of physically softened onlookers.

The alarming number of those rejected for military service because of physical defects in all wars in this century has been appallingly high. The failure of American children to pass certain fitness tests in comparison to European children resulted in President Eisenhower's recent National Conference on Physical Fitness. Likewise obesity, heart involvements, mental illness, and death from degenerative diseases are all on the increase. The constant threat of internal social upheaval, war, and tragedy undermines our morale. As a nation it is imperative that we be strong, healthy, and ready to maintain our position of world leadership, or even to survive, if need be, in time of still another great crisis.

People voluntarily do in their free time those things which bring them joy and satisfaction. They will choose to play only when they have an interest in doing so, a feeling that from such activity they can gain something of value, or when they possess enough skill to receive real satisfaction from doing so. Unfortunately, many youngsters and adults have developed such a strong dislike for active sports from their physical education teachers and classes in school that they shun these activities during their leisure time. Often these are the victims of poorly prepared teachers and other instructors who have spent too much precious class time teaching intricate drills, or perfecting isolated game skills (such as the hockey dribble) so that the students rarely are given the opportunity to use these mastered techniques in a real game situation. Fortunately, more and more physical educators are realizing their great responsibilities to teach not only isolated skills but also game play to their students. Such inspired instructors teach sports and games masterfully enough that the learner *wants* to and *does* play them in after school hours in her youth as well as in her free time during her later years.

Every living person has the same amount of daily time—always 24 hours, no more or no less. What one *does* with this free time is quite another matter. Likewise, if one has not been educated to the necessity of allowing so many hours each day for recreational activities, she is not only ignorant of a needed revitalizing process necessary to maintain health, but also has developed detrimental life-shortening habits.

Leisure time can be spent in positive or negative ways. The former are made up of those activities which benefit each person and society, the latter are both detrimental to the individual and the group. Society-set standards for both work and play of what is good or bad have come down through the centuries. Playing on a basketball team can be as highly beneficial as robbing a store is detrimental. Consequently, recreation is more than what one does when she wants to when she has the time to do it, for both the game or the criminal act fits this description. How one's leisure time is spent is vastly important to the individual and to civilization, for leisure time offers rich opportunities which, when rightly used, benefit us all. An upright citizen is more than one who votes in all elections or collects donations for the annual Community Chest drive; she is hale, hearty, and healthy, and fully realizes the role exercise plays in keeping her in that state of well-being. Such a sojourner contributes as well as gets in her own pursuit for the good life.

DISCUSSION QUESTIONS

1. What are the unique contributions team sports make to the individual as well as to society?
2. How is our cultural heritage passed on through sports and games? What is this heritage?
3. What evidence do you have that many in your school and city are the victims of "spectatoritis"?
4. Record during the next seven days how you spend your leisure time. Evaluate your findings.
5. Observe a poorly coordinated and unskilled student in any physical education class over a period of time. Find out as much about this person as you can. Discover if there is any evidence that the lack of ability to play well influences social or emotional adjustment in any way. If so, in what ways? What is significance of this finding to you as a teacher?
6. In order to understand yourself better, make a list of your strong and weak points. Discuss this list with another classmate.
7. Summarize any article you read in the *Journal of Health, Physical Education and Recreation* on physical fitness. List ways in which you can increase your own fitness.

SELECTED AUDIO-VISUAL AIDS

Films

Country and Community Recreation in Action. (29 min., sound, b & w). Audio-Visual Center, Indiana University, Bloomington, Indiana. (Rental)

Live Like a Champion. (20 min., sound, b & w). Sterling Morris, U.S.A., 43 West 61st Street, New York, N.Y. (Free)

Playtown, U.S.A. (23 min., sound, color). The Athletic Institute, 209 S. State Street, Chicago 4, Ill. (Rental)

Social Change in a Democracy. (29 min., sound, b & w). United World Films, 542 S. Dearborn Street, Chicago, Ill.

They Grow Up So Fast. (20 min., sound, color). American Association for Health, Physical Education, and Recreation, 1201 16th Street, N.W., Washington 6, D.C. (Rental)

We Plan Together. (20 min., sound, b & w). Bureau of Publications, Teachers College, Columbia University, New York, N.Y. (Rental)

Filmstrips

Your Education Philosophy—Does It Matter? Visual Materials Consultation Bureau, Wayne University, Detroit, Mich. (Rental)

SUGGESTED READINGS

Allen, Robert: *Time for Everything,* New York, Thomas Crowell, 1955.
A literary gem showing readers how to have more leisure time daily with suggested ways for using it wisely.

Durant, John, and Bettman, Otto: *A Pictorial History of American Sports,* New York, A. S. Barnes, 1952.
This unique volume is the first complete word-and-picture history of the sports in this country from 1607 to the present. It includes materials from auto racing to walking.

Gumpert, Martin: *The Anatomy of Happiness,* New York, McGraw-Hill Book Company, Inc.
In this unique and helpful book a prominent physician analyzes the leading physical and emotional causes of unhappiness and shows how one can achieve a full amount of happiness and inner contentment in life.

Life Magazine. *The Good Life* (Special Issue) Vol. 47, No. 26, December 28, 1959.
This issue contains outstanding articles and photographs about the increased leisure time problems America must face. Noteworthy are the articles, *A $40 Billion Bill Just For Fun; How About Tomorrow—A Practical Prophecy;* and the editorial *Leisure Can Mean a Better Civilization.* The article, *Happy Idle Hours Become A Rat Race* is excellent.

Prudden, Bonnie: *Bonnie Prudden's Fitness Book,* New York, Ronald Press, 1959.
A master plan of exercises to help women and girls build and maintain fitness. Based on her series featured in "Sports Illustrated," aired on TV, and personally sold to hundreds of Americans who want to be fit and feel on top of the world.

Soule, George: *Time for Living,* New York, The Viking Press, 1955.
This exciting book describes what the coming years have in store for us, and the impact on civilization of ever increasing productivity and the resulting increase in leisure time.

Sports Illustrated: *The Spectacle of Sports,* New York, Prentice-Hall Book Company, Inc, 1958.
An amazing collection of photographs of the top sport events in the world in 1957–58, with a brilliantly described summary.

Van Keuren: *The Game of Living,* New York, Charles Scribner's Sons, 1953.
This little inspirational book is filled with sound, practical advice and good psychology.

2

Learning and Teaching

The best teachers of sports and games are those who know fully each game and can both perform and help others learn how to play them well by using the many intricate skills necessary for successful play. Each such master instructor has a clear and workable understanding of (1) learning and how it takes place, (2) a wide variety of teaching methods, and (3) students, both as individuals and as a class group.

HOW LEARNING TAKES PLACE

Learning is a process of adjusting to experience and results in changed behavior. It is a personal, progressive, linked experience. Everyone reacts differently to learning experiences according to interest and desire to learn. Since knowledge comes through one's senses and is closely associated with emotions, it is impossible to separate physical from mental mastery. A person has learned when she can repeat at will actions which bring desired results, when she can place the served tennis ball where she wants to, or accurately dribble and pass the hockey ball on to a teammate. All who profit from experiences both in and out of school have many social skills and wide understandings, and can see into things quickly or grasp easily how to do things. They possess many interests and are eager to acquire still more; can readily develop new habits and skills, and aspire to explore even more fields of knowledge. In short, such persons are above average, skill hungry, well adjusted individually and socially, and seekers of ways to become even better than they are. They are truly educated.

Learning is of three types. *Primary learning* revolves around the mastering of a specific skill, such as learning to punt correctly in speedball. *Secondary learning* is marginal and is largely concerned with knowledge about the skill, such as game rules or the names of champion players. *Concomitant learning* involves character education and the shaping of proper attitudes. All physical education activities are rich in opportunities to teach honesty, player consideration, and other valued concepts. Although many accomplished instructors can teach activity skills to others, a relatively small number are potent enough as educators to shape another's future or concept of life's values. People of all ages copy those whom they most admire. Consequently, easily impressed youth especially need leaders worthy of emulation who realize that character can best be "caught," or is shaped through positive examples in numerous ever changing situations.

SOME PRINCIPLES OF LEARNING

Principles are the end products of expert opinion, research, and experience which serve as action guides enabling one to form her own teaching philosophy. Basic beliefs of learning which will prove helpful to all teachers in forming such a philosophy are:

1. Learning is largely a *doing*, not a listening or watching activity.
2. The role of motivation in helping others want to learn is of paramount importance. It is the key to teaching others successfully.
3. Short practice periods are superior to long ones. All such periods should vary in length according to the learner's interest or fatigue level.
4. The student masters only what she deems important, or has a felt need to learn.
5. Every person learns in her own unique way and at her own rate of speed. Each learner is as different in this respect as each of the five fingers of your own hand.
6. Practice makes perfect, but only if one practices the correct pattern repeatedly in the right way. Practice of the imperfect is costly, indeed.
7. Overlearning results in longer retention.
8. Emotions and a strong will to learn spur on the rate of learning. Lack of interest or desire to learn results in little, if any, learning. You can teach only those who want to learn. Your main job is to instill this desire to know or do in others.
9. The learner teaches herself. The teacher's role is to help her eliminate error, catch on how to do it, and be able to repeat at will the process which led to success.
10. Teaching is helping people discover what they could do all the time and did not know they could.
11. Transfer of a thing learned from one experience to another will occur only if there is a conscious effort made. Such transfer occurs only when two experiences are joined and one knows such a union exists.

12. Evaluation is a vital part of all learning, for mistakes, when understood, play an important part in the mastery of anything.
13. Education is for use.

TEACHING METHODS

Just as adequate professional preparation is the prerequisite for successful teaching, so also is the careful planning of each lesson. This can best be done by the *whole-part-whole* method, wherein the teacher begins by (1) planning the course content for a semester or a single unit, (2) devising plans for each class period of this larger whole, and (3) evaluating the results at the unit's completion.

Group plans are the prerequisites for successful group experiences. Consequently, the teacher and pupils (rather than the pupils and teacher) should set up desired individual goals and class objectives, choose the materials to be mastered, share a teaching-learning experience, and measure their success or failure to obtain their goals.

Each of the many teaching methods is valuable but there are times when one is superior to another. The one best to use depends upon ever changing factors which the successful instructor learns to sense or feel. Certainly, any method is only worthy of use if through it, desired results can be obtained and it is socially approved. Also, a teaching method which has proven to be successful for one teacher may be a failure when used by another. Ways of teaching others are patterns which must be tailored to fit one's own situation. The many techniques for successful teaching include:

Chalk Talks	Experiments
Drills	Class discussions
Lectures	Workshops
Questions and answers	Forums
Reports	Assignments
Demonstrations and participation	Field trips
	Debates
Supervised practice	Workbooks
Role playing	Projects
Visual aids	Combinations of all listed

TEACHING MOTOR SKILLS

The teaching-learning situation must be a controlled one. The instructor who tries to out-talk or speak without the attention of the group is wasting both time and energy. The inability to get and hold the learner's attention is characteristic of the beginning teacher and also the poor one. One has only to observe someone teaching a dog to "sit" or "heel" successfully to realize the role the following play in getting fast and sure results: (1) complete attention, (2) firmness of voice, (3) repetition or conditioning by using the same pattern of movement and voice repeatedly, and (4) a reward (a head pat for the dog, verbal praise for the student). It is recommended that all those who desire to become master teachers gain experience and increase their greatly needed patience by practicing on pet animals or birds before teaching human beings. There are many elements common in teaching all age groups. One must "learn" to be a teacher, for it is impossible to become a superior one without much hard work and capitalizing upon past errors. Just as the way *to learn* is to start learning something which is to be mastered, so the way to teach is to *teach*. The time to learn is now, not when one gets a job as a teacher in one, two, three, or four years. Practice, evaluate mistakes, and learn how as you go along is the only magic formula for obtaining success as a teacher.

In teaching any skill the instructor should:

(1) briefly explain what she is doing and how to do it, (2) show others how to do it by means of demonstration, (3) give individual assistance to all who are having difficulty copying her movements, and (4) help each evaluate the progress made.

Some teachers prefer to explain and demonstrate simultaneously by first facing the class lined up in a single line(s) so she has good eye contact with the group, doing each movement to count, and then having the class repeat, through mimetics, with her both the movement and count. The entire class again watches her demonstrate with her back to the group as they say the count, followed by all of them counting and doing the movement with her. For example, when teaching the softball throw the instructor should have the group on count One hold the ball in both hands in front of the body, on count Two bring the hand and arm holding the ball down below the waist, on count Three up and around making almost a complete circle, and release the ball on count Four.

Regardless of how the teacher drills class groups learning new skills, all skills should be used in a game as soon as possible. Movement accuracy should precede the development of agility, speed, timing, and body flexibility.

It is important that teachers demonstrate skills correctly, for students learning through trial and error and insight who copy an incorrect movement pattern soon develop habits difficult to break. Drills, relays, and novelty games are all valuable for skill practice purposes, but *only* when done with the specific goal in mind of assisting the student in mastering the needed skills for successful game play. Movement accuracy should be acquired first, followed by the development of speed, correct timing, and the ability to change direction suddenly.

When the learner, with the teacher's help, gains an understanding of what she is doing incorrectly and can avoid doing it, she has learned. Skill "polish" results when the learner can do movements correctly and they become easy, rhythmic, automatic responses. Thus teaching is both remedial and diagnostic. It is imperative that the teacher can pick out faulty movement patterns, and know how to correct them. Just as the patient quickly loses confidence in the physician who declares, "Now your trouble *may* be this" or "I *think* your difficulty may be," so students tend to disregard the guesses of teachers who cannot immediately spot what is being done incorrectly. One has only to catch the face of any student with its glow of triumph, as she hits the target's bull's-eye after making the movement correction her teacher recommended, to realize the tremendous value correct diagnostic ability plays in learning. Likewise, one has only to note the expression of frustration in any student as she tries this, that, and many more teacher suggestions for improvement (and none of them work), to comprehend the importance of the teacher helping the student discover *what* is wrong, *why* it is wrong, and *how* to avoid repeating the same mistake again and again.

TEACHING GAME RULES

The best way to teach game rules is in relation to skills to be mastered. For example, the rules for serving a volleyball and techniques for doing so correctly should occur simultaneously, just as would the teaching of the basketball free throw and the reason a player is awarded it. All players must know and understand that game rules are necessary for safe but fast play. Teacher or student demonstrations showing how rules are broken and what happens when they are afford splendid ways to help players learn them. Pencil and paper tests aid the instructor to spot quickly those who have a hazy or false concept of the laws of any game. All such tests should be discussed with the group and the correct answers given for all questions. Oral review, for several days, of certain test sections may be followed successfully by another revised written rule test.

The instructor should help her class know each rule and why it is a rule, as well as the penalty for breaking it. When players discover that rules have been devised for their protection and for the improvement of the quality of the game, they are often more interested in learning them. The use of student officials increases a desire for rule mastery, especially when it is considered an honor among peer groups to be chosen for such a leadership position. Physical education majors are usually required to complete an officiating course for many sports as part of their professional training and must call many games in the intramural program in order to fulfill requirements of the course. Both such younger and older students often help teams and classmates learn game rules more quickly than can the teacher.

All practice and competitive games should be played according to the rules. The game should be stopped in classes or at practice periods at *teachable moments* when rule infractions occur. In class situations the teacher may ask the group what someone did incorrectly which caused the game interruption, rather than calling out the penalty or awarding the offended player her earned privilege. Inferior instructors tend to answer such teachable moment questions themselves, then go on automatically calling a game, and thus deprive their students of many fine learning experiences.

The use of clinics and workshops is also often a successful way to teach rules to large groups. Since most of our learning comes through our eyes and ears, actual demonstrations with explanations of all rules is superior to the use of movies, or slides. The latter, however, may be successfully used as a means of summarizing materials for a class, a clinic, or other groups.

TEACHING GAME STRATEGY

The techniques of offensive and defensive play may be taught by first helping groups discover the object of the game, how scores are made, what each score counts, and how to prevent the opponent from scoring. Since the object of most team games is to advance a ball, the offensive team should develop skills for doing so through defensive territory. A player *without* the ball tries to move into a free area to be in a receiving position. A player *with* the ball tries to pass into an open space to a free teammate.

There are numerous ways to teach the techniques of offensive and defensive play. The use of magnetized boards is highly recommended, for the teacher can use them for showing almost every kind of play possible in a game situation. Such boards are relatively inexpensive and can be purchased from companies advertising them in the monthly *Journal of Health, Physical Education, and Recreation.* Chalk talks, movies, filmstrips, and still pictures have proven successful also. Drills of set plays, and variations to use when the first-learned combinations fail, are valuable techniques for teaching advanced game tactics to players. However, no team or individual player should be drilled to excess, so that they or she become "burned out" from this experience to the extent that skill in actual game play is destroyed or game enjoyment damaged.

DISCUSSION QUESTIONS

1. Make a list of things you want to teach others under the three types of learning, using the headings Primary, Secondary, and Concomitant.
2. Teach someone to do a skill you have mastered using the four steps for doing so described in this chapter. Which of the steps were easiest for you to do? Which ones the hardest? Why?
3. How would you motivate a class group to want to learn to serve a tennis ball correctly?
4. Explain the statement that "Teaching is helping people discover what they could already do but didn't know they could." What learning experience have you ever had which substantiates this?
5. Write a brief paper on the best teacher you have ever had and why. At the end of your paper add a statement of why you want to be a teacher.
6. Give an example from your own experience that character is better "caught" than taught.
7. If we learn by doing, how much time should be given in a 40 minute class to teacher explanation, how much to demonstration, how much to class drill, and to play using the skill taught that period?

8. Chart the offensive and defensive play you would teach your students in hockey, speedball, basketball, soccer, and volleyball.

Selected Audio-Visual Aids

Accent on Learning. (30 min., sound, b & w). Department of Photography, Ohio State University, Columbus, Ohio. (Rental)

Children Growing Up With Others. (30 min., sound, b & w). National Film Board of Canada, Ontario, Canada. (Rental)

Water Ski Fun. (14 min., sound, color). Florida Development Commission, Caldwell Building, Tallahasse, Fla. (Free)

Training You To Train Your Dog. (A series of 3: 32, 20, 21 min., sound, b & w). Gaines Dog Research Center, 250 Park Avenue, New York, N.Y. (Free)

Suggested Readings

American Association of Health, Physical Education, and Recreation, *Physical Education for High School Students,* Washington, D.C., 1955.

American Association of Health, Physical Education, and Recreation, *Fit To Teach,* Washington, D.C., 1957.

Dale, Edgar: *Audio-Visual Methods in Teaching,* rev. ed. New York, The Dryden Press, 1954.

Division of Girls and Women's Sports, AAHPER: *Social Changes and Sports.* Report of the National Conference on Social Changes and Implications for Physical Education and Sports Program.

Haskew, Lawrence: *This is Teaching,* Dallas, Scott, Foresman, 1956.

Highet, Gilbert: *The Art of Teaching,* New York, Alfred Knopf, 1950.

Hussey, Delia, and Murray, Ruth: *From Student to Teacher in Physical Education,* New York, Prentice-Hall Book Co., Inc, 1959.

Kozman, Hilda, Cassidy, Rosalind, and Jackson, Chester: *Methods in Physical Education,* Ed. 2, Philadelphia, W. B. Saunders Company, 1958.

Mitchell, Elmer, Editor: *Sports for Recreation,* Revised Edition, New York, A. S. Barnes, 1952.

Muldoon, Mary Warren: *Learning to Teach,* New York, Harper Brothers, 1958.

Vannier, Maryhelen, and Fait, Hollis: *Teaching Physical Education in Secondary Schools,* Philadelphia, W. B. Saunders Company, 1957.

3

Class Organization

Class organization, planned and routinized, is necessary if the teacher is to make the most of each precious instruction period. Roll taking, done speedily and accurately, may be successfully accomplished by any of the following methods:

1. Assigning each student a floor number and recording the numbers of the uncovered spaces.
2. Assigning each student a number which is called out as the instructor moves down a squad line composed of ten or less and recording the unspoken number.
3. Giving each student a name on a tag board and recording absentees shown by the unturned discs.
4. Having squad leaders check and report absentees in their lines.
5. Calling each person's name.

CLASS EXCUSES

Written policies regarding excuses should be read aloud to each class and posted on a bulletin board. Those having difficulties during their menstrual periods should be encouraged to take part in as much of the class as they deem possible. Requiring all to dress when they have their monthly periods encourages those having difficulty to take part in milder forms of activity.

UNIFORMS

In physical education classes, students should dress in regulation uniforms. One piece uniforms, preferably blue, green or some color other than white, are recommended for high school girls. College women seemingly prefer wearing dark shorts and white blouses, although hockey tunics are favored in some sections of the country. Wearing the proper clothing for each sport will increase player comfort for in, as well as out of, class play. Rubber elevated shoes should be worn for hockey, speedball, soccer, and lacrosse. Light wool socks are usually better than heavy ones for girls and women. Goalie pads and shin guards for hockey and lacrosse, finger tabs for archery, a face mask, body pads and gloves for fencing are all necessary equipment. Loose, attractive, and comfortable clothing is best for all games and sports. Tank or lightweight woolen swimming suits are easy and inexpensive to launder. Sport uniforms may be student or school furnished, and rented for a small fee which usually includes laundering.

The teacher should insist that all class members look attractive and be in clean uniforms. Some instructors prefer to wear a costume which is different from that worn by a group, remembering that a leader is one who looks and acts like a leader. Some prefer to wear an all-white uniform with a colored blazer.

USE OF SPACE AND ASSISTANTS

It is imperative that all class members take an active part in as much of each class program as possible. The teacher must devise ways to utilize best all allotted space. The use of squads and squad leaders will enable her to move from group to group, giving individual help when needed. All student leaders should be carefully selected, given leadership tips, as well as receive additional skill instruction so that they can best assist their squads. Ideally, such chosen assistants should either dress differently from their peers, or wear some awarded emblem which distinguishes them. The use of such young leaders will only prove successful, however, if (1) it is a real honor to be selected, (2) all who are chosen are really outstanding, and (3) this picked group receives extra help in skill mastery and training in the techniques of leading others successfully.

DRILL FORMATIONS

Skill drills play a vital part in skill mastery. Students should be conditioned to move quickly into the desired drill formation. See specific group formations for each sport as it is discussed in detail later.

EVALUATING RESULTS

Records which will enable a teacher and students to see their accomplishments or failures, and standing among others are of great value—but only if they are used for evaluation and motivation purposes.

Measuring techniques which will prove helpful include:

1. Knowledge tests
    a. True-false, right-wrong, same-opposite, yes-no
    b. Short answer, completion questions, association

    c. Multiple choice of choosing most correct answer, selecting all correct answers in a question of four or more parts, choosing the wrong answer

    d. Matching key words with phrases

    e. Use of pictured playing areas requiring the student to mark and name the position of each offensive and defensive player

2. Skill tests

    a. Isolated game skills for speed and accuracy[1]

    b. Ability rating scales in which each player is ranked in relationship to others on a team or in a class; a diagnostic check list for rating each student's ability to perform isolated techniques making up a specific skill (e.g., if the racket is held correctly for a tennis serve, the ball contacted at the right place, etc.)

    c. Game incidence charts showing how many goals were made out of how many tries; number of successful blocks made in volleyball, number of successful traps completed in soccer, etc. Such checklist charts show up both skill and game strategy strong and weak points

3. Physical fitness tests of endurance, speed, strength, agility, motor capacity

4. Attitude tests

5. Social development tests

6. Posture tests

7. Others

Evaluation is vital to good teaching, especially when used for motivation purposes, self-appraisal, grouping, spotting weaknesses, guidance, or ranking. However, to be of value a test must be easily understood, easy to give, record, and grade. It must be valid and reliable, as well as prove challenging and meaningful to the person taking it. Here again, student assistants can be invaluable in assisting small groups in taking a test, recording their efforts, keeping time accurately in speed tests, as well as getting necessary score sheets or needed equipment ready. It is also important that each student know her test results and class standing.

DISCUSSION QUESTIONS

1. Which of the suggested ways for checking roll seems to you to be superior? Why should or should not roll be taken in a class, for intramural practice, or intramural play?

2. Bring to class pictures taken from advertisements appearing in any issue of the *Journal of Health, Physical Education, and Recreation* of the uniforms you would like your class to be required to wear.

[1] See Scott, Gladys, and French, Esther: *Better Teaching Through Testing*, St. Louis, C. V. Mosby Company, 1950; Larson, Leonard, and Yocum, Rachael: *Measurement and Evaluation in Physical Education, Health and Recreation*, St. Louis, C. V. Mosby Company, 1951; and Issues of *The Research Quarterly* of the A.A.H.P.E.R. for recommended skill tests for all sports included in this book.

3. List and discuss five qualities you would want your selected student leaders to have.
4. Devise a ten lesson training period for your selected student assistants for a unit on field hockey or advanced swimming.
5. Show in a diagram assigned class space and duties for each squad in a class of 40 students for instruction in basketball.
6. Find, take, and give to a fellow student a test in physical fitness. What are your conclusions as to (1) your own fitness in relation to others, and (2) your ability as a tester?
7. Find, take, and give to a fellow student any skill test in your best sport. Record your reactions to this test as a means of determining player ability in a game situation.
8. Read and write a brief summary of any chapter in any of the books listed in the suggested reading or from Scott and French, or Larson and Yocum. What is your reaction to this material?

Selected Audio-Visual Aids

After School Activities for Boys and Girls. (Filmstrip, silent, b & w). American Council on Education, Washington, D.C. (Free)
Beginning Swimming. (11 min., 16 mm., b & w). Coronet Instructional Films, 65 East South Water Street, Chicago, Ill. (Rental)
Beginning Archery. (Filmstrip—4 units). The Athletic Institute, 209 S. State Street, Chicago 4, Ill. (Rental)
Beginning Bowling. (Filmstrip—3 units). The Athletic Institute, 209 S. State Street, Chicago 4, Ill. (Rental)

Suggested Readings

A.A.H.P.E.R., *Measurement and Evaluation Materials in Health, Physical Education, and Recreation,* 1950.
Miller, Donna Mae, and Ley, Katherine: *Individual and Team Sports for Women,* New York, Prentice-Hall Book Company, Inc., 1956.
Powell, Elizabeth, and Howe, Eugene: Motor Ability Tests for High School Girls, *Research Quarterly,* Vol. 10, December, 1939.
Vannier, Maryhelen, and Foster, Mildred: *Teaching Physical Education in Elementary Schools,* Ed. 2, Philadelphia, W. B. Saunders Company, 1958.
Voltmer, Edward, and Esslinger, Arthur: *The Organization and Administration of Physical Education,* Ed. 3, New York, F. S. Crofts and Company, 1958.
Yocum, Rachael, and Hunsaker, H. B.: *Individual Sports for Men and Women,* New York, A. S. Barnes, 1947.

4

Equipment and its Care

Sports equipment is of three types: *permanent*, which lasts over many years, such as tennis posts and diving boards; *semi-permanent*, which must be replaced after several seasons of hard use, such as archery targets and tennis nets; and *expendable*, such as badminton rackets and birds which often must be restocked yearly. Instructors have an obligation not only to make the best use of what materials they have, but also to increase the life span and usefulness of these materials.

THE PURCHASE OF EQUIPMENT

Regardless of whether one does her own buying or this is handled by the school's purchasing agent, the following suggestions will prove helpful in obtaining the best value from allotted funds:

1. All orders should be made on a purchase order blank and kept on file.
2. When buying uniforms or other articles of clothing, factors to keep in mind are: attractiveness of appearance, comfort, quality, durability, guarantee, and amount of laundering or cleaning needed.
3. Buy quality products in quantity; take advantage of legitimate discounts and off-season sales.
4. Buy multi-purpose equipment when possible.
5. Avoid salesmen's gifts, for their acceptance usually entails an obligation or hidden cost.
6. See and test what you buy; avoid ordering only from catalogs.
7. Use all alloted funds. Check regularly the amount of money still available. Buy throughout the year rather than purchasing unneeded items at the close of the fiscal year in order to use up all of your budget.
8. Make a yearly inventory and running seasonal check of all equipment. Buy needed items at the close of each sport season.

9. Buy from local merchant's only when they can offer values equal to those from larger, better known firms.

THE CARE OF EQUIPMENT

Costumes.   Woolen, cotton, and rayon uniforms should be cleaned and stored in dry, well ventilated places. Moth protection will increase their use over a longer period of time.

Leather Goods.   Leather is best protected by cleanliness and oil. Neat's-foot oil, carefully applied, is best for softball gloves. Balls (inflated to normal pressure) and other leather goods, should be kept in a cool dry place to prevent mold. Wet balls should be dried out gradually at normal room temperature. Saddle soap and neat's-foot oil will keep the leather soft. Stored balls should be only partially inflated, and all balls should be carefully inflated. If a pump is used for this purpose, the needle should be dipped into glycerin before it is inserted. A pressure gauge should be used also and all equipment inflated to recommended size and degree of hardness. Overinflation will strain as well as lessen the life and use of all balls.

Rubber Balls.   Many schools are now buying rubber instead of leather balls since they are less expensive and are proving as serviceable. Proper cleaning with a mild soap and warm water plus careful storage in a cool, dry area will increase the length of their usefulness. Cleaning fluids should never be used on this equipment.

Wooden Equipment.   Bats, hockey and lacrosse sticks, and other similar wooden equipment should be carefully wiped, rough spots sandpapered out, and oiled before storing.

Archery Equipment.   Targets should be laid out flat for storage and be stacked or laid singly on a platform several inches from the floor. Powdered sulfur spread among the butts will keep animals away.[1] Target faces can be reinforced by cardboard or heavy paper backings. A thin coating of paraffin will increase the life of corrugated cardboard targets.

Bows should be unbraced, hung vertically on wooden pegs, and stored in a cool, humid place. Simoniz or Johnson's wax should be rubbed on the bows at the end of the season to protect their finish, and those with leather handles should be saddlesoaped. Strings should be beeswaxed at least once weekly and frayed strings replaced.

Arrows should always be stored in a rack instead of in a box. An arrow tray, made by drilling holes in lines for six arrows through three boards nailed in three layers about 8 inches apart to two upright boards is ideal for this purpose. Arrows numbered on the shaft in sets of six to correspond to numbered holes in the tray will enable students to replace them quickly. A thin coating of wax, applied at the end of the season, will protect the finish.

---

[1] Robertson, Grace: Elementary Care and Repair of Archery Tackle, *Archery-Riding Guide,* June 1958–June 1960, p. 33, Division of Girls and Women's Sports, A.A.H.P.E.R., Washington, D.C.

Finger tabs and leather quivers should be saddlesoaped regularly.

Tennis and Badminton Equipment.   Wooden tennis and badminton rackets should be in presses and hung on a wall. Rubberized coverings are recommended for expensive rackets. Although steel and fiberglass rackets do not need to be in presses, they should never be stacked together but rather stood upright in a box or metal container. Tennis balls can best be kept in separate boxes with the correct number for each class, if the school furnishes balls to the players. Plastic birds must be stored in a moist environment, for dryness causes them to become brittle. A commercial humidifier, or a breadbox, is best for this purpose. Many schools, now using plastic birds for large classes, are finding them inexpensive and satisfactory, especially for beginners. Regardless which type of bird is used, students need careful instruction in handling shuttlecocks properly. Cotton or woolen practice balls used for beginners are often economical, although these students should use regular birds as soon as they have learned basic game strokes.

Outdoor tennis nets should be tarred or made of metal. Woven nets should be dipped yearly in creosote and stored on pegs (never rolled or folded) in a cool, dry place. Indoor badminton nets may be rolled or folded when not in use. Rips and breaks should be mended immediately. Both tennis and badminton nets should be loosened when not in use to relieve tension.

Mats.   Rubber and plastic mat covers should be carefully cleaned with soap and water. Uncovered mats should first be vacuumed and then carefully scrubbed with either commercial mat cleaner or soap and water by washing only a small area at a time and wiping it dry. Mats should never be dragged across the floor but be carried and hung on pegs or racks. They should never be rolled but always kept flat.

Metal Equipment.   This type of equipment should be oiled or painted in order to prevent rust. Steel tapes, jumping standards, and other such equipment may be cleaned with steel wool and lightly oiled instead of painted.

REPAIRING OF EQUIPMENT

Numerous firms specialize in this service and give relatively inexpensive service. Prompt attention should be paid to all items needing repair. Simple repairs, such as sewing ripped balls, can be made by the teacher or students. A liquid fabric cement called **Lam-A-Fab** can be used to repair minor rips and tears in cloth or canvas.[2] All broken racket strings should be repaired at once. Although arrows which are cracked or splintered should be discarded, slightly warped ones can be straightened by heating them over a steam kettle and gently reshaping them. Damaged plastic nocks can be best removed by scraping and pasting new nocks on with Duco cement. Splin-

[2] Voltmer, Edward, and Esslinger, Arthur: *The Organization and Administration of Physical Education,* Ed. 3, New York, Appleton-Century-Crofts, 1958, p. 48.

tered piles, beyond repair, should be cut off (the arrow thus becomes shortened) and new ones put on with Ferruletite cement. All broken or damaged feathers should be removed with a knife, and new ones pasted on with Duco cement. Repainting dulled crests with bright, quick drying enamel will add to their attractiveness.

The Equipment Room. This room should be dry, well ventilated, kept locked, and located near the gymnasium floor and instructor's office. A half door or small window through which equipment can be issued is recommended.

Checking Equipment In and Out. If no custodian is available for this task, a student can be assigned this responsibility. Large laundry sacks for carrying bats, boxes for enough balls for each class, or targets placed on a stand with rollers will enable squad leaders or others to move needed equipment to playing areas quickly. Each instructor should (1) carefully study what equipment she has and know what condition it is in, (2) devise best ways for getting it out to each class (here a student committee can often come up with some fine ideas), and then (3) strive to decrease the time needed for getting a properly-equipped group ready for instruction.

Marking Equipment. All equipment should be stenciled. Uniforms should be stamped according to size (large, medium, or small or 38, 34, 32) along with the name of the school and date of purchase (S.M.U., 8/16/60). Although stealing is not often as serious a problem with girls, it does exist in some schools. Each teacher must work out the solution to this difficulty for herself and devise written policies to combat it. Students usually cooperate when they come to realize that they are really hurting themselves and others by their "borrowing habits" in that the budget is limited and the purchase of new equipment is impossible if part of it must be used to replace missing items. Unfortunately, some few women instructors encourage students to wear school property as a means of advertising a would-be well-known coach. Such misguided youth leaders will even appear before a class all decked out in a school-stenciled uniform and then, ironically enough, some time during the term preach loudly to the group against the pilfering or use of the property of others.

IMPROVISED EQUIPMENT

"Where there is a will there is, indeed, a way," as any creative teacher knows when faced with a lack of, or poor equipment. In most every phase of the program, certain pieces of equipment can be made by either the school's mechanical arts or home economics department. Imaginative leaders, with student assistance, can add much to this list of suggested things that can be devised from inexpensive or cost free materials:

Archery. Arm guards from heavy cardboard and rubber bands; quivers from mailing tubes or tennis ball cans; target backstops from bales of hay or heavy cardboard; archery strings from Barbour's No. 12 Irish

Linen or heavy carpet thread; finger tabs from shoe tongues or inner tubes; golf tees, coke bottle tops with nails driven through them, or spools for toe markers; points of aim from used ice picks; bow sights from adhesive tape and big-headed pin; tassels for wiping arrows from discarded yarn.

Softball. Use discarded lumber for home plate and bases, covering them with heavy canvas. Make batting tees with a heavy wooden base and a hard rubber tube. Make a backstop with old lumber and inexpensive chicken wire.

Basketball. Make outdoor backboards and goal posts from discarded lumber. Goals can be made of heavy iron rings or be cut from heavy metal cans.

Golf. A miniature golf course can be made by driving opened cans of various size into the ground and using broomsticks as clubs.

Stunts and Gymnastics. A balance beam and Swedish Box from old lumber; broom-sticks for balancing and body flexibility stunts; a chinning bar, ladder walk, rope climb from discarded materials. Mats from old mattresses or from army surplus stores.

Soccer, Hockey, Speedball, Lacrosse. Goal posts from discarded lumber and chicken wire.

Swimming. Buoys from rope and unsinkable wood.

Tennis, Badminton, Volleyball. Net posts and practice backboards from old lumber; heavy ropes for nets.

Track and Field. Starting blocks, jump standards, broad jump take-off board, etc., can all be made from old lumber.

DISCUSSION QUESTIONS

1. Discover how athletic goods are purchased in your school. What do you consider to be the weaknesses and strong points of such a practice?
2. Write a short paper on how the methods used in the storage of athletic equipment in your school could be improved.
3. How is the problem of student "borrowing" of equipment handled in your own and other schools? Give your reactions to these methods. How do you plan to solve this problem if it occurs?
4. Bring to class any article of athletic equipment you have repaired. What did you learn from this experience which will prove profitable for your classmates?
5. Bring to class any piece of athletic equipment you have made from junk or inexpensive material. Show your classmates how you made it. Collect other ideas from your group and, as a class, select the best article submitted.

SELECTED AUDIO-VISUAL AIDS

ABC of Hand Tools. (Two parts, each 18 min., sound, color). General Motors Corporation, Detroit, Mich. (Free)

Keeping Your Boat Shipshape. (24 min., sound, color). DuPont de Nemours and Company, Advertising Department, Wilmington, Del. (Free)

Leaders for Leisure. (21 min., sound, color). The Athletic Institute, 209 S. State Street, Chicago 4, Ill. (Rental)

Basic Net Mending. (16 min., sound, color). Fish and Wildlife Service, Department of Visual Information, Washington, D.C. (Free)

The Inside Story of a Golf Ball. (10 min., sound, b & w). United States Rubber Company, Advertising Department, 1230 Avenue of the Americas, New York, N.Y. (Free)

The Spalding Story. (30 min., sound, color). Spalding and Brothers, 4850 N. Harlem, Chicago, Ill. or, 1505 Hi-Line Drive, Dallas, Texas. (Free)

Two Weeks With Pay. (15 min., sound, color). Carborundum Company, Niagara Falls, New York. (Free)

Working For Fun. (31 min., sound, color). MacGregor Company, Advertising Department, 14861 Spring Grove Avenue, Cincinnati, Ohio. (Free)

You Asked For It—How Bowling Balls Are Made. (5 min., sound, b & w). Brunswick-Balke-Collender Company, 623–633 S. Wabash Avenue, Chicago, Ill. (Free)

Suggested Readings

Bourguardez, Virginia, and Heilman, Charles: *Sports Equipment: Selection, Care and Repair,* New York, A. S. Barnes, 1950.

Damron, C. Frazier: *Improvised Equipment for Physical Education,* A Mimeographed Report, University of Florida, 1952.

Gabrielson, Milton, and Caswell, Miles: *Sports and Recreation Facilities for School and Community,* New York, Prentice-Hall Book Company, Inc., 1958.

Vannier, Maryhelen, and Fait, Hollis: *Teaching Physical Education in Secondary Schools,* Philadelphia, W. B. Saunders Company, 1957.

Individual Sports

"A MAN WOULD HAVE NO PLEASURE IN DISCOVERING ALL THE BEAUTIES OF THE UNIVERSE, EVEN IN HEAVEN ITSELF, UNLESS HE HAS A PARTNER WITH WHOM TO SHARE HIS JOYS." . . . . . CICERO

Archery

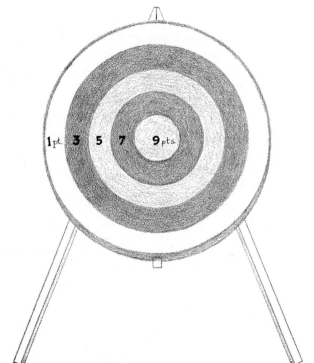

Figure No. 5–1.   An Archery Target Showing Scoring Values.

Archery is a year-round sport for both sexes of all ages, the physically strong or the muscularly weak. Properly played either indoors or outdoors as an individual or group activity, it can improve posture and develop chest, arms, and back strength as well as general physical fitness. Its carry over value is among the highest of all sports, for it is equally for the younger player and the older hobbyist who makes her own bow and arrows or collects arrow-heads. It is one of the few sports which offers new challenges—when one has mastered target shooting she can learn to hunt for adventurous fun with a bow and arrow at home or while on a safari with the big game hunters of Africa.

This ancient sport of Robin Hood, William Tell and Hiawatha has strong romantic appeal, especially to youth. Its history includes the primitive who both protected himself and provided food with his crudely fashioned bows and arrows. It contains the colorful panorama of Egyptian, Greek, Turkish, Japanese, English, and French armies standing shoulder to shoul-der, or mounted on heavily padded horses shooting hundreds of arrows in unison at the approaching enemy. Museums in almost every nation have exhibits of these ancient weapons—the short heavy bow of only 4½ feet with even shorter arrows, the oddly-shaped C bow from which six feet long arrows were shot, or the highly polished English or Oriental crossbows, the unattractive but deadly weapons of the Indian hunters, or the poisoned ar-rows of uncivilized tribes.

Since the beginning of the 17th century, archery has continued to gain widespread popularity as a sport. Today over 500,000 people of varying age are enjoying this inexpensive activity in schools, colleges, parks, forests, and at camps. In the past 20 years the Camp Archery Association has given over 200,000 proficiency certificates to youth in summer camps. The National Archery Association, organized in America in 1879, annually sponsors a national tournament in this activity. The Olympic Bowman's League con-ducts winter indoor meets that are nationwide, and sponsors the annual Intercollegiate Telegraphic Tournament. Interest in archery continues to soar due largely to the great impetus given this game by the thousands who have thrilled to this challenging and rewarding sport.

THE NATURE AND PURPOSE OF THE GAME

The purpose of archery is to hit the target and preferably the bull's-eye with each arrow shot. Competition may be based upon individual or team (a group of four or less) or individual and team scores. Standard archery rounds for competitive purposes for women are:

American Round—30 arrows from 60 yards, 50 yards and 40 yards respectively.

Junior American Round—30 arrows from 50 yards, 40 yards and 30 yards respectively.

Columbia Round—24 arrows from 50 yards, 40 yards and 30 yards respectively.

Junior Columbia Round—24 arrows from 40 yards, 30 yards and 20 yards respectively.

Scholastic Round—24 arrows from 40 yards and 30 yards respectively. Junior Scholastic Round—24 arrows from 30 yards and 20 yards respectively.

Range Round—60 arrows from a single distance; either 50 yards or 40 yards or 30 yards or 20 yards on regulation targets.

Miniature Round—60 arrows from 15 yards on a *two-foot* target, scaled to the same proportions as is the regulation target.

SCORING

Gold	9 points
Red	7 points
Blue	5 points
Black	3 points
White	1 point

Arrow cutting two circles is given the higher point value.

Arrow that hits and bounces off the target is given 5 points.

Arrow that hits the petticoat is given 0 points.

Arrow that touches the line between two rings counts as hitting the higher value ring.

NEEDED FACILITIES AND EQUIPMENT

The Bow.   Semi-flat lemonwood bows are recommended for beginners because they are both inexpensive and durable. Bows are made all of one piece (a self-bow), or strengthened by thin pieces of fiber, felt, or wood (a backed bow), or constructed from two pieces or billets (also called half staves) which are spliced together. Bows made of osage orange, yew, or plastic have proven to be most satisfactory.

Bow length is largely determined by arrow length. Light bows are recommended for beginners so that they can develop good form quickly and make a full draw each time they shoot. A bow 5 feet 6 inches in length and weighing 18 to 22 pounds is ideal for this group, with intermediates using a 20 to 24 pound bow, and advanced students using one from 24 to 28 pounds.

Bow strings made from linen or latex are best. All strings should be kept well waxed. Single loop ones are recommended, because they can be made to fit any length bow.

Arrows.   Arrows should be true or straight and weigh between 250 and 300 grams. Port Oxford cedar arrows are superior to birch arrows, for the latter tend to warp easily. Self-arrows (made of a single piece of wood) or footed arrows (those having a foreshaft of hardwood) may be used. The feathers, or vanes, are taken from the wings of a turkey. The cock feather is at right angles to the nock and is of a different color than the hen feathers. The crest, or group of varicolored rings, adds attractiveness to arrows. Commonly used lengths range from 24 to 28 inches. The correct

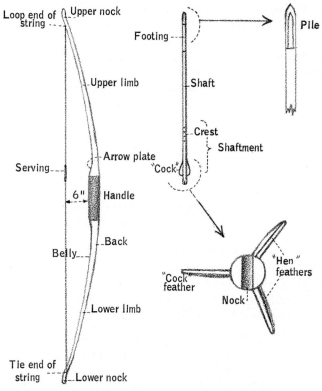

Figure No. 5–2.   Archery Equipment.

length for each student can be determined by measuring her arm distance from the knuckle of the first finger of the shooting hand to her chin. It can also be found by placing the arrow against the chest and reaching extended arms and fingertips around it. The arrow will be of correct length if it extends just beyond the fingertips of each hand.

Finger Tabs.   These are made from smooth, pliable leather. Finger stalls or tips, fashioned for each archer, are desirable but expensive unless each makes her own by cutting out the finger ends of an old glove. Advanced archers often use a shooting glove which has an opening for the thumb and little finger.

Arm Guards.   Such guards made of leather thick enough to protect the arm should cover the whole inner forearm. Laced guards are superior to those which buckle on.

Quivers.   Ground quivers are usually made of iron, circle shaped at the top with a pointed tip at the bottom and a hook near the circle on which to rest the bow. Leather quivers can be worn on a belt.

Targets.   Although bales of hay or heavy cardboard boxes stuffed with straw or hay can be used, rye straw targets are the best. The target

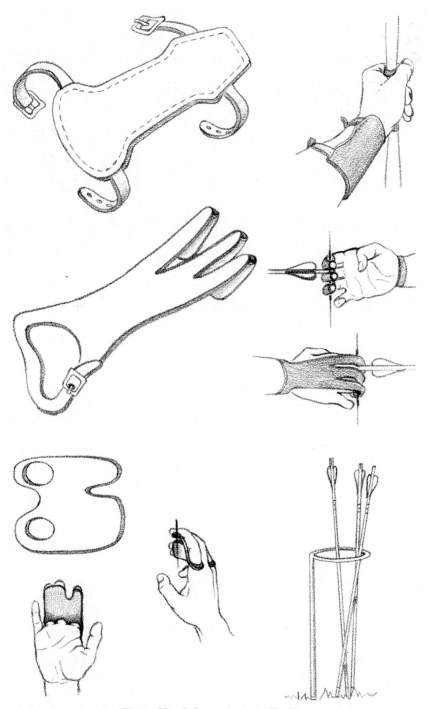

Figure No. 5–3.   Archery Tackle.

Name Audrey Bullett **Round** Jr. Col. Round **Date** May 20, 1955

At 40 yds.						Hits	Score
9	7	7	7	5		5	35
9	7	7	7	7	5	6	42
9	7	7	7	7		5	37
9	9	7	7	7	7	6	46
						22	160

At 30 yds.						Hits	Score
9	7	7	7	7	5	6	42
7	7	7	7	7	5	6	40
9	9	9	9	5	5	6	46
7	7	7	5	5	5	6	36
						24	164

At 20 yds.						Hits	Score
9	9	9	9	7	7	6	50
9	9	9	9	9	9 (6)	6	54
9	9	9	9	9	7	6	52
9	9	9	9	7	7	6	50
						24	206

Total Score 70 530

Name Mary McEwan **Round** Jr. Col. Round **Date** May 20, 1955

At 40 yds.						Hits	Score
9	5	5	5	3		5	25
7	5	5	5	3	1	6	26
5	5	1	1			4	12
9	5	3				3	17
						18	80

At 30 yds.						Hits	Score
9	9	7	5	5	3	6	38
9	7	7	5	5	5	6	38
7	7	7	7	3	3	6	34
7	7	5	5	5	3	6	32
						24	142

At 20 yds.						Hits	Score
9	7	7	7	5	3	6	38
7	7	7	7	5	3	6	36
9	7	7	7	5	5	6	40
9	7	7	5	5	3	6	36
						24	150

Total Score 66 372

Name Joan Lord **Round** Jr. Col. Round **Date** May 20, 1955

At 40 yds.						Hits	Score
9	9	7	7	5	3	6	40
7	7	7	5	5	5	6	36
7	7	7	5	3	1	6	30
9	9	7	5	5	5	6	40
						24	146

At 30 yds.						Hits	Score
9	9	9	9	9	7	6	52
9	9	9	9	9	7	6	52
9	9	7	7	7	5	6	44
9	9	9	9	9	7	6	52
						24	200

At 20 yds.						Hits	Score
9	9	9	7	7	1	6	42
9	9	9	9	9	7	6	52
9	9	9	9	9	7	6	52
9	9	9	9	7	7	6	50
						24	196

Total Score 72 542

Name Nancy Hoag **Round** Jr. Col. Round **Date** May 20, 1955

At 40 yds.						Hits	Score
7	7	7	5	5		5	31
7	7	5	3	1	1	6	24
7	7	7	7	5	5	6	38
9	9	9	7	7	3	6	44
						23	137

At 30 yds.						Hits	Score
7	7	7	7	5	3	6	36
9	9	7	7	7	5	6	44
9	9	9	7	7	5	6	46
9	9	7	7	7	7	6	46
						24	172

At 20 yds.						Hits	Score
9	7	7	7	7	7	6	44
9	7	7	7	7	5	6	42
9	9	9	7	5	5	6	44
9	9	9	7	7		6	50
						24	180

Total Score 71 489

Team Score 279 – 1933

SAMPLE SCORE SHEET

Figure No. 5–4.

should be 48 inches in diameter, 4 to 6 inches thick and hung so that the center of the gold is 4 feet from the ground. The face is tilted slightly toward the sky.

Target Stands. Regulation stands are made of cedar or cypress boards, six feet long, three inches wide and one inch thick and are bolted into a tripod at the end. On windy days ropes or ground hooks should be used to secure the target. One target blown over full of arrows is an expensive (but preventable) loss.

Target Faces. Oilcloth faces should be painted in bright colors with a gold center 9.6 inches in width surrounded by four concentric circles 4.8 inches wide and colored red, blue, black, and white and with the outer edge (or the petticoat) beyond the outer white ring one inch wide.

The Shooting Range. The outdoor range should be in a remote spot (preferably inside a fenced or roped-off area when located in a heavily populated play space) and be on well mowed, level ground. The target backdrop may be a hill, cliff, or bales of hay. An open area may be used providing there is at least 30 feet of open space behind the farthest target. The range should be at least 75 yards long with white marked shooting lines at 20, 30, 40, and 50 feet. Target centers should be 10 feet apart. Not more than five persons should shoot simultaneously at the same target. Although, if a partner system of alternate shooting and checking form is used, as many as ten may be assigned to the same target.

An indoor range of 35 to 45 feet may be used successfully. All room exits and entrances must be kept locked while shooting is in progress. Targets should be placed 10 feet apart and 3 feet from the back wall. Heavy felt mats, canvas, or fiberboard backdrops will protect the wall and arrows. Floor quivers made of tennis ball cans nailed to square boards can be used. Both a 20 and 30 foot range can be set up in such an area.

Score Cards.   Carefully kept scores help motivate skill mastery among individuals as well as class groups. Charts showing individual progress marked in red can be kept by either the student or teacher.

Points-of-Aim.   Brightly painted ice picks, wooden blocks one inch square and three inches long painted white and placed crosswise on the ground, or rolled up pieces of paper, a mound of grass or a leaf may be used for this purpose.

Bow Sights.   A glass-headed colored pin inserted on a piece of sponge rubber glued to the back of the limb of the bow makes an excellent bow sight. Hair and bead sights, prisms, and those made of metal are available commercially.

First Aid Kit.   A standard kit should be at the shooting range at all times. It should contain an additional supply of band aids, tweezers, antiseptic, and tape. Tincture of benzoin should also be included, since it will assist in toughening the fingers of the shooting hand. It should be applied at the first sign of soreness.

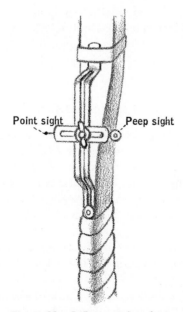

Figure No. 5-5.   Point-of-Aim.

TEACHING UNITS

Suggested course content for beginning and advanced students include:

Unit for Beginners	*Unit for Advanced Students*
Brief history	Discussion of archery clubs and
Selection of proper tackle	tournaments
Care of equipment	Review of safety rules
Safety rules	Review of fundamental skills
Fundamentals	Shooting at 20, 30, 40, 50 yards
Stringing	Field archery
Nocking	Flight shooting
Pulling	Clout shooting
Releasing	Archery golf
Point-of-aim, use of range	Cardboard animal shoot and other
finder and bow sight	novelty tournaments
Scoring	Basic hunting skills
Shooting at 20, 30, 40 yards	Evaluation
Evaluation	

Rainy Day Materials
(For classroom use where indoor archery is an impossibility)

Historical background
Parts of the bow and arrow
Care and repair of equipment
Films, filmstrips, and still pictures
Purchase of equipment
Tournament organization and etiquette.

BASIC SKILLS

Bracing and Unbracing the Bow. The lower end of the bow is placed against the inside arch of the left foot with the back of the bow held toward the body. The bow tip does not touch the ground but is pressed against the foot. The heel of the right hand is held near the bow tip while the left hand pulls the bow toward the body. The right hand presses the bow down while the thumb and index finger slide up the bow and slip the noose up to the nock.

To unstring the bow, the same bow, hands, and body positions are used. The string is lifted from its nock by the forefinger as the bow is pulled toward the body.

The Stance. The archer stands astride the shooting line with body weight equally divided. The left shoulder and head face the target, and the feet are spread shoulder width. The body is held in a relaxed, yet erect and comfortable position. The bow is held upright with the string side toward the body and the wood toward the target.

The Grip, Draw, and Release.   All fingers of the bow hand lightly encircle the bow as the bow rests against the fleshy part of the thumb and hand. The first three fingers of the other hand should reach under the string and hook over it at the first joint. As the draw is made, the bow arm is raised to shoulder height, the elbow is bent slightly and held in this position as the other hand pulls the string back to touch the nose and chin while the outer forefinger anchors under the jaw and against the neck. The fingers are opened to release the arrow and it shoots toward the target.

Nocking the Arrow.   The cock feather is held up while the arrow is placed on the string. The bow is held horizontal to the ground with the strings toward the body. The arrow is ready for shooting when it is on the string to the left side of the bow at the top of the bow grip, the cock feather is away from the bow, and the arrow is placed not too tightly on the string and can be easily released.

Aiming.   Only arrows shot at a short distance travel in a straight line, as they lose speed they curve to the ground. The arrow flight pattern is called its trajectory, and knowledge of the trajectory leads to successful scoring. A bow sight aids in shooting but it must be adjusted for each shooting distance. If the arrows are grouped high on the target, the sight is raised; lowered when they are grouped low.

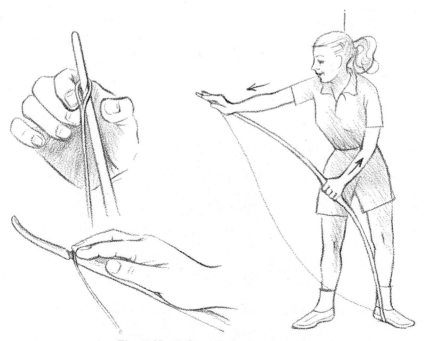

Figure No. 5–6.   Stringing the Bow.

The point-of-aim method of shooting is using a spot on the ground, target, or background at which the archer aims. It should be directly on the arrow tip, and must be adjusted for each distance shot, bow weight and arrow length, and changing environmental conditions. For shooting a long distance, the point of aim should be above the target; on the target for

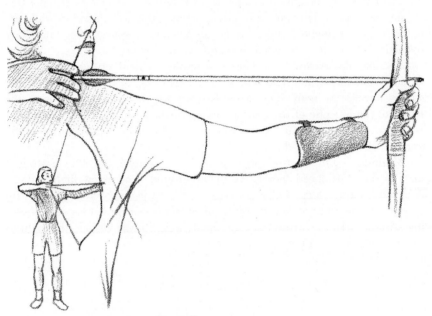

Figure No. 5–7.   Drawing the Bow.

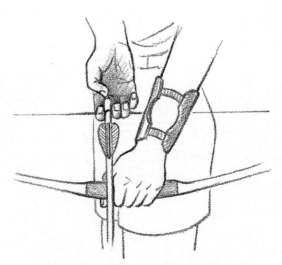

Figure No. 5–8.   Nocking the Arrow.

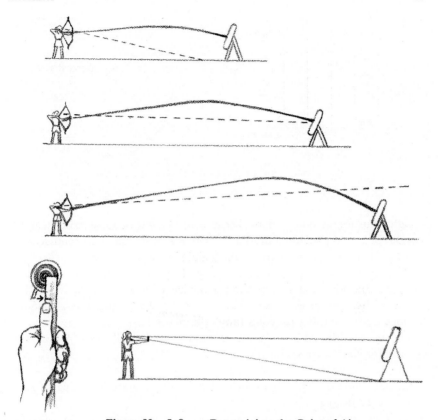

Figure No. 5–9.   Determining the Point-of-Aim.

medium distance; and in front of it for short range shooting. The point-of-aim should be lowered when arrows go over the target, and raised when they go below it. When arrows scatter or go to either side of the target consistently, shooting forms should be rechecked if the point-of-aim has been found to be correctly placed as shown by previous scores.

A range finder, made of a short stick or tongue depressor, can be used successfully when it is held so the top of the thumbnail matches with a ground point-of-aim. The stick is held perpendicular to the arrow's length and lined up with the gold target center.

CLASS ORGANIZATION

Ideally, each student should have her own tackle. However, two can share equipment with one shooting and the other checking form. Definite shooting lines should be marked off at 20, 30, 40, 60, or more yards and students trained to move as a group, upon a signal from the teacher, to retrieve arrows or shoot from new areas. A semi-circle is better than a

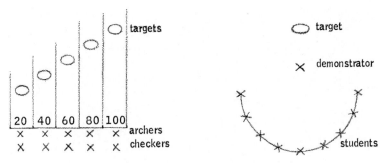

Figure No. 5–10.   Suggested Class Organizations.

straight line for demonstrations, because it enables all to see and hear the teacher better. Squad organization is best for large classes; groups can be rotated for shooting at various distances and scoring.

Homogeneous pupil grouping is favored by some instructors, but many feel that the advantages of placing a novice with a more experienced or skilled archer produces faster learning results. For tournament shooting, homogeneous grouping provides fairer competition.

Safety rules should be emphasized and followed at all times. A minimum of these for class purposes include:

1. All students must remain behind the safety line until a signal is given for retrieving arrows.
2. The bow is to be drawn only when one is standing on the shooting line. All arrows are to be nocked in unison at a given signal.
3. Only safe equipment will be used, and all splintered arrows, cracked bows, etc., given to the instructor for repair.
4. On the field range, "Fast" should be called out to warn others that an arrow is being released.
5. No one shall be careless with equipment, leave it unguarded where children or others can use it, or shoot an arrow high into the air without regard for the safety of others.

TEACHING PROGRESSION

As soon as all tackle has been properly fitted to each student and a brief rundown given on safety rules, the class should practice and gain a clear understanding of the basic steps for shooting: the stance, nock, anchor, aim, and release. These are first done mimetically with the teacher demonstrating the correct procedure for each step by (1) facing the group, and (2) with her back to them, having the group imitate her movements. This is followed by a repetition of these basic skills using the bow and arrow. The teacher may break down the complete movement by using counts and key-words, such as:

Count 1.	(The stance)	Straddle the shooting line
Count 2.	(The nock)	Nock your arrows
Count 3.	(The anchor)	Draw your arrow back, anchor under your chin
Count 4.	(The aim)	Aim carefully
Count 5.	(The release)	Open your fingers slowly, and hold position

Since one only learns when she has a need to do so, each individual should shoot towards the target at 20 yards in the first lesson in order to gain a quick realization of the necessity for following all instructions care-fully. Next, the group should be taught the bare essentials of aiming. Throughout the remainder of the unit, the teacher should give individual attention to all students and help them correct shooting faults and form. A suggested course outline for a beginner's unit includes:

Lesson I

1. Fit the needed tackle to each student
2. Explain the safety rules
3. Demonstrate mimetically, without tackle, explain, and count out the five basic steps for shooting
4. Have the class mimetically, without tackle, repeat these first basic steps for shooting
5. Have the class, with the tackle, do the basic steps for shooting
6. Shoot one end of arrows at 20 yards

Lesson II

1. Review mimetically the five basic steps
2. Shoot at 20 yards
3. Teach the point-of-aim shooting method
4. Teach scoring

Lesson III

1. Review the five basic steps, check each student's form
2. Shoot two ends at 20 yards
3. Have each student record her own scores
4. Shoot one end at 30 yards
5. Explain a progress chart showing scores and assign each student to keep her own

Lesson IV

1. Teacher demonstration of correct form and review of five basic steps
2. Teach the use of a range finder
3. Shoot two ends at 30 yards

Lesson V

1. Pupil demonstration (using one or two of the best) and review of correct shooting form
2. Teach the sight method of shooting
3. Shoot at 40 yards using a range stick and the sight method
4. Give advanced coaching hints for those scoring highest in the past two lessons

Lesson VI

1. Shoot and score at 20, 30, and 40 yards
2. Check the progress charts of each student and have each pinpoint her own weaknesses to the instructor

Lesson VII

1. Shoot and score at 30, 40, and 50 yards
2. Confer with each student again regarding her difficulty as previously expressed and help each improve shooting form

Lesson VIII

1. Introduce novelty animal or clout shooting
2. Brief review of materials covered
3. Teacher-student evaluations of class results. Individual student's written evaluation of her own efforts along with a list of the most important things in order of rank that each gained from the class

Lesson IX

1. Skill test
2. Oral review of all materials covered in class

Lesson X

1. Written test

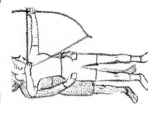
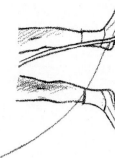
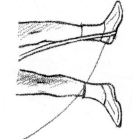
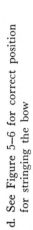
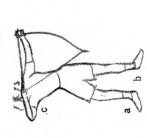

SKILL DIFFICULTIES AND THEIR CORRECTION

Difficulty

1. Stringing the bow

a. Inability to bend the bow far enough

b. Turning the bow away from the body

c. Inequality of pull strength of one arm with the push strength of the other

d. Pushing the bow end into the ground instead of bracing it against the instep of the foot

2. The Stance

a. Body weight unequally distributed, carried usually on the foot nearest the target

b. Stance too wide or too narrow, not straddling the line, feet not parallel

c. Leaning toward or away from the target

Correction

1.

a. Use a lighter bow

b. Have student repeat and do "Turn the bow toward the body" several times until the movement becomes automatic

c. Use a lighter bow

d. See Figure 5–6 for correct position for stringing the bow

2.

a. Teacher holds hands on student's waist to give her an idea of equally distributed weight

b. Insist on a stance shoulder width

c. Teacher stands behind archer and holds waist to prevent body movement until student avoids doing so

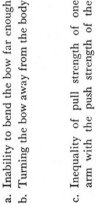
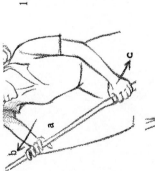
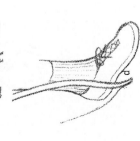

SKILL DIFFICULTIES AND THEIR CORRECTION (*Continued*)

Difficulty	*Correction*

3. *Holding the Bow*

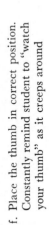

3.

a. Holding it only with encircled thumb and forefinger

b. Separation of the bow hand forefinger from the second; separation of all fingers

c. Wrist stiff and inflexible

d. Forefinger above or below the top edge of the handle

e. Turning the hand too far to the left or right

f. Hooking the thumb over the forefinger

a. Insist on the whole hand encircling the bow

b. Place small pieces of paper between fingers and tell student to keep them there until arrow is shot. Repeat until student gains the concept of fingers being held together

c. Teacher taps archer's wrist lightly, saying "relax" as she does so

d. Place tongue depressor or pencil on the hand until student can balance it by holding hand straight. Shoot from corrected position

e. Place student's fingers in proper position and watch her shoot two or more ends in order to get the "feel" of the correct hand position

f. Place the thumb in correct position. Constantly remind student to "watch your thumb" as it creeps around

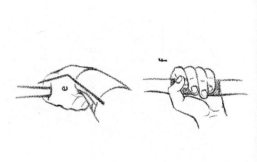

Difficulty

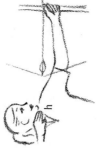

g. Bending the head forward to sight the arrow

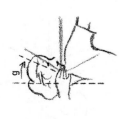

h. Moving the string hand forward and collapsing the bow arm when shooting the arrow

i. Holding the string too far back in fingers

Correction

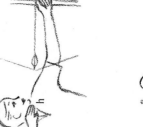

g. Teacher holds the student's head steadily in correct position as she shoots several times

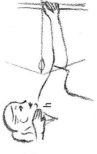

h. Remind the student to hold shooting position a bit longer after arrow leaves the bow

i. Remind student to hook the string before the first joint

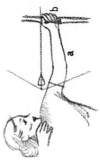

SKILL DIFFICULTIES AND THEIR CORRECTION (*Continued*)

Difficulty	*Correction*
4. Nocking the Arrow	**4.**
a. Having the cock feather down	a. Have the student reverse the feather and say, "The cock feather is up"
b. Failing to nock the arrow so it is in a straight line	b. Have the student nock arrow, teacher checks arrow position before student shoots
5. The Release (Causing arrows to go high or over the target)	**5.**
a. Straightening the bow arm	a. Have student repeat and do "bend arm slightly and hold this position" several times as the teacher watches her shoot
b. Lifting the bow arm or index finger	b. Have the student repeat and do "keep bow arm (or index finger) in the same position" several times as the teacher watches her shoot
c. Dropping the elbow or string hand	c. See b above, with student using the phrase "keep elbow in a straight line" or "do not drop string hand"
d. "Peeking" or looking up too soon to see arrow flight at short ranges	

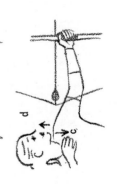

Difficulty	*Correction*

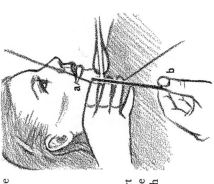

e. Opening the mouth causing the anchor point to be lowered

f. Overdrawing the bow by bringing the string back behind the anchor point

g. Jerking the hand back and inward on the release

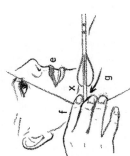

d. Teacher holds student's head in desired position as she shoots

e. Remind student to keep lips together

f. Watch student draw, anchor, and shoot. Help her "feel" when to release the arrow

g. Hold the student's fingers in anchor position until she releases the arrow

6.

6. *The Release* (Causing arrows to go low or below the target)

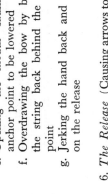

a. Creeping or pushing the arrow forward as it is released

a. Insist that student anchors before releasing the arrow

b. Anchoring too high, failing to anchor under jaw, or holding anchor and drawn position too long before releasing

b. Teacher touches with finger or short stick to exact anchor point on the student's face and stands by to watch her shoot several arrows

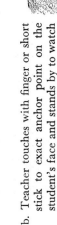
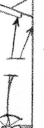
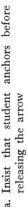
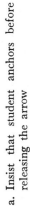
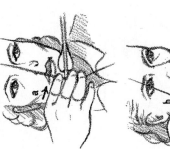
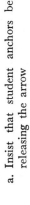

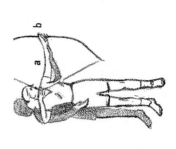

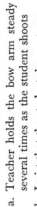

SKILL DIFFICULTIES AND THEIR CORRECTION (*Continued*)

Difficulty	*Correction*
c. Lifting the chin forward to reach the string.	c. Teacher holds the student's hand in desired position until she gets the concept of keeping her head steady
d. Using a point-of-aim that is too near, or not keeping the aiming position steady	d. Move point-of-aim further away. Have student keep point-of-aim for four counts, releasing on count 3
7. *The Release* (Causing the arrows to go to the right)	7.
a. Moving the bow arm to the right	a. Teacher holds the bow arm steady several times as the student shoots
b. Turning the bow to the right just before or during shooting	b. Insist that the student does not move the bow after correct drawing position is made

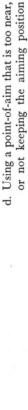

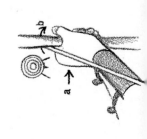

c. Remind student to distribute weight evenly

d. Have student count 1, 2, 3, 4 and release on count 3

8.

a. Teacher holds the bow arm steady several times as the student shoots

b. Teacher touches correct anchor shot under student's jaw and watches her draw, anchor, and shoot several times from this spot

c. Teacher holds left shoulder in correct position as student shoots several arrows

d. Have student repeat and do "relax hand," or "relax fingers"

e. Remind student of correct position and watch her shoot several ends

f. Stress again the necessity of keeping the hand at anchor point until the arrow hits the target

g. Have student review the directions for sighting. She usually does not know the correct ones given periodically in class

c. Body weight carried on toes instead of whole foot

d. Releasing too quickly (sometimes is called "Shooting Indian Style")

8. *The Release* (Causing the arrows to go to the left)

a. Moving the bow arm to the left

b. Incorrect anchor, usually at cheek-bone or beside lips

c. Hunching left shoulder

d. Gripping the bow and/or arrow too tightly

e. Bending the bow arm too much

f. Moving the string hand away from the anchor point

g. Sighting with the left eye

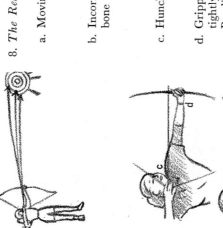

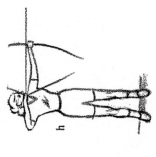

Difficulty	*Correction*
h. Weight on heels and body line held backward	h. Remind student to distribute weight on the whole foot and not lean away from the target
9. *The Arrow Falling to the Ground Before It Can be Shot*	**9.**
a. Improper hand shelf on which the arrow rests	a. Repeatedly check bow hand position by teacher and student
b. Pinching the **arrow nock**	b. Have student recheck fingers of drawing hand to be sure all fingers are pulling equally
10. *A String Burn of the Bow Arm*	**10.**
a. Moving the bow arm as arrow is released. Turning bow arm and hand too far to the left	a. Reemphasize the "hold" bow arm position
11. *Cutting the Forefinger of the Bow Hand With the Arrow*	**11.**
a. Improper shelf for arrow before and during shooting	a. See previous suggestions for remedying this fault. Also check the condition of all feathers as well as the trueness of all arrows

NOVELTY EVENTS

The following novelty events can do much to maintain or increase student interest in archery after the basic skills of the sport have been mastered.

Balloon Shoot. Place brightly colored balloons around the target face. Devise a novel scoring system for awarding points for each broken balloon. For variations, shoot at many balloons tied on a long rope which is extended between two target stands or upright poles parallel to the ground.

Big Game Hunt. Cut silhouettes of various African game out of cardboard and paint them. The object of this sport is to hit the greatest number of animals or gain the greatest score by hitting the most vital spots (award 5 for hitting the heart area, 4 for between the eyes, etc.). Commercial animal silhouettes can be obtained from many sporting goods companies or from the Ben Pearson Archery Company, Pine Bluff, Arkansas.

Wand Shooting. Drive a thin strip of wood two inches wide and six feet high into the ground. The winner scores the greatest number of hits from 36 arrows shot at 60 yards. For variation, a strip of cardboard can be attached to the target, in first a horizontal then a perpendicular position, and shot at for the highest number of hits.

Clout Shooting. Shoot 36 arrows from first 120 then 140 yards at a target laid flat on the ground and marked by a red flag in the center. Score as in regular archery.

Flight Shooting (Also known as Free Style Shooting). The winner shoots the fartherest arrow using either regular equipment or special flight shooting equipment (shorter, thicker bows with lighter arrows made especially for resisting air pressure). In "free style shooting," the archer lies on her back, has the bow strapped to her feet and draws the bowstring with both hands. (The present record for such shooting is 575 yards and 2 feet.)[1]

Archery Golf. The winner is the one making the hole in the fewest number of shots. The game is played on a regular golf course with a small target placed on each green instead of the cup.

OFFICIATING TECHNIQUES

The presiding official for tournament competition is known as Lady Paramount. Her official duties are to:

1. Examine and approve the shooting area.
2. Check all target assignments.
3. Supervise the three preliminary target practice ends.
4. See that all rules are enforced.
5. Answer all questions from target captains or archers after the preliminary practice and before the competition begins.
6. Signal by one whistle blast for all shooting to start, by two whistle blasts for an emergency and all shooting to cease.

[1] Menke, Frank: *The Encyclopedia of Sports,* New York, A. S. Barnes, p. 23.

7. Make the final decisions for all questionable hits by personally removing the arrow in question and placing it in the area in which it is to be scored.

8. Penalize an archer after repeated rule infractions have been called to her attention by enforcing the following progressive penalties: a. loss of the highest scoring arrow during the end in which a rule was broken; b. removal of archer and her score from the round being shot; c. withdrawal from the tournament.

9. Sign all score cards.

A target captain at each target assists the Lady Paramount by performing the following duties:

1. Sees that each archer shoots in order.
2. Settles all local questions.
3. Draws out all arrows from the target and calls out the score made.
4. Takes an archer's place in the shooting line in case of an accident or delay.

Two official scorers should be assigned at each target to record the number of hits and scores for each end, group ends and range scores, and the total number of hits and scores for each round. The method used for tournament scoring is like that followed in non-competitive shooting except for the following differences:

1. An arrow that has passed completely through the target so it cannot be seen on the target face counts 7 at 60 yards or less.

2. All arrows rebounding from the target, as witnessed by others, count 7 points.

3. Both penetrations and rebounds are checked in red by the target captain after the target has been checked for line hits.

4. An arrow which hits and is embedded into another arrow on the target counts the same as the arrow in which it is embedded.

5. All tie scores shall be broken by counting the greatest number of golds, reds, blues, and blacks in that order. If the tie remains, it is to be resolved by the greatest number of perfect ends. If it is still tied, it remains so.

6. All arrows withdrawn by anyone other than the target captain are not counted.

7. In the event that any archer shoots more than six arrows in any end, she must forfeit as many of the highest scoring arrows as the number of extra arrows shot.

8. Any hit or score made on a target unassigned to an archer is not scored.

9. Arrows scoring highest are drawn first from the target.

10. The archer may not repeat the shot if her tackle breaks during the act of shooting.

The official rules for field round shooting and other types of archery competitive meets can be found in the DGWS Archery-Riding Guide for 1958-1960.

EVALUATING THE RESULTS

Since evaluative tools help motivate student progress as well as help teachers grade students fairly, the following means for evaluating results are recommended:

1. A written objective test of rules, shooting techniques, and safety precautions.
2. Archery tournaments (ladder, single and double elimination) in which each archer keeps and records her own final tournament standing.
3. A progress chart, marked in red, of the daily scores of each student and kept by each one.
4. An analysis form technique chart based upon the correct shooting fundamentals used by each partner to check the other. Score one point for each fundamental done correctly, none for those incorrectly performed.
5. The use of the Hyde Archery Test,[2] in which students shoot and score 120 arrows at 30, 40, and 50 yards.
6. The use of the Columbia Round:

24 arrows at 50 yards

24 arrows at 40 yards

24 arrows at 30 yards

TERMINOLOGY

Anchor—The string hand position which is fixed under the jaw when the archer is shooting or aiming

Brace—Stringing the bow

Cock Feather—The feather at right angles to the nock. It is usually a different color than the other feathers

Creeping—The edging forward of a fully drawn arrow before it is released

End—Six arrows shot in succession

Fistmele—The distance between the bow belly and the string (approximately six to seven inches but more for recured fibre glass) that is the ideal bracing height for most arrows

Follow-Through—Holding the release position until the arrow hits or lands

Grouping—A cluster of arrows which have landed approximately in the same place on the target

Hanging Arrow—An arrow which has landed on the target only at the tip end and hangs down

Hen Feathers—The two feathers on the arrow which are not at right angles to nock (these are usually the same color)

[2] Mathews, Donald: *Measurement in Physical Education*, Philadelphia, W. B. Saunders Company, pp. 157–158.

Nock—The grooves at the bow ends into which the string is slipped for bracing the bow; also the end of the arrow into which the string is fitted for nocking the arrow

Point-of-Aim—The point below, above, or in front of the target at which the archer aims

Release—Rolling the fingers off the string to send the arrow on its way

Six Golds—A perfect end; all six arrows scoring 9 points

Trajectory—The arrow's path of flight

Discussion Questions

1. Demonstrate and briefly explain the five mimetical steps for teaching beginners to shoot correctly.
2. Demonstrate and explain the reason why arrows would consistently go (a) below the target, (b) to the right, (c) above the target, (d) to a seven o'clock position on the target face.
3. Bring to class an arrow you have repaired. What have you learned from this experience?
4. Draw up a plan for teaching an archery unit of ten lessons to a class of 35 students in a situation where only 18 bows, the needed number of arrows for each student, and four targets are available.
5. Demonstrate and explain the use of (a) point-of-aim, (b) a range finder, and (c) a bow sight. Which method for aiming would you endorse? Why?
6. Draw up plans for an archery tournament for 60 participants. What (a) entry qualifications, (b) safety regulations, (c) methods of officiating, (d) type of tournament, and (e) kind of awards would you endorse?

Selected Audio-Visual Aids

Archery For Beginners. (12 min., silent, b & w). United World Films, 542 S. Dearborn Street, Chicago, Ill. (Rental)

Archery for Girls, 1949. (10 min., sound, b & w). Coronet Instructional Films, 65 East South Water Street, Chicago, Ill. (Purchase)

Archery Technique Chart, Mrs. E. B. Miller, 450 West 24th Street, 16A, New York, N.Y. (Purchase)

Activities at Teela-Wooket Archery Camp. (10 min., silent). Mrs. E. B. Miller, 450 West 24th Street, 16A, New York, N.Y. (Rental)

Beginning Archery. (Filmstrip, 4 units, 10 min. each, color). The Athletic Institute, 209 S. State Street, Chicago 4, Ill.

Suggested Readings

A.A.H.P.E.R., *Archery-Riding Guide,* 1958–1960, Division for Girls and Women's Sports, Washington, D.C., 1958.

Armbruster, David: *Basic Skills in Sports,* St. Louis, C. V. Mosby Company, 1953.

DeWitt, R. T.: *Teaching Individual and Dual Sports,* New York, Prentice-Hall Book Company, Inc., 1953.

Reichart, Natalie, and Keasey, Gilman: *Archery,* New York, A. S. Barnes, 1940.

Shane, Adolph: *Archery Tackle, How To Make and Use It,* Peoria, Manual Arts Press, 1936.

Wilson, Lura R.: Aids in Running an Archery Tournament, *Official Archery-Riding Guide,* 1954–56, pp. 29–31.

Periodicals

Archery, Post Office Box H, Palm Springs, California. $2.25 for 12 issues.

The Archer's Magazine, 1200 Walnut Street, Philadelphia, Pa. $2.50 for 12 issues.

Badminton

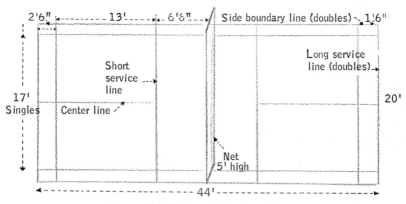

Figure No. 6–1. Badminton Court.

Badminton originated from the ancient game "Battledore and Shuttlecock" played in Siam and China over 2,000 years ago. A modified version of this sport known as "Poona" in India caught the attention and enthusiasm of British Army officers stationed there who later brought the game home to England with them around 1870. The Duke of Beaufort gave real impetus to the game at his estate, Badminton House, in the rural hamlet of Badminton in Gloucestershire. The game spread rapidly throughout the world and reached America via Canada. Since 1929 it has gained thousands of enthusiastic players and spectators in America. Numerous tournaments are sponsored by the American Badminton Association, and many individuals subscribe to "Bird Chatter," the official publication of this organization.[1] The game is taught and played in many of our secondary schools and colleges throughout the land.

[1] For information regarding this magazine, write to the Editor, *Bird Chatter,* 7518 Orin Court, Seattle 3, Washington.

As a co-educational and family activity, badminton has no equal. It is a sport with great appeal for all ages, as well as for those of varying skill levels and degrees of physical stamina. Although the beginner can quickly learn to hit the bird back and forth across the net, it is the advanced player, who has mastered game strategy and bird placement, that receives the greatest satisfaction from the game. Since badminton requires little space and can be played outdoors as well as indoors on an imperfect or perfect surface, and since accident possibilities and game hazards are minimized, and needed equipment is inexpensive, it is an ideal activity for schools, camps, organizations, and backyard family fun.

THE NATURE AND PURPOSE OF THE GAME

Badminton can be played as a singles or doubles game with one or two players on a side. The object of the game is to hit the shuttlecock, or bird, back and forth with a racket across a net 5 feet from the floor at its center and 5 feet and 1 inch at the sides.

SCORING

A game of women's singles is 11 points, whereas for men's singles and mixed doubles it is 15 points. The doubles service court extends from the short service line to the long service line, and from the center line to the side boundary line. The singles service court extends from the short service line to the back boundary line, and from the center line to the side boundary line. The court service boundaries are long and narrow for singles, short and fat for doubles. After service the singles playing court remains the same, whereas the doubles playing area becomes long and wide. Points are scored only by the serving side with loss of a point known as "side out," as in volleyball.

The server serves only one bird into alternate courts (as in tennis) and begins in her right-hand court. To be good, the bird must go diagonally across the net and land in the receiver's box. In doubles, only one player serves at the beginning of the game (this is called "one hand down in the first inning"), but for the rest of the game both the opposing partners alternate serves. Service in doubles always starts in the right court. In singles the service begins in the right court, but thereafter it is made only in this court when the score is even for that side, and in the left court when the score is odd for that side. The singles player first to reach nine points when the score is 9-All may choose to play for 3 more points, or for 2 more when the score is 10-All. In doubles, when the score is tied 13-All, those first reaching 13 determine whether to finish the game at 15 or to "set" it for five more points. At 14-All the game may be set at 3 more points.

It is a fault (a service or hand loss for the server, or point loss for the receiver) when:

(*a*) the bird is served above the waist or the racket head is higher than the hand on a serve

(*b*) the bird is hit out of bounds, into the net, or hits a player or any obstruction outside the court

(*c*) anyone other than the intended receiver returns the bird

(*d*) the server feints a serve or baulks her opponent

(*e*) a player reaches over the net to hit the bird or touches it with any part of her body or racket

(*f*) a player hits the bird twice, "tosses" or "holds" it, or "hits wood" instead of stroking it correctly

(*g*) a player fails to return the bird, hits it twice in a row, or it is hit by one player and then her partner successively before it goes over the net

(*h*) the shuttlecock hits the net on service

NEEDED FACILITIES AND EQUIPMENT

Badminton rackets weigh between 4½ and 5 ounces and are much more delicate than tennis rackets. The strings are made of nylon, gut, steel or linen; the body of aluminum, fiberglass, plastic or wood. All steel rackets are both inexpensive and durable for large groups. Advanced players, however, prefer and should play with wooden rackets strung either with nylon or gut. When not in use, all such rackets should be kept in a press. A badminton cart with multiple presses is recommended for both proper storage and ease of distribution of rackets for class use.[2]

Shuttlecocks may be made of cork, 14 to 16 goose feathers covered with fine leather, or of plastic. The former is best for skilled players. The best birds are stitched in three places to keep the 16 feather spines and quills straight. Beginners may be taught to play with fleece balls commercially obtained or homemade of yarn, wool or cotton practice balls, or birds made of synthetic materials or chicken feathers before using the more costly ones. Students should be taught to straighten out the feathers before hitting the bird each time, as well as be cautioned against damaging it by kicking or stepping on it or putting it into play with overhead strokes. All feathered birds should be kept in a humidifier in a temperature between 60 and 65° and a humidity of 70 to 75 per cent before using them again after each play period. A modified humidifier can be made by placing a smaller tin can filled with water on a well filled sponge into a larger can. Place a wire screen over the smaller can and scatter the birds over it; then cover both cans to retain the moisture.[3]

The net should be made of fine meshed cord, kept folded, and stored in a dry place when not in use.

[2] Hale, Patricia: Design For a Badminton Cart. *Official Tennis-Badminton Guide, 1956–1958*, National Section for Girls and Women's Sports, AAHPER, Washington, D.C., pp. 94–98.

[3] Bourguardez, Virginia, and Heilman, Charles: *Sports Equipment, Selection, Care and Repair*, New York, A. S. Barnes, 1950, p. 214.

Rubber-soled tennis shoes or sneakers are required for safe indoor play and are also recommended for outdoor use.

TEACHING UNITS

Suggested areas to be included in the units for beginners and advanced students are:

Units for Beginners	*Units for Advanced Students*
Brief history	Selection and care of personal equipment
Care and use of equipment	
Fundamental skills	Review of fundamental skills
Serving	Advanced skills
Forehand stroke	High, deep serve placement
Backhand stroke	Low, short serve placement
The smash	Cross court shots
The clear	Undernet hairpin shots
The round-the-head shot	Doubles strategy
The drop shot	Up-and-back
Footwork	Side-by-side
Rules	Rotation
Singles and doubles playing strategy	Mixed doubles play
Ladder and/or single elimination tournament play	Singles strategy stressing speed and game pace variance
Evaluation	Types of tournaments and play in as many kinds as possible
	Evaluation

BASIC SKILLS

The Grip.   A flexible wrist snap is imperative for correct form. This can best be accomplished by grasping the racket handle as though shaking hands with it and holding it toward the net with the racket face at right angles to the ground. The fingers are spread slightly apart and the racket held in an easy grip, primarily with the pressure of the thumb, forefinger and little finger. The "V" between the thumb and forefinger should be at the handle top and in direct line with the racket head. The racket should appear to be an extension of the arm. Swing the racket back and forth, snapping the wrist to get the feel of the needed, quick definite movement.

The Forehand Stroke.   This stroke, which is similar to throwing a softball, is a flowing, free movement in which the follow-through plays an important part. It is a natural movement used when returning the bird from the right side of the body. The head of the racket should be kept over the wrist, the left foot forward, the body leaning slightly (toward sideward angles to the net). The backswing should start at the same time the left foot is brought forward. The wrist should be slightly ahead of the racket head and snapped at the moment of contact. If the player wants to hit the bird upward, she should swing low, then up to it, whereas to hit it downward, the forward swing is in a downward arc. The arm should be extended and relaxed, and the bird hit squarely in the racket center by a quick wrist flick.

Figure No. 6–2.   Forehand Grip.

Figure No. 6–3.   Forehand Stroke.

Figure No. 6–4.   The Backhand Grip.

Figure No. 6–5.   The Serve.

The Backhand Stroke.   Opposite to the forehand stroke, this one is made with the right shoulder facing the net. As the bird is hit with the reverse side of the racket, the weight is shifted with the feet in a stride position from the rear to the forward foot. When the bird is played in front of the body, the thumb may be held so that it rests flat against the non-hitting side of the racket for more power and better control.

The Serve.   The shuttle should be struck in front of the body with the full arm stretched for a relaxed but forceful movement. The body weight, distributed evenly, feet held in stride position, shifts from the forward foot to back, then is returned to forward as the bird is hit. The wrist flick, forward arc swing and follow-through should be easy, natural movements. Beginners should drop the bird from the thumb and index finger, held at the extreme feather tip, and play it in front of the forward foot. Advanced players may master the toss serve by throwing the bird slightly into the air and contacting it with a well timed forward stroke. The majority of serves in singles should be high and deep; in doubles, low and land just inside the service court or on a boundary line. To be a legal serve, the bird must be contacted below the waist with no part of the racket higher than the server's hand.

The Overhead Stroke. On this shot the bird is hit above the head to the right of the body for the forehand and to the left for the backhand overhead stroke. The feet are held shoulder width apart in stride position. As the bird is contacted, body weight shifts from the rear to the forward foot. The arm is slightly bent and is extended when the bird is hit slightly in front of the body with a forceful wrist flick. The racket follow-through makes a half circle. Quick judgment, timing, and accuracy are required to hit the approaching bird at least six inches in front of the body and to bring it down just over the net and well placed in the opponent's court.

The Round-the-Head Shot. Similar to the overhead stroke, this one is stronger and often more effective. The narrow stride stance and shift of weight from the rear to the forward foot are similar to those used in most

Figure No. 6-6.   The Overhead Stroke.

Figure No. 6–7.   The Around-the-Head-Stroke.

shots except that the weight should end well-balanced on the left foot. The bird is contacted above the shoulder and around the head on the left side by extending the bent stroking arm in order to hit the bird on the racket forehand side.

Strokes As Determined By Bird Flights.

The High Clear.   Played either by the fore or backhand, the high clear is a defensive stroke used to gain time, to move the opponent into the back court or draw her to the net, or change game pace. The bird is played just as it is in either the fore or backhand and should land far into the back court after sailing high into the air. It is similar to the tennis lob.

The Drive.   This attacking stroke should barely clear the net. It can be played with either the fore or backhand to force the opponent to switch to alternate court sides. The bird can best be controlled for this stroke at shoulder height but can be also played successfully from knee level. Variance in bird speed must be mastered in order to use this shot most effectively.

The Drop Shot.   The name of this stroke best describes it, for it is a shot which causes the bird to drop sharply close to the net into the opponent's front court. Played as any other shot, it requires control, placement ability, and is used as a surprise attack to change game pace, or to fool the opponent who, expecting a drive or clear into the back court, has moved

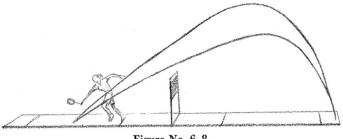

Figure No. 6–8.

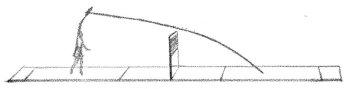

Figure No. 6–9.   Types of Shots.

back for it and is thus out of position. Cross court drop shots are especially effective. Overhand strokes are best for making such a shot while in the back court, and underhand ones wisest to use when close to the net.

The Smash.   Although the smash is used more in doubles than in singles, it is best played in midcourt and should be aimed directly at the opponent, to her weakest defensive body side (usually backhand for right-handed players and forehand for left-handed players), or for open court spaces. It should be a powerful, fast stroke and can be best done with a forehand. In the forehand smash the left foot should be ahead and the racket swung far back behind the head and shoulder by a flexible wrist. The bird should be hit ahead of the forward left foot and weight put into the stroke by a forceful body shift as the bird is contacted. The term "smash" is both descriptive of this stroke and how to do it correctly.

The Net or Hairpin Shot.   Played close to the net, this shot can send the bird just barely over it, diagonally across it, or far into the back court as a high clear. The bird should be hit near the net top, and the racket held face up by the extended arm as it gently taps the shuttlecock with a slight wrist action. Careful aiming, coupled with this restricted wrist motion will direct the bird most effectively. The net clear is similar to the drop shot but is done with a delayed, more pronounced wrist flick. This stroke is ideal for changing game pace, gaining time, wearing the opponent down, and restricting the possibility of any diagonal or outward angles to a returned shot.

PLAYING STRATEGY

Badminton is a game of brain as well as brawn. In the pre-game warm up, players should discover each other's weaknesses whether they be in stroking or inability to move quickly around the court and then, during the game, play to that weakness. Hitting the bird *away* from the opponent or into uncovered court areas is usually the best strategy to use. Wearing her out by running her up the court then back is ideal for this purpose. Since one can only score points each time she serves or is "in," the skilled player who realizes this will never *beat herself* by careless mistakes such as serving incorrectly or hitting the bird into the net or out of bounds.

Singles Strategy

1. Although deep, high serves near the center line are best for singles, they should be varied in height and direction. The server's best position is about four feet behind the short service line, but she should return after the serve to the middle of the court (or "home base"). The receiver's best position is in midcourt slightly centered.
2. Return a high serve with a drop to the opponent's forehand, or clear to her backhand, or a sparingly used smash.
3. Return a short serve with a high clear in the back court.
4. Avoid returning a net shot with a net shot unless you can do a quick diagonal one away from your opponent.
5. Anticipate returns. Hit the shuttle back to the court area your opponent is leaving.
6. Always play the bird in front of you, remembering that if it goes back over your head you are lost, and that it is easier to move forward than backward.
7. Cross court smashes are generally the most effective.
8. Return a smash with a drop shot away from the area from which your rival smashed.
9. Change game pace often; plan your strokes ahead.
10. Take the offensive by making accurate, well placed shots from a well prepared defensive position which moves your opponent from front to rear, side to side.
11. Deception is the key to winning. Deceive your opponent by making the same preparatory stroke for the smash, drop, and clear, then fool her by using the one for which she is least prepared.

Doubles Play

Four methods for playing doubles are:

1. *Side-by-side*—with each player being responsible for her half of the court.
2. *Up-and-back*—with one player at the net and her partner covering the back court.
3. *A combination*—in which the side-by-side system is used for defense and the up-and-back method for offense.
4. *Rotation*—best for advanced players who circle counterclockwise in order to play the bird forehand as much as possible. As the right player ad-

vances to the net, the left one drops back, crosses into the right court, and moves into the original player's right court position, as both continue in the circle. Both players should be right-handed if the system is used.

Strategy

1. The best defensive position is partners side-by-side near the center of the court. The best attacking formation is for one to smash, with her partner forward ready to "kill" a weak forecourt return.
2. Most serves should be short and low, but long, deep ones should be used occasionally.
3. Hit most shots down and away from the opponents.
4. Gain the attack and keep it by hitting the bird low so the opponents will have to hit it up and it can be smashed back at them.
5. Use hard smashes directed to the body.
6. Drive the bird occasionally down the midcourt line in order to draw both opponents to the center with the hope that they will both go for it, or if one is left-handed and her partner right-handed.

CLASS ORGANIZATION

The teacher faces the group which has been formed into a single line in front of her as she explains and demonstrates the correct grip, footwork, and other aspects of the correct form for each stroke. The group then does each of these without the bird as the teacher passes along the line giving individual help and correcting faulty movements. The forehand, backhand,

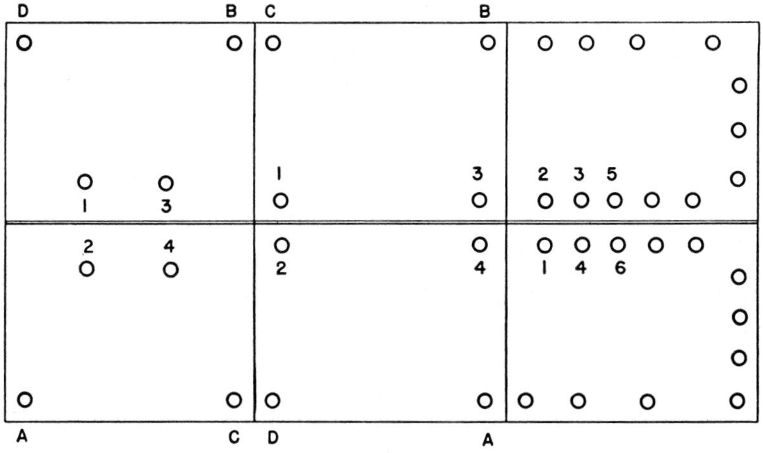

Figure No. 6–10.   Class Organizational Plan for a Large Class.

Court 1: A serves deep to B, C to D. 1 + 2, 3 + 4, net shots. Players rotate positions.
Court 2: A + B, line drives; C + B, line drives. 1 — 2, 3 — 4, net shots. Players rotate positions.
Court 3: 1 — 2, 3 — 4, 5 — 6, net shots. Rest—wall practice. Players rotate positions.

and serve strokes are taught mimetically before the group is divided into two facing lines, with each student working with opposing partner as the bird is hit back and forth across the net.

Although ideally only four persons should be assigned to a court, as many as six may be assigned, with three on each side. Since court markings are unimportant to beginners, in large classes additional practice space can be made by stretching ropes across unused court border areas. Those having difficulty can be moved to a wall space for individually coached racket practice with a synthetic based bird.

Above all, every student should be kept actively engaged throughout each period learning to play, officiate, or master the game strategy of badminton. In large classes using four courts it is suggested that one student be assigned to rate on a scorecard one, two, or all four partners playing doubles depending on class size, and to go over the tallied results with them. Such a method increases the scorer's awareness of how the game is being played in relation to how it should be played. Extra players can also keep score and officiate games.

TEACHING PROGRESSION

Students are first taught the serve and are given basic information followed by teacher demonstration of the grip, arm swing, wrist action, timing, and footwork. Next comes the forehand, the backhand, and underhand clear —in that order. Judging from pupil progress, the class begins playing a game as soon as possible. Miller and Ley suggest that the following related strokes (Figure 6–11) be taught when the class is ready to learn them:[4]

⎰ Short serve—1 ⎱ Underhand clear (long serve)—2	⎰ Drive—7 ⎱ Overhead drop shot—8
⎰ Overhead clear—3 ⎱ Smash—4	⎧ Long serve (underhand clear)—9 ⎨ Overhead clear—10 ⎩ Smash
⎰ Underhand drop—5 ⎱ Net shots—6	⎧ Underhand drop ⎨ Short serve ⎩ Net strokes

Students are assigned to squads, court, and practice areas by subjective grouping after the first lesson so that the instructor can rotate from those having difficulty on to those ready to learn a new skill, or how to polish the one already mastered, or to those making some progress. The Miller Badminton Wall Volley Test, given in the fourth lesson, will serve to regroup the class more objectively.[5]

[4] Miller, Donna Mae, and Ley, Katherine: *Individual and Team Sports for Women,* New York, Prentice-Hall Book Company, 1956, p. 110.
[5] Mathews, Donald: *Measurement in Physical Education,* Philadelphia, W. B. Saunders Company, 1958, pp. 159 to 161.

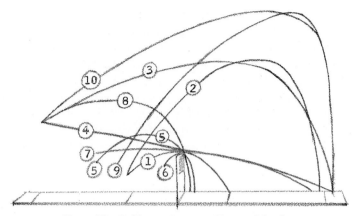

Figure No. 6–11. Common Types of Strokes.

The class should rally first in partners the major portion of the first lesson, and then with one bird in groups of four on each court. Competitive counting among partners as they hit the shuttle back and forth to each other until one couple reaches 15, then 25 points first (after starting back to count one each time the bird is missed), serves both as a learning incentive and increases aiming accuracy. Those able to do this successfully are ready to learn to hit the bird *away* from their partners, an idea and technique most difficult for many players to gain.

By the second lesson the class should see a demonstration game played by experts. Although a film may be used for this purpose, it is second best, especially for beginners who are usually more motivated by seeing a fast game skillfully played on the same court they are using. Simplified scoring rules can also be demonstrated at this time, whereas other rules (such as serving) can best be understood as the strokes are learned. The cartoon method for teaching rules, perfected by the Athletic Institute of Chicago, via filmstrip or bulletin board materials, is highly recommended.

Overhand bird throwing drills are suggested for those having trouble learning the smash. Have partners (1) stand at midcourt and throw the bird over each other's head, (2) against a large wall space, and (3) into wall circles of diminishing size. Bouncing-against-the-wall drills, again using (1) large wall space ten feet high while standing ten feet away, (2) one five feet high, and (3) into circles of diminishing size, are recommended for practicing the serve, forehand, and backhand strokes.

Footwork drills to learn changing body positions and racket grip can best be taught with the class in a single line behind the teacher, who demonstrates and has the class copy her movement patterns as she shifts and says "forehand, backhand, forehand, backhand." Sideline coverage slides, moving quickly forward, backward, and the correct footwork for turning with a pivot into a driven clear and other basic footwork patterns should be taught as each new stroke is introduced and done as a warm up drill every class period for beginners.

The use of magnetized boards, films, and filmstrips is ideal for teaching game strategy, especially if the class has another opportunity midway in the unit to again watch an expert demonstration game.

Although few schools have enough courts that class groups can play singles, it is suggested that an after school singles ladder and elimination tournament be drawn up, as well as one in mixed doubles in order to give students this type of playing experience. All should be encouraged also to play at local clubs or community courts in after class hours.

A sample teaching unit of ten lessons for beginners may well contain the following:

Lesson I

1. Brief history
2. Equipment and its care
3. The grip and footwork
4. Hitting the bird back and forth in couples
5. Hitting one bird back and forth among four players
6. The serve, low and high
7. Teacher explanation and demonstration of bird flights

Lesson II

1. Review of previous lesson
2. Serve practice against the wall
3. Grip, footwork, and practice of the forehand and backhand
4. A demonstration game
5. Simplified rules
6. Students play game

Lesson III

1. Review of previous lesson
2. Serve, forehand, backhand wall practice
3. The underhand clear
4. The overhead clear
5. The smash

Lesson IV

1. Review of previous lesson
2. Homogeneous grouping of students using the Miller Wall Badminton Test
3. The drive
4. Net shots
5. Students play game

Lesson V

1. Review of previous lesson
2. Strategy for singles
3. Strategy for doubles
4. Methods of playing doubles
5. All rules discussed
6. Demonstration game by experts
7. Students practice strokes

Lesson VI

1. Review of previous lesson
2. The round-the-head shot
3. Bird placement practice
4. Round robin doubles tournament

Lesson VII

1. Review of all strokes
2. Brief review of rules and playing strategy for singles
3. The drop shot
4. Practice net shots
5. Round robin doubles tournament

Lesson VIII

1. Practice drop and net shots
2. Work on bird placement hitting into marked-off court areas
3. Review of doubles strategy
4. Round robin doubles tournament

Lesson IX

1. Round robin doubles tournament ends
2. Short review of rules, game strategy, and player courtesies
3. Begin skill test

Lesson X

1. Written test of factual materials covered
2. Grade papers in class and discuss errors in order to straighten out misconceptions
3. Finish skill test

SKILL DIFFICULTIES AND THEIR CORRECTION

Difficulty	*Correction*

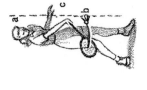

1. *The Grip*

a. Choking the **racket**

b. Holding the racket too tightly, muscles too tensed

c. First finger up behind racket; thumb extended along handle

d. Failure to modify grip for the backhand

1.

a. Move student's hand down

b. Stress relaxation

c. Remind student to keep fingers down. Tape finger in proper position of those having the most trouble remembering

d. Review correct backhand grip

2. *Hitting the Bird*

a. Missing it entirely

b. Hitting it on the racket edge

c. Stiff tennis arm swing

2.

a. Use a wool practice ball. Suspend a bird with string and have student stroke it many times to get the proper timing. Wall practice. Have student hit bird gently with racket face up 15 to 20 times. Shorten grip. Stress "watch the bird"

b. Stress hitting in the correct part of the racket. Use suggestions above

c. Stress wrist flexibility. Have student flop hand up and down, side to side without, then with, the racket

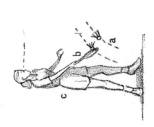

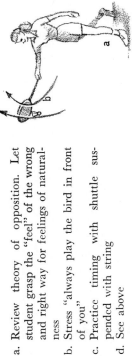

Correction

3.

a. Have student flex knees more and bend closer to the bird. Use wall practice with a slightly dropped shuttle. See suggestion 2a

b. Stress timing and rhythm. Demonstrate and have student copy. Show where bird should be contacted. Check grip to see if student is choking racket

c. Review serving rule

d. Teacher demonstration and correction of error

e. Drop bird nearer forward foot instead of too far in front

f. Let wrist lead racket head until bird is hit, then bring racket head up slowly for good follow-through

4.

a. Review theory of opposition. Let student grasp the "feel" of the wrong and right way for feelings of naturalness

b. Stress "always play the bird in front of you"

c. Practice timing with shuttle suspended with string

d. See above

Difficulty

3. *Serving*
a. Missing the bird

b. Driving it into the net

c. Moving the feet while serving
d. Holding the bird too close to the body
e. Serving too short and high

f. Serving too low

4. *Footwork and Timing*
a. Wrong foot forward, especially on serve

b. Letting the bird get behind the head

c. Swinging too late

d. Standing too close to the bird while stroking

71

SKILL DIFFICULTIES AND THEIR CORRECTION (Continued)

Difficulty	Correction

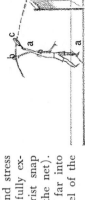

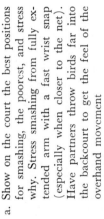

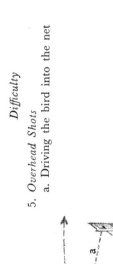

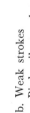

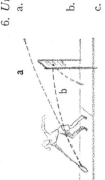

5. Overhead Shots

a. Driving the bird into the net

b. Weak strokes

c. Bird sails too long before dropping down

6. Underhand Shots

a. Driving the bird out of bounds

b. Weak stroke

c. Missing the bird in game play

7. Strategy and Court Positions

a. Hitting the bird back and forth to the opponents

b. Both partners on same court side

c. Failure to think ahead, or to place the bird instead of just hitting it

d. Failure to return to "home base" after making a shot

e. Backing up for deep shots instead of pivoting and running back

5.

a. Show on the court the best positions for smashing, the poorest, and stress why. Stress smashing from fully extended arm with a fast wrist snap (especially when closer to the net). Have partners throw birds far into the backcourt to get the feel of the overhand movement

b. Stress wrist snap

c. Stress hitting bird at highest point of the reach and the wrist flick

6.

a. Review form for the clear and drop shots. Stress again the necessity for a full backswing and snap from a wrist, and correct follow-through

b. Stress wrist snap. Practice close to net, then move back

c. Stress keeping the eye on the bird at all times

7.

a. Stress that the object is to hit the bird *away* from the players

b. Show through exaggerated movements, using a class member, how foolish it is to leave one side of the court unguarded

c. Stress the necessity of anticipation and planning ahead

d. Teacher observes game play and constantly reminds player to "go home"

e. Through exaggerated movements teacher demonstrates why one should

NOVELTY EVENTS

Around-The-Court Badminton. Played like Around-The-Table ping pong. Two groups of players on each side of the net move in a circle taking turns hitting the bird and are eliminated for missing it.

Sponge or Balloon Badminton. This game is especially fun for skilled players. Substitute a soft sponge or balloon for the shuttlecock.

Hand Badminton. The shuttle, or wool practice ball, is hit with the bare hand. Several players can be on each side. The game is scored as volleyball with only the side "in," or serving, scoring points. Outside boundaries are needed but no area is designated for serving or receiving.

Paddle Badminton. This game can be played by any number on a team, as above, and has the players using ping pong paddles instead of rackets.

Tin Plate Badminton. Played as regular badminton. Players use tin plates as rackets and ping pong or wool practice balls as birds.

Mass Badminton. Using a volleyball or tennis court, any number of two equally divided teams can play. The game is scored as volleyball. The same person on each team may serve throughout the game from any place on the court, or players may rotate and serve from the back or a midcourt line, rotating as in volleyball. Each player should have a racket.

One Racket—Four Player Badminton. Played as regular badminton. The two players on each side must alternate hitting the bird and racket use.

Shuttle Badminton. Players in several single files in shuttle formation on a volleyball court hit the bird and give the racket to the next in line before going to the end of her line. Those who miss are eliminated. The winning line plays the longest.

Call Shot Badminton. As the shuttle is hit, the player calls the shot she wants her opponent to use in returning it. Score one point if this is done, subtract one if it is not. Play for 21 points. Either player can start the play but must serve diagonally into the opponent's court.

OFFICIATING TECHNIQUES

Except during tournaments, players may call their own games and can thus develop good sportsmanship, honesty, and consideration for the other player. In tournament play, however, games should be called by a rated official assisted by linesmen stationed near both back courts. The specific costume and duties of this official include:

I *Dress, Equipment, and Position*
    Preferably all white and a colored blazer or sweater
    Have a coin for tossing, rule book, pencil, scorecard, shuttles
    Stand near the outside lines at net in order to have a clear view of
      the whole court

II *Procedure*

    Check net height, test shuttles

    Make introductions of self and players

    Toss for court assignments

    Give players warm up time

    Instruct linemen to call out or have palms down for good shots, thumbs up for outside ones

    Announce (for singles), "Love All—play"

                    (for doubles), "Love All, one hand, play"

III *During Match*

    Watch for and give rule violations in calling out the score, "Fault— give violation (feint)—side out"

    Record score in book after each point and announce the score before next service delivery

    Ask the player first reaching the right to "set" if she wishes to do so (at 9-All and 10-All in singles; at 13-All and 14-All in doubles). If the player wishes to "set," announce the score as "Love All" and allow the game to continue

    Announce "Game point" when there is but one point remaining

    Announce "Game and match point" when there is but one point needed by the serving side to win

    Never change called decisions but always be sure those announced are correct

IV *Match Conclusion*

    Announce the score, giving that of the winning side first

    Have players change sides if the match is to continue, allowing the side winning the first game to serve first

    Give five minutes time out if there is to be a third match. During this game, if it is played, have players change sides at 6 points in singles or at 8 points in doubles

    Announce, record, and post final score at conclusion of match, giving the winner's score first

EVALUATING THE RESULTS

Although both the student and teacher should constantly be cognizant of the former's progress in learning to play badminton well, this subjective rating can serve chiefly as a means of ranking students in relationship to each other, rather than in measuring the amount of actual skill mastery gained. A suggested way for best evaluating progress is in comparing written game knowledge test scores and skill test scores given at the beginning and end of the entire unit.

Rating Scales.   Teacher devised rating scales for class use by extra players as well as for herself to use in judging learning progress are highly recommended. Such a scale might be constructed around the following suggested pattern:

PLAYER RATING SCALE

STROKES	*Failure* (No point scored)	*Success* (Score 1 point)
Serve		
Short	_____	_____
Long	_____	_____
Clear		
Underhand	_____	_____
Overhand	_____	_____
Net Shot		
Hairpin	_____	_____
Diagonal	_____	_____
Drive		
Smash	_____	_____
Around-the-Head Shot	_____	_____
GAME STRATEGY		
Hit Bird to Opponent	_____	_____
Hit Bird away from Opponent	_____	_____

Final number of points scored_____

Rating of Player: _____Fair _____Good _____Very Good

Although this is a time consuming process, it can be used to gain insight into one's teaching ability, as well as to help students gain satisfaction or insight from knowing whether their efforts to learn the game have been fruitful or not.

Knowledge Tests. Standardized knowledge tests available include:

Fox, Katherine: Beginning Badminton Written Examination, *Research Quarterly 24:*135, May, 1953.

Phillips, Marjorie: Standardization of a Badminton Knowledge Test for College Women, *Research Quarterly 17:*48, March, 1946.

Scott, Gladys: Skills and Knowledge Tests of Badminton for College Women Research Committee, Central Association of Physical Education for College Women.

Scott, Gladys: Achievement Examination in Badminton, *Research Quarterly 12:*242–250, May, 1941.

A chart can also be obtained from the AAPHER, Division for Girls and Women's Sports, Washington, D.C., "Badminton Technique."

Skill Tests. The Miller Badminton Wall Test, previously mentioned, is recommended for measuring general playing ability. In this test, a one inch line is extended across the wall 7 feet, 6 inches from, and parallel to, the floor. The wall space width is 10 feet and height 15 feet or higher. The student, given one minute to practice, on the signal "ready, go," legally serves the bird behind the 10 feet floor line and plays it on the rebound. One point is scored for every time the shuttle hits on or above the $7\frac{1}{2}$ foot wall line. If the foot or any body part goes over the line, no point is scored, or if the shuttle goes below the $7\frac{1}{2}$ foot wall line. However, when this occurs, the player may keep the bird in play. It may also be stopped and restarted at any time behind the 10 foot line, including when it is missed. Any stroke can be used. A "carried bird" or double hit counts if hit and it goes above the $7\frac{1}{2}$ wall line. The player may go across the line to pick up the bird, but must be behind it to start play again. Three 30 second trials are given and the final score consists of the sum of three trials.

Other suggested skill tests are:

French, Esther, and Salter, Evelyn: Study of Skill Tests in Badminton for College Women, *Research Quarterly 20:*257, 272, October, 1949.

Scott, Gladys: Achievement Examinations in Badminton, *Research Quarterly 12:*242, May, 1941.

Scott, Gladys, and French, Esther: *Evaluation in Physical Education,* St. Louis, C. V. Mosby Company, 1950.

Lockhart, Aileene, and McPherson, Frances: The Development of a Test of Badminton Playing Ability, *Research Quarterly 2:*113–131, December, 1949.

TERMINOLOGY

Ace—One point, also called "score," "point"

Alley—Used in doubles play, strips one and one-half feet wide between two boundary lines

Balk—To hinder an opponent

Change Ends—Used in match play at the beginning of each new game. The match at the third game, players change ends when the leading score is one point beyond the halfway mark, i.e., in an 11 point game change ends at 6; at 8 in a 15 point game; at 11 in a 21 point game

Down—Loss of serve given when serving side fails to score. In doubles, the side first serving has only one down

Fault—A bird which falls short, hit into the net, or lands out of bounds

Hairpin (Net) stroke—A bird just barely crossing over the net and falling close to the other side. The bird flight resembling a hairpin

Home Position—Ideal court spot for awaiting opponent's return; usually at midcourt near center line

Lob—Also called a high clear or driven clear that goes over opponent's head

Love All—The game score at the beginning of the game and after "setting"

Odd and Even Courts—In singles the right half court is "even" and the left half is "odd." When the server's score is love or an even number, the service is taken from the right-hand court, from the left when it is an odd number. In doubles, the server in the right court is called the "even" player and her partner the "odd." When the "even" player is serving from the right, the score is even, and odd when from the left. The reverse is true of her partner

Out Side—The receiving side

Playing For An Opening—Getting the opponent into position for a "kill"

Rally—Rapid returns made by players. The winner of a rally usually serves, except in tournament play

Rubber—The best of three games

Setting—Increasing game play at a tied score, at 9-All, 10-All, 14-All. In a 15 point game when the score is tied, a player may set for 5 points, or at 3 points when tied at 14. In an 11 point game, when the score is tied at 9, one may set for 3 points, or when tied at 10, may set for 2. The one reaching the tied score first, "sets"

Sling or Throw—An untrue hit, usually the result of catching the feathers in the strings or drawing the racket away from the bird as it is stroked; a fault

Wood Shot—An untrue hit in which the bird hits the racket frame

DISCUSSION QUESTIONS

1. Demonstrate and describe the serve, high clear, round-the-head shot, the diagonal net stroke.
2. Draw up court and space assignments for a class of 42 students in a gymnasium where there are only four courts. Show how you would rotate and assign all students so that each would be actively engaged after the third lesson.
3. Draw up a teaching unit of eight lessons for beginners and intermediate players.
4. Make a sample rating sheet to use as you observe each student play in a game, such as the one suggested in this chapter.
5. Discuss and demonstrate the care and repair of all badminton equipment.
6. Visit a sporting goods store and examine the badminton equipment for sale there. What kind of racket and shuttles would you want to buy for your own use? What would you recommend buying for a school that has large classes and a limited budget?
7. Devise a sample objective badminton knowledge test composed of 25 items using several true-false, matching, multiple choice, and fill-in-blanks type of questions.

SELECTED AUDIO-VISUAL AIDS

Badminton Fundamentals, 1950. (10 min., sound, b & w). Coronet Instructional Films, 65 East South Water Street, Chicago, Ill. (Rental)

Beginning Badminton. (Instructor's Guide and Handbooks, slide films, 4 units, color). The Athletic Institute, 209 S. State Street, Chicago 4, Ill. (Rental)

Good Badminton. Teaching Film Custodians, 25 W. 43rd Street, New York, N.Y. (Rental)

Let's Play Badminton, 1947. (10 min., sound, b & w). General Sportcraft Company, 215 Fourth Avenue, New York, N.Y. (Rental)

Tips For Better Badminton. Sports Tips and Teaching Aids, 16801 Parkside Drive, Detroit, Mich. (Purchase)

SUGGESTED READINGS

AAHPER, Division for Girls and Women's Sports, *Selected Tennis and Badminton Articles*, Washington 6, D.C., 1958.

Davidson, Kenneth, and Gustavson, Lealand: *Winning Badminton,* New York, A. S. Barnes, 1951.
Devlin, J. F.: *Badminton For All,* New York, Doubleday and Company, 1937.
Dewitt, R. T.: *Teaching Individual and Team Sports,* New York, Prentice-Hall Book Company, 1953.
Jackson, Carl H., and Swan, Lester A.: *Better Badminton,* New York, A. S. Barnes, 1939.

PERIODICALS

Bird Chatter, American Badminton Association, 7518 Orin Court, Seattle, Washington.

Bowling

The sport of bowling, which attracts 22,000,000 Americans to 70,000 lanes across the nation each year, developed from a German religious ceremony. Although the true origin of the game is questionable, most German men in the third and fourth century carried a *kegel*. The kegel, a small club resembling the present day Indian club, was used for strengthening wrists and forearms, for recreation, and for religious ceremony. In the religious ceremony a man called by the priest to prove he was leading an honorable life had to set up his kegel, called *Heide* (heathen) and knock it over with a small round stone.

The monks and laymen recognized the recreational value in bowling and continued the sport long after the religious ceremony was abolished. Martin

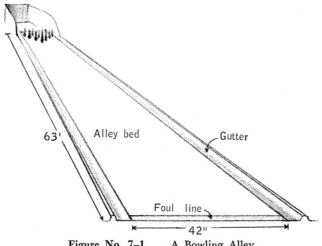

Figure No. 7–1.   A Bowling Alley.

Luther, an enthusiastic bowler of the 15th century, published a set of rules for a game of nine pins.

The nine pin game came to America with the Dutch settlers and became so popular that indoor lanes, the Knickerbocker Alleys, were built in New York in 1840. Bowling suffered a setback when the nine pins game was prohibited by the Connecticut legislature because of gambling and rowdiness. It remained for an ingenious hero to add a tenth pin to circumvent the law. The additional pin resulted in a triangular set and the birth of present-day bowling.

During the past 70 years improved equipment and playing surroundings have resulted in increased participation. In the late 19th century the American Bowling Congress organized and standardized rules, equipment and alleys. As bowling lost its rowdy, saloon-like atmosphere women and youth moved in as enthusiastic keglers. In 1916, the Women's International Bowling Congress was organized and has continued to conduct national tournaments and give leadership to the sport. The American Junior Bowling Congress sponsors tournaments and helps boys and girls receive reduced rates and free instruction as preparation for a lifetime of fun and recreation in this sport.

Bowling is now enjoying a "boom" period uncommon to many American sports. The alertness of national organizations toward meeting the needs of all ages, emphasis given the sport by television in bringing an understanding and appreciation into many homes, and the "new look" of bowling establishments are primarily responsible for increased public interest. The well decorated, air conditioned alley with automatic pinsetting equipment is an attractive, desirable place for the entire family's recreation.

THE NATURE AND PURPOSE OF THE GAME

The object of a bowler is to roll well aimed balls down a wooden alley and knock down as many of the triangularly set ten pins at the end of the alley as possible. The maximum number of pins which can be scored in a single game of ten frames is 300. The bowler stands in an approach area,

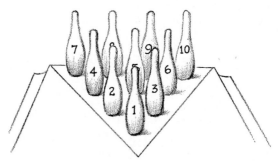

Figure No. 7–2.   Properly Set and Numbered Pins.

walks or runs toward the alley and delivers the ball beyond the foul line so it rolls toward the pins. Competition can be individual, with from one to five persons on an alley, or it may be in units with as many as five on each team. A handicap scoring system allows for equitable competition among all skill levels.

Long hours of physical conditioning and body building are not necessary for skillful bowling. Since coordination and rhythm are more important than great speed, strength or endurance, bowling is an ideal sport for co-educational instruction at the high school or college level. As a social activity, bowling allows time for conversation between turns and provides an opportunity for the consideration of other players.

SCORING

The number of pins knocked down during the ten frames of a game is the bowler's total score. Each pin falling is scored one point. The player bowls two balls for each frame, unless she delivers a strike—upsetting all ten pins with the first ball. When this occurs a second ball is not delivered in that frame. However, if a strike is delivered in the tenth frame, two more balls are delivered immediately. If a spare is made (all ten pins upset by the first and second balls) in the tenth frame, one more ball must be rolled at a new brace of pins immediately to complete the game score.

When all pins are knocked down by the first ball in a frame, a strike is recorded by an (X) in a small square in the corner of the score box of that frame. Eventually, the score in that frame will be the ten pins scored for the strike plus the total number of pins knocked down by the next two balls.

If pins are left standing after the first ball is rolled (called a spare leave), but all remaining pins are knocked over by the second roll, a spare is indicated by a diagonal line (/) in the square of that frame. The player's score in the spare frame is a cumulative total of all pins knocked down in the preceding frames, the ten pins scored for the spare and the pins knocked down on the next ball delivered. To keep an accurate check on the cumulative score, the number of pins knocked down by the first ball should be recorded at the top of the frame.

When pins are left standing after both balls are rolled, an error is indicated by a straight line (—) in the score box and only the total pins knocked down with both balls are recorded.

If, after the first ball is delivered, the head pin is down and two or more pins are left standing with at least one pin knocked down between them, a split is recorded by a circle (O). If the remaining pins are knocked down by the second ball, a spare is indicated (Ø) in the score box. When pins remain standing after the second ball, only the number of pins knocked down by the two balls is scored.

An understanding of the foul rule is basic to accurate scoring. There are

Figure No. 7–3.   Some Common Fouls.

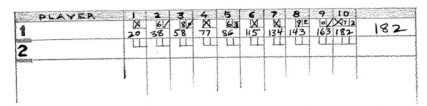

Figure No. 7–4.   Scoring: A Sample Game.

many ways in which a foul is committed, but the most common is crossing the foul line with any part of the body during or after delivery.

When a foul is committed, the ball rolled shall count as a turn but any pins knocked down or displaced are respotted and no pins are scored.

A game description and illustration of recording scores are helpful in mastering scoring techniques:

Frame   1—1. All pins are knocked down by the first ball (a strike)
Frame   2—1. Six pins are knocked down, head pin remains standing on first ball
         2. Remaining pins are knocked down by second ball. A spare is recorded and the score totaled for the first frame
Frame   3—1. Eight pins fall on the first delivery, leaving pins 7 and 9. A split is recorded and total can be reached for second frame
         2. Second ball knocks down the remaining pins. A spare is recorded
Frame   4—1. A strike is recorded
            Total score recorded in frame 3
Frame   5—1. Six pins are knocked down
         2. Three pins are knocked down by second ball
            A miss is recorded in the score box
            Total score is recorded in frames 4 and 5
Frame   6—1. A strike is recorded
Frame   7—1. A strike is made
Frame   8—1. Nine pins are knocked down on the first delivery
            Score is totaled in frame 6
         2. The second ball hits the remaining pin but the bowler's foot crosses the foul line
            An error is recorded in the score box and the score is totaled

Frame   9—1. The first ball runs into the gutter and no pins are knocked over
            2. The second ball knocks down all pins
               A spare is scored
Frame 10—1. A strike is scored
               Score in frame 9 is totaled
            2. Next ball delivered knocks down 7 pins
            3. Last ball rolled knocks down 2 of the 3 remaining pins
               The completed game score is recorded

NEEDED FACILITIES AND EQUIPMENT

One of the appeals bowling has for the beginner is that it is not necessary to own a single piece of equipment to participate. An enthusiastic kegler will want to own her personal shoes, ball and equipment bag eventually, but commercial establishments and most student unions rent shoes at a nominal fee and furnish balls.

Dress. No special uniform or costume is required. A comfortable, full skirt and a washable blouse are acceptable bowling attire. Many women wear slacks but this practice should receive approval of the class instructor. Well fitting socks should be worn. Bowling shoes are essential for safety and skill development. For a right-handed bowler the left sole is leather or buckskin to allow for sliding on the approach and the right sole is rubber for braking this action. The sole materials are reversed for left-handed or "wrong foot" bowlers. A leather-soled shoe or heavy sock on the sliding foot and a tennis shoe on the braking foot may substitute for regulation shoes during instructional periods in the gymnasium or corridors.

Ball. The American Bowling Congress rules that balls may not be more than 27 inches in circumference or weigh more than 16 pounds. Balls with two or three finger holes are permissible. Most beginning women bowlers are more comfortable with a three hole ball weighing 12 to 14 pounds, while junior bowlers select smaller balls weighing around ten pounds. In keeping with the "new look" of bowling establishments, colored balls are increasing in popularity over the solid black ball. Color is a personal preference and does not necessarily indicate weight or size of the hard rubber compound balls.

Alley. The terms alley and lane are synonymous and include the total area where the preparation, delivery, and contact of the pins take place. The area includes the approach, foul line, alley bed, gutters, and pit. The ball return and rack are also part of a complete lane.

The approach is a level runway extending from the seating area and scoring table to the foul line. A minimum of 15 feet is necessary for the approach. The 63 foot long alley bed begins at the foul line and extends to the pit area. The alley bed is constructed of maple and pine lengths laid vertically so that the balls roll on the thickness of the boards. The harder and more durable maple wood is laid at the beginning of the foul line for 12 or 15 feet, then pine, then maple again on the deck area where the pins are knocked over on the lane. Many alleys have range finders to help in selecting a point of aim in spot bowling. These darts, or dots, are usually placed where the maple and pine lengths first join on the alleybed.

On the deck, ten pin spots are marked for accuracy in setting pins. The spots are 12 inches apart, from center to center, in a triangular pattern with the apex toward the bowler. Particular attention should be drawn to these spots if a class does its own pinsetting.

The pit, at the rear of the alley, is a depressed area into which pins are knocked and the human or automatic pinsetter works. Installation of fully *automatic* Pinsetters[1] and Pinspotters[2] is increasing across the country with approximately 22,000 installations in 1958; however, many establishments have semi-automatic machines. If this is the case, the techniques of pinsetting should be included in the instructional unit.

On each side of the alleybed, there is a rounded and depressed gutter. This trough carries a poorly aimed ball to the pit where it is placed manually or automatically on the ball return track and thus to the ball rack next to the approach area.

Pins.   Official pins for American Ten Pins are hard, clear, maple, 15 inches in height, and weighing between 3 pounds and 3 pounds, 8 ounces. Proper balance and design is assured by reputable manufacturers.

TEACHING UNITS

Suggested units for beginning, intermediate, and advanced students follow. If instructors find that two groups, rather than three, are more manageable, the intermediate and advanced units may be combined.

Unit for Beginners	*Unit for Intermediate Students*	*Unit for Advanced Students*
Brief history	Review of equipment,	General review
Orientation to alley or	pinsetting, scoring,	Game bowling
setting	etiquette, safety	Back-up ball (optional)
Explanation of game	Review straight ball	Curve ball
Equipment	delivery	Explain average and
Beginning safety	Review spot and cross	handicaps
precautions	alley bowling	Intensive practice on
Dress	Spare bowling	designated spare
Selection of equipment	Hook ball delivery	leaves
Shoes	Game bowling	Explain "fast" and
Ball	(League bowling)	"slow" alley beds
Grip		League bowling

---

[1] Name of automatic equipment manufactured by Brunswick-Balke-Collender Company.

[2] Name of automatic equipment manufactured by American Machine and Foundry Company.

Unit for Beginners	Unit for Intermediate Students	Unit for Advanced Students
Explanation and demonstration of pinsetting (not necessary with automatic equipment)	Evaluation Written Practical	Elimination tournament Evaluation Written Practical
Fundamentals of straight ball delivery Grip Four step approval Delivery Aiming		
Scoring		
Spot bowling Use of range finder		
Cross alley bowling		
Etiquette		
Game bowling		
Beginner's tournament		
Evaluation Written Practical		

BASIC SKILLS

Ball Selection and Grip. Selecting a ball that permits a comfortable natural grip is basic to successful scoring. Although balls weigh from 10 to 16 pounds, most women prefer 12 to 14 pound balls. Ball choice is determined by an individual's strength, size and, most important, comfort in handling, according to the location, size, and direction of the finger holes. Few women use a two hole ball because of the additional finger strength needed to control the delivery. Most experts recommend a three finger ball.

Size and pitch of the finger and thumb holes, and span of the bowler's hand determine the proper fit of a ball. The holes must be small enough to allow the thumb, middle and ring finger to maintain contact with the edge of the hole toward the palm of the hand, yet loose enough for an easy release without scraping the fingers. Proper span for the conventional three hole grip is determined by inserting the thumb about three-quarters of its length into the hole drilled on the center line of the ball. Spreading the hand so the middle and ring fingers extend to the left and right of the centerline, the middle knuckles of both fingers should extend about ¼ inch past the inside edge of the holes. If the holes are bored at the usual ⅜ inch angle, a naturally balanced grip results when the thumb is inserted three-

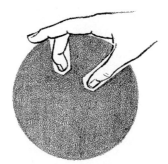

Figure No. 7–5.   Selecting a Proper Ball.

quarters of its length and the fingers inserted up to the second joint. The first and little fingers are straight and spread over the outside of the ball for control. A bowler can check the grip by asking: (1) Is my hand comfortable? (2) Do I have a feeling of control? and (3) Can a pencil be slipped between my hand and the ball without changing the grip?

Stance and Approach.   These two important skills are best taught as a unit because each is dependent upon the other. Stance involves grip and how and where to stand on the approach area. The bowler determines her stance position for the four step approach by taking four regular steps and allowing several additional feet to account for increased strides and slide in an actual approach. Starting from a designated spot so delivery will be consistent, the bowler places her feet close together with left foot slightly forward (right-handed bowler). The feet, hips, and shoulders are facing the pins squarely. Standing position varies among the experts, some stoop forward with ball held at the waistline, while others stand erect with the ball at chest level. In either case the upper back is straight. Beginners are encouraged to stand upright, weight on the heels, bending slightly forward from the hips while holding the ball at the waistline. One hand grips and the other hand, palm up, supports the ball weight. Each bowler should find a comfortable, relaxed position.

The approach is a series of well coordinated movements that end in the release and delivery of the ball. Successful bowlers vary in their approaches from three to five steps, but the four step is popular as the easiest and most rhythmical for group instruction. From a selected stance position the bowler follows a straight line to the foul line and point of ball release. The right-handed bowler moves the right foot forward in a slow, short, rhythmical step; the second step (left foot) is slightly longer and faster. Forward momentum increases as the right foot extends in a longer, faster third step leading to the fastest and longest fourth step on the left foot. Forward momentum stops as the fourth step ends in a slide with the toe of the left foot, pointing to the head pin, nears the foul line. The right foot swings behind the body for balance and for braking action of the forward movement. The approach begins from an upright position and as the bowler picks up momentum she increases her forward leaning position. The final steps into the slide end with the left knee bent, hips tucked under the body, and the upper body straight and inclined forward.

Coordinated Approach. Preparation for delivery requires coordination of approach steps, arm swing, and body action. As the right-handed bowler takes her first step (right foot), the ball, held by both hands in front of the body, elbows close to body, is pushed directly forward. While the second step is taken (left foot) the right arm gripping the ball, swings down and straight backward in a pendulum-like motion with the ball leading the backswing. At completion of the second step the arm should be pointing straight down, alongside of the leg. The ball swings back on the third step. The left arm is free to swing outward to maintain balance as the body moves in a straight line toward the pins.

On the third step (right foot) the right arm and ball continue upward as the backswing nears shoulder height. As the fourth step (left foot) begins the forward slide, the left knee bends and the weight of the ball pulls the right arm downward and forward. The right arm and left foot move forward together. The ball passes the left leg and is released about a foot beyond the foul line. The right foot swings behind the body in a natural position to maintain balance as the right arm follows-through toward the pins and upward to eye level. The shoulders stay parallel to the foul line and the left foot finishes on the same board it has followed from the stance position.

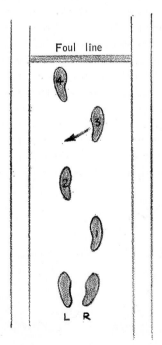

Figure No. 7–6.   The Four Step Approach.

Figure No. 7–7.   Coordinated Approach.

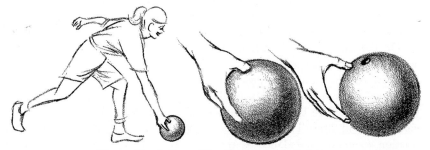

Figure No. 7–8.   The Straight Ball Release.

Straight Ball Delivery.   The straight ball delivery is considered the most successful for beginners. Throughout the coordinated approach the ball hand and arm parallel the floor boards. As the ball approaches the foul line, the thumb is pointing toward the pins and the fingers are under and behind the ball. As the release begins the thumb slides from the hole and the ball rolls off the finger tips approximately one foot beyond the foul line and six to eight boards in from the right gutter (see aiming). After the ball is released, the open hand, with palm up and fingers and thumb pointing toward the pins, continues in an upward arc.

Back-up Ball Delivery.   This is perhaps the most difficult ball to deliver effectively and consistently. It is not a desirable skill to teach, yet it is a common delivery among women and should be recognized and corrected. The hand is almost directly under the ball with the thumb pointing to the

Figure No. 7–9.   Back-up Ball Delivery.

right of the pins (right-handed bowler). As the ball is released, a left to right twist causes a reverse spin and the ball travels the left side of the alley and breaks right to enter the pins.

Hook Ball Delivery.   The hook is the fastest of all deliveries and when controlled has a high strike percentage. The ball hits the pins at a most effective angle with a spinning motion which scatters the pins. Positioning for the approach is similar to that of a straight ball delivery, with the bowler standing right of center of the approach area about 6 to 12 inches from the right gutter. The right-handed bowler turns the ball hand so the little finger is toward the floor, and the thumb near the body during the swing. The "V" between thumb and forefinger points toward the 1-3 pocket. The ball is released beyond the foul line, six to twelve boards in from the right gutter. The thumb is released first with the fingers following. The delayed finger release causes a right to left spin as the hand and arm follow-through outward and upward toward the pins. The ball travels parallel to the right gutter toward the 3 or 6 pin, depending upon the "break" of the hook. About two-thirds of the way down the alley the ball angles sharply toward the pins and travels into the 1-3 pocket to the 5 pin.

Curve Ball Delivery.   The curve is a slow, wide sweeping ball which travels in an arc toward the 1-3 pocket (right-handed bowler). The width of the ball's arc determines where the bowler stands for delivery. A right-handed bowler using a small arc stands slightly to the right of the head pin.

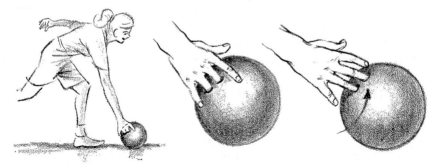

Figure No. 7–10.   Hook Ball Release.

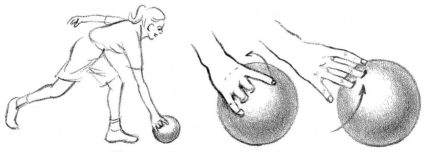

Figure No. 7–11.   Curve Ball Release.

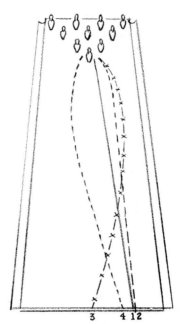

Figure No. 7–12.   Four types of deliveries: Straight ball (1), hook ball (2), curve
ball (3), and back-up ball (4).

With wide arcing balls she may move farther to the left of the approach
area, possibly to the left of the head pin. The bowler's hand is placed on the
ball as in a hook delivery; however, the thumb is rotated back and to the
left until it is at "nine o'clock." On release, the thumb leaves the ball first
and the hand and wrist twist from right to left and impart spin. This is a
difficult skill to master for consistent strike bowling and even more difficult
to control in picking up spare leaves.

   Aiming.   There are two distinct theories of aiming and a third is gaining popularity.

   Head Pin bowling.   On the first ball the bowler looks at the pins and
aims for the 5 pin through the 1-3 pocket. After the first delivery she aims
directly at the pin and area she hopes to contact. Pin bowling is less accurate than spot bowling because of the distance the bowler must sight to the
target, but is recommended for beginners as it requires less concentration.

   Spot Bowling.   The bowler selects a spot part way down the lane, between the point of release and the desired point of contact with the pins,
over which she tries to roll her ball. Most modern alleys have a range finder
on the alley bed to make spot selection easier. On the first ball using a
straight ball delivery, the bowler selects a spot 12 to 15 feet down the alley
where the maple and pine boards join and approximately eight to twelve
boards in from the right gutter. Once the spot is selected and becomes a
target, any change in delivery will be in angle, speed, or approach position.
The bowler concentrates on the spot until the ball passes over and beyond

it. Some bowlers prefer two spots. One, where the ball is laid down on release, and the second, a spot over which the ball should roll. Beginners
should not try to use two spot aiming.

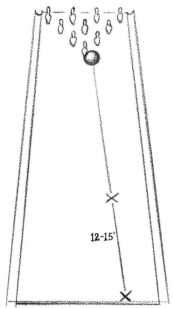

12-15'

Figure No. 7–13.   Spot Bowling.

Line Bowling.   This is a combination of pin and spot aiming methods. The line bowler draws an imaginary line from the stance position to the
1-3 pocket. She has four check points: the starting position, the slide position, the chosen spot, and the strike pocket. At any time she can select another spot and then change the other check points. This is a precision method
of aiming which requires concentration and practice.

Spare Bowling.   The bowler who hopes to score well must be proficient in picking up spare leaves and splits. The basic principle of cross alley
bowling is that as much of the alley width as possible should be between the
delivery spot and the standing target. Therefore, when a pin or pins are on
the right side of the alley the bowler moves to the left of her regular first
ball delivery spot. Conversely, when the leave is on the left, begin to the right
of the regular delivery spot. The leave and type of delivery dictate how far
the bowler moves in each direction.

Speed and pin deflection are important to spare bowling. A fast ball may
cause the pins to move so that they do not fall horizontally, knocking down
additional pins. Yet, a slower ball may itself be deflected to the right or
left if it does not hit a pin head-on, or have sufficient momentum to carry
through. The bowler should remember that some leaves are three feet behind
the head pin and additional thought should be given to speed and type of
delivery to these pins.

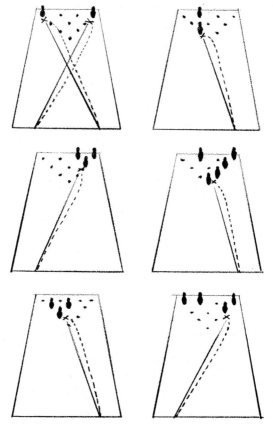

Figure No. 7–14.   Common Spare Leaves: Cross Alley Bowling.

Courtesy Skills.   Developing bowling etiquette is a social skill necessary for game enjoyment. In brief:

1. Always observe the foul line
2. Walk directly back from the foul line after delivery
3. Be alert and ready for your turn
4. The bowler addressing the pins has the right of way. If players on adjoining alleys address the pins simultaneously, the bowler on the right has the privilege of bowling first
5. Avoid talking and jesting with a bowler addressing the pins
6. Select one ball and use only that ball throughout the game
7. Control your temper. Bowling is a game to be enjoyed. It should not defeat the bowler

CLASS ORGANIZATION

Class organization is largely dependent upon the instructional setting. If possible, no more than five students should be assigned to each alley. Forty-five students is the maximum desirable number for a single instructor who hopes to give some individual assistance. A class period should be at least 45 minutes so a full game can be completed.

Some instructors, by choice, or when alleys are not available, teach basic skills in the gymnasium, corridor, or hard surfaced outdoor area. Plastic bowling balls and pins are used successfully on wooden floors, whereas rubber pins and balls can be used on other surfacing. A portable alley is now on the commercial market for gymnasium use.[3] If none of this equipment is available Indian clubs and softballs or playground balls can be used. The basic skills of stance, approach, and delivery, as well as scoring, etiquette and strategy can be taught effectively.

When five persons are assigned to each alley, one student sets pins, one scores, and the others bowl. Students rotate, in a pre-determined order, so each has an opportunity to work on skills in the early session. If automatic pinsetters are used, develop a rotation plan of one scoring, one coaching, and three bowling.

Alleys requiring student pin setters present a problem in co-educational classes. Girls should not set for boys because of the increased hazards of fast balls and flying pins.

Classification of students by ability levels is advisable for instruction and ease and increased competitive interest. The following suggested criteria aid in initial classification:

Beginners

   1. Those who have never bowled
   2. Those who have bowled very little

Intermediate

   1. Those who have passed successfully the beginning bowling skills test
   2. Those who have averaged 90 or above in the first three games

Advanced

   1. Those who have passed successfully the intermediate skills test
   2. Those who have received high skill marks in beginning bowling

Since bowling is a comparatively safe activity, rules can be kept at a minimum. Minimum regulations should include:

   1. Dress properly. Wear regulation shoes and avoid tight, restricting clothing
   2. Select a ball that is comfortable and easy to handle
   3. Use only one ball. Wait for your ball to be returned from the pit
   4. Make certain the pinsetter is out of the pit before delivery
   5. Stay away from the approach area when another person is preparing to bowl

[3] Consult any issue of the Journal of the American Association for Health, Physical Education, and Recreation for advertised sources.

TEACHING PROGRESSION

The instructional unit can be introduced in the gymnasium through selected novelty games such as duckpins, candle pins, skittles, or improvised games using Indian clubs. As soon as possible students should be assigned to instructional groups of their own skill level. Working in their groups in the gymnasium, students learn scoring methods and techniques of stance, approach, and delivery.

Once in the alley, the instructor helps the student select shoes and a ball for permanent use. The teacher makes temporary alley assignments and explains class organization and conduct while in the lane. She then introduces basic rules of safety and courtesy and explains pinsetting, if necessary.

Suggested course outlines for beginners and intermediate-advanced bowlers follow:

BEGINNERS UNIT

Lesson I

1. Acquaint students with equipment, costume, and facilities
2. Explain and demonstrate ball selection and grip
3. Assign balls and alley
4. Teach pinsetting, safety precautions, and courtesy skills

Lesson II

1. Review proper grip
2. Review guides to safety and courtesy
3. Demonstrate and explain stance and four step approach
4. Students select stance spot and practice approach without ball
5. Explain and demonstrate coordination of arm swing with steps. Stress push away, free pendulum-like swing, and release
6. Explain and demonstrate straight ball release
7. Practice straight ball delivery at pins 1, 3, and 5

Lesson III

1. Review starting spot, stance, coordinated approach with straight ball delivery
2. Explain strike bowling and practice at the 1-3 pocket
3. Explain speed and deflection
4. Bowl at all ten pins

Lesson IV

1. Review complete approach and delivery
2. Explain and demonstrate scoring using terminology of strike, spare, split, and error
3. Practice session at all pins. Score five frames

Lesson V

1. Review head pin aiming
2. Describe and demonstrate spot and cross alley bowling
3. Practice bowling at seven pin and ten pin
4. Informal evaluation by teacher and pupils of group progress

Lesson VI

1. Practice session—review scoring procedures
2. Informal skills test

Lesson VII

1. Regulation game bowling
2. Students record scores on official records

Lesson VIII

1. Show film demonstrating straight ball delivery and theory and technique of spot bowling
2. Show film which demonstrates difference among straight ball, hook, back-up, and curve ball

Lesson IX

1. Bowl
2. Teacher gives individual assistance

Lesson X

1. Bowl
2. Discuss spare bowling

Lesson XI

1. Skills examination
2. Begin ladder tournament

Lesson XII

1. Oral review of unit
2. Continue ladder tournament

Lesson XIII

1. Written test
2. Complete tournament

In additional lessons stress individual improvement in delivery and practice at designated splits and spare leaves.

INTERMEDIATE-ADVANCED UNIT

Lesson I

1. Review fundamentals of grip, stance, and approach
2. Review safety fundamentals and etiquette
3. Assign balls and alleys
4. Bowl. Teacher checks individual form

Lesson II

1. Review fundamentals of straight ball delivery
2. Review scoring
3. Bowl

Lessons III to VI

1. Concentrated practice at designated leaves
2. Bowl
3. Discuss deflection and pin action

Lesson VII

1. Demonstrate and explain hook ball delivery
2. Students bowl using hook ball delivery

Lesson VIII

1. Explain method of determining individual and team handicaps
2. Explain varying alley bed conditions on ball action
3. Bowl

Lesson IX

1. Novelty games
2. Practice sessions

Lesson X

1. Conduct class tournament on league basis

Lesson XI

1. Complete tournament

Lesson XII

1. Written and oral examination

Subsequent lessons should include intensive individual practice under the instructor's direction and films showing advanced skills.

SKILL DIFFICULTIES AND THEIR CORRECTION

Difficulty

Correction

1. *Selecting the Ball*

1.

a. Hand tires quickly from weight of the ball

a. Select a lighter ball; assure the student she will soon get used to the ball weight

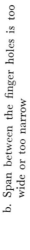

b. Span between the finger holes is too wide or too narrow

b. Review techniques for selecting a well fitting ball. Teacher checks proper span by inserting a pencil between palm of the hand and ball

c. Thumb and finger holes are too tight, too loose, or incorrectly angled

c. Select a ball which does not scrape or irritate the thumb or fingers on release, or tire the hand by tense gripping of closely set holes. Have the student release the ball in order to recheck before the final choice is made

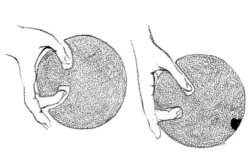

SKILL DIFFICULTIES AND THEIR CORRECTION (*Continued*)

Difficulty	*Correction*
2.	**2.**
The Stance	
a. Body weight unequally distributed. Wrong foot forward on release	a. Teacher suggests a comfortable standing position with feet apart and left foot (right-handed bowler) slightly forward for greater balance base. Exaggerate the clumsiness of the wrong stance to help student see how awkward and unnatural it is
b. Tension in the knees and body	b. Take a deep breath and relax. Flex the knees and allow the body weight to settle. Remind student to "relax"
c. One shoulder turned toward pins forcing poor body alignment	c. Stress that shoulders should be squared toward pins at all times. Have one student check only this as her partner bowls
d. Variation in distance from starting spot to the foul line causing fouls, uneven approach steps, and variance in timing	d. Teacher reviews method of selecting stance position and guides the four steps to position. Teacher marks student's starting position with chalk

3. *Four Step Approach*

a. Completing approach too far from the foul line or over the foul line

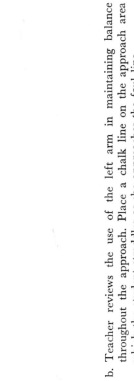

b. Approaching in a zig zag fashion

c. Bobbing up and down during the approach

d. Approaching too fast or too slow resulting in rushed or delayed delivery

3.

a. Student practices the approach mimetically with back to the foul line before selecting spot for stance

b. Teacher reviews the use of the left arm in maintaining balance throughout the approach. Place a chalk line on the approach area which the student straddles as she approaches the foul line

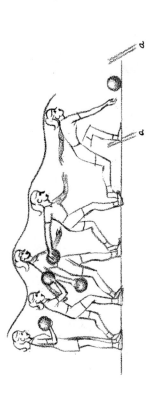

c. Teacher suggests that a bucket of water might be carried on the head without spilling during a rhythmical approach

d. Suggest a rhythmical pattern for the student to repeat while practicing mimetically. For example, "Slow, fast, faster, fastest," or "Short, long, longer, longest"

SKILL DIFFICULTIES AND THEIR CORRECTION (*Continued*)

Difficulty

Correction

4. Coordinated Approach

4.

a. Failure to push the ball straight forward to begin the downward arc

b. Tension in arm and shoulder inhibiting a free swing

c. Taking too short a backswing resulting in a slow ball, improperly delivered on the alley

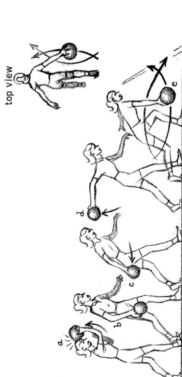

top view

d. Taking unnecessarily long backswing resulting in uncoordinated delivery

e. Swinging ball in an outside-to-inside or inside-to-outside arc causing the ball to curve or angle toward side of the alley

f. Bending forward from the waist causing poor balance at time of delivery

a. Push the ball straight ahead as if handing the ball to someone

b. Relax and allow the ball weight to swing the arm

c. Review length and timing of approach steps and be certain there is enough time for a full arc. Teacher should stress the forward, rather than upward, push of the ball that begins the arc. Let the elbow straighten in the backswing

d. Teacher checks approach, and initial forward, not downward, push of the ball. Emphasizes the importance of keeping the shoulders from twisting during the delivery. Has other students watch for shoulder rotation

e. Concentrate on keeping the shoulders parallel to the foul line. Relax the arm and let the ball swing freely. Teacher helps the student get the feeling of a "pendulum" swing by moving her arm in correct arc

f. Teacher demonstrates how the knees bend and hips come under the upper body while the upper back remains straight

a. point of release

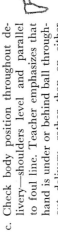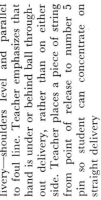
b. EASY OUT
c.

g. Dropping the shoulder of bowling arm causing ball to be delivered early and ineffectively

g. Avoid twisting shoulders and "listing" toward bowling arm

5. *Straight Ball Delivery*

5.

a. Releasing ball too early or dropping it behind the foul line

a. Be certain fingers keep contact until the ball touches the alley. Teacher reviews the arc pattern and shows how ball is released at bottom of the arc

b. Bouncing or throwing ball on alley bed

b. Keep body low and let ball release naturally at end of arc. Say aloud "easy out" as the ball is released

c. Ball curves as it travels down the alley

c. Check body position throughout delivery—shoulders level and parallel to foul line. Teacher emphasizes that hand is under or behind ball throughout delivery, rather than on either side. Teacher places a piece of string from point of release to number 5 pin so student can concentrate on straight delivery

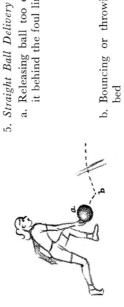

point of release

SKILL DIFFICULTIES AND THEIR CORRECTION (*Continued*)

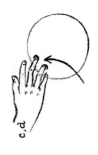

Difficulty	*Correction*
d. Ball consistently rolls too far across the alley	d. Teacher stresses follow-through with the bowling arm following the ball, then upward until the thumb touches the ear on bowling arm side
6. Hook Ball Delivery	**6.**
a. Ball skids or slides as it is released	a. Teacher demonstrates hand position at time of release. Hand is at the side of ball, with fingers pointing down, the "V" of the hand points toward head pin
b. Stopping swing as ball is released	b. Follow-through stressed. Show mimetically the follow-through in throwing or in hitting a golf ball
c. Ball spins erratically	c. Avoid using wrist action; sufficient spin is given by fingers as they leave the ball
d. Inconsistency in degree ball hooks	d. Practice is needed to perfect delivery. Avoid twisting hand or wrist, or jerking movement at end of swing arc

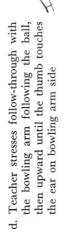

piece of string

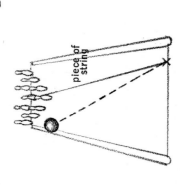

Difficulty	*Correction*
7. *Curve Ball Delivery*	**7.**
a. Ball fails to break or curve	a. Impart spin with wrist and fingers by a right to left twisting action
b. Curve is consistently short or long	b. Change delivery position or point of aim. A slow or fast alley can change the action of a curve ball
8. *Aiming*	**8.**
a. Failure to concentrate on 1–3 pocket in head pin bowling	a. Look at the pocket until the ball strikes the pins. Follow-through should be directed to the pocket
b. Looking away from target as ball is delivered	b. Avoid watching ball. In spare leaves and splits look to the target until ball hits wood
c. Failure to get best angle on leaves	c. Teacher should remind student to get as much alley width as possible between delivery point and standing pins
d. Ball consistently breaks into head pin or other pin when spot aiming	d. Select another spot to guide aiming
e. Failure to pick up common splits	e. Teacher reviews principles of velocity and deflection causing pin action. Review aiming

103

NOVELTY EVENTS

Novelty bowling games that use the standard bowling instructional area and equipment add interest to the program and may be used to improve basic skills. The more closely the game relates to the difficulties the students are meeting, the greater its value.

Blind Bowling.   Played and scored as in regulation bowling except a light curtain is hung approximately one-half of the way down the alley so pins are unseen by the bowler throughout the game. Automatic recorders show spare setups or they may be called to the bowler by an observer. (Excellent game for practicing skills of spot bowling.)

Cocked Hat.   Set only three pins each frame on the 3-7-10 or 2-7-9 spots. Two balls are allowed in each frame. The method of scoring is similar to ten pins; however, a strike scores three points plus the total of the next two balls. A spare scores three points plus the pins of the next ball. (Good practice for spare pickups.)

Cocked Hat Feather Bowling.   Set up pins 1-5-7-10. Use two balls each frame. Bowler attempts to score by knocking down pins 1-7-10. Strikes and spares score three pins plus bonus balls. If the 5 pin, the "feather," is knocked down there is no score in the frame. Variation: Use only one ball per frame. (Valuable practices for spare bowling.)

Strike Setup.   Set up pins 1-3-5. Bowler rolls only one ball a frame. No score is recorded unless all pins fall. Strike score is three plus next two balls (if all pins fall.) (Valuable practice for delivery of the strike ball.)

Surprise Setup.   Set up a series of common spare leaves of two or more pins. For example 6-10, 1-2-4, and 4-7. Repeat the series throughout 10 frames. Each bowler has one ball each frame. All pins, whether two, three, or four, must be knocked down to score five points. Maximum game score is 50. (Valuable practice for spare setups.)

Scotch Bowling.   A mixed doubles game played and scored as official tenpins. One partner rolls the first ball, the second partner the next and alternate delivery continues until game is completed. (Primarily of social value.)

OFFICIATING TECHNIQUES

Bowlers who understand scoring can enjoy a recreational game without officials; however, league and tournament bowling should be governed by a board of directors and conducted by a secretary, team captains, foul judges and scorers. Their official actions are determined by the American Bowling Congress (ABC)[4] and the Women's International Bowling Congress (WIBC).[5]

In brief, officials' responsibilities include:

[4] American Bowling Congress, 1572 E. Capital Drive, Milwaukee, Wisconsin.
[5] Women's International Bowling Congress, 4319 W. Irving Park Road, Chicago, Illinois.

I Board of Directors
1. Decide controversies
2. Hear and decide protests and appeals
3. Declare disputed games invalid or forfeited
4. Decide upon postponements
5. Act as judge in all other league or tournament matters

II Secretary
1. Declares forfeited game if player or team refuses to play within five minutes after warning
2. Allows appeals if rules are misinterpreted or foul called against wrong contestant
3. Disqualifies a player who deliberately fouls or uses abusive language. Arranges player substitution
4. Disallows a protest on a foul if it is recorded and next player has bowled
5. Advises teams on plan to end tie games or tournaments
6. Arranges entries for teams entering district or national tournaments

III Team Captain
1. Assumes responsibility for conduct of her team
2. Files protests with secretary

IV Foul Judge
1. Decides on fouls committed on or over the foul line

V Scorers
1. Check official score sheets and bowlers' names
2. Record every frame and total game score of each bowler
3. When there is no foul judge, may call obvious fouls not recorded by foul detector

Those conducting official tournaments may refer to WIBC *Rules for Sanctioned Leagues;* however, the following simple guides may be helpful in conducting class tournaments:

1. Conduct individual and team matches of three games
2. Competing teams (four or five members per team) bowl on adjoining alleys, exchanging alleys after each completed frame
3. Team winning the greatest number of games is match champion
4. Adopt a point scoring system for league play. For example, award one point for each single game won and one point to the team having the largest game total. In a five game match, six points are awarded.

EVALUATING THE RESULTS

The evaluation program should show a fair measure of the student's skill and knowledge of rules, courtesies, safety, terminology and strategy. It may include:

1. A written examination of rules, scoring, etiquette, history, and game strategy.
2. Tournament results (ladder, double elimination, league results) and individual tournament records.
3. Observation of student's form, effectiveness, skill development, and understanding of playing courtesies and periodical rating of each of these items on a devised scale.
4. Skills tests including:
   a. Strike ball delivery
   b. Spare pick-up
   c. Split bowling
   d. Spot bowling
5. Progress charts kept by individual students of all games bowled.

TERMINOLOGY

Alley Bed—Alley surface between foul line and pit
Anchor—Person who bowls last in team's lineup
Baby Split—Split leaving 2–7, or 3–10 pins
Back-up—A reverse hook
Big Four—4–6–7–10 split
Blow—An error; failure to convert pins standing (other than a split) to a spare
Brooklyn—A ball that crosses over and hits left of head pin in 1–2 pocket
Chop—(Cherry) To knock down the front pin or pins of a spare leave
Double—Two successive strikes
Foul—Act of touching or going beyond the foul line
Foul Line—Line separating the approach and alley bed
Full Hit—Ball that hits center of pin
Gutter Ball—A delivered ball that drops into either gutter before reaching the pins
Handicap—In competition, a predetermined number of pins given to lower average individual or team
Head Pin—Number 1 pin
Hook—A ball that travels a straight line then breaks toward the pins
Kegler—A bowler
King Pin—Number 5 pin
Lane—An alley
Lead-off—Person who bowls first on team
Line—A game or ten frames
Mark—To make a strike or spare
Perfect Game—Twelve successive strikes and a game total of 300
Pit—Area where pinsetter works
Pitch—Angle at which finger holes are bored
Pocket—Space between 1 and 3, and 1 and 2 pins
Railroad—A split
Sleeper—A pin hidden by another pin
Spot—A mark or location on the alley where the bowler aims
Strike—All pins are knocked down by the first ball of a frame
Strike Out—Three successive strike balls in the tenth frame
Turkey—Three successive strikes
Woolworth—Split leaving pins 5–10

DISCUSSION QUESTIONS

1. Demonstrate mimetically and explain the four step coordinated approach.
2. Briefly explain the straight ball delivery, hook, back-up and curve. Teach each of these to any beginner with or without using a ball. Chart the path of each ball from the foul line to the pins. Which delivery is most successful for the beginner? Why? Do the authors of this book agree with your findings?
3. Score and explain a complete game including situations of a double, spare, error, split pickup, and a tenth frame turkey.
4. Explain the terms "head pin bowling," "spot bowling," and "line bowling." What are the advantages and/or disadvantages of each method of aiming?
5. Demonstrate and explain how a beginning bowler should select a ball.
6. Plan several novelty games for use in the gymnasium which are suitable for teaching the approach and scoring.
7. Plan a mixed doubles round robin tournament for ten team entries. Explain how you would determine each team's handicap.

SELECTED AUDIO-VISUAL AIDS

America Bowls. (25 min., 16 mm., sound). Brunswick-Balke-Collender Company, 623–633 S. Wabash Avenue, Chicago 5, Ill. (Loan)
Beginning Bowling. (Filmstrips and recordings). The Sport, The Delivery, Aiming and Scoring. The Athletic Institute, 209 S. State Street, Chicago 4, Ill.
Better Bowling—How It's Done. (20 min., 16 mm., color, sound). Ebonite Company, Division of Stow-Woodward, Inc., Newton 64, Mass. (Loan)
The following are all available from: Brunswick-Balke-Collender Company, 623–633 S. Wabash Avenue, Chicago 5, Ill.
  Bowling Fever. (12 min., 16 mm., sound.) Loan
  Bowling Kings. (12 min., 16 mm., sound.) Loan
  King of the Pins. (12 min., 16 mm., sound.) Loan
  Let's Go Bowling. (25 min., 16 mm., sound.) Loan
  Pin Games. (12 min., 16 mm., sound.) Loan
  Splits, Spares, and Strikes. (12 min., 16 mm., sound.) Loan
  Strike to Spare. (12 min., 16 mm., sound.) Loan
  Ten Pin Aces. (12 min., 16 mm., sound.) Loan
  Ten Pin Titans. (12 min., 16 mm., sound.) Loan
  Young America Bowls. (25 min., 16 mm., sound.) Loan

SUGGESTED READINGS

AAHPER: *Individual Sports Guide,* Current edition, Division of Girls and Women's Sports, Washington, D.C., 1958.
Brunswick-Balke-Collender Company: *Better Your Bowling Score,* American Junior Bowling Congress, 1913 W. 103rd Street, Chicago, Illinois, 1952.
Brunswick-Balke-Collender Company: *More Pins More Fun,* American Junior Bowling Congress, 1913 W. 103rd Street, Chicago, Illinois, 1952.
Day, Ned: *How to Bowl,* Boston, Halcyon House, 1948.
Day, Ned, and Raymer, Milton: *How to Improve Your Bowling,* The Athletic Institute, 209 S. State Street, Chicago 4, Illinois.
Falcaro, Joe, and Goodman, Murray: *Bowling for All,* New York, A. S. Barnes, 1943.
McMahon, Junie, and Goodman, Murray: *Modern Bowling Techniques,* New York, The Ronald Press, 1958.
Miller, Donna Mae, and Ley, Katherine L.: *Individual and Team Sports for Women,* New York, Prentice-Hall Book Company, Inc., 1955.
Vannier, Maryhelen, and Fait, Hollis F.: *Teaching Physical Education in Secondary Schools,* Philadelphia, W. B. Saunders Company, 1957.

Women's International Bowling Congress: *Bowler's Manual,* revised edition, Women's International Bowling Congress, Inc., 4319 W. Irving Park Road, Chicago, Illinois.

PERIODICALS

Bowling: American Bowling Congress, 1572 E. Capital Drive, Milwaukee, Wisconsin.
Prep Pin Patter: 1913 W. 103rd Street, Chicago, Illinois.
Woman Bowler: Women's International Bowling Congress, 4319 W. Irving Park Road, Chicago, Illinois.

8

Fencing

The growth of fencing as a popular international sport is a tribute to the progress of civilization. From its beginnings, and through the years of organized training in fencing, the skill was used as a method of war and a device for settling personal disputes. Today fencing attracts 50,000 Americans to organized group participation in a friendly, competitive sport demanding agility, speed, and endurance.

Through the years the weapons of fencing reflected the purposes and types of combat of each era. The warriors of the Middle Ages used a two-handed sword for destruction and submission of their foes. The heavier weapons were eventually replaced by light rapiers with sharp points and sharp edges.

After gun powder was introduced, the sword lost its value in warfare, but the aristocracy continued to use fencing as a method of settling personal disputes. The tragic number of injuries and deaths from combat caused na-

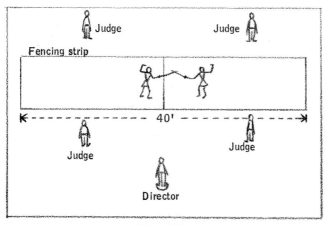

Figure No. 8–1.

tions across the world to banish the sword as a weapon. The nineteenth century saw fencing rise as a new and acceptable sport of skill and strategy rather than sheer strength and brute force. Women entered into fencing when protective equipment was developed and techniques of foil fencing were refined.

Fencing is gaining in popularity where its inherent values are recognized and the sport becomes better known. Although fencing has not gained the rapid popularity of some sports in the United States, it remains a drawing activity in European countries. The formation of the Amateur Fencers of America in 1891 and the Intercollegiate Fencing Association in 1894 gave necessary leadership and sponsorship to competition and league formation across the United States. In a recent National Collegiate Athletic Association championship, 37 colleges participated and over 100 institutions indicated active fencing teams. Fencing clubs affiliated with Amateur Fencing League of America are active in major cities across the nation and encourage participation from both sexes and all age groups.

The foil, lightest of all fencing weapons, encourages good body mechanics through balance and posture control. Whether a beginner or advanced fencer competing with other women or with men, fencing requires quick decisions, speed of movement, energy, and endurance.

THE NATURE AND PURPOSE OF THE SPORT

Fencing is a game of attack and defense by two opponents who attempt to score touches on one another with a designated weapon. Women use only the foil as a weapon; however, men fence with the sabre and epeé as well. The bout is conducted in a designated area—the strip—and continues until one contestant scores four valid touches against her opponent.

The foil, theoretically, is a pointed instrument capable of inflicting a puncture wound on the opponent's torso. The point of the foil must touch upon the target area which includes any portion of the body from the collar bone to an imaginary horizontal line passing across the hip bones on both front and back of the trunk. Touches on arms, legs, hands or masks are not valid.

To score touches a contestant must attack her opponent. A successful attack requires precision and accuracy in selecting proper distance and timing. An arm extension, a lunge, or steps and a lunge bring the attacker to striking distance.

To avoid touches the defender uses a system of parries, or blocking actions, which deflect the attack. The defender may then return an attack to score a touch.

SCORING

Winner of women's standard fencing bout is the person who first scores four legal touches on her opponent. In some bouts, usually direct elimination, a winner may be required to score eight touches with a two touch advantage. In other competitions two out of three bouts must be won.

Scoring of a bout is recorded by the official scorer as each touch is awarded by the director of the bout.

The most common tournament is the round robin. A sample score sheet (Fig. No. 8–2) of a five person round robin tournament best illustrates scoring.

The contestants are assigned numbers prior to competition. Thereafter, the scorer calls the participants by number. To begin the bout, the scorer calls contestants 1 and 4 to appear "on strip" for an immediate bout and contestants 2 and 3 "on deck" for the next bout. As bouts are completed, each is crossed out or checked off on the Order of Bouts.

As contestants are called, a (————) horizontal line is placed in the squares corresponding to the competitors. Reading from left to right, marks above the horizontal line indicate touches the contestant received; below the line, the W (won) or L (lost) indicates the outcome of the bout. For example, contestant #1 (S. Smith) received two touches from #4 (H. Fox) and #1 won the bout. Contestant #2 received four touches from #3 and lost the bout. Number 2 failed to make a valid touch on #5 during the bout. A similar recording is made on each participant in a bout.

At completion of the tournament, total scores, touches and placement are recorded. Bouts won and lost are added from the horizontal line; touches received are added in the horizontal column corresponding to the participant's number. Touches rendered are added in the vertical column corresponding to the participant's number.

First place is awarded the fencer winning the greatest number of bouts, second place to the next greatest bout winner and so on. When a tie for first

NAME	#	1	2	3	4	5	BOUTS		TOUCHES		PLACE
							WON	LOST	REC'VD	SCORED	
Smith, S.	1		1 / W	0 / W	11 / W	0 / W	4	0	3	12	1
Brown, L.	2	111 / L		1111 / L	1111 / L	1111 / L	0	4	12	5	5
Davis, J.	3	1111 / L	11 / W		1111 / L	1 / W	2	2	11	9	4
Fox, H.	4	1111 / L	11 / W	1 / W		1111 / L	2	2	11	12	3
Walker, S.	5	1111 / L	0 / W	1111 / L	11 / W		2	2	10	9	2

ORDER of BOUTS

1 – 4	2 – 4
2 – 3	5 – 1
4 – 5	4 – 3
1 – 2	5 – 2
3 – 5	3 – 1

Figure No. 8–2. Round Robin Tournament.

place occurs in the finals among two or more fencers, they fence each other to determine places. If ties occur for other than first place, highest placement is given the fencer with the least number of touches received. If a tie still exists, the fencer scoring the largest number of touches receives higher placement. If a tie still remains and placement must be determined, the tied contestants fence each other.[1]

NEEDED FACILITIES AND EQUIPMENT

Schools and colleges probably will find it necessary to furnish basic materials for instruction as fencing equipment is not usually owned by young people. As is true with many activities, equipment and facility areas can be improvised and result in a full instructional program. However, basic safety requirements demand some carefully selected equipment.

Ideally, a separate fencing room in the physical education area should serve for instructional and recreational purposes. The gymnasium area should not be filled with wall targets, mirrors or the fencer's equipment because of the possible danger to participants in other activities. Beginning fencing skill may be taught in or outdoors on various surfaces; however, the strip for bouting should be carefully laid out.

The fencing strip is the area upon which the bout is conducted. An official strip is between 5 feet 11 inches to 6 feet 7 inches in width and 50 feet in length. Absolute minimal dimensions are 3 feet wide and 40 feet long. Preferred surfacing is of linoleum, rubber, or cork composition; however, hardwood floors are satisfactory. The strip is divided by five parallel lines, one inch wide across its width. In the middle by a center line: two "on guard" lines on either side and 6 feet 6¾ inches from the center line, and two warning lines, 3 feet 3⅜ inches from each end of the strip. If the strip is marked in accordance with men's intercollegiate rules, the markings may be used. If it is not possible to paint lines on the floor's surface, because of multi-use, commercial plastic tapes can be laid and later removed with no floor damage.

Mirrors, stall bars, mats, and wall targets are among the aids helpful in teaching fencing skills. Mirrors are valuable in analyzing footwork and body position, enabling each student to observe her faults and make necessary adjustments; stall bars provide a device for checking body alignment. Wall targets and dummies are invaluable for warming up and in practicing accuracy while lunging.

Foil.   Women fence with both the French and Italian foils; however, the French foil is more popular for instructional purposes. The total weight of the foil must be less than 17.637 ounces and the length less than 43.3 inches. The foil is composed of four major parts—the blade, guard, handle, and pommel. The steel blade, of fine machine steel, is quadrilateral (rectan-

---

[1] See A.F.L.A. *Fencing Rules and Manual* for complete discussion of scoring individual and team competition.

gular or square cross section) and tapers to a blunt end. The pliable blade measures from 32 to 35 inches from guard to tip.

Guard.   The steel or aluminum guard is a round or oval protection of the weapon hand. The round guards are 3½ to 4 inches in diameter. The oval or "figure eight" guards cannot exceed 4⅝ inches. A thumb pad or cushion is inserted between the guard and the handle to prevent friction between the metal guard and the fencer's knuckles.

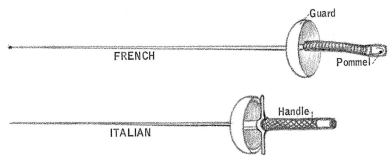

Figure No. 8–3.

Handle.   The handle is rectangular and curved to fit the contour of the hand. The wooden handle is wrapped with cord or covered by leather to aid in a secure grip.

Pommel.   The pommel is a threaded steel knob which screws to the tang of the blade (threaded end) and secures all parts of the weapon together. The pommel acts as a balance to the weight of the blade.

Martingale.   The martingale or similar strap holds the weapon near the hand so the foil will not be knocked toward fencers or spectators in case of disarmament. This is not necessary during instructional classes.

Mask.   A mask is as important to the sport of fencing as the foil itself. Prevention of injury and fencer's confidence in safety make it essential. The mask and attached bib cover the entire front portion of the head and neck. The mask is constructed of strong wire mesh reinforced with leather or cord straps, a heavy padded cloth or canvas bib, and wire headpiece (tongue) covered with cloth which bends to adjust to a fencer's head.

Jackets.   Fencing jackets and plastrons serve as protection for the upper body. The full jacket is the most desirable protection for women, although the adjustable half-jacket is more practical for group instruction. The jacket is made of heavy white material padded in front and in the upper sleeve with shoulder seams corresponding to arm and shoulder lines. It should fully cover neck, arms, and torso and overlap the fencing breeches or skirt. Extra breast protection of padded material, plastic, or aluminum should be worn under the jacket.

Footwear.   Absorbent socks which cushion the feet and absorb perspiration are essential. Although flat leather-soled fencing shoes are desirable on regulation strips, tennis shoes or low heeled rubber-soled shoes are practical for classwork.

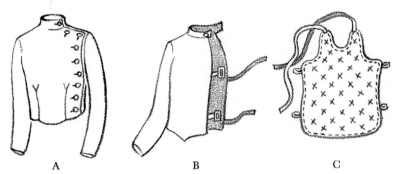

Figure No. 8–4.   Fencing Jackets. A. Full Jacket; B. Half Jacket; C. Full Plastron.

Glove.   A padded leather glove should be worn on the foil hand. If students share gloves, they should wear a thin inner cotton glove to absorb perspiration.

Storage and Care of Equipment

Multi-use of equipment requires care for cleanliness and safe condition of equipment. Students should assume some responsibility in maintenance. A few suggestions:

1. Construct a "Fencers' Caddy"[2] which is movable and light, yet serves as a storage area for equipment not in use. If such a device is not practical store equipment in a central location; foils hanging so blades are not damaged, and masks, jackets, and gloves located for maximum ventilation.
2. Foil tips should be padded with rubber tips or adhesive tape. Pommels should be secured to prevent guards and blades from wobbling.
3. The blade should have a slight bend so that when a touch is scored the tip is lower than the bend in the blade. To bend or straighten the blade, rub it between the shoe sole and floor. By friction the blade is heated and becomes more pliable. Avoid using hands to straighten a blade.
4. Replace and repair protective cushions and handles before damage to fencer's hands. Thread or cord wrapped around the handle and glued at each end is satisfactory. Felt pads or padded leather serve as guards.
5. Check masks frequently for gaps or rust spots in the mesh. If a mask cannot be repaired to complete satisfaction remove it from use. When masks are used by several persons wash material and bibs with soap and water, or brush with disinfectant after each wearing.
6. Jackets should be checked often to make certain buttons and zippers are functioning. Any tears or rips should be repaired immediately. Encourage women to remove makeup to prevent collar stains. Wash and fluff dry jackets regularly.

[2] See Bernhard, Frederick and Edwards, Vernon: *How to Fence,* Dubuque, Wm. C. Brown Company, 1956, pp. 10–11.

7. Gloves should be aired and cleaned with disinfectant powder after use. Inner gloves should be aired and washed frequently.

TEACHING UNITS

Suggested course content for beginners and advanced students include:

Units for Beginners	*Units for Advanced Students*
Brief history	Selection and care of personal
Care and use of equipment	equipment
Safety fundamentals	Review exercises
Fundamental skills	Review safety precautions
Preparatory position	Review fundamental skills
Salute	Advanced skills
Guard position	Parry of seventh
Reassemblement	Compound attacks
Advance	Parry of eighth
Retreat	Compound parries
Warm up and conditioning ex-	Advanced parries (If appropri-
ercises	ate for individual)
Lunge	Cutover
Lunge and recovery	Remise
Grip	Jump lunge
Salute in 5 counts	Stop thrust
On guard in fourth	Strategy
On guard in sixth	Officiating
Parry of fourth	Individual and team tournaments
Parry of sixth	Evaluation
Straight thrust	
Disengage	
Counter parry	
Riposte	
Attack on blade: Beat, one-two	
attack	
Feint	
Rules	
Strategy	
Beginning officiating	
Bouting (individual)	
Evaluation	

BASIC SKILLS

Guard Position. The guard is the best body balanced position for offensive and defensive play. The fencer enters the guard position from an erect or preparatory position, knees straight and heels together at 90° angles. Forward foot points toward opponent's foot. The body is turned so forward

Figure No. 8–5.   Preparatory Position.

shoulder and hip are toward opponent. The front of the body is angled in the same direction as rear foot. The foil arm is straight and extended forward and down so that the tip of the foil is held slightly off the ground. The back arm is straight, pointing downward and slightly away from the body. The hand is straight, palm up.

In assuming the crouched guard position, move forward foot approximately two foot-lengths forward. The heels remain at right angles, the knees are bent so the kneecaps are directly over the toes of each foot. The torso is erect, as if sitting on a bench, with weight equally distributed on each foot. The back arm is bent with elbow at shoulder height and held in body line behind the torso. The wrist of the rear arm is relaxed, palm toward the head. The foil arm is bent and comfortably carried toward the opponent. The elbow of the foil arm is rotated toward the body line and in about 6 to 9 inches (a hand span) from the side of the body. The foil is in a straight line with the forearm, pommel resting on the wrist as the foil tip points at opponent's eye level.

Salute.   The salute is a traditional movement of courtesy and greeting to the opponent. The two movement salute begins from the preparatory position (as described under guard position) with feet at right angles, foil extended forward and downward and rear arm away from body. On the first movement the foil is raised sharply bringing the guard to the chin, the pommel is centered in the forearm, toward the fencer, and the foil tip is directed toward the ceiling. With the second count, the fencer briskly returns to preparatory position.

The Advance.   The advance is a forward body movement used when the fencer needs to get close to her opponent for an attack. The advance is made from the guard position with small, even steps. The forward foot leads, as the toe pushes and heel leads, into a step of several (3 to 7) inches. The rear foot follows immediately with a step covering the same distance. The guard position is maintained and distance between the feet is constant. Weight is low and the torso in an erect position.

The Retreat.   The retreat is the reverse of the advance movement. It is a defense action which takes the fencer out of her opponent's reach. The

Figure No. 8–6.   Guard Position.

Figure No. 8–7.   Salute (in two movements).

Figure No. 8–8.   The Lunge.

rear foot moves rapidly backward followed immediately by the front foot as
the toe pushes off and the heel leads to the floor. The feet do not rise far
from the floor as the guard position is maintained and weight is distributed
to insure rapid movement in any direction.

Lunge.   The lunge is an extension of the arm and body from the
guard position for the purpose of delivering an attack to the opponent. The
lunge must be executed with split second timing in this sequence: (1) extension of the foil arm toward opponent in line of attack (fingernails of hand
up and pommel against wrist); the arm is straight and elbow and shoulder
are firm; (2) Straighten back leg and knee as the forward foot moves toward opponent (to a position where kneecap is over instep of forward foot);
(3) Simultaneous with leg movements, the rear arm straightens, parallel to
leg, with palm up to aid in balance and in preparation for recovery. The
ankle of the rear foot is flexed so the foot can maintain firm floor contact.

Recovery of the Lunge.   The recovery to a guard position is accomplished by simultaneous movements: (1) bending rear knee as rear arm
pulls to guard position, (2) pushing back with the forward toe and bringing
foot to guard distance from rear foot, (3) bending foil arm to guard position. The recovery must be a smooth, rapid movement as a slow recovery
presents a weak defensive position.

Grip.   A proper grip is essential to effective foil fencing. The handle
of the foil is curved and shaped to fit the hand. Looking down on the handle, the convex portion fits in the palm of the hand, as the thumb and forefinger serve as holding digits while the remaining fingers guide the fine foil
action. The index finger is placed near the cushion so the handle rests
on the second joint of the finger. The thumb is placed on top of the
handle pointing toward the blade. A pinching motion is assumed. The fleshy
tips of the second, third, and fourth fingers rest lightly along the concave
surface and pull the handle into the palm. The wrist is straight and the
pommel rests against the middle of the wrist. In this position there is a
straight line from elbow to foil tip. Precision and accuracy are dependent
upon the coordinated grip—with the thumb and index finger directing the

gross action of the blade and the other fingers controlling the direction of the foil tip.

The Target.   The target area is any portion of the body from the collar bone to an imaginary horizontal line passing across the hip bones on the front and back of the torso. Touches off the target area are invalid. To aid in defining attacks and parries, the target is divided into four sections by imaginary lines. Such a division results in high and low lines and inside and outside lines.

Parries and Guard Positions.   A parry is a defensive movement that blocks or deviates the opponent's attacking blade. There are eight fundamental parries, each designed to defend a section of the target area. Properly named and numbered in French, parries are given corresponding numbers in English for ease of understanding during instruction.

Parries should be looked upon as movements to guard positions and taught as movements from one guard position to another. That is, when a

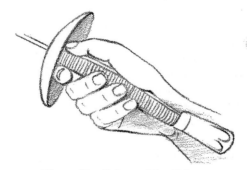

Figure No. 8–9.   The Grip.

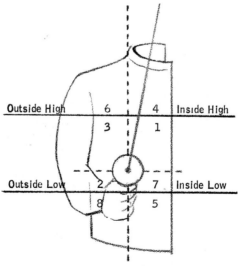

Figure No. 8–10.   The Target Area.

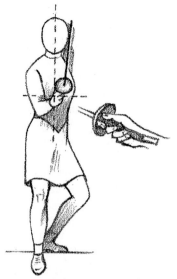

Figure No. 8–11.   Parry of Fourth.

Parry of Sixth.   The hand moves from guard position of fourth to right to defend upper outside target. With the hand at breast height, point at opponent's eyes, the forearm carries the weapon from pivot point of elbow so attacking blade can be carried by the strong part of the blade to the right of the body.

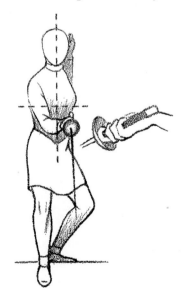

Figure No. 8–13.   Parry of Seventh.

Parry of Fourth.   This defends upper inside target area. The hand moves from guard position of sixth to the left to protect the high inside line. The hand moves to the left, at breast height, to outer limits of the body to remove the threatening foil tip of the attacker. The hand is supinated, thumb up, and slightly higher than the elbow. Point of the blade remains at opponent's eye level but slightly to the right.

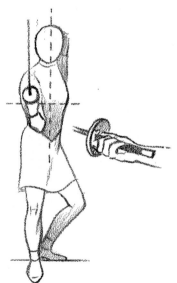

Figure No. 8–12.   Parry of Sixth.

Parry of Seventh.   This defends low inside line. Foil tip moves in a clockwise semicircle toward opponent's knee level, hand to the left with palm facing upward.

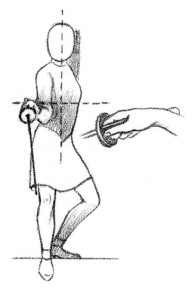

Figure No. 8–14. Parry of Second.

Parry of Second. This defends low outside line. Foil tip drops to opponent's knee level by rapid counterclockwise semicircular movement. Hand to the right with back of hand upward.

Parry of First. This defends high inside line. Foil tip points toward opponent's feet as forearm is raised to horizontal plane, elbow to the right. The hand is pronated, thumb down and fingers pointed toward opponent.

Figure No. 8–15. Parry of First.

Figure No. 8–16. Parry of Third.

Parry of Third. This defends high outside line. Foil and pronated hand move to the right; foil tip pointed toward opponent's eye level.

121

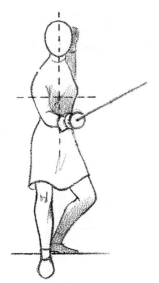

Parry of Fifth. This defends low inside line. Pronated hand moves to the left and drops below the elbow. Point of the blade is higher than the hand.

Figure No. 8–17.   Parry of Fifth.

Parry of Eighth. This defends low outside line. Hand moves to the right, palm up with pommel directed past body line. Point of blade toward opponent's knee level.

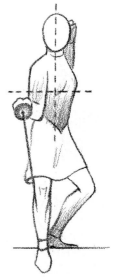

Figure No. 8-18.   Parry of Eighth.

fencer executes a parry of sixth, she is properly moving to the guard position of sixth. For the beginner, guard of fourth and sixth are defensive positions.

The parries for right-handed fencers are briefly described in the logical order of presentation. Instructors should stress mastery of parry of fourth and sixth for beginners and be reminded that a fencer can be competent with skill of four parries—one for each target section.

Counter Parry. A counter parry not only deviates the opponent's blade, but sweeps it into another line of attack with a circular motion of the defender's blade. By using the fingers, rather than the entire hand, the defender drops the blade point, rotates it around the attacking blade (clockwise from fourth position and counterclockwise from sixth position) and deviates the blade.

Simple Attacks. Generally, an attack is considered a forward movement of the foil, with or without a lunge, toward the opponent's target. A simple attack comprises only one movement such as a straight thrust, disengage or cutover.

The Straight Thrust. This is the simplest of all attacks. It involves a quick, smooth extension of the foil arm (shoulder high and palm up), in the line of engagement. The arm extension may be followed by a lunge if distance to the opponent requires it.

The Disengage. This is a change of line of attack made by passing the blade under the opponent's blade to an opposite line of engagement. Execution begins with an extension of the arm, shoulder high, palm up. Keeping the foil close to opponent's blade, the fingers drop the tip under opponent's blade circumscribing a small semicircle or a moving "V." The rapid change from the closed to open line is immediately followed by a lunge.

The Cutover. This is accomplished as the blade passes over the point of the opponent's dropped blade to change the line of engagement. It is used against an opponent's lowered blade, as an opponent applies pressure with weak sections of blade against strong parts of the defender's blade, and when an opponent holds a parry too long. To execute the cutover the arm remains bent as the fingers and wrist lift the blade so the tip circumscribes a small semicircle or inverted "V" as it crosses opponent's blade. The arm is extended immediately when the foil tip clears and the lunge follows.

Riposte. The riposte is a return attack that follows a successful parry. The return may be a simple single thrust or compound attack. In either case, an immediate riposte has the right-of-way over a second attack by the original attacker.

Feint. A feint is a false attack intended to deceive an opponent so she will close the line (parry) of attack and open a new line. A feint may take such form as a straight thrust, disengage, beat or press, but to be deceptive it must be rapid and vigorous.

Figure No. 8–19.   The Lunge and Parry.

Compound Attacks.   Compound, or composite, attacks are made in two or more movements by feints, attacks against the blade, or a combination of these. They include:

Double Disengage (One-Two Attack).   This consists of two disengages executed in rapid succession. The first disengage, with an extended arm, is made into an open line forcing the opponent to parry. The second disengage follows immediately in opposite direction to go on target in a newly created opening. The lunge begins with the second disengagement.

The One-Two-Three Attack.   An additional disengage is added to the "one-two" attack in an attempt to make an opening and a touch.

The Double.   An attack involving two disengagements in the same direction.

Attacks on the Blade.   Attacks on the blade serve to create an opening in a closed line, to confuse the adversary by causing reaction to pressure on the blade and thus deception of the parry. They also serve as invitations for attack.

The Beat.   A short, sharp movement executed so the middle part of the attacker's blade raps sharply against the middle or weak part of opponent's blade. The wrist and fingers control the attacking blade action. From an engagement in the former line the blade moves to the right as the grip of the last three fingers relaxes. Quickly the fingers pull to the hand and the blade snaps sharply. If an attack, rather than a feint, is intended, the lunge follows immediately.

The Press.   Pressure is applied against the opponent's blade to remove it from the line. Without warning, it is executed similarly to the beat;

however, it is a smooth, strong action. As pressure is answered the attack may move (1) in the same line, or (2) a release of attacker's pressure and a disengage and attack in another line.

The Glide.   An advanced technique wherein the attacker moderately pressures her own blade along opponent's blade until thrust is complete.

The Pressure Glide.   A difficult technique of exacting pressure downward and forward against the opponent's blade from the weakest point of the blade to the guard.

Attacks Taking the Blade.   These attacks are developed to dominate the opponent's blade by removing the foil point from line by controlling the defending blade.

Opposition.   Similar to the glide. However, the guard of the attacking fencer is in continuous opposition to opponent's blade. This must be a simple attack.

Bind.   A method of moving an opponent's blade from high to low line or low to high line. The action is taken against a stiff extended arm by applying the strong part of the foil blade to weak portion of opponent's and forcing with one's own blade and forearm. For example, when making eighth bind from guard position of sixth, make a small circle over the top of the defender's blade and lower blade and forearm. This action carries the blade to eighth. A slight lateral and forward motion to the right will carry the opponent's point outside the body line.

Envelopment.   This is executed against a straight arm similar to the bind. However, it is a continuous motion carrying the opponent's blade in a complete circle and returning to original position.

Counter Attacks.   These involve split second timing as they are simply arm extensions toward the fencer preparing to attack.

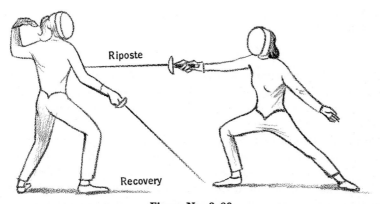

Riposte

Recovery

Figure No. 8–20.

Time Thrust.   A simple arm extension aimed to touch opponent who has not taken the right-of-way. It is most effective against an advancing opponent.

Stop Thrust.   The defender extends her arm as the opponent, preparing to attack, moves into the extended foil. It is effective against compound attacks.

Secondary Attacks.   Secondary attacks follow an initial thrust and are effective when the opponent's riposte is delayed.

Redouble.   This is a second attack in a changed line, executed immediately after the first is parried. It is successful when defender delays or fails to riposte.

Replacement.   This consists in replacing the point of the foil in the same line after it is parried.

A touch can be attempted by replacement when the riposte is delayed, or the opponent attempts a compound return.

STRATEGY

The successful bout fencer is aware of her personal resources and alert to the actions of her opponent. Several basic guides to attack and defense are helpful:

1. As the bout begins observe opponent's stance, lunge, guard position, length of reach, preferred attacks. Knowledge of an opponent is most important in planning bouting tactics.
2. Use simple attacks when possible. A well planned, simple attack is preferable to compound attacks. Always lunge with an extended arm.
3. Develop and use rapid, positive feints for opponent's deception.
4. Recover from attacks, successful or otherwise, immediately to avoid a return.
5. Delay parries until last moment to avoid being deceived by change of line. Keep parries under control—a wide parry invites touches in an open line.
6. Keep footwork smooth and rapid. Keep feet and body as alert as the mind.

CLASS ORGANIZATION

Basic fencing skills are taught best in carefully organized and supervised class situations. The potentially hazardous nature of the sport demands more organization than some sports skills. The group should be small enough so some individual instruction can be given.

During demonstrations the group can be drawn in a semicircle close to the instructor. In a large group, the front row may kneel or sit and the back row stand. As the class begins skill practice, each individual should be assigned to a pool (squad) of at least six girls. The squad may be given names or numbers which identify them for teacher assignment to mirror or dummy practice, couple skill drill, or bouting.

The double line is an excellent formation for basic instruction, checking form, and observing general class progress. The squads form parallel lines facing each other so students are paired off. Facing an opponent, the student practices footwork, attacks, parries, and beginning bouting technique. In order to vary opponents, have one line rotate with the leader going to the end of line at a designated time interval. When double line formation is used in a crowded area the opposing line should execute a single skill, rather than individual skill practice, to avoid accidents. For example, line #1 attacks as line #2 retreats; line #1 executes a disengage lunge into the fourth line as line #2, back to the wall, parries and ripostes.

A pool serves as a unit for a round robin tournament as the student's skills develop. As two girls fence, the other members officiate and score the bout.

TEACHING PROGRESSION

A short and inspiring history of fencing helps girls and women develop the spirit and attitude for a new experience in a combative sport. At the beginning of a unit an explanation of safety precautions, demonstration, and explanation of fencing and of equipment is essential. Basic exercises and novelty games are helpful in developing strength and agility and in releasing tensions often present.

Prior to class practice of a skill, the teacher should demonstrate and explain its use in a bout. Basic skills of the guard position, grip, advance, retreat, lunge and recovery should be stressed for form, agility, and effectiveness. The salute and call, taught early in a unit, add dignity and courtesy to informal practice.

Emphasis on the basic parries of sixth and fourth gives a fencer confidence to work against simple attacks. Addition of skills of riposte encourage agility and alertness and increase practice pleasure. Each fencer practices skills against an opponent, first on the teacher's command and later in bouting sessions. Early bouting and novelty events are desirable to break tedious, but necessary, drills. Selected films and demonstration bouts help maintain interest.

As students progress, attacks on the blade, compound attacks and counter parries are introduced. Bouting and officiating should encourage students to participate with community fencing groups.

A sample teaching unit for beginners might include the following:

Lesson I

1. Brief history
2. Equipment and its care
3. Safety fundamentals
4. Explanation of the game (target, touches)
5. Demonstration bout

Lesson II

1. Review of previous lesson
2. Preparatory position
3. Salute
4. Guard position
5. Call and reassembly
6. Advance
7. Retreat
8. Novelty games for agility and speed

Lesson III

1. Review salute, call, reassembly
2. Review guard position, advance, and retreat
3. Grip
4. Drill of advance and retreat (Simple Simon game)
5. Student discussion and evaluation

Lesson IV

1. Review
2. Lunge
3. Lunge and recovery
4. Combined practice of guard position, advance, retreat, lunge, and recovery
5. Straight thrust

Lesson V

1. Review
2. Engagement
3. Demonstration and explanation of parries
4. Parry of fourth
5. Beat and parry four
6. Practice attack and parry

Lesson VI

1. Review—stressing attack and parry of fourth
2. Parry of sixth
3. Begin officiating skills
4. Beginning bouting

Lesson VII

1. Review—emphasize parries
2. Disengage

3. Group drill on attacks and parries
4. Bouting strategy

Lesson VIII

1. Selected film
2. Novelty events
3. Informal evaluation

Lesson IX

1. Review
2. Riposte
3. Drill parries and ripostes in combination
4. Drill parries and ripostes with footwork
5. Counter parries

Lesson X

1. Review—stress form in movements
2. Attack on the blade: beat
3. Drill and bouting
4. Review finer rule points as:
   a. Right-of-way
   b. Stopping the bout
   c. Acknowledgment of touch

Lesson XI

1. Review
2. Explain and demonstrate feint
3. Introduce one compound attack; beat disengage
4. Practice bouting

Lesson XII

1. Review officiating
2. Begin round robin tournament

Lesson XIII

1. Complete tournament
2. Class evaluation of fencing unit

Lesson XIV

1. Written evaluation
2. Demonstration and explanation of advanced skills

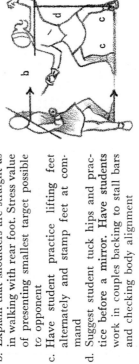

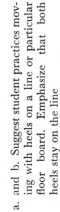
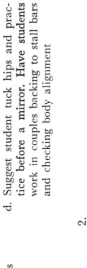

SKILL DIFFICULTIES AND THEIR CORRECTION

Difficulty	Correction
1. Guard Position	**1.**
a. Feet too close or too far apart	a. Review sequence of movements to guard position stressing a comfortable step forward and balance
b. Turning body toward opponent	b. Explain that shoulders are straight as in walking with rear foot. Stress value of presenting smallest target possible to opponent
c. Weight transferred to one foot	c. Have student practice lifting feet alternately and stamp feet at command
d. Body inclined forward from hips	d. Suggest student tuck hips and practice before a mirror. Have students work in couples backing to stall bars and checking body alignment
2. Advance and Retreat	**2.**
a. Body does not move forward or back in a straight line	a. and b. Suggest student practices moving with heels on a line or particular floor board. Emphasize that both heels stay on the line
b. Feet and heels lose their relationship and cause improper body balance	

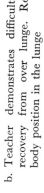

Difficulty

c. Knees are straightened as body moves (indicated by fencer's head bobbing)

d. Feet are dragged

e. Feet become too close or too far apart for proper balance

3. Lunge

a. Body precedes arm thrust

b. Fencer lunges too far

c. Forward foot is lifted high and lunge is slow and attack carried out of line by raised body

Correction

c. and d. Have the student move slowly as the instructor counts or calls foot action emphasizing body position

e. Suggest the student stop often and check balance and foot position

3.

a. Explain the rule of "right away" and the necessity of rapid arm extension. Teacher demonstrates proper timing and leads group by command of "thrust-lunge," "one-two," or "bing-bing"

b. Teacher demonstrates difficulty of recovery from over lunge. Review body position in the lunge

c. Teacher explains that the forward heel need not be raised more than an inch during the lunge. Student practices lunge with extended arm until body movement is smooth

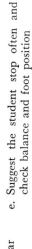

SKILL DIFFICULTIES AND THEIR CORRECTION (*Continued*)

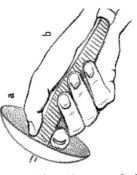

Difficulty	*Correction*
d. Failing to hit target because of under lunging	d. Teacher demonstrates how too short a step carries the knee past the toe. Student practices lunging at wall target to learn distance
4. Recovery of Lunge	**4.**
a. Recover to a standing position	a. Teacher demonstrates and stresses return to a balanced guard position for coming action
b. Failure to use rear arm in recovery	b. Suggest student recovers without use of arm and then compare with properly executed recovery
c. Slow, hesitating movements	c. Stress the importance of coordination of all the body into one movement
5. Grip	**5.**
a. Foil held upsidedown or sideways	a. Demonstrate proper grip and check each student
b. Foil held too tightly	b. Demonstrate proper grip and check each student
c. Foil held too loosely	c. Teacher may tap blades to show how a fencer can lose control with an improper grip

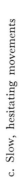

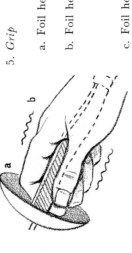

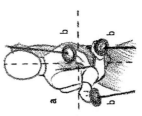

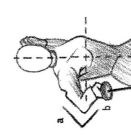

Difficulty	*Correction*
6. Simple Attacks	**6.**
a. Failure to extend arm prior to body lunge	a. Explain the right-of-way rule and importance of arm extension. Repeat response to command exercises "one-two," "bing-bing"
b. Arm moves foil tip in disengage and cutover causing tip to move too far out of line leaving target unprotected	b. Stress importance of maintaining protection of target area—demonstrate use of fingers in moving foil tip. Student draws imaginary pictures with foil tip while keeping arm in extension and in guard position
c. Grip becomes so loose foil control is lost	c. Suggest student practice simple attacks slowly, maintaining control as opponent beats or pressures against the blade.
7. Simple Parries	**7.**
a. Parries are made by arm resulting in slow recovery and large unguarded target area	a. Practice parries with tip of foil against wall so student concentrates on flexible wrist and finger movement and foil direction
b. Extending arm or dropping hand as attack begins	b. Explain parries are made from a guard position to another guard position. Teacher gives commands "parry fourth, parry sixth, etc.," so action becomes easy before bouting begins
c. Lack of skill in selection of proper parry	c. Explain parries designed to protect each target area and suggest opponents lunge slowly during practice sessions

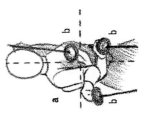

133

SKILL DIFFICULTIES AND THEIR CORRECTION (*Continued*)

Difficulty	*Correction*
8. *Riposte*	8.
a. Failure to complete a parry before beginning riposte	a. Student should practice the riposte mimetically, then at teacher's command, and against a slow lunge before bouting
b. Delaying so opponent can redouble or replace	b. Suggest student practice to command "parry-extend-lunge." Increase speed and add disengage and cutover. Instruct opponent to wait for riposte until skill is developed

NOVELTY EVENTS

Balloon Bouting.   Conduct as a regular bout with a small balloon attached to some valid target area. A winner is declared only when the balloon is broken, no matter how many touches may be made before.

Variations may include: 1. "Prize Picking" when a touch is valid only if it is made on candy or gum hung on the jacket, 2. "Party Day" when a heart (Valentine's Day), shamrock (St. Patrick's Day) or other symbolic design becomes the target.

Decision Making.   A game directed by the teacher or class leader to encourage agility and alertness. Two lines are formed facing one another, with predetermined opponents. The leader speaks to one line and commands, "advance, retreat, lunge, etc." The opposing fencer must react to avoid being touched, but may not make any defensive moves unless given a command.

Ladder Climb.   All fencers are given a ladder tournament position. Fencers may challenge the person one or two positions above. On signal, bouting begins; on a second signal bouting ceases. The fencer with the largest number of touches is declared winner. Ladder positions are changed and bouting begins again. Allow enough time and have enough ladders so fencers on the last "rungs" can reach the top.

Indian Fencers.   Excellent novelty game for developing agility. Played as Indian Club Snatch with two lines facing each other. Each team member is numbered with her opponent diagonally opposite. As a number is called, the opposing team representatives run forward each attempting to snatch the club and return safely to her team.

Variation: Play as above, but players must advance and retreat in the guard position.

Story Telling.   Novelty game designed to encourage quick reaction. Two lines facing. Each line is given a color designation. The teacher or leader begins telling a story. When the color is mentioned, the fencers in that color line may attack and make one thrust. The story continues, using the name of either line's color until both lines have had opportunities to test their agility and alertness.

OFFICIATING TECHNIQUES

Officiating a fencing bout requires a jury consisting of a director, and two to four judges. A scorekeeper and a timekeeper assist the jury. All officials should be thoroughly familiar with the current bout rules as stated by the Amateur Fencers League of America. The director stands midway between the fencers, approximately 13 feet from the strip. The judges stand on each side of both fencers. The judges to the right of the director observe touches on the fencer to the director's left. Conversely, the judges to the left observe materiality of touches on the fencer to the director's right. When only two judges are used, they are positioned to observe maximum

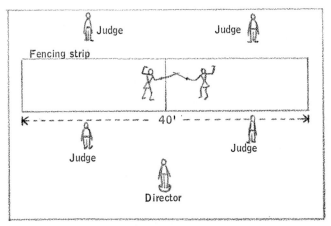

Figure No. 8–21.

target area. If both fencers are right-handed, the judge in the lower left corner and the one in the upper right corner in Figure No. 8-21 are in judging position.

Director.   The director is in full charge of the bout. She has jurisdiction over all fencers, officials, and spectators. She is responsible for preparation, conduct, and conclusion of the bout. Only the director can award touches, inflict penalties, and decide all questions concerning rules and bout conduct.

Once the director orders "fence" she should turn her attention to the ensemble of plays and phrasing to decide validity (whether a touch should be awarded), although she may aid in determining materiality (whether or not there has been a touch).

Judges.   Judges assist in establishing the materiality of a touch. When a judge sees, or thinks she sees, a touch or a direct foul she gains the director's attention by raising an arm. The bout stops and the director calls upon the judges to verify the materiality of a touch on the fencer she is watching. The judge answers orally by "yes," "no," "foul," or "abstain." Each judge has one vote and the director a vote and a half. Abstention does not count as a vote. The majority of votes determines the decision on materiality. The director then determines validity and awards the touch.

Beginning fencers should be encouraged to call their touches in practice fencing and learn more formal officiating rules and techniques for use in their pool. A review of basic rules of judging is valuable.

1. Every touch, to be valid, must arrive on target clearly and cleanly on the point.
2. A direct foul is a good touch on foul territory—arms, legs, mask, hand.
3. An indirect foul is one that is applied into foul territory by either contestant.

4. A direct foul annuls any action that follows. The bout stops for a direct foul, but not an indirect foul.
5. On double touches the first touch landed is scored. If it is not determinable which fencer had right-of-way, no touch is scored.
6. Right-of-way. The attacker has the right-of-way, the defender gains the right-of-way by a riposte or evasion by body movement. A counter riposte gains the right-of-way again.

EVALUATING THE RESULTS

Evaluation in fencing classes is complicated by the numerous parts contained in a single skill. An effective evaluative plan should consider the student's knowledge and understanding of rules of bouting, safety, officiating, and skills. Her ability to fence effectively should reflect her skill development.

Rating Basic Skills. It is desirable to evaluate a student's progress and skill individually. A rating scale may be developed for each skill taught. For example, the teacher may wish to evaluate fifteen separate skills of: (1) guard position, (2) advance, (3) retreat, (4) advance and lunge, (5) cutover lunge, (6) disengage lunge, (7) feints, (8) one-two, (9) double, (10) beat attack, (11) parry of fourth, (12) parry of sixth, (13) riposte, (14) parry of seventh, and (15) parry of eighth.

Aside from the simple execution of the above skills, the teacher may evaluate their execution considering the student's 1. ability to advance, retreat, and lunge in good form with good judgment of distance; and 2. her ability to execute attacks and parries with precision and speed.

The Schutz Fencing Achievement Scales[3] use the lunge for speed and accuracy, and the speed in footwork and lunge to measure elements important in the sport. The scales may be used successfully if the teacher remembers no attempt is made to measure general fencing ability.

Rating scales used by student officials are helpful in evaluation of general fencing ability. Tournament play in a round robin pool may be arranged so each person evaluates all other pool members on fencing ability, strategy, and officiating ability.

The complete picture of the student's progress includes a written examination of the rules, history, and safety of the sport.

TERMINOLOGY

Advance—Forward movement of the body toward opponent
Attack—An attempt to hit an opponent by a thrust of the foil (usually followed by a lunge)
Attack on the Blade—Beats, pressures, binds, and glides used to open a line of attack or deceive opponent

[3] Schutz, Helen J.: Construction of an Achievement Scale in Fencing for Women, Abstract of Master's Thesis, University of Washington, Seattle, Washington.

Call—Stamping forward foot twice to stop the bout
Closed Line—A line closed to attack due to position of foil and arm of opponent
Compound Parry—Two or more parries used in combination
Contraction Parry—A combination simple and counter parry
Counter Parry—Defender's blade is disengaged as opponent attacks and defender parries
Cutover—Passing foil over tip of opponent's blade
Deceive—Escaping and avoiding control of blade by opponent
Disengage—Pass the point of foil under opponent's blade to another line
Double Touch—Two correct simultaneous attacks. They do not score
Engagement—Contact of opposing blades
Invitation—Actions which invite attack by an opponent
Line of Attack—Used to describe position of the attacking weapon
Parry—Blocking an opponent's thrust by contact with foils
Pass—Point of foil grazes target, failing to hit properly
Phrase—A period of continuous bouting
Pool—A group of fencers competing in round robin play
Retreat—Backward movement of body away from opponent
Right-of-Way—The right of attack gained by fencer who first extends the foil arm. May be gained by riposte and counter riposte.
Riposte—A return or counter attack following a successful parry
Salute—Acknowledgement to opponent and judges
Thrust—An extension of the arm in a feint or an attack
Touch—A legal hit on opponent's target area

Discussion Questions

1. Suggest warm up exercises for use in and out of class which help in conditioning for fencing.
2. Explain and demonstrate the difference between simple and compound attacks.
3. What safety precautions are necessary in conducting a fencing class?
4. Explain the "right-of-way" rule. How does a fencer secure right-of-way? Demonstrate.
5. Plan a ten lesson teaching unit for beginning fencers.
6. Organize a round robin tournament for a pool of eight fencers. Explain tournament conduct, necessary officials, and the responsibilities.
7. Discuss evaluative procedures for a class of beginning fencers.

Selected Audio-Visual Aids

Beginning Fencing. The Athletic Institute (Filmstrip and Recording). 209 S. State Street, Chicago 4, Illinois.
Fencing. (15 min., 16 mm., sound). Ford Foundation TV Workshop, 477 Madison Avenue, New York 22, N.Y.
Foil Fencing. (10 min., 16 mm., silent, instructor's use only). Castello Equipment Company, 30 East 10th Street, New York, N.Y.
A Series of Slides for Beginners in Foil Fencing 1955. (44 slides color). Produced by Leonora Kateman. Lafayette High School, Brooklyn, N.Y. Inter-Library Loan, Woman's College, University of North Carolina, Greensboro, N.C.
Sport of Fencing. (9 min., 16 mm., sound; for instructor level only). Wholesome Film Service, Inc., 20 Melrose Street, Boston, Mass. (Rental)
Techniques of Foil Fencing, 1942. (10 min., 16 mm., silent). University of California, Extension Division, Department of Visual Instruction, Berkeley 4, California. (Rental or Sale)

Techniques of Foil Fencing, 1954. (10 min., 16 mm., silent). University of California, Extension Division, Educatonal Sales Department, Los Angeles 24, California. (Rental or Sale)

SUGGESTED READINGS

A.A.H.P.E.R.: *Bowling-Fencing-Golf Guide.* Latest edition, Division for Girls and Women's Sports, 1201 16th Street, N.W., Washington 6, D.C.

Ainsworth, Dorothy S. *et al.: Individual Sports for Women,* Philadelphia, W. B. Saunders Company, 1958.

Amateur Fencing League of America: *Fencing Rules and Manual,* (obtained from Mrs. M. Rocko, 40–62nd Street, West New York, N.J.)

Barbasetti, Luisi: *The Art of the Foil,* New York, E. P. Dutton and Company, 1932.

Bernhard, Frederica, and Edwards, Vernon: *How to Fence. A Handbook For Teachers and Students,* Dubuque, William C. Brown Company, 1956.

Cass, Eleanor Baldwin: *The Book of Fencing,* Boston, Lothrop, Lee and Shepart Co., 1930.

Costello, Julio Martinez: *The Theory and Practice of Fencing,* New York, Charles Scribner's Sons, 1933.

Crosnier, Roger: *Fencing With the Foil,* New York, A. S. Barnes, 1955.

Deladrier, Clovis: *Modern Fencing,* United States Naval Academy Institute, Annapolis, Md., 1948.

Hett, George V.: *Fencing,* New York, Pitman Publishing Corporation, 1939.

Nadi, Aldo: *On Fencing,* New York, G. P. Putnam's Sons, 1943.

Nobbs, Peter E.: *Fencing Tactics,* New York, Charles Scribner's Sons, 1936.

Vince, Joseph: *Fencing,* New York, A. S. Barnes, 1937.

PERIODICALS

Amateur Fencing League of America: *American Fencing* (bimonthly) Write W. L. Osborn, 2709 Grand Central Terminal, New York 17, N.Y.

National Fencing Coaches Association of America: *The Swordmaster.* (Quarterly) Write Irving Dekoff, Columbia University, New York, New York.

9

Golf

The game of golf undoubtedly grew from field hockey, the forerunner of all stick and ball games. The origin of many such games is lost in antiquity. It may actually be as old as the spirit of play when men devised games of striking stones with sticks. It is believed by most authorities that golf, as it is played today, originated in Scotland in the 14th century, and was played by many sports loving Scotchmen by 1440. Even Parliamentary action forbidding the game as a threat to the development of skill at archery, and thus of national defense, deterred the game only briefly until King James IV became a fan and golf was played openly.

Unlike many sports, golf has been a woman's game for centuries. Mary Queen of Scots was an enthusiastic and skilled golfer. Her attentive army cadet was the forerunner of the caddy of today.

Golf crossed the Atlantic to Canada and America in the latter part of the 19th century. John G. Reid introduced the game to his friends in a cow pasture in Yonkers, New York, in 1885. This Scotsman, who became known as the "Father of American Golf," was instrumental in establishing the first golf club, St. Andrews of Yonkers, in 1888. Five of the private clubs in the Eastern United States joined together to form the United States Golf Association in 1894. From its beginning, the U.S.G.A. has been the ruling body for amateurs and the sponsoring body for prominent tournaments.

During the early years most golf courses were open only to men. Even as women were allowed playing privileges, the cost of equipment and club membership restricted the game to the wealthy. However, the addition of public, municipal, and college courses and the mass manufacture of golfing equipment have given great impetus to the ever increasing popularity of the game. Today over 6,000 courses attract three and one-half million participants while numerous driving ranges and instructional classes serve millions more.

THE NATURE AND PURPOSE OF THE GAME

Golf is a game of skill and accuracy played by both sexes from youth throughout life. The development of mechanical carts enables handicapped or aged persons to participate and benefit from good fellowship and exercise in the out of doors.

The game consists of hitting a small, hard ball with selected clubs across various surface areas known as fairways, hazards, and roughs to smooth patches of grass, known as greens, and into small holes, or cups, in the greens. The object of the game is to use as few strokes as possible on each hole and over the entire course.

Although golf courses are laid out in units of nine holes, most official ones have 18; however, a few courses have 27 or 36 holes. Par golf scores are based on eighteen holes.

The 18 hole course is planned to balance play and avoid player congestion. It is divided into the "front nine" (out) and "back nine" (in). These are indicated on the score card. An 18 hole course includes 5200 to 7200 yards of playing area, roughly equalized between the front and back nine. Each hole is assigned a par value, or an arbitrary standard of excellence, determined by length of the hole. This value is established to allow a certain number of strokes to get to the green and two putts on the green. Course distances for par are:

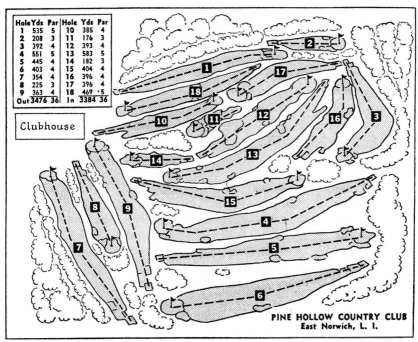

Hole	Yds	Par	Hole	Yds	Par
1	535	5	10	385	4
2	208	3	11	176	3
3	392	4	12	393	4
4	551	5	13	583	5
5	445	4	14	182	3
6	403	4	15	404	4
7	354	4	16	396	4
8	225	3	17	396	4
9	363	4	18	469	·5
Out	3476	36	In	3384	36

Clubhouse

PINE HOLLOW COUNTRY CLUB
East Norwich, L. I.

The New York Times

Figure No. 9–1.   The Layout of a Typical 18 Hole Golf Course.

Men	*Women*
Up to 250 yards, par 3	Up to 210 yards, par 3
251 to 450 yards, par 4	211 to 400 yards, par 4
451 to 600 yards, par 5	401 to 575 yards, par 5
601 yards up, par 6	576 yards up, par 6

Par for an 18 hole course is usually 71, 72 or 73 with a planned balance of three, four and five par holes. A distribution on the front nine holes of par 4, 5, 3, 4, 4, 5, 4, 3, 4 would indicate sound planning. The first hole is relatively easy, the second spreads out the players, and the third is short and less difficult. A well planned course has approximately ten 4 par holes, four 5 par holes, and four 3 par holes.[1]

Two, three or four players may compete in one group. At the first tee, the order of teeing is decided by lot. Thereafter, the honor of playing first is awarded the winner of the preceding hole. In case of a tie, the honor is awarded the individual or side which held it at the previous tee. After the players have teed off the person farthest away from the hole, whether on the fairway, in the rough, or on the green, shoots first. After players "hole out" they move off the green and record their scores before going to the next teeing area.

SCORING

Several methods of scoring are used in golf competition. Generally, competition is by medal or match play. In medal, or stroke, play the winner is the golfer using the least number of strokes over the designated course. In match play, or hole play, the victor is the player who wins the greatest number of holes from her opponent, regardless of the final stroke total. In match play where opponents have the same number of strokes on a hole, they have "halved" the hole and neither scores a point. Stroke play is considered more exacting since each stroke is of equal value; whereas in match play a loss of several strokes and the loss of a hole may be recouped by a one stroke victory on a later hole.

Use of a scorecard is helpful in teaching scoring procedures, for it usually gives name and location of the course, entries for date, event, scorer's name, attestor and four players, and local rules on the back of the card. The inside scoring section indicates the number of yards for each hole, total course yardage, par for men and women, the handicap stroke ranking awarded each hole, and columns for total score for match or medal play.

An example of both medal and and match scoring follows:

1. Ellen and Alice play the out nine by medal. Ellen has a total of 41 strokes, Alice records 46. Ellen is the winner.

2. On the back nine Ellen and Alice choose match play. During the

---

[1] A teacher responsible for planning or administering a golf course will find help from the National Golf Foundation, 407 South Dearborn Street, Chicago 5, Illinois.

nine holes, they halved holes 10, 13, 14 and 18. Alice won holes 11 and 17; Ellen won holes 12, 15, and 16. Although both players had 43 strokes on the last nine holes, Ellen was the victor.

Golf utilizes a handicapping system as a method of equalizing competition among players of different ability. The United States Golf Association gives detailed explanations for computing handicaps.[2] Briefly, these state that the number of handicap strokes is determined by a percentage of the difference between course par and the player's average score. Player A with a handicap of six is competing against Player B with a handicap of eight. In the match Player B is allowed to subtract one stroke on each of the holes numbered one and two in the score card column marked handicap strokes, regardless of the sequence of the holes on the course. If A had a four handicap and B an eight handicap, Player B would receive a stroke on each of the holes numbered one through four.

The Nassau system of scoring is used only in singles or doubles match play. In a single match (two competing) each match is worth three points. One point is given the winner of the first nine holes, one point for the winner of the second nine holes, and one point to the player winning the greatest number of holes of the 18. In doubles match play additional possible team points are added.

Novelty golf events and improvised class tournaments often use other methods for scoring and awarding points.

[2] See *The Conduct of Women's Golf,* United States Golf Association, 40 East 38th Street, New York 16, N.Y.

Hole	Yards	Bogy	Par	ELLEN	ALICE	Handicap Strokes		W+ L— HO	Hole	Yards	Bogy	Par	Ellen	Alice	Handicap Strokes		W+ L— HO
1	325	5	4	5	5	7			10	325	5	4	4	4	8		0
2	185	3	3	4	3	15			11	185	3	3	4	3	16		+
3	325	4	4	4	5	9			12	325	4	4	4	5	10		—
4	500	5	5	5	6	1			13	500	5	5	6	6	2		0
5	375	5	4	6	7	5			14	375	5	4	6	6	6		0
6	150	3	3	3	4	17			15	150	3	3	3	4	18		—
7	450	5	5	5	6	3			16	450	5	5	5	6	4		—
8	300	4	4	5	6	11			17	300	4	4	6	4	12		+
9	300	4	4	4	4	13			18	300	4	4	5	5	14		0
Out	2910	38	36	41	46				In	2910	38	36	43	43			
									Out	2910							
									Total	5820							
									HANDICAP								
									NET SCORE								

DATE   EVENT

SCORER....*Alice*....

ATTEST....

Figure No. 9–2.   A Completed Golf Scorecard. The out nine illustrates scoring for Medal Play, the back nine illustrates scoring for Match Play.

NEEDED FACILITIES AND EQUIPMENT

Most schools and colleges will find it necessary to furnish minimum equipment for golf instruction, for most students do not own clubs. Golf equipment for the instructional program need not be too expensive as most club professionals and driving range operators are anxious to increase golfing interest and will sell serviceable used equipment reasonably. When possible better equipment should be purchased as an investment for the growing golf program.

Clubs.   The U.S.G.A. limits the golfer to the use of 14 clubs during a match. All 14 are not necessary for the beginning player, but a minimum set of five clubs should be available to a student on a golf course. The teacher should be cautious when advising students about purchasing clubs. Perhaps the safest recommendation is that they buy medium priced clubs of a reputable manufacturer, preferably on "open stock" which can be added to later. The basic set should include a brassie, number 2 wood, or a spoon, number 3 wood, numbers 3, 5, and 7 irons, and a putter. Early additions to the basic set include a 9 and 2 iron and a driver (number 1 wood).

Clubs are generally classified into the two groups: woods and irons. The designation originally referred to the composition of the club heads; however, "woods" may have heads of plastic, magnesium, laminated, or persimmon wood. Essentially, iron and wood clubs have the same parts.

The main parts of the club are the grip, shaft and clubhead. The golfer

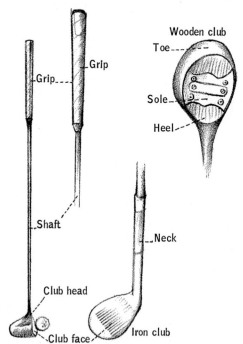

Figure No. 9–3.   Components of Woods and Irons.

holds the club by the leather or composition covered grip at the top of the shaft. A cap at the top of the handle protects the upper portion of the grip and secures the wooden plug to strengthen the hollow shaft. The shaft is a tension steel tube over which the grip is placed and into which the clubhead attaches.

The clubhead is below the neck of the club where the head and shaft join, and it includes the sole—the lower part of the club that rests on the ground; the heel, or part nearest the shaft; the toe—the outer tip of the head, and the club face with its scored or grooved striking surface. Wooden clubs have a metal sole plate to protect the bottom as it swings across the ground. Iron clubs often have a metal flange on the back of the head to give it additional weight.

Wooden clubs are named and numbered to designate their use as the following:

Number 1—driver: used only for tee shots and gives a low, flat trajectory with maximum distance to the ball. For the average woman it is 41 to 43 inches long and weighs 13 to 14 ounces.

Number 2—brassie: used for long shots with good lies from the fairway and from the tee. The club face has more loft, causing a ball to go higher in the air with less forward direction than when hit with a driver.

Number 3—spoon: used for short tee shots and for long shots from the fairway and rough from mediocre lies. More loft to the face and often a shorter shaft than number 1 or 2 woods which allows better control.

Number 4—cleek: used for long shots from a poor lie, as the smaller head and shallow face penetrate to the ball. It gives higher flight and less distance than other woods.

Wooden clubs should be dried carefully after use to avoid swelling and eventual warping and cracking. Students should be encouraged to wipe the shaft and head with light oil (linseed) several times a year and wax the head. Wrappings around the clubhead and the grip should be checked frequently. Often a durable glue will serve; however, black linen line can be applied to the head and shaft and leather stripping to the shaft. Head covers of knit, plastic or leather protect the highly polished surface from scarring. Clear sacks may be used for protecting instructional clubs.

Iron clubs are informally grouped as long, medium, and short irons. This classification refers to both the length of the shaft and ball flight distance gained by the use of each club. The construction of the irons gives an immediate teaching cue for beginning golfers. "The larger the club number, the shorter the shaft, the more loft to the face, consequently, the higher and shorter the ball flight."

The long irons include numbers 1, 2, and 3:

Number 1—driving iron: used for long, low full shots from a good lie. The long shaft and straight face make it a difficult club for beginners. It is often replaced by a 3 or 4 wood.

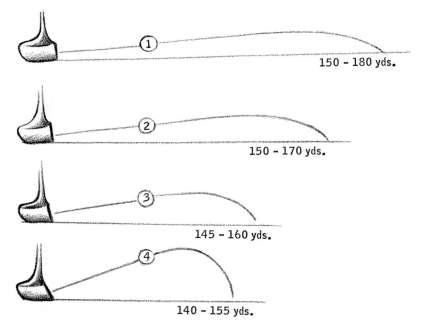

150 - 180 yds.

150 - 170 yds.

145 - 160 yds.

140 - 155 yds.

Figure No. 9–4.   Woods. Anticipated Distances for Average Women Golfers.

Number 2—midiron: a utility club for comparatively long fairway and tee shots.

Number 3—mid-mashie: used for less distance than a number 2 iron but the loft of the face allows a stroke from a relatively bad lie.

The medium irons include numbers 4, 5 and 6:

Number 4—mashie iron: used from the fairway and rough for medium distances; for occasional tee shots on short holes and on "drag" strokes from the edge of the green.

Number 5—mashie: an excellent utility club for the beginner. As the medium length club among all, it is used from the fairway and rough; for pitching a ball high to the green; for pitch and run shots to the green when a safe approach is desired; and as a tee club on short holes.

Number 6—spade mashie: used from high rough, for pitch shots to the green and from clean lies in a sand trap when distance is needed.

The short irons include numbers 7, 8, 9 and wedge:

Number 7—mashie niblick: used for short pitch shots from fairway, traps, and over trees and obstacles.

Number 8—pitching niblick: used for quick rising shots over hazards or as an approach from the fairway. An excellent club when obstacles prevent a follow-through.

Number 9—niblick: the iron with the greatest loft. It is used primarily from heavy sand traps and deep rough. Some manufacturers produce wedge-type niblicks with a heavy flange to prevent the clubhead from a deep entry into the sand or turf. These "sand wedges" have additional weight to assist in the follow-through.

The *putter* is an essential club for all golfers. In a category of its own, this short shafted club with a straight face is the only one used on the green. Although the putter is used from the lip area for holing out, it is constructed to roll the ball along the ground to the hole.

Little care is required to maintain irons other than drying and oiling them occasionally to prevent rusting. A golfer should avoid hitting rocks or hard objects which will nick the club, change its balance, as well as cut balls. Club nicks should be filed smooth when they appear on the face.

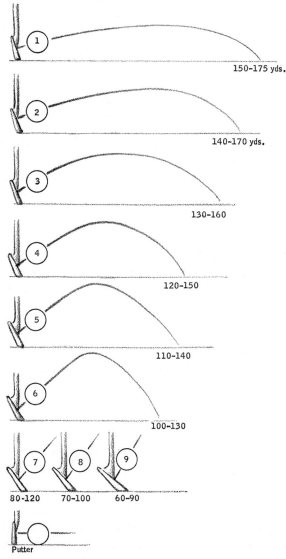

Figure No. 9–5. Irons. Anticipated Distances for Average Women Golfers.

Balls. Golf balls are constructed of liquid, rubber or plastic centers tightly bound by wound rubber yarn and encased in a balata rubber cover of dimpled design and painted white. There is constant controversy over the merits of selected ball construction, but a golfer will eventually find a ball in her price range. Beginning players need not buy expensive balls as the covers may not stand up under inaccurate stroking. Personal balls should be clearly marked for rapid identification.

Large instructional groups can purchase low grade "range" balls, used ones or manufacturers' rejects for outdoor practice. Practice balls of plastic, cotton, felt, and woolen yarn are available for indoor use. Although accurate distances cannot be measured indoors, the safe and relatively noiseless balls are superior to homemade paper or tape balls.

Tees and Tee Mats. Tees are used to elevate the ball for the first drive on each hole. On a course most golfers use wooden or plastic tees. Inexpensive tees should be selected as they are often broken and lost. If tee mats are used outside, rubber tees may be placed below the mat for semi-permanency.

Indoor practice mats are usually made of rubber tire strippings, or cocoa. The heavy duty rubber mats are satisfactory for tee shots; however, cocoa mats are better for iron club practice as they "give" with the impact of the hands and wrists and allow the clubhead to contact the ball below ground level. When using mats in or outdoors, the instructor should lower the mats or elevate the player's stance area so the surface simulates actual playing conditions. Strips of close pile carpeting can be used for indoor putting surfaces.

Bag. A light fabric "Sunday" bag is ideal for the beginning golfer with limited equipment. The more durable and attractive leather or fabric one with shoe and ball pockets, a carry strap and handle, and a hood is a heavy burden for the woman golfer with a full set of clubs who cannot afford regular caddy service.

Golf Carts. An increasing number of "do-it-yourself" golfers are seen on public courses pulling a two wheel cart loaded with bag and raingear. The cart is a boon for the golfer of limited financial resources, but it does not replace the help of a caddy. Some courses prohibit the use of carts but allow power driven golf cars for those who prefer to ride the course.

Accessories. There are numerous accessories for the woman golfer. Among the necessities are gloves, full or half, which aid in gripping and prevent calluses, umbrellas for the inevitable thundershowers, and a shade hat. Other useful accessories include stroke counters to aid the novice in keeping her score and ball holders worn on the belt to eliminate bulging pockets.

Costume. Golf shoes with spikes are a valuable part of a golfer's equipment. Some players find that rubber lug, or ribbon-soled shoes serve satisfactorily. Jewelry should not be worn as rings may be injurious to the hands and wrist watches may be ruined by the stroking impact. When in doubt of club regulations concerning dress, women should wear a semi-full skirt and a loose fitting, neat blouse or a manufacturer's golf dress, all of which are comfortable when walking and swinging a club. Long walking shorts or slacks are acceptable on the majority of courses.

Indoor Equipment. In addition to balls, tees and mats, an indoor instructional program can be more complete with putting cups, driving cages, targets, and sand approach areas. Nearly all of this equipment is sold commercially, yet much of it can be made inexpensively.[3] A movable golf cage is a valuable piece of indoor equipment which can be used outside, and is an instructional timesaver in both settings.

TEACHING UNITS

The suggested units for beginning and advanced students follow:

Unit for Beginners	*Unit for Advanced Students*
Nature and value of golf	General review
Brief history	Swing
Care and use of equipment	Stances
Beginning golf terminology	Chip
Safety precautions	Pitch
Fundamental Skills	Approach
Grip	Long irons
Stance	Woods
Address	Putting
Pivot	Medal tournament
Backswing	Sidehill lie
Top of swing	Uphill lie
Wrist action	Downhill lie
Downswing and follow-through	Sand trap play
exercises	Intentional slice
Use of #5 iron	Intentional hook
Pitch and run shot	Advanced rules
Pitch and chip	Handicap procedure
¼, ½ and ¾ swing	Evaluation
Putting	Written
Approach shots	Practical
Long irons	
Wood shots	
Etiquette	
Rules	
Course play	
Evaluation	
Written and skills test	

[3] For suggestions see Orlando, Anthony E.: *Journal of A.A.H.P.E.R.* Make Your Own Indoor Golf Area. February, 1955.

BASIC SKILLS

The Grip. The same basic grip is used for all clubs except the putter. Three grips are commonly used by golfers: the overlap, the interlock, and the natural or "baseball." Although several championship golfers use the interlocking and natural grips, the overlapping (Vardon) technique assures more club security and greater hand coordination for most women.

To assume the overlapping grip, the clubhead rests on the ground in normal position as the golfer places her extended left hand slightly over the top of the shaft (A) and grips the club across the base of the fingers (B). The shaft lies diagonally across the hand pulled toward the fleshy portion of the palm. The grip is secured by the last three fingers with the thumb and index fingers forming a "V" which points toward the right shoulder. With the left hand thumb to the right of the shaft, the thumb and index fingers exert a pinching pressure. Looking down the shaft, the golfer should see three knuckle joints.

The right arm swings freely until the right hand reaches below the left so the little finger grasps between the index and second fingers of the left hand. The palm of the right hand is squarely facing the right side of the club shaft. The next three fingers grasp the shaft as the right hand pulls left

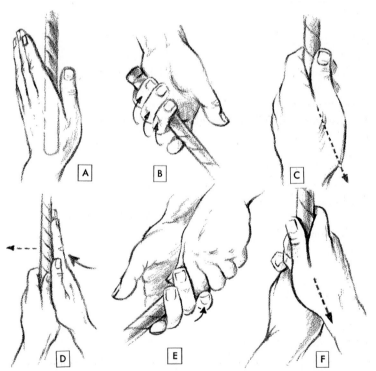

Figure No. 9–6.   Placing the Hands for the Proper Grip.

so it smothers the thumb of the left hand in a valley formed by the fatty portion of thumb and index finger. The inverted "V" of the right hand also points to the right shoulder. With both hands close together and working as a unit, power and control are attained.

The reverse overlap grip is used by many for putting. The right hand is placed a handspan from the top of the club with the thumb pointed directly down the front of the shaft to the clubhead. The left hand, palm opposite right palm, is underneath the shaft with thumb down the front of the shaft. The index finger of the left hand overlaps the little finger of the right hand.

Stance and Address.   A firm, comfortable stance assures the balance necessary for a swing. In preparation for all strokes, except putting, weight is equally distributed on both feet from the heel to the ball of the foot, toes are pointed outward with feet about shoulder width apart. The body is fairly erect with knees flexed. The body curves as if it is sitting on a ball. With eyes on the ball, extend the left arm so it is firm and straight. The arms hang but do not reach so as to pull the body off balance. Sole the club directly behind the ball so the bottom is evenly placed on the turf and the face directly pointing along the desired line of flight.

There are three general stances which a golfer assumes for a designated stroke:

Square or Parallel Stance.   The feet are parallel to, and equally distant from, the imaginary line of flight of the ball. With the knees, hips, and shoulders parallel to flight line, this is a good beginning stance as it gives a feeling of balanced swing motion with an equally balanced backswing and follow-through. It is the most commonly used stance for long and medium irons.

Open Stance.   The left foot is drawn back from the imaginary flight line. The body is turned slightly toward the direction of ball flight, leaving the right hip forward, thus restricting body rotation in the backswing and correspondingly increasing follow-through. The open stance is used primarily for short irons, chipping, and pitching when less distance, power, and greater accuracy are needed. It may be used for intentional slices.

Closed Stance.   The right foot is drawn back from the flight line thus increasing backswing rotation and limiting follow-through. This stance is used for power when teeing and on some fairway shots, as well as for an intentional hook shot.

Body-Ball Position.   The position of the ball in relation to the body and club greatly controls ball spin. A forward spin resulting from a blow as the clubhead is traveling upward causes low ball flight and increased forward roll on the ground. A horizontal blow at the center of the swing arc results in a slight backspin as the ball is hit below center. A definite backspin is caused as the clubhead contacts the ball before the center of the swing arc is reached and the club continues downward across the back of the ball.

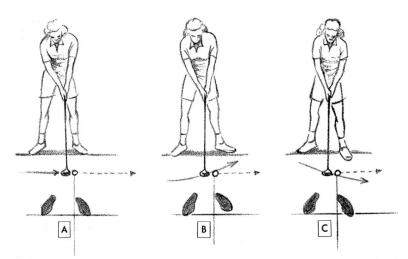

Figure No. 9-7.   Types of Stance. A. Square Stance; B. Open Stance; C. Closed
Stance.

Generally, tee shots and wood shots are made from a closed, or square,
stance with the ball placed forward of center for a horizontal or upward
impact of the club. The long and medium irons are most often played from
a square stance off or near the center of the body. The length of the club
shaft determines the golfer's relation to the ball, but the arms are easy, not
forcibly reaching, and the wrists are down and firm. With shorter irons, the
golfer moves closer to the ball, open stance, moves feet closer together and
plays the ball off-center or right of center of the body for more loft and
less roll.

Swing.   The backswing, downswing and follow-through are the swing
segments which ultimately control the flight of the ball. A description of a
full swing precedes the fractional swings.

The backswing begins from a proper stance, body bent slightly at the
waist, hands comfortably close to the body, club face square to flight line.
Hips begin the coordinated body movement by a rotation toward the right
around the spine as an axis. The arms and body drag the clubhead backward along the flight line and upward. As the pivot becomes deeper the
right hip is forced backward and the left hip forward, shifting the body
weight toward the outside of the right foot and inside of the toe and ball
of the left foot. The left knee relaxes and bends toward the right toe.
Shoulders turn as the upper body pivots with the hips. As the arms reach
approximately waist height, the wrists begin to break as the arms continue
in an upward arc. The left arm and right leg remain firm with the right
elbow bent and pointing downward.

At the top of the full swing, the body is in coiled readiness with the club
shaft approximately horizontal to the ground and held with a firm grip,
right wrist under the shaft and head steady.

The left hip initiates the downswing leading the body and pulling the arms into the hitting area. The club descends along an arc inside that followed in the backswing. As the hips turn, the wrists, hands, and club are brought down approximately half way in the arc before they begin to uncoil. The body weight shifts toward the left side of the body, the left hip moves out of the club path and the arms and wrists reach straight alignment with the club at the instant of ball contact. The golfer hits against a firm left side at the moment of impact.

The clubhead follows the line of intended flight until forward motion becomes naturally restricted and wrists begin to turn. With the golfer still over the ball, the body pivots around the axis and head. Weight continues to shift to the left side with the right foot pushing from the toes. Hips turn with arms and shoulders turning around naturally. At the completion of the swing, the weight is on the left foot and the head is turned, not lifted, to follow the ball.

Quarter Swing.   Hips initiate a weight shift, rather than a rotation and clubhead follows back of ball until arms are outside of the right leg, wrists cock bringing club parallel to the ground. The downswing and follow-

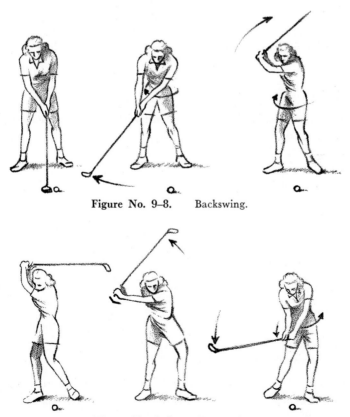

Figure No. 9–8.   Backswing.

Figure No. 9–9.   Downswing.

Figure No. 9–10. Fractional Swings.

through carry the club to a position parallel to the ground on the left side of body.

Half Swing. Executed as a quarter swing with backswing arc continuing until the cap of the grip points directly toward the ground. Follow-through position equals the backswing.

Three-Quarter Swing. Executed as the full swing except less depth is taken in the ascending and descending arcs. At the top of the backswing the clubhead points to two o'clock; on the follow-through it points toward 10 o'clock.

Wood Shots

1. Use a square or slightly closed stance with feet 10 to 14 inches apart depending on comfort.
2. Play ball off left heel on the tee.
3. Use full swing.

Long and Medium Iron Shots

1. Use square stance for normal flight.
2. Stand closer to irons than woods so swing will be more upright.
3. Hit the ball a descending blow as if trying to bury the ball, take turf and continue through.

Short Iron Shots

1. Use square to open stance with feet 6 to 10 inches apart.
2. Use a fractional swing for desired distance.
3. Play ball almost in center of stance position.
4. Allow body crouch, easy and relaxed.

Chip Shot. A chip shot is made from 25 to 35 yards from the green when there is no obstacle, as the ball is pitched part of the way and rolls the rest of the way.

1. Use a number 4, 5, 6 or 7 iron.
2. Use an open stance, feet close together, short backswing with a minimum of body action (use hands and arms).
3. Keep hands ahead of the ball throughout the stroke.

Pitch Shot.   The pitch carries the ball through the air in a high approach toward the green where it stops immediately upon contact with the ground.

1. Select a number 7, 8 or 9 iron.
2. Use an open stance close to the ball with right elbow close to right hip.
3. Use minimum body action with a quarter or half swing.
4. Hit the ball a descending blow to impart backspin so it will stay when landing.
5. Follow-through with clubhead pointing toward target.

Sand Trap Shots.   The chip shot and blast are the most fundamental strokes for getting out of a sand trap. The chip is used when the ball is resting on top of the sand. A number 6 or 7 iron is used as in a short approach; however, the club must not be grounded or touch the sand on the backswing.

The explosion shot is the safest when the ball is buried or must rise over a bank.

1. Select a sand wedge or number 9 iron.
2. Anchor the feet and aim an inch or two behind the ball and take more sand.
3. Play the ball off of the left heel.
4. Take a full swing and a complete follow-through.

Putting.   Putting is the most individualized of all golfing skills. Although the criterion of a good putt is its effectiveness, beginners should understand the basic techniques:

1. Use the reverse overlap grip.
2. Use a fairly light grip for relaxed control.
3. Stand fairly erect with feet comfortable in a square or slightly open stance.
4. Play the ball close to the feet and look directly at the ball.
5. Use a square or slightly open stance with ball played off left heel.
6. Right elbow rests against the right hip, left elbow points toward the hole.
7. Head, hips, and shoulders are steady as the hands and arms move.
8. Clubhead comes straight back and through the ball, following-through directly toward the hole.
9. Putter blade remains close to the green throughout the stroke.

Putts account for approximately one-half the strokes in a round of par golf, therefore putting deserves concentration and practice from the golfer. "Line up" a putt by determining the slope of the green, the grain of the grass, and ultimately the course of the ball to the hole. It is helpful to pick a spot about six inches along the imaginary ball course and concentrate on rolling the ball over that spot.

Playing Difficult Lies

Rough.   A club is selected which will give the necessary loft to the ball. The stance is more open, the club face slightly open, and the swing upright with as full a follow-through as possible.

Downhill Lie.   Normally play the ball off the rear foot with an open stance and a minimum of body pivot so the body will maintain balance. Select a club which will give height as the ball leaves the ground.

Uphill Lie.   The ball should be played off the forward heel, using slight body pivot. Use a low trajectory club as the height normally attained with a club is over accentuated by the ground contour.

Sidehill Lie.   This stroke must be made with the golfer standing either above or below ball level. When the ball is below the stance, a longer club is used with a square stance. The golfer bends over the ball and compensates for natural tendency to slice by aiming left.

If the ball is above foot level, the golfer selects a shorter club, opens her stance, moves farther away from the ball and plays the ball off the right foot. The aim is usually to the right to compensate for a pull stroke.

Stroke Adjustments.   Advanced golfers can take several strokes from their game by learning to direct the ball in flight.

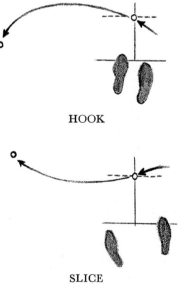

HOOK

SLICE

Figure No. 9–11.

Intentional Hook. To accomplish a deliberate curve of the ball from right to left, the golfer uses a closed stance with the ball almost opposite the right foot. Using a flat swing arc, the club contacts the ball from the inside to the outside. The degree of hook can be controlled by placing the right hand beneath the shaft and the left hand on top.

Intentional Slice. A deliberate slice curves from left to right in flight because of the spin imparted to the ball. The golfer uses an open stance with the ball approximately off the center of the stance. Swing arc is almost upright with the clubhead contacting the ball from the "outside-in." For more decided slice the right hand moves to the top of the shaft and the left hand under the shaft.

High Ball. The beginning golfer should attempt to select a club with enough loft to carry the ball over obstacles or into the wind; however, advanced golfers may play the ball off the left foot and stroke the ball on the upswing with an open club face.

Low Ball. The ball is played off the right foot and hit with a closed clubface from a flat swing arc. Hit down on the ball and take turf after ball contact.

BASIC RULES

The United States Golf Association establishes the rules of golf. Since these rules are numerous and difficult for a beginning player, the following basic guides suggest conduct for the first golf 'rounds':

1. The player should be able to identify her own ball by its markings.
2. At the beginning of each hole the ball should be teed between the tee markers and not more that two club lengths behind the markers.
3. An intentional swing at the ball, whether a hit or a miss, counts as a stroke.
4. Loose impediments may be removed if hindering a stroke; however, no growing vegetation may be removed. To facilitate a golfer's stance, shrubs, bushes, and the like may be temporarily held or moved.
5. A ball lying near an unnatural obstacle, such as a bench or hydrant, may be moved not more than two club lengths and never nearer the hole without penalty.
6. A ball in casual water (rain water, leakage, etc.) may be dropped over the golfer's shoulder with no penalty.
7. If a ball is unplayable because of a hazard it may be removed and dropped over the shoulder of the golfer who is facing the hole and a one stroke penalty is added.
8. A ball is considered lost after a five minute search.
9. When a ball is lost or goes out of bounds the player places another ball as near as possible to the spot where the original ball was played. The penalty is the loss of distance (of the first stroke).

ETIQUETTE

Since golf demands delicate coordination and concentration from players, a definite code of behavior is followed by experienced players. These courtesies are intended to prevent distraction and increase player safety. Beginning players should be aware that:

The player should not:

Talk or move while a player is stroking.

Swing clubs while a player is stroking.

Hit until players ahead are out of range and have taken at least their second shots.

Approach the green until players ahead have putted out and are off the green.

Stand near the cup when another is shooting.

Stand in line with the one putting and the cup.

Allow one's shadow to cross the line of a putt.

Place a golf bag in a sand trap, thus roughing up the sand for players following.

Place a golf bag on the green, for fear of marring the surface.

Place a golf bag on the near side of the green where it might stop the ball of a player following.

Record scores while standing on the green.

Practice putts or play them over if missed.

Invite players to play through when a ball is lost and then start shooting before they are out of range.

Take practice swings in the direction of the hole. (By taking them at right angles to the line of flight you eliminate possibility of being questioned by opponents.)

Concede, or ask to be conceded, a putt.

Take a careless stroke at a short putt and expect to take another trial if the hole is missed.

Pick up a ball for identification.

Stand close enough to the rim of the cup to disturb turf.

Press down grass or weeds to get a better stroke. This is improving the lie and is against the rules.

The player should:

Shoot from behind the markers on the tees.

Hold the flag for your opponent or see that the caddy does.

Allow the player winning the honor to tee first.

When lost, or in a slow match, invite players following to play through and allow them to get out of range before proceeding.

Always replace divots.

Back out of sand traps, leveling off holes made by your club and foot tracks. Admit penalty stroke.

Allow the player farthest away, whether on green or in field, to stroke first.

Call "Fore" only if there is danger of a ball hitting a player ahead.

Drop the ball over one's shoulder when taking a penalty stroke.

CLASS ORGANIZATION

This is determined largely by the available equipment, facilities, and instructional personnel. Instruction can be given entirely indoors in a gymnasium or large all-purpose room; however, it is desirable to have access to an indoor area, outdoor play fields, a driving range and putting area, and a 9 or 18 hole golf course.

Instruction may begin indoors and include the game, grip, and basic swing. As many as 25 to 30 students can be taught by a single instructor standing in the center of the circle of learners if there are student assistants available. Advanced golfers can profit from a review of the basic skills. As the class moves to an outdoor area, a threesome or foursome of those with similar skills can work together to economize on equipment and instructor's time. Selected skill drills are assigned each group. Group members may coach one another, retrieve balls, and share observations.

When possible, all students should have a playing experience on a course. A threesome or foursome should play a minimum of three holes and preferably nine. During course play the instructor roams the course to observe each individual and answer questions, but should not coach if it delays the play of outside groups on the course.

TEACHING PROGRESSION

There is no single "best" progression for teaching golf. Instructors will select the methods best suited for utilization of equipment, facilities, and their style of teaching. Many teachers believe skills should progress from the grip, stance, and swing to the use of a basic club (#5 iron), to short irons and approach shots, putting, long irons, and woods.

BEGINNERS UNIT

Lesson I

1. Explain the nature and value of golf
2. Explain and demonstrate use of equipment
3. Discuss the golf course and selected terminology

Lesson II

1. Brief discussion of the history of golf
2. Explain and demonstrate the grip

3. Explain and demonstrate stance, stressing the square stance for beginners
4. Film on the game, grip, and stance

Lesson III

1. Review grip and stance
2. Explain and demonstrate the full swing
   a. pivot; b. backswing; c. top of swing; d. wrist action; e. down-swing; f. follow-through
3. Demonstrate swing exercises

Lesson IV

1. Review grip, stance, and swing
2. Introduce the short irons and their use
3. Discussion of the chip shot and fractional swings

Lesson V

1. Review short irons
2. Review chip shot
3. Explain and demonstrate pitch shot
4. Informal contest using chip and pitch shots

Lesson VI

1. General review
2. Discussion of putting
   a. lining a putt; b. grip; c. stroke

Lesson VII

1. Practice approach shots
2. Practice putting

Lesson VIII

1. Explain and demonstrate use of long irons
2. Begin rule discussion
3. Film on iron play

Lesson IX

1. Review long irons
2. Group competition for accuracy and distance on long irons
3. Competition for accuracy of chip, pitch, and putting

Lesson X

1. Explain details of rules and scoring necessary for beginning course play
2. Explain and demonstrate wood shots using the full swing
3. Individualized coaching

Lesson XI

1. Intensive practice and review of clubs. Stress proper club selection
2. Individual coaching

Lesson XII

1. Introduce trap shots
2. Student-teacher evaluation of course progress

Lesson XIII

1. Intensive practice
2. Written evaluation of knowledge, rules, and etiquette

Lesson XIV

1. Skills examination
2. Begin tournament or course play

Lessons XV to XVII

1. Continue course play
2. Introduce "difficult lies" and stroke adjustment to advanced players
3. Individual attention to skill improvement

SKILL DIFFICULTIES AND THEIR CORRECTION

Difficulty	*Correction*
1. Grip	**1.**
a. Gripping club so tightly the wrists and fingers become immobile	a. Teacher suggests student releases grip, then places left hand on club and lifts it toward the body. Place the right hand on shaft and swing club slightly to get idea of relaxed movement
b. Club grasped in palm of hand	b. Teacher demonstrates how control is lost at top of backswing by moving the club. Stress the importance of feel and sensitivity in the fingers
c. Improper placement of hands resulting in open or closed club face	c. Remind student that the club should rest naturally on the ground. Demonstrate what happens to the ball in flight when struck by open or closed face

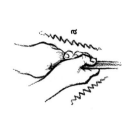

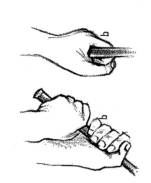

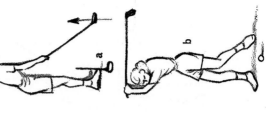

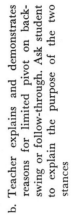

d. Review proper grip, stressing the left hand's firm grip with last three fingers and the right hand's thumb and first two fingers. Remind the student that the hands must work as a unit—always in firm contact with the club

e. Suggest that student's arms swing freely, comfortably grasping the club, then adjust grip

2.

a. Teacher may draw chalk line or place club across student's toes to show variance in aiming and body position

b. Teacher explains and demonstrates reasons for limited pivot on backswing or follow-through. Ask student to explain the purpose of the two stances

d. Index finger and thumb do the gripping, resulting in a loss of control at top of swing

e. Grip uncomfortable and seemingly unwieldy

2. *Stance and Address*
a. Failure to align body with the imaginary flight line

b. Using closed and open stance indiscriminately

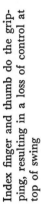

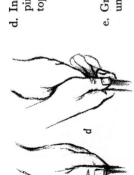

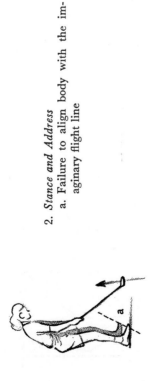

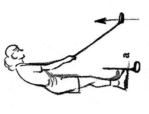

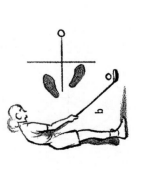

163

Difficulty	*Correction*
c. Stiffened knees and body	c. Stress relaxation and have student practice "sitting on the ball" with easy arm position
d. Standing too close or too far from the ball with weight forward on the toes	d. Explain the principles of centrifugal force, thereby showing weight must be back to balance tendency of the swing to pull the golfer off balance

3. The Swing

a. Making a false pivot or slide, rather than a rotation	a. Explain to student that she could pivot in a barrel, rolling and shifting weight so the axis does not move, and her hips do not touch the sides of the barrel
b. Improper shift of weight	b. Suggest that the student stand "duck footed" toeing out both feet on ground. With club through her arms and behind her back she rolls. A proper pivot is achieved or she loses balance

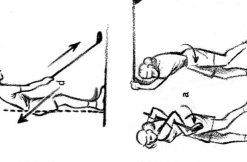

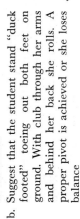

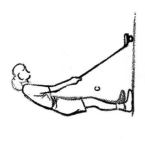

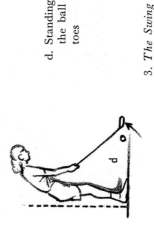

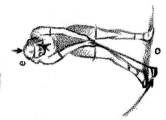

c. Controlling stroke by arms in such a way that club leaves the ground abruptly, resulting in "arm golf"

c. Review proper sequence of the co-ordinated pivot: hips begin the action as arms and hands drag the club back along the flight line

d. Bending the left arm on upswing and raising right elbow, or reverse on follow-through

d. Teacher places a practice ball or cloth under right armpit and suggests "push the left arm"

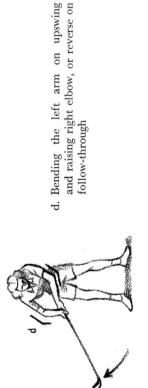

e. Moving or lifting the head thus changing level of swing pattern and "topped" ball

e. Teacher or fellow student places a club shaft on student's head so she becomes aware of her movement by club pressure

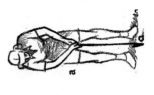

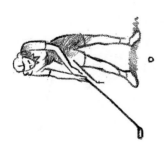

SKILL DIFFICULTIES AND THEIR CORRECTION (*Continued*)

Difficulty	*Correction*
f. Uncocking wrists too soon resulting in loss of power and control	f. Stress control and relaxed, normal hand action. Review the action of the hands and wrists on downswing and follow-through
g. Swinging too hard	g. Slow backswing and relax. Power can be imparted later
4. *Putting*	4.
a. Tense grip and rigid arm movement	a. Relax. Teacher reminds student that putter action is like a pendulum— easy and smooth

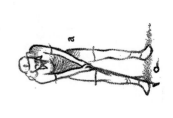

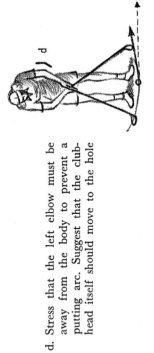

Difficulty

Correction

b. Punching or jabbing the ball

b. Stress follow-through. Teacher can mark a backswing and follow-through line on the green over which the club should pass

c. Inability to line a putt

c. Suggest student thinks and concentrates on grass, slope, and distance. Ask her to explain the steps for lining up a putt

d. Pulling a putt

d. Stress that the left elbow must be away from the body to prevent a putting arc. Suggest that the clubhead itself should move to the hole

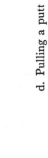

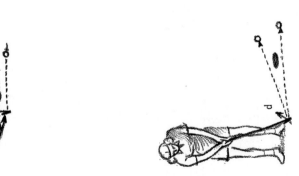

FAULTY GOLF SHOTS AND THEIR REMEDIES

Causes	*Remedies*

I.

I. Slice

Slice is a ball that curves to the right (for right-handed players). A slice is the result of an "outside-in" swing with the club face in an open position at the moment of impact, thus giving the ball a clockwise spin

a. *Causes*

1. An incorrect grip—right hand may be too far under or left hand not enough on top

2. Too open a stance—cuts down pivot

3. Right hand lifting the club on backswing—throwing right elbow out of position

4. Improper cocking of wrists on backswing

5. Throwing the hands forward or away from body at start of downswing

a. *Remedies*

1. Grip—three knuckles of left hand showing. Both V's toward right shoulder

2. Club face at top—must be half closed

3. Right wrist at top, under shaft. Left not under

4. Left hand at top, fingers closed. Grip firm

5. Backswing. At start all in *one piece*. Dominated by left side, around head as fixed point

Causes

6. Bending left arm on backswing

7. Pulling the arms in at impact
8. Lifting head too soon on downswing

9. Starting backswing on "outside"

10. Locking left knee on follow-through

11. Overworking left arm

Remedies

6. Position at top—shaft point across line of flight, shoulders 90°, much more weight on right foot
7. Check sway. Head must not move
8. Hitting from top, position of hands at finish will show it
9. Downswing. Hip turn must be first move
10. Hips not too far around to left on first movement
11. Dip of left shoulder should not be. Shoulders in horizontal plane

II. *Push Ball*

II.

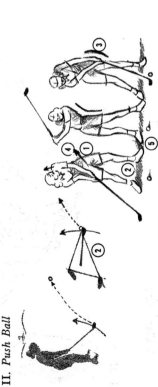

Push is a ball that travels straight to the right. A push is caused by an "inside-out" swing, with an open club face at impact

a. *Causes*
1. Improper hip shift
2. Stance too closed

a. *Remedies*
1. Check jerking head up
2. Check sway to right on backswing

169

FAULTY GOLF SHOTS AND THEIR REMEDIES (*Continued*)

Causes	*Remedies*
3. Hands too far ahead at impact	3. Check backswing starting all in one piece
4. Body too far ahead at impact	4. Check stance in relation to ball
5. Ball played too far back	
6. Flat swing	

III. *Hook*

III.

Hook is a ball that curves to the left. A hook is caused by an "inside-out" swing with a closed face at the moment of impact. Although a hook is not considered a bad shot in golf, it has disadvantages when hitting to the green. The counterclockwise spin imparts overspin to the ball, which upon landing has considerable roll. It is an error of the good, not average player

a. *Causes*	a. *Remedies*
1. Closed club face due to incorrect grip. Left hand too much on top or right hand too far under	1. Check left hand

Causes

2. Closed club due to incorrect wrist cock
3. Wrist roll to right in backswing. Start back all in one piece
4. Stance too closed
5. Exaggerated inside-out swinging
6. Collapse of left arm with wrist roll
7. Hands breaking at top of swing (may cause hook or slice)
8. Right hand domination

Remedies

2. Be sure right wrist is under shaft
3. Check right hand control
4. Start back in one piece

IV.

IV. *Pulled Ball*

Pull is a ball that travels straight to the left. A pull is the result of an "outside-in" swing, with a closed face at moment of impact

a. *Causes*
1. Grip right hand too far over
2. Using closed stance—limits follow-through
3. Overworking right hand—check position at top
4. Punching at ball. Check shoulders on backswing

a. *Remedies*
1. Check right hand
2. Closed stance not good
3. Be sure of top position
4. Watch shoulders

FAULTY GOLF SHOTS AND THEIR REMEDIES (*Continued*)

Causes

Remedies

V.

V. Skulling

Topping, often called "skulling"

a. *Causes*

1. Jerking head up. Many people look up but do not alter the position of the head. Only as head pulls shoulder out of place do we need to worry

2. Swaying moves the arc, because lowest point of arc is behind ball if you sway back

3. Raising the arc of the swing. Done on backswing by raising shoulders, body, and head. Body bend too far on address. Too much weight on left leg straightening and locking right knee at top of swing

a. *Remedies*

1. Check jerking head up

2. Check swaying either to right or left

3. Check arc of swing

4. *Avoid* stooping and locking right knee

5. *Smooth, rhythmic correct swing.* Tension caused by hitting at top of swing removed

Causes

VI. *Smothering*

Smothering occurs when ball goes into ground quickly. Reason is hooded club face as it strikes ball. This causes ball to head for the ground. Degree depending upon amount

a. *Causes*

1. Grip. If either or both hands are to the right on the shaft, it will close the club face at top of swing

2. Position at top; right wrist must be under shaft. If left is under then the weaker left lets go of club

3. Weight on right leg instead of left at moment of impact

a. *Remedies*

1. Pulling head and shoulders up on downswing

2. Check club face at top. Should be half closed, never completely closed

3. Check fingers of left hand at top. Make certain that they grip firmly not loosely

FAULTY GOLF SHOTS AND THEIR REMEDIES (*Continued*)

Causes	Remedies

VII. *Sclaffing*

VII.

Sclaffing means hitting behind the ball

a. *Causes*

1. Transference of weight. Must go from left to right on backswing and not from right to left
2. Dipping knee on backswing
3. Dropping right shoulder either at address or downswing
4. Beginning of backswing. Starts all in one piece. Head fixed
5. Hitting from top. Don't turn club from top. First motion is hip

a. *Remedies*

1. Check weight transference
2. Check shoulder sway
3. Check hitting from top
4. Check backswing

VIII. *Skying*

VIII.

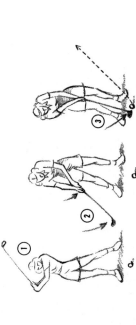

Skying occurs when the ball soars into air and doesn't go very far

a. *Causes*

1. Forward sway with a chop due to lifting of club head on back-swing

2. Turnover of club head, due to right hand control on down-swing or rolling wrists

a. *Remedies*

1. Check swing for chop

2. Check lifting club quickly

3. Check sway to left

4. Check weight on left front at address and impact

5. Check turning over club head at impact

6. Check right wrist at top, under shaft

NOVELTY EVENTS

There are numerous games which can be conducted with improvised equipment to teach isolated skills and game conduct. The following ones are designed for skill improvement:

Target Golf.   This may be improvised for use of any club, other than the putter. From a designated area each player "shoots" for a target laid on the ground in concentric circles like an archery target. Circles carry 1, 3, 5, 7, and 9 point value. The target should be large enough to encourage beginners and may be decreased in size as skill develops. The game may be played with indoor equipment.

Hole in One.   Each participant is given two or three well marked balls on a short hole or on an area with a flagmarker. Players attempt to make a hole in one. The ball closest to the cup is the winner.

Bingle-Bangle-Bongle.   This event is designed to encourage players to get on the green and near the cup. Three points are awarded on each hole: 1. one to the first player to reach the green, 2. one to the first player to hole out, and 3. one for the ball nearest the cup when all players are on the green.

Flag Tournament.   The tournament is played on a course with each player given her average number of strokes for three, six, or nine holes and a flag with her name on it. Play proceeds as a regular round until all strokes are used. At that point, she must plant her flag to indicate the point of course penetration. The object is to progress as far as possible with the restricted number of strokes. (This is excellent for showing individual student progress.)

Blind Bogey.   Tournament officials select certain holes to be counted toward score. Winners may be declared on low total or on low of selected holes.

Dogfight.   An event for foursome competition in which points are awarded for particular types of scoring. For example, one for a bogey; two for par; three for a birdie; four for an eagle; and six for a hole in one. A variation: the group can play for low ball for five points.

Specialty Tournament.   Played by a group of four, each with a club in which she specializes. The foursome plays three, six, or nine holes in competition with the total score of other groups. The club needed for each shot dictates who will play the shot. As a variation, have players rotate clubs on each hole.

Scotch Foursome.   A team consists of two players who alternate stroking only one ball over a designated course. Low medal score determines the winning team.

OFFICIATING TECHNIQUES

Rarely in the life of an amateur golfer will there be occasion for officials to govern the match, for all have a responsibility to learn and use the

U.S.G.A. rules. Tournaments sponsored by the Professional Golf Association are conducted under its rules.

Officials of a tournament include the (1) executive committee, (2) rules committee, (3) referees, and (4) scorers. In brief, the executive committee is in charge of competition, makes arrangements for competitors to participate, supervises and decides pairings, and generally supervises pretournament and tournament conduct.

The rules committee designates rules of conduct of a tournament and rules on any point made by a referee in tournament play.

A referee is assigned to each group, is in charge of play, and should be constantly alert to infractions of rules. She handles disputes and rulings during play and carries a rule book and tape measure for settling disputes.

A scorer is responsible for following a group from the first tee to the completion of a round. She records the number of strokes each player makes on a hole and gives the strokes per hole for each player upon request. She later attests the scorecard and has it signed by the player. The scorer assists in controlling the conduct of spectators.

EVALUATING THE RESULTS

As in all individual sports, the true evaluation of the game of golf is in the individual's ability to play a game properly with good score results. Often, it is not possible for students to play several rounds, but a fair measurement should be devised when grades and marks are given. Skill can be measured by (1) mechanical devices, (2) rating scales, and (3) accuracy tests on a designated area. In addition to skill, the student's understanding of rules, etiquette, and game play should be evaluated.

Suggestions for testing include:

I. Subjective performance rating scale (observed by teacher)
   a. Proper grip
   b. Stance
   c. Address
   d. Swing execution
   e. Ability to select proper club
II. Objective skills test
   a. Putting
      1. Stance
      2. Stroke technique
      3. Ability to two-putt a green from 20 or 25 feet. (For example, using seven golf balls, the putter may score four points on each of best five putts. Thus, a maximum score of 20 and minimum of 14 for passing.)
   b. Chip Shot. A player shoots from 30 feet from edge of green attempting to hit within 12 feet of cup with a #5 or #6 iron. (Using seven

balls the golfer may score four on each of best five balls, evaluated on hitting ball properly and destination of the shot. Maximum score 20.)

    c. Pitch shot. A player shoots 75 feet from the green. Score as the chip shot.

    d. Five iron. To test the player's ability to carry five out of seven balls 90 yards to the green. Score as pitch and chip.

    e. Wood shot. To evaluate the student's ability to hit a clean, controlled shot from the tee and fairway for distance.

III. Written test on rules, knowledge, and etiquette

IV. Tournament results

 V. Course scores and individual progress

TERMINOLOGY

Addressing the Ball—Placing the body and club in a position to hit the ball

Ace—Hole in one

Approach Shot—The shot that is intended to put the ball on the green

Away—Ball farthest from the hole and to be played first

Birdie—Making a hole, in one less than par

Bisque—Handicap set, but strokes to be taken on any hole as designated by the recipient

Bogey—A phantom's score against which players may compete—usually one over par for each hole

Brassie—Wooden club No. 2

Bunker—Hazard, usually artificial

Caddie—Assistant to the players—watches the ball, carries bag and clubs

Carry—Distance the ball travels through the air

Club—Implement used to propel the ball

Course—Ground within playing limits

Cup—Hole into which the ball is played

Dead—Ball does not roll after hitting

Divot—Slice of turf cut out with iron clubs

Dodo—Three under par for any hole

Dormie—As many holes up as there are remaining and one cannot be beaten

Down—Number of strokes or holes one is behind an opponent

Driver—Wooden club No. 1

Eagle—Two under par for any hole

Face—Lofted part of club heads

Fairway—Area between a tee and the green where the grass is cut short

Flag—Flag indicating position and number of hole, the staff being inserted in the center of the cup

Fore—Warning to those ahead when a ball is traveling toward them

Foursome—Two players on a side

Green—Putting green around the hole

Grip—Part of a club that is gripped; also method of grasping

Halved—Tied score on a hole or complete game

Handicap—Number of strokes conceded by a stronger to a weaker player

Hazard—Natural or artificial obstacle other than the ordinary grass of the course

Head—Striking portion of the club

Heel—Part of head nearest shaft
Hole—Cup into which the ball is played
Hole Out—Final stroke for a hole
Honor—Right to play first from a tee
Hook—A shot that curves to the left
Iron—Club with iron head
Lie—Position of ball on course
Links—The entire course
Loft—Height or elevation of ball; also angle of clubhead
Match—A game
Match Play—Competition based on holes won and lost
Medal Play—Competition based on total strokes per round
Neck—Angle between shaft and head of club
Par—Perfect score for a hole
Pivot—Body turn
Press—Effort to hit ball unusually hard
Putt—Stroking ball with putter toward hole
Rough—Rough ground and long grass on either side of fairway
Shaft—Handle of a club
Slice—Hitting across the ball so that the ball curves to the right
Stance—Position of feet
Stroke—Act of hitting ball
Stymie—When one ball lies on the green directly in line of another and the balls are more than six inches apart
Tee—Elevation—wood, ivory, etc.—upon which ball is placed for drive
Teeing Ground—Marked out area at start of each hole
Top—Hitting the ball above its center
Trap—Hole with bed of sand, which forms a hazard
Up—The number of holes or strokes one is ahead of opponent
Waggle—Preliminary movements with the clubs as you address ball
Winter Rules—Rules which allow player to improve the lie of the ball on the fairway

DISCUSSION QUESTIONS

1. Discuss golf etiquette and explain its importance to the game. What consideration should you have for fellow players a. on the tee; b. on the fairway; c. on the green?
2. Name all of the clubs a golfer may use and discuss the proper use of each club on the course.
3. Demonstrate the correct grip, stance, and swing of:
   a. A driver used off the tee
   b. A #2 iron used for maximum distance
   c. A #5 iron for 120 yard approach stroke
   d. A #9 iron from a deep sand trap
   e. A 25 foot putt
4. Briefly explain the different techniques for playing a sidehill lie, an uphill lie, and a downhill lie.
5. Explain scoring methods used in golf. How would you establish a handicap at the local course?
6. Plan a ten lesson instructional unit outdoors for beginning golfers, including films, novelty games, and teaching aids. The unit should terminate with a class tournament.

Selected Audio-Visual Aids

Beginning Golf. (Filmstrips and recordings. Four units, 10 min. per unit, color). The Game. Grip, Stance and Swing. Iron Shots and Putting. Rules Simplified. The Athletic Institute, 209 S. State Street, Chicago 4, Ill. (Rental)

Better Golf. (16 mm. and 8 mm., sound, b & w). Series of 14, three minute films on stance and grip of each club. Valley Film Service, 16121 Sherman Way, Van Nuys, Calif. (Purchase)

Famous Fairways. (32 min., 16 mm., sound, b & w). A. G. Spalding & Brothers, Inc., 161 Sixth Avenue, New York, N.Y. (Loan)

Follow Through. (10 min., 16 mm., sound, b & w). Shick Film Service, Box 131, 404 N. Goodwin Avenue, Urbana, Ill. (Rental)

Golf Advanced. (10 min., 16 mm., sound, b & w). American Film Registry, 24 E. 8th Street, Chicago 5, Ill. (Rental and Sale)

Golf Fundamentals. (7 min., 16 mm., sound, b & w). Shick Film Service, Box 131, 404 N. Goodwin Avenue, Urbana, Illinois and American Film Registry, Chicago 5, Illinois. (Rental and Sale)

Golf Techniques, 1956. Loop series and script on: 1. Grip; 2. Full Swing; 3. Pitch Shot; 4. Chip Shot; 5. Putt; 6. Explosive Sandtrap Shot. Miss Billie Burrill, Department of Physical Education, Connecticut College for Women, New London, Conn. (Purchase)

How to Play Your Best Golf with Tommy Armour. (16 mm., sound, b & w, 3 reels, 10 min. each). Castle Films, Division of United World Films, Inc., 1445 Park Avenue, New York 29, N.Y. (Purchase)

Play Better Golf. (Two parts: Golf Fundamentals and Golf Advanced, 16 mm., sound, b & w). Professional Golfer's Association, Broadway and Main, Dunedin, Fla. (Loan)

The Basics of Better Golf. (30 min., 16 mm., sound, b & w). Palm Beach Company, 200 Fifth Avenue, New York 10, N.Y. (Loan)

The Nine Bad Shots of Golf. (10 min., 16 mm., sound, b & w). Lewis Film Service, Inc., 1425 East Central, Wichita 7, Kansas. (Rental)

The Rules of Golf Etiquette. (17½ min., 16 mm., sound, color). National Educational Films, Inc., 165 W. 46th Street, New York 36, N.Y. (Rental)

Saving Strokes with Sam Snead. (10 min., 16 mm., sound, b & w). University of Wisconsin, Bureau of Visual Instruction, 1312 W. Johnson Street, Madison 6, Wis. (Rental)

Slamming Sam Snead, 1948. (10 min., 16 mm., sound, b & w). Wilson Sporting Goods Company, 2037 N. Campbell Avenue, Chicago 47, Ill. (Loan)

Suggested Readings

A.A.H.P.E.R.: *Bowling, Fencing, Golf Guide,* Current Edition, Division for Girls and Women's Sports, 1201 16th Street, N.W., Washington 6, D.C.

Ainsworth, Dorothy, editor: *Individual Sports for Women,* ed. 3, Philadelphia, W. B. Saunders Company, 1955.

Armour, Tommy: *How To Play Your Best Golf All The Time,* New York, Simon and Schuster, 1953.

Boros, Julius: *How To Play Par Golf.* Englewood Cliffs, N.J., Prentice-Hall Book Company, Inc., 1956.

Hicks, Betty, and Griffin, Ellen: *Golf Manual for Teachers,* St. Louis, C. V. Mosby Co., 1949.

Hogan, Ben: *Five Lessons.* New York, A. S. Barnes, 1957.

Miller, Donna Mae, and Ley, Katherine L.: *Individual and Team Sports for Women.* Englewood Cliffs, N.J., Prentice-Hall Book Company, Inc., 1955.

National Golf Foundation: *Golf in Physical Education; Golf Fundamentals; Golf Facilities; The Easy Way to Learn Golf Rules; Golf Lessons; Golf Events, Golf Plan for Schools.* 407 S. Dearborn Street, Chicago, Ill.

National Golf Foundation: *How to Improve Your Golf.* The Athletic Institute, 209 S. State Street, Chicago 4, Ill.

Rehling, Conrad H.: *Golf for the Physical Education Teacher and Coach.* Dubuque, Wm. C. Brown Co., Inc., 1954.

United States Golf Association: *The Rules of Golf.* 1959 Edition. U.S.G.A., 40 East 38th Street, New York 16, N.Y.

PERIODICALS

Golf Digest, Box 629, Evanston, Illinois.

Golfdom: The Business Journal on Golf, 407 S. Dearborn Street, Chicago 5, Illinois.

Golfing, Golfing Publications, Inc., 407 S. Dearborn Street, Chicago 5, Illinois.

Golf World, Golf World, Inc., Pinehurst, North Carolina.

Sports Illustrated, 540 North Michigan Avenue, Chicago, Illinois.

Swimming, Diving, and Synchronized Swimming

It is difficult to know when and how man first learned to swim. Perhaps he swam in search of food, to survive a pursuer, to fulfill a religious rite, or totally by an accident which threw him into water. Progression of man's skill in water has been slow because of his structural handicaps. A beginning swimmer quickly realizes the eyes, ears, nose, and mouth are not ideally placed for natural efficiency in the water.

Pictures on the walls of caves in the Libyan Desert indicate man's ability to swim as early as 9000 B.C. Throughout history there is mention of "bathing" for hygienic, military, or pleasurable purposes and there is written evidence that swimming instruction was given to select groups in Egypt around 2160 B.C.

The art and skill of swimming as it is practiced today may be traced to Nicolaus Wynman, a German professor of languages, who wrote the *Art of Swimming* in 1538. This description of the breast stroke served as a basis for technique until the desire for speed resulted in adaptations of the side stroke, side overarm, and trudgen.

It is believed the ancient Indians of the Western Hemisphere were capable swimmers, and some experts attribute the overarm stroke to their technique. Swimming was vigorously pursued in early America, and a swimming school flourished in Boston by 1827.

Great progress has been made in stroke development in less than 100 years. The Australian crawl, American crawl, inverted breast stroke, back crawl, butterfly breast stroke, the dolphin (fishtail), butterfly and a refinement of the trudgen, have expanded the interest, skill, and recreational value of this sport. The development of synchronized swimming has refined a sports skill into an aesthetic art form. Development of scientific equipment and underwater skills have revealed an underwater world for study and pleasure.

Diving combines the skills of tumbling and swimming into a form of aerial acrobatics. A newcomer to the sports field, the first diving competition was in England in 1905, and today has developed into a skillful and exciting activity for millions.

THE NATURE AND PURPOSE OF SWIMMING AND DIVING

Swimming serves us today as it has for centuries—survival, food, and pleasure. As a healthful and beneficial form of exercise, it attracts more participants of all ages than any other form of sport. Swimming skills are basic to all aquatic activities, from fishing, canoeing, boating, water skiing, synchronized swimming, to skin and scuba* diving. The age-old struggle for self preservation and survival is a strong motivating factor in our space age.

Regardless of one's motive in swimming, the principles basic to a co-ordinated stroke are the same. The body on its front, side, or back is pro-pelled through water by movements of the arms and legs. Skill development is complicated by the different body position from normal active position, and by the human being's inability to breathe under water. Effective stroke development is dependent upon learning to inhale on top of the surface and exhale below the water's surface.

Diving serves to get the swimmer into the water in the most efficient way. Fancy diving is primarily a spectacular and skillful sport.

SCORING

The Division for Girls and Women's Sports of the American Association for Health, Physical Education, and Recreation recommends the following competitive events:

75-foot Pools

Free style, back crawl, breast stroke and butterfly stroke
25 yards   50 yards   100 yards
75-100 yard individual medley
(25 yards breast stroke; 25 yards back crawl; OPTIONAL: 25 yards butterfly stroke; 25 yards free style)
75-100 yard medley relay
(1st swimmer, 25 yards back crawl; 2nd, 25 yards breast stroke; OPTIONAL 3rd, 25 yards butterfly stroke; 4th, 25 yards free style)
100-yard free style relay
(4 swimmers, 25 yards each)

60-foot Pools

Free style, back crawl, breast stroke, and butterfly stroke
20 yards   40 yards   100 yards
60-80 yard individual medley
(20 yards breast stroke; 20 yards back crawl; OPTIONAL 20 yards butterfly stroke; 20 yards free style)
60-80 yard medley relay
(1st swimmer, 20 yards back crawl; 2nd 20 yards breast stroke; OPTIONAL 3rd, 20 yards butterfly stroke; 4th 20 yards free style)
80-yard free style relay
(4 swimmers, 20 yards each)

* Scuba is an abbreviation for "Self-contained underwater breathing apparatus."

75-foot Pools	*60-foot Pools*
Diving	Diving
Form Swimming	Form Swimming
Elementary back stroke	Elementary back stroke
Side stroke	Side stroke
Breast stroke	Breast stroke
Crawl	Crawl
Back crawl	Back crawl

Places for swimming events, other than form swimming, are determined by the fastest times.

Dual meets are scored as follows:

a. In the free style relay race:

First place	8 points
Second place	4 points

b. In the medley relay race:

First place,	4 contestants	8 points
	3 contestants	6 points
Second place,	4 contestants	4 points
	3 contestants	3 points

c. In all other events:

First place	5 points
Second place	3 points
Third place	1 point

d. In the event two tie for first place, the first and second place awards shall be added and half the sum shall be awarded to each contestant in the tie; there shall be no second place. If three tie for first place, the first, second and third places shall be added and one-third of the sum shall be awarded to each contestant in the tie; there shall be no second or third place. The same is true for those tying for second place, third place, and whatever other places there may be.

Group meets are scored as follows:

a. In the relay races, both free style and medley:

First place	10 points
Second place	8 points
Third place	6 points
Fourth place	4 points
Fifth place	2 points

b. In all other events:

First place	6 points
Second place	4 points
Third place	3 points
Fourth place	2 points
Fifth place	1 point

c. In case of ties see d above.

The team having the greatest number of points shall be declared the winner of the swimming meet.

Diving competition is based upon compulsory and voluntary dives, each one being evaluated by three or five judges on a point value scale of 0 to 10. The winner is the contestant earning the greatest point total. If two receive the same number of points, the one with the greatest sum of points for compulsory dives wins. If a tie still exists, the points award for the compulsory dive with highest degree of difficulty determines the victor.

Form swimming is considered one event with three places in a dual meet and five places in a group meet. Judges award scores of 0 to 10 on each stroke which is properly executed for a length of the pool. Points for each place are given as in other swimming events and figure in team total.

NEEDED FACILITIES AND EQUIPMENT

The Swimming Area.   Although swimming can be pleasurable in many bodies of water, a sound instructional program should be conducted in a well controlled, sanitary swimming area. Instructors training competitive swimmers and divers should work in 75 or 60 foot areas with one meter and three meter diving boards. The most common teaching area is a pool, although lake and river fronts serve many camps. An increasing number of schools, recreation departments, and Y.W.C.A's are including regulation pools in their building plans. Elementary school children are also being increasingly served by school, private, and commercial pools.

Teaching Accessories.   Many instructors prefer to teach without any artificial aids; others like the feeling of security and isolated practice offered by swimming jackets, kickboards, leg floats, and shoe fins. All swimming areas should have minimum equipment for the safety of swimmers. The area dictates the use of ring buoys, bamboo poles, shallow water markers, canoes, boats, and other equipment.

Phonograph equipment, amplifiers, underwater speakers, and adequate lighting are necessary for synchronized routines and desirable for general instructional periods. Properly selected music is helpful in developing relaxation, coordination, and stroke rhythm.

Costume.   Women should wear full suits which do not interfere with body movements. Competitive swimmers seem to prefer the one-piece nylon or durene speed suits. Caps not only protect the swimmer's hair and prevent annoyance, but also keep the natural hair oil and hair out of the pool and filtration system. Bobby pins and clips should be removed to prevent loss, falling to pool bottom, and eventual rusting on bottom.

Slides or clogs may be used when walking to and from the swimming area.

Regulations Concerning Pool Use.   Students and teachers should establish basic safety and sanitary rules for every swimming area. These should include:

1. Soap shower without suit before swimming.
2. Remove all jewelry and accessories.
3. Expectorate only in designated receptacles.
4. Chewing gum and candy are prohibited.
5. Street clothes and shoes are prohibited in pool area.
6. Running and "horseplay" are not allowed on pool deck and in the pool only with instructor's permission.
7. Persons with ear and eye infections, cuts and abrasions, and athlete's foot should not be permitted in pool.

TEACHING UNITS

Suggested topics for a swimming unit include:

Unit for Beginners-Intermediates

Value and purpose of swimming
Safety procedures and class conduct
Relaxation and breath control
Jellyfish and turtle floats
Prone and back floats and recovery
Prone and back glides
Prone and back kick guides
Human stroke (optional)
Finning
Sculling
Changing body positions
Elementary back stroke
Rhythmic breathing
Crawl stroke
    Flutter kick
    Overarm stroke
    Breathing
Jump into water
Side stroke
    Scissors kick
    Arm stroke
    Breathing
Elementary surface dives
Elementary land dives
Treading water
Side overarm stroke
Trudgen
Simple water stunts and games
Evaluation

Unit for Advanced Swimmers

Review safety procedures
Review fundamental swimming and
   diving
    Trudgen crawl
Back crawl
Breast stroke
    Kick
    Arms
    Breathing
Inverted breast stroke
Diving
Lifesaving skills
Racing starts and turns
Butterfly stroke
Underwater swimming
Advanced stunts,
   routines and water games
Officiating meets
Evaluation

BASIC SKILLS

No matter the age of a beginning swimmer, there are certain steps of skill development to be mastered.

Water Adjustment and Beginning Skills.   The beginner wades into waist deep water, splashing her wrists, body and arms to lessen the shock and become accustomed to a new environment. She should dunk to chin depth, jumping up and down cautiously. Standing with feet apart for balance, inhale and hold breath for five or six counts, exhale. Move to shoulder depth, bending forward to submerge the face, repeat breath holding. Lengthening the time of breath holding, repeat until the beginner shows confidence and ability to submerge the entire head. Open eyes under water and count toes, fingers or objects on the pool floor.

Jellyfish Float.   In waist deep water bend from the hips, submerge face, and slowly reach for the ankles. As feet rise from the bottom grasp ankles, hold for three counts, then slowly release, extend legs and recover to standing position.

Turtle Float.   Begin as in jellyfish float, raising knees to chest, arms encircling knees. Allow the water to move the body, then extend legs and recover.

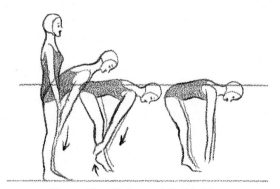

Figure No. 10–1.   Jellyfish Float.

Figure No. 10–2.   Turtle Float.

Figure No. 10–3.   Prone Float.

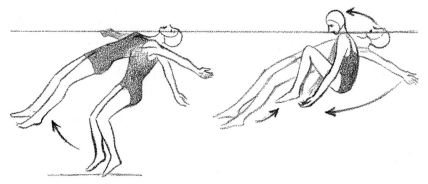

Figure No. 10–4.   Back Float.

Prone Float.   Assume a turtle float and go to full extension, gently pushing arms forward and legs back. Hold the float ten counts and recover by bringing knees to chest and extending legs toward bottom.

Prone Glide.   Place one foot against the side of pool, bend forward at hips, take a breath and put face in the water. Gently push against the side of the pool and glide forward. Recover to standing position.

Back Float.   Submerge with shoulders below the surface, in waist deep water. Raise arms to the sides, palms up. With partner supporting the back of the neck with one hand and back with the other, push off gently. Lift the hips and extend arms, palms up. The head is back and ears are in the water.

A partner aids in recovery until the beginner can return to standing position by dropping the chin forward and bringing the knees toward the chest as the hands scoop down and forward.

Back Glide.   Hold the pool bracket with both hands, facing wall. With head back, ears in the water, draw both feet against the side. (In shallow water push from the bottom.) Remove hands from the side and firmly straighten the legs, pushing away. Hands close to the side for balance, and the legs close together. Recover as in a back float.

Kick Glide in Prone Position.   With the body in a prone position, the legs move up and down alternately from the hips in a thrashing action with loose knees and relaxed ankles.

Kick Glide in Back Position.   From a back glide flatten the back and tuck the chin, look toward the toes. A flutter kick from the hips, with relaxed knees and emphasis on the "up kick" moves the body forward.

Arm Movements on the Back

Finning.   To combine arm movements with back glide and kick, start with the arms straight and hands at the side. Elbows bend as hands simultaneously move up the body about a foot. With fingers pointing away and heel of hand near hips, the hands thrust out and down with a wrist flip to original position.

Winging.   In a back glide, hands and arms work together. Begin with arms straight and hands at side. Hands move up, elbows bend and follow the line of the body until fingertips are at waist level. Arms extend to side (45° angle) and pull to original position. Combined with a resting phase, this is an excellent lead-up for elementary back stroke.

Sculling.   From a back glide, palms near the legs, paired arm action begins by turning hands (rotating wrists) so thumbs are down and back of hands toward legs. Press the hands out and slightly down for about eight inches. Turn thumbs up, and move each hand back to the legs with palms facing body. Keep wrists flexible, and arms firm.

Arm Stroke in Prone Position.   Take a prone glide position, face in water, arms extended. Pull the left arm below the surface straight toward bottom of pool. The elbow bends and shoulder relaxes so the left hand touches the midline of the abdomen. As the left hand extends toward the chin and moves underwater toward its beginning position, the cupped right hand and arm begin a similar pattern.

Combined Elementary Movement

The Back.   Combine simple flutter kick with finning, winging, or sculling while breathing naturally through the mouth.

The Front.   Combined leg and arm movements result in the human stroke or dog paddle. The head is held above the surface with hips below the surface and back arched. The arms reach and pull alternately, recovering below the surface (see "Arm Stroke in Prone Position"). The kick is the elementary flutter with a pronounced knee bend. As the left arm pulls, the right leg bends downward and kicks. Legs alternate with two beats for each arm cycle. Later, three leg beats to a single arm stroke can be developed in preparation for the crawl.

There will be greater stroke efficiency when the face is in the water and raised only for inhalation. Develop a pattern of inhaling from the side and exhaling breath in the water. If the right side is the most comfortable, turn the head to the right, lifting it slightly for a breath as the right hand pulls

Figure No. 10–5.   Human Stroke.

through and the left arm recovers. As the right arm begins recovery the face turns into the water and exhalation begins.

Changing Body Positions and Directions.   Confidence and control are gained by the beginner who can move on the front and back and change positions easily.

Turning from Front to Back.   From an extended glide position with both arms overhead, bring the right arm down and cross the body and roll left as the head turns left.

Turning from Back to Front.   Head and shoulders remain low and horizontal with arms at side. As right arm and right leg reach across the body, both arms extend to an overhead prone position.

Turning Right, Left, or Around.   Stop swimming action and allow the body to drop to a near vertical position. Extend hands and pull in the direction of desired change. Return to front or back position and resume stroke.

Treading Water.   This is a support skill which has value for personal safety. Combine a scissors, frog, or breast stroke kick with a sculling or finning hand and arm action. Treading is done in a vertical position and requires individualized adaptations.

STROKE SKILLS

Elementary Back Stroke.   This resting stroke enables one to cover long distances without undue exertion. Since it is easily mastered by beginners it should be taught after the horizontal float. The body is on the back with head up, chin slightly tucked, ears in the water. The legs are extended and straight with arms at the sides, palms downward.

Arms.   The hands begin the stroke as they move up along the side, thumbs close to the body, elbows bent and shoulders back. As the fingers reach toward the armpits, the wrists rotate and the fingers lead the arms upward and outwards to a "V" position. The arms pull firmly back to the starting position in the power phase and then rest as the body glides through the water.

Legs.   Powered leg action begins as the fingers reach the top of the ribs. With heels together, the legs draw toward the body with soles of the feet toward the bottom of the pool. The knees bend and move away from the body. Heels separate and ankles flex turning the toes outward, as knees remain bent. The legs then sweep outward and together pressing the sole of the foot against the water. Squeeze thighs together as legs return to starting position.

Breathing.   Breathing is regular with inhalation during the recovery and exhalation as the body moves.

Coordination.   The stroke can be phrased in four flowing counts: 1. Arms begin action; 2. legs move up and knees extend as arms move outward; 3. legs spread and whip together as arms complete pull; 4. glide in initial position.

Figure No. 10–6.   Elementary Backstroke.

Crawl Stroke.   The crawl is an efficient and graceful speed stroke using the flutter kick and overhand arm action with rhythmical breathing. The body is in an extended prone position.

Arms.   With both arms extended overhead the left arm pulls firmly straight toward the bottom. The pull turns to a push as the hand passes the shoulder and continues until it is almost under the left hip bone. Left arm begins recovery as the elbow bends and shoulder action lifts the elbow and relaxed hand clear of the water. The forearm is relaxed and forward as the fingers enter the water and begin a new pull with a slightly cupped hand.

The right arm begins identical action as the left begins its recovery forward. The hands enter the water at natural arms' length in front of the face, slightly inside the shoulder line.

Legs.   The kick begins with slightly "pigeon-toed" leg extension. Right leg bends slightly at the knee as it drops downward from the hip. As the right leg snaps back to extended position, the left leg drops. The action is primarily from the hips with relaxed knee and ankle action. Legs pass close together as they penetrate 12 to 16 inches into the water and rise almost to the surface.

Breathing.   Turn the head to inhale as the arm opposite the breathing side is set and forward for support. A quick "bite of air" is taken, the head turns back into the water and exhalation begins. It continues as the head turns for a breath when the "breathing arm" pulls by the shoulder and the support arm is forward.

Coordination.   The complete rhythmical stroke is a coordinated movement of six* evenly measured leg beats to a complete cycle of both arms with a breathing ratio of one inhalation and exhalation.

Side Stroke.   A side stroke is a restful, powerful stroke that is a necessity in executing lifesaving skills. Its mastery makes the overarm, side and

* Some competitive swimmers use an eight beat kick; some a four beat synchronized cycle.

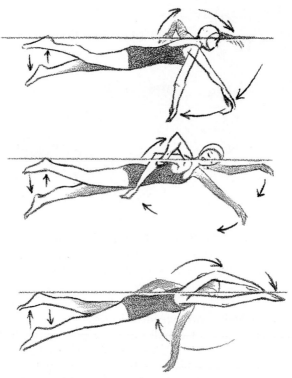

Figure No. 10–7.   Crawl Stroke.

trudgen strokes relatively easy. The side stroke should be learned on both sides with conventional and inverted kicks. The following description is for the right side.

Ready position is reclining on the right side, body straight, feet together and legs extended. The left arm is resting on the front of the thigh of the left leg, right arm is extended in the water, palm down. The head is supported by the water and right shoulder comfortably.

Arms.   The right arm begins a downward pull toward a line directly beneath the head. The left arm, elbow bent, glides across in front of the body toward the right armpit. The right elbow bends and the hand is brought in toward lower shoulder, fingers leading. Right arm slides forward beneath the surface, palm down as the left hand "catches" and presses toward the feet and starting position.

Legs.   The legs execute a scissors kick. From an extended position the knees flex drawing the heels backward in line with the back. Legs remain close together. The toes lead in a lateral leg extension as the top (left) leg reaches to the front of the body and lower leg behind. Top foot flexes and lower foot remains extended. The legs, still flexed, begin driving backward and together with sole of the top foot and instep of lower foot pressing the water, then meeting, stopping, and remaining extended during the glide.

In the inverted scissors kick the top leg goes to the back of the body and the bottom leg moves forward. It serves as a change of pace and an excellent lifesaving skill for carrying a victim.

Breathing.   Breathing is natural as the head is out of the water. Most swimmers prefer to inhale during the power phase and exhale during the glide.

Coordination.   The lower arm pull downward is the initial movement. Immediately, the top arm begins moving forward and the legs bend. As the lower arm completes a power phase and the top arm prepares for power delivery, the legs separate and drive as the arms return to starting position.

Ride the glide.

Single Overarm or Side Overarm.   The side overarm is a comparatively simple stroke following mastery of the side stroke. The basic timing is the same in both strokes except for the recovery by the top arm above the surface.

Arms.   From the side stroke position the lower arm begins a pull to

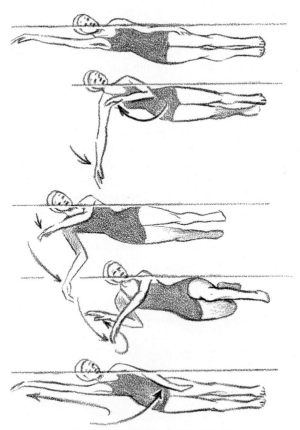

Figure No. 10–8.   Side Stroke.

Figure No. 10–9.   Side Overarm Stroke.

shoulder level. As it starts upward the top arm, elbow relaxed, recovers over the water and the fingers enter slightly in front and above the forehead. Stroke continues as in side stroke.

Legs.   Scissors kick.

Breathing.   Same as with side stroke.

Coordination.   The coordinated stroke is similar to the side stroke.

Trudgen.   An excellent stroke for distance as it is fast, steady, and not as tiring as the crawl to the average swimmer.

Arms.   Overhand (crawl) stroke.

Legs.   Single scissors kick.

Breathing.   Similar to crawl stroke on selected side.

Coordination.   Beginning from a prone glide position, face down, the left arm begins a pull. Legs trail motionless. As the left arm begins recovery the right arm pulls and the legs draw to a modified scissors position. With the left arm forward for support, the body rolls slightly right, mouth clears the water for inhalation and re-enters the water as the right arm recovers and the scissors kick is delivered. The body has rolled back onto the face and exhalation continues as arm cycle is completed.

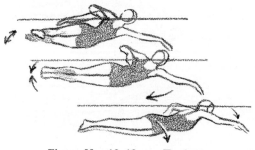

Figure No. 10–10.   Trudgen.

Trudgen Crawl. An efficient stroke using hand over hand arm strokes and scissors and flutter kicks. While executing a trudgen, simply add three or four flutter kicks between scissors kicks instead of allowing legs to trail. When learned from a crawl, roll to the breathing side and add a scissors kick as inhalation occurs.

Back Crawl. This is the fastest stroke executed on the back. In most respects it is a graceful and rhythmical inverted American crawl.

Arms. The arm pull may be deep or shallow with a bent or straight arm recovery. The shallow pull, straight recovery is described below. On the back with chin tucked and hips slightly dropped, eyes focus where toes will kick the surface, extend both arms to a "V" position overhead. The right arm pulls directly toward the right side with palm leading a cupped hand traveling two or three inches below the surface. As the recovery begins, the hand rotates so the palm is away from the body as the little finger leads a straight arm upward and slightly sideward. Wrists are relaxed as the fingers reach toward the water to begin a new cycle. The left arm works alternately and begins its power phase as the right arm recovers.

Legs. The inverted flutter kick is used with legs extended, one knee bends and the foot drops 12 to 16 inches toward the bottom. A hip lift forces the leg upward, toes extended so instep presses against the water. The toes break the water as the knee remains below. As one leg begins upward

Figure No. 10–11.   Back Crawl.

pressure the other drops in alternating action. Six or eight "pigeon-toed" kicks are done with each arm cycle.

Breathing.   As the head is out of the water, inhalation time is optional.

Coordination.   As one arm begins a pull, the opposite leg begins a kick lift. A rhythm of six to eight beats is set, alternating arms and legs.

Breast Stroke.   The breast stroke was the first competitive stroke and has been refined more than any single stroke. It is basic to the fast and powerful butterfly. The orthodox breast stroke is a smooth, graceful movement done from a prone position. The body is in extension with arms beyond the head several inches below the water with thumbs together and palms down. Legs are straight and together.

Arms.   Arm action begins as palms turn outward, thumbs down and pull begins downward and backward until arms approach shoulder level. Elbows bend and the hands lead inward toward the chest with elbows coming close to the sides. As the fingers meet beneath the chin, palms down, arms extend forward to starting position.

Legs.   Leg action begins from extension, knees draw toward the body, dropping slightly and separating easily. Feet flex outward and reach away from the body. The power and drive is accomplished by a whipping sweep out and backward with ankles and feet leading to an extension for riding the glide.

Breathing.   As the arms press back against the water on the first movement there is a natural lift to the upper body that allows for a quick bite of air before submerging the face.

Coordination.   Coordination and timing are often difficult. Using a four count pattern the following occurs:

Count   one: arms begin press; head rises for breath

Count   two: arms move toward chest as legs draw toward body; face submerges

Count three: arms slide forward and legs whip outward and backward

Count   four: glide in extended position

Inverted Breast Stroke.   This is a resting stroke similar to the elementary back stroke. The body is flat on the back with legs straight and arms extended beyond the head, thumbs touching.

Arms.   Slightly cupped palms turn away from each other and pull out, down, and in to the sides. With arms still several inches below the water the elbows bend outward allowing the palms-down hands to follow the body toward the armpits where the hands turn over and fingers lead past the shoulders and under the head to initial position.

Legs.   Knees bend and separate slightly as heels drop toward the bottom. Toes point sideward and back. The legs extend and whip out and together.

Breathing.   Inhale as arms pull toward the body and exhale as legs kick and arms recover.

Coordination.   Arms come to the sides before legs prepare for the kick. As the arms recover along the body, the legs recover and drive together as the arms extend to glide position.

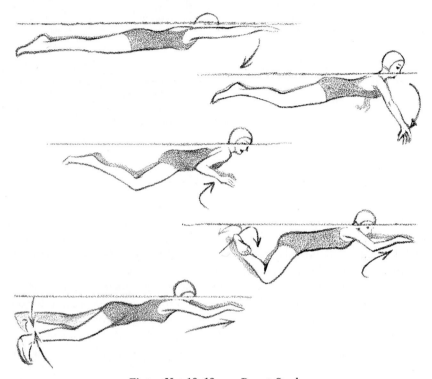

Figure No. 10–12.   Breast Stroke.

Butterfly Stroke.   For this stroke "both arms must be brought forward simultaneously over the water and brought backward simultaneously. All movements of the legs and feet must be executed simultaneously. Simultaneous up and down movements of the legs and feet in the vertical phase (dolphin kick) are permitted."[1]

Arms.   With arms extended upward from the shoulders, the hands begin a downward and backward pull straight for the bottom until arms are fully extended, then hands press back toward the thighs. Arms lift out of the water and sweep forward with relaxed elbows. Arms extend and reenter in front of the shoulders.

Legs.   Although the breast stroke kick may be used with slight modification in timing, speed can be increased by the dolphin (fishtail) kick. The dolphin involves a vertical movement of both legs together. Similar to the flutter kick, except that the legs are extended in prone position with

[1] New ruling of Aquatic Committee of DGWS as printed in Guide 1957–1959, p. 79.

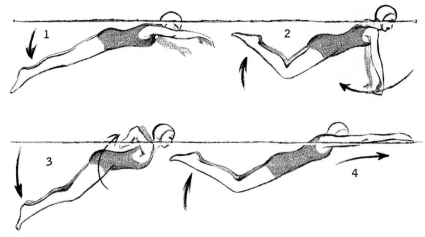

Figure No. 10–13.   Butterfly Stroke.

heels, toes, and knees together; the feet are drawn toward the body by bend-ing knees and hips and flexing ankles. Heels break water slightly before body and leg extension begins. Extension is completed by hip flexion and legs rise upward before another sequence begins.

Breathing.   The head is brought out on the downward pull of the arms and inhalation occurs when chin lifts to water level. As the hands press backward the chin tucks and exhalation begins. Competitive swimmers often prefer a two cycle stroke for each breath.

Coordination.   A properly executed stroke has two kicks to an arm cycle. In four counts:

Count   one: arms pull downward; legs begin bend; head lifts to inhale

Count   two: head enters water; arm pull continues; legs push down-ward and straighten

Count three: hands continue backward pull and start upward; legs bend upward

Count four: arms recover; legs push downward and straighten

Underwater Swimming.   Underwater skills are increasingly necessary for skin and scuba diving (See note p. 182). Many strokes can be used but a modified breast stroke seems superior.

Arms.   Arms pull all the way to the sides with little or no downward pressure.

Legs.   The kick is identical with the breast stroke. Flutter or scissors kick may be used.

Breathing.   Take several deep breaths at the surface, then a normal breath before submerging. Hold the breath as long as there is no tension in the chest, then release it slowly.

Coordination.   The timing may be identical with breast stroke or with simultaneous arm and leg action.

DIVING SKILLS

Diving is an exciting skill which should develop with swimming. Before actually diving from the deck or float, students should learn to jump into water of various depths. While in the water, a beginner should push off in a prone glide and direct the body below the surface by dropping the head and arms. By turning the head and hands upward the body rises to the surface. Next, standing in waist deep water with arms overhead, thumbs locked together, the swimmer takes a breath, bends forward at the hips and pushes up and forward into the water.

Surface Dives.   Generally, surface dives are easily learned as the swimmer is in the water and does not need additional courage for a ledge or board entry. Considerable skill must be developed in the use of hands, arms, and head.

To begin a head first surface dive with a tuck, the body is in prone position on the surface. Take a deep breath and duck head sharply. As the arms pull back toward the shoulders the body is drawn into a flexed position with knees and hips bent. The arms continue a pull through to the thighs. Immediately the hips and knees straighten above the surface. The weight of the legs above helps the body glide toward the bottom as palms turn toward the head and scoop downward.

The head first surface dive with a pike is similar to the previous dive except there is no bend in the knees. As the dive begins the body bends into a jackknife position. The hips straighten and extend the legs, feet together and toes pointed to complete the dive.

The foot first surface dive begins with the body in a vertical position, arms at sides, palms in. Palms turn toward the bottom and with a kick, force the upper body out of the water. As the body sinks, legs come together and toes point as the arms turn, palms away, and begin pressure upward against the water as the head goes below the surface. In a completed dive the body and extended arms are submerged.

Elementary Diving.   Diving from the pool deck should follow "in-water dives." The following progression leads to a standing dive:

Sitting Dive.   Sit on pool or float edge with feet braced against the side. Place extended arms overhead, upper arms by ears and thumbs locked together, palms down. Bend between spread knees, take a breath through the mouth and as the body falls forward gently push with the legs. Bring legs together and straighten and extend toes.

Kneeling Dive.   Place one knee close to the edge of the pool and toes of the other foot over the edge. With arms above head roll forward toward the water. The head remains down and between the arms, and the eyes are fixed on the entering spot. Alternate knees.

Standing One Leg Dive.   Standing on one leg with toes over the edge, the other leg bends behind the body for balance. Arms over head, head down, the upper body bends forward and the balance leg lifts aiming the

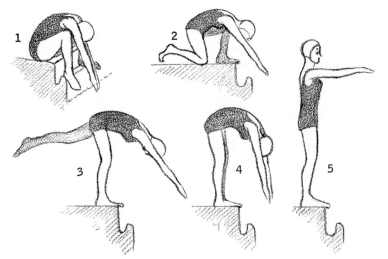

Figure No. 10–14.   Diving Progression.

Figure No. 10–15.   Running Dive.

body downward. Roll into the water bringing the stationary leg up to meet the other.

Standing Semi-Crouch Dive.   Stand on both legs with toes over the edge. Knees are easily bent, arms extended. Bend forward at the hips and push up and into the water.

Standing Stationary Dive.   Stand erect with toes over pool edge, legs together and arms at sides. Raise arms forward to shoulder height, bending knees. Lift the heels and push up and slightly out as the head and shoulders drop between the arms and the diver enters the water. After this is mastered begin in an erect position and swing arms upward as the legs push. Extend legs and toes.

Springboard Diving. Instruction should begin on the one meter board. Many teachers like students to progress through a series of jump dives prior to "headers." Foot first practice should precede each new dive. Beginning dives are done from a standing position at the take-off end of the board and later with an approach and hurdle.

The Front Jump. Standing several inches from the take-off end, jump up, down, and push (riding the spring) with balls of the feet as the arms reach forward and upward. To keep the body from falling forward, press the head and shoulders back against the arm pull. At first let the arms stay extended overhead for the feeling of lift; later bring arms down along side of the body before entering the water.

Standing Front Header. Preparation for the take-off is the same as the foot first entry. Allow the body to follow arms upward then turn over and enter the water with legs together and extended, and toes pointed.

Figure No. 10–16. Swan Dive.

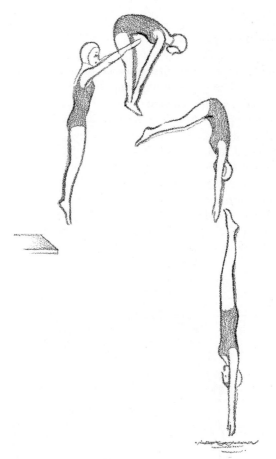

Figure No. 10–17.   Front Jack Knife.

Running Front Dive.   All running dives have an approach which includes the stance, walk, hurdle, and take-off. A beginner determines where to begin her approach by placing her heels on the take-off end of the board and mimetically taking desired steps and a hurdle. Once the spot is determined, begin each dive there unless the approach pattern is changed.

Stance.   Stand erect with chest and chin up and eyes focusing on end of the board and to the desired height of the dive. Arms are firmly by the side, palms in, feet together and parallel.

Walk and Run.   A minimum of three steps must be taken in the approach and many divers prefer four. The steps are natural, increasing in momentum. The arms move slightly forward with the first step, slightly backward on the second step, and then forward with the third step. Eyes focus on the end of the board and the head is up.

Hurdle.   As the leg and knee lift for the hurdle, the arms move strongly forward and upward pulling the diver off the board. Both feet then come down together on the end of the board as the arms move downward toward the hips to add weight to bend the board. As the board rebounds, legs and ankles straighten, arms lift upward and chin and chest rise with eyes on an object at the end of the pool.

Action Position in the Air.   The diver leaves the board in an upward and slightly outward direction with arms reaching overhead, legs straight and toes extended. The back arches very slightly.

Entry.   The point of entry is in front of the board, directly beneath the body and descending downward toward the pool bottom. In a header, the fingertips touch the water first, with the body following in a straight line at right angles to the water surface. On a foot first entry the body is erect and extended with arms at the sides.

Fancy Dives.   There are five groups of dives as categorized by the Division of Girls and Women's Sports: forward, backward, reverse (gainer),

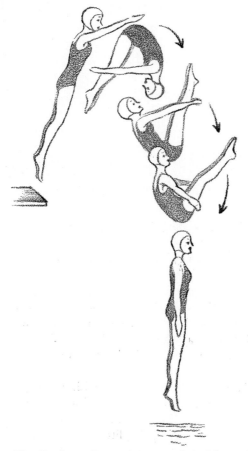

Figure No. 10–18.   Forward Somersault in Pike Position.

Figure No. 10–19.   Back Dive.

inward (cutaway) and twisting. The handstand group is not given official competitive status. Selected dives from the five groups will be described.

Forward Group—Swan, Jack knife, Forward Somersault, Forward 1½ Somersault.

Swan Dive.   In competitive events the running front and swan are considered the same. The difference is in the arm movements. As the diver leaves the board her hands are lifted from the hips and spread straight from the shoulders with a slight forward angle. At the peak of the dive the body rotates and the head slowly drops between the arms as they close for entry.

Front Jack Knife.   The diver climbs with hands extended. At the end of the reach, the arms reach down as legs and toes are pressed forward with hips higher than the head. Hands contact the feet and the body remains piked for an instant before the legs lift slowly for a vertical entry with head between the arms.

Forward Somersault.   This may be done in a tuck, pike or layout position. In a tuck the knees are close to the body, in pike position the body is bent at the hips with legs straight, and in the layout the body remains straight and in the same plane throughout the dive.

In a tuck or pike the somersault is made by bringing the heels backward and upward as the head and chest pull to the knees. In a tuck the knees bend and heels come to the buttocks with arms below the knees. In a pike, place the hands at shin level. Before the body reaches a vertical position the legs extend and feet begin entry.

Forward One and One-Half Somersault.   This is like forward somersault with additional rotation for a head entry.

Backward Group—Back Dive and Back Somersault.

Back Dive.   This is a standing rather than a running dive. Standing at the end of the board, eyes focused on the back wall, raise arms to shoulder height in front of the body. Toes and balls of the feet carry body weight as heels are extended over the end of the board. To lift from the board, arms lower to side and heels lower simultaneously. The arms then raise above the head, in front of the face and upward.

The diver leaves the board straight upward with arms extended. At height of the upward momentum, the head stretches backward, back arches

Figure No. 10–20.   Back Somersault in Tuck Position.

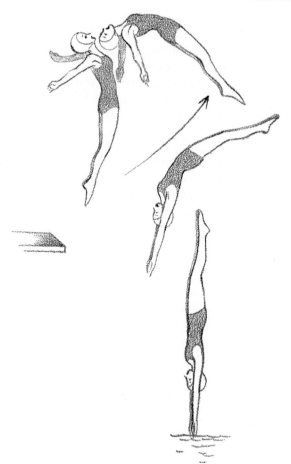

Figure No. 10–21.   Half Gainer.

and eyes focus on the water. For a swan, the arms move out at shoulder level and come together as they pass the end of the board on descent.

Back Somersault.   Can be done in pike or tuck position. From take-off position, rise and lift the arms forcibly. Immediately lift the knees to chest in a tuck, or bend at the hips for a pike. The head pulls backward and continues backward until the body falls in line for a vertical descent. Legs straighten, toes point downward as arms straighten by the thighs.

Gainer Group—Half gainer.

Half Gainer. (Islander). A beautiful dive that requires excellent hurdle and take-off control. Simply, it is a backward dive from a forward take-off. At the end of the lift with arms in spread position, the head, arms, and shoulders pull backward and the chest, hips, and legs are lifted in a stretched position. As the body reaches a horizontal position the legs remain lifted and relatively stationary as arms, shoulders, and head continue rotation downward. Arms close to the head at board level and lead a vertical entry.

Cutaway Group—Back Jack knife.

Back Jack Knife.　　Begin as if a back dive. Lift from the board, forcing hips upward and bring hands down to touch the instep in pike position. Raise hips and legs and lower head between the arms for head first entry.

Twisting Group—Front Dive with half twist; Front Dive with full twist.

Half Twist.　　Take-off as in a front header with arms reaching up and out from the shoulders. At the peak of the reach, if the twist is made to the right, lower the right shoulder and direct the right arm toward a spot of entry in the water. The head turns and eyes focus on the lowered right arm. Entry into the water is straight with back toward the board.

Full Twist.　　Rise from the board in a swan position. If twisting to the right, thrust the left arm across the hip and downward. The right arm raises above the head as legs bear upward during rise and descent. A half twist is completed while rising and continues as head turns forcibly right and left arm extends by head with right upon entry.

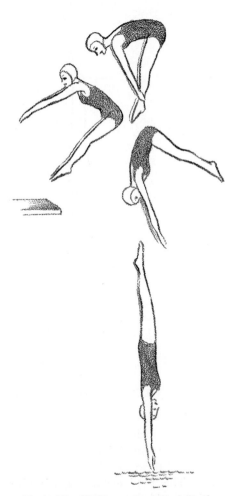

Figure No. 10–22.　　Back Jack Knife.

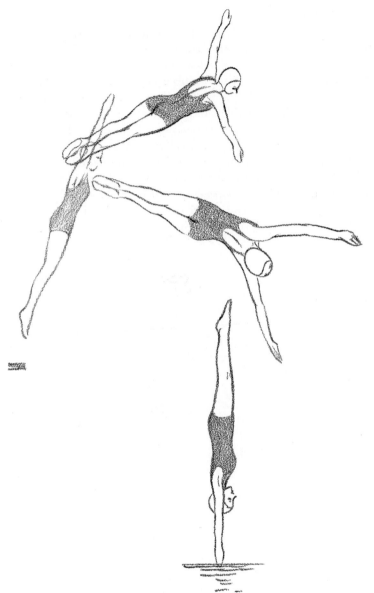

Figure No. 10–23.   Front Dive with Half Twist.

SYNCHRONIZED SWIMMING SKILLS

Synchronized swimming involves setting swimming movements and stunts to a rhythmical accompaniment. Basic water skills and a sense of rhythm and creativeness are essential. The water skills are standard strokes and stunts, and derivations of these combined by a creative pattern.

Beginning Skills.   The fundamentals which give a swimmer confidence and skill include breathing, back float, sculling, and rolling.

Breathing.   Stress rhythmical breathing for ease and timing at approximately a two count inhalation and four count exhalation. Teach breath holding with most of the air expelled and combine with glides, prone floats, and flutter kick.

Back Float.   Floating on the back should be mastered in horizontal position, working at every angle to finally a vertical position. A basic horizontal float includes straight legs, pointed toes with arms extended above the head. At this point the powered butterfly stroke can be taught with partners floating side by side with heads in opposite directions. Arms and legs spread as partners hold one another near ankle with inside hand. Partners move in a circle by stroking with free outside arm.

Sculling.   For head first sculling see p. 189. Sculling feet first in a floating position with arms at sides is accomplished by turning palms out and pulling against the water from feet toward head.

When sculling feet first with arms and hands overhead, palms are turned away from the body and pressure is applied outward and downward against the water.

Practice in line formations and small groups. Add simple stunts like the tub and single ballet leg.

Rolls.   Simple rolls are executed by turning the head in the direction of the roll with lower arm extended under the head and upper arm on top of the thigh. For a description of moving from front to back and back to front, see p. 190.

Simple Stunts.   A more complete description is published by A.A.U. and reprinted in selected D.G.W.S. Aquatics Guides.

Tub.   From a back floating position draw knees to chest as hips sink. Turn in a circle by sculling.

Ballet Legs.   From a back float with legs together and ankles extended begin sculling for support. One knee bends toward chest, then rises to a vertical position, bends back to chest and to starting position. Alternate legs to develop equal skill. A double ballet leg is accomplished by simultaneous leg movements.

Shark.   From a side position, body arches with top arm extended overhead in a continuing arc. Propel the body in a circle by using scooping motion with lower arm.

Porpoise.   From a horizontal breast stroke position, body extended, pull arms as in breast stroke, bend at the hips lifting legs straight above the head. Submerge straight toward the bottom and return to the surface vertically, feet leading.

Catalina.   From a back float bring the right knee to the chest and extend as in a ballet leg. Drop the head and turn under the left arm still maintaining the ballet leg while in a vertical position with the head down, slide the left leg along the right until both are extended. Slowly submerge.

Corkscrew.   From a side stroke position with top arm on thigh, lower arm extended, roll the body in a complete revolution.

Dolphin.   From a back float drop the head back as back arches.

Scoop outward and upward from the shoulders while pulling the body in a complete underwater circle.

Oyster.   From an extended back float bend at the hips bringing the arms and toes together above the hips. Submerge in this piked position.

CLASS ORGANIZATION

Class conduct is dependent upon the varying skill level, facilities, and equipment available. Swimming and diving skills are best learned by the whole-part-whole method of presentation. The teacher demonstrates and explains (1) the whole movement, (2) then breaks it into component parts for mastery before, (3) coordinating them into a stroke.

Following a progression of land drills and shallow water drills prior to deep water, the arms, legs and breathing skills are developed. Land drills may be done standing, lying on the deck or partially on the deck leaning into the pool. In shallow water arm drills can be done in both stationary and moving positions. Leg strokes are practiced in bracket drills at pool side.

In both shallow and deep water practice formations are helpful in observing class progress. When mass practice is desirable in a large group divide the class into one, two, or three squads and use a wave formation.

Figure No. 10–24.   Prone, side, and back positions for bracket drills.

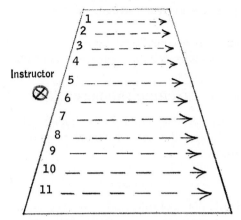

Figure No. 10–25. Wave Formation.

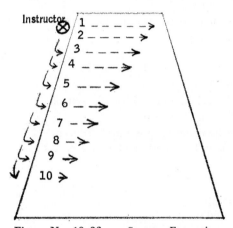

Figure No. 10–26. Stagger Formation.

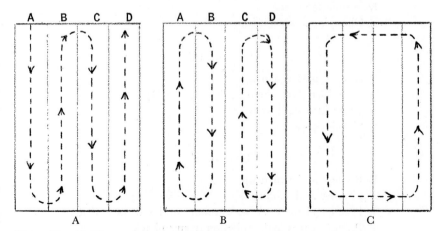

Figure No. 10–27. A. Long Practice Course; B. Short Practice Course; C. Circle Course.

If teachers want to observe each swimmer for a few strokes use a stagger formation.

Distance swimming is accomplished by dividing the pool into lines, or courses, with swimmers staggering their starts to avoid collisions.

TEACHING PROGRESSION

The following plans are suggested for beginning swimmers. Progression will vary considerably and the teacher should prepare for increasing variance within a class.

Lesson I

1. Explanation of pool rules and class progression
2. Nature of swimming
3. Brief history
4. Adjustment to the water
5. Simple game

Lesson II

1. Warm up
2. Practice relaxation and breath control
3. Jellyfish and turtle floats
4. Prone float, prone glide and recovery
5. Back float, back glide and recovery

Lesson III

1. Warm up
2. Kick glides
3. Elementary arm movements
4. Simple tag game
5. Changing body positions

Lesson IV

1. Review and warm up
2. Introduce the human stroke (optional)
3. Jump into shallow water
4. Simple game

Lesson V

1. Review and warm up
2. Finning and sculling
3. Practice elementary backstroke—land and water drills
4. Practice turns and strokes on front to back.
   Reverse

Lesson VI

1. Review and warm up
2. Begin crawl by practicing a. flutter kick, b. overarm stroke, c. breathing
3. Play a water game using elementary backstroke skills

Lesson VII

1. Review all parts of the crawl
2. Coordinate the crawl
3. Begin elementary diving, perhaps introducing a surface dive
4. Play water game requiring surface dives

Lesson VIII

1. Review and practice coordinated crawl
2. Practice elementary backstroke
3. Continue diving progression

Lesson IX

1. Review and warm up
2. Begin side stroke, stressing the scissors kick
3. Elementary land dives—sitting and kneeling

Lesson X

1. Review and warm up
2. Drill arms for the side stroke
3. Coordinate arms and legs in the side stroke
4. Continue diving

Lesson XI

1. Distance swim in the crawl
2. Practice side stroke
3. Water game involving diving skills

Lesson XII

1. Continue stroke development
2. Treading water
3. Evaluation

It is common for some students, retarded by fear, to be in the early stages of the lesson progression after several weeks, while others, advancing rapidly will be working on the springboard and developing the trudgen, trudgen crawl, and back crawl.

SKILL DIFFICULTIES AND THEIR CORRECTION

Difficulty	*Correction*

1. Basic Water Adjustment

1.

a. Tension caused by fear

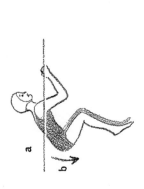

a. Teacher stresses the fun and security in the water. Play games and encourage the student with any progress

b. Inability to float

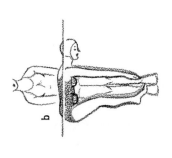

b. Encourage the student to relax. Have a partner help her into a comfortable float. Demonstrate the buoyancy of the body

c. Inability to recover from floats

c. Demonstrate slowly and place hands on student to assist in developing timing

Difficulty	Correction

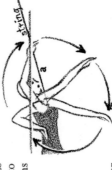

2. Elementary Backstroke

a. Legs sink or break water

b. Arms move upward rather than by side on recovery

c. Failure to glide

2.

a. Keep the head back and avoid bending at the waist. Suggest the stroke be practiced slowly

b. Explain principles of water resistance

c. Explain and demonstrate the value of the glide in moving the body and as a resting phase

3. Crawl Stroke

a. Arms crisscross in front of body and pull sideward

b. Pull is too shallow and done with a bent arm

3.

a. Teacher may demonstrate the loss of power in the stroke. Tie strings to suit inside the shoulder line so arms cannot cross unnoticed

b. Suggest that the student "reach for the bottom" to get maximum power

SKILL DIFFICULTIES AND THEIR CORRECTION (*Continued*)

Difficulty	*Correction*
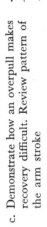 c. Arms overpull	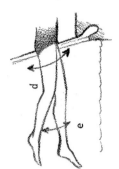 c. Demonstrate how an overpull makes recovery difficult. Review pattern of the arm stroke
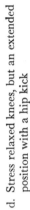 d. Knees bend too much, lifting feet out of the water e. Pressing down with legs so body is stationary or moves backward	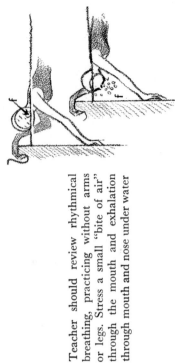 d. Stress relaxed knees, but an extended position with a hip kick e. Suggest student practices in shallow water so the push comes from the bottom of the pool upward
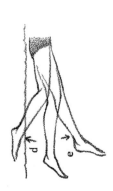 f. Inability to breathe properly	 f. Teacher should review rhythmical breathing, practicing without arms or legs. Stress a small "bite of air" through the mouth and exhalation through mouth and nose under water

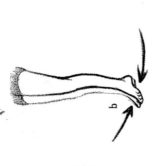

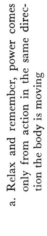

4.

a. Relax and remember, power comes only from action in the same direction the body is moving

b. Suggest that the student becomes pigeon-toed so toes will catch and stop negative action

c. Review and practice kick in bracket drill

4. Sidestroke

a. Forcing the legs apart

b. Legs pass after they close, pulling against glide action

c. Bending the hips as legs recover so body sinks

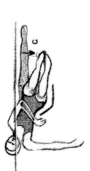

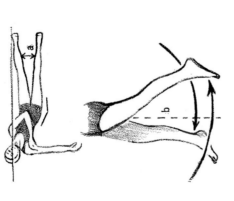

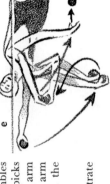

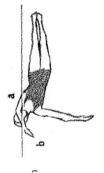

SKILL DIFFICULTIES AND THEIR CORRECTION (*Continued*)

Difficulty	*Correction*
d. Improper force during arm action	d. See 4a
e. Poor relationship and coordination of arms	e. Suggest that the stroke resembles peach picking. The lower arm picks the peach, giving it to the top arm in front of the chest and top arm throws it into a basket toward the feet
f. Poor stroke coordination	f. Review entire stroke, demonstrate and assist student individually
5. *Side Overarm Stroke* (in addition to sidestroke errors)	**5.**
a. Body lunges out of the water as arm recovers over water	a. Stress a relaxed recovery with arm low over water
b. Body rolls on face	b. Avoid overreaching
6. *Trudgen and Trudgen Crawl* (In addition to crawl arm strokes and flutter and scissors kicks)	**6.**
a. Incorrect coordination	a. Review crawl coordination and demonstrate the insertion of the scissors kick
b. Failure to maintain an "uneven" rhythm	b. Student is reminded that the scissors kick causes a natural uneven rhythm and a slow recovery for arm on breathing side

Difficulty

7. Back Crawl

a. Legs are rigid and cause body thrashing

b. Ankles are rigid

c. Body is too flat in the water

d. Elbows drag through the water on recovery

e. Completing one arm cycle before the other arm starts

f. Hands recovering too far over head causing loss of power pull and stiff body

Correction

7.

a. Relax. Teacher may suggest that the kick is like riding a very small bicycle with flexible ankles and "rubber" knees

b. Develop floppy ankles by pretending there is mud on the instep and the swimmer is trying to kick it off

c. Suggest that the student "sit" and look toward her toes

d. Emphasize the backpull of this error and suggest a lift up and back

e. Suggest land drills practicing alternating action

f. Remind the student that the power comes from the downward pull from shoulders to side. Arms should form a "V" as they enter the water

219

SKILL DIFFICULTIES AND THEIR CORRECTION (*Continued*)

Difficulty	*Correction*
8. *Breast Stroke*	8.
a. Overpulling arms causing a bobbing motion through the water	a. Review arm stroke stressing an even relaxed movement
b. Using incorrect kick, generally the scissors	b. Suggest the student practice on pool bracket with body parallel to pool side. Leg movements are paired and identical. Practice with kickboard
c. Failure to glide	c. To prevent the arm pull too soon, student may lock her thumbs during arm recovery and hold for the glide
d. Inability to coordinate, usually due to simultaneous arm and leg action	d. Review complete stroke
9. *Inverted Breast Stroke* (In addition to the common errors of the breast stroke)	9.
a. Throwing water onto face and upper body as arms recover	a. Arms should recover below the head with slight force
b. Bending knees out of water resulting in body sinking	b. Review breast stroke kick

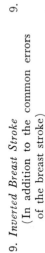

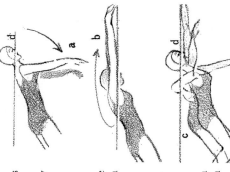

Correction

10.

a. Reach for bottom with straight arms

b. Straighten arms and keep head low in water as arms fling forward

c. Relax hips and ankles and allow the body to undulate. Practice kick with arms at the sides

d. Review arm-breathing coordination

e. Teacher reviews stroke rhythm

f. The student should work toward a continuous arm pull and leg action

Difficulty

10. *Butterfly Stroke*

a. Failure to keep elbows straight on arm pull, thus destroying leverage

b. Arms trail through water on recovery

c. Hips are rigid, and feet and knees apart

d. Improper timing for inhalation

e. Only one leg kick for complete arm cycle

f. Gliding

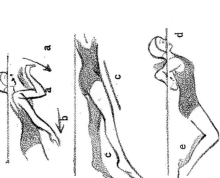

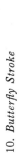

SKILL DIFFICULTIES AND THEIR CORRECTION (*Continued*)

Difficulty	*Correction*
11. *Elementary Diving*	11.
a. Legs overthrow the head 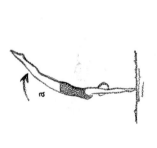	a. Student should avoid dropping the head too soon or pull the arms down with excessive force
b. Landing flat or too far out 	b. Teacher should remind student "as the head and arms go—so goes the body." Duck head between the arms and push *up* rather than *out*
c. Knees collapse upon entry 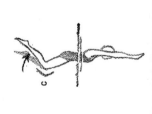	c. Stress body extension with legs firm and ankles extended

NOVELTY EVENTS

Games for beginning students

Ball Tag.   Played by 10 to 20 persons with a light water ball. One player is selected as "it" and must tag someone else by tossing the ball. The one tagged becomes "it."

Balloon Ball.   Two teams, each selects a goalkeeper to keep the balloon from passing over the goal. All other players line up in the center facing one another. A balloon is put in play and players try to advance the balloon by batting it with an open hand. If the balloon touches the water, a member of the team, not touching it last, begins play.

Ping-Pong Ball Retrieving Contest.   Two teams of any number of players are seated on the pool deck facing each other. Ping-pong balls are thrown in the shallow end of the pool. On signal, players jump into the pool and attempt to catch a ball in their mouths. Hands may not be used. When a ball is caught, players return it to their side, receive a point and return to play until the allotted time is over.

Games for intermediate and advanced students

Water Volleyball.   Played with a regulation water polo ball or hollow ball of similar size. The number of players is limited by size of the pool. The game proceeds as regulation volleyball, modifying the rules to permit the ball to be caught and thrown, but not held. The height of the net above the water can vary between 3 and 5 feet. Rotate "courts" if one team can touch bottom and the other cannot.

Water Basketball.   Played with a regulation water polo or similar ball. Regulation size backboards and baskets are used. The rim of the basket should be 3 to 4 feet above pool surface. Six players comprise a team as in an official basketball game. A personal foul allows the offended player two free shots from a distance of 5 feet in deep water and 10 feet in shallow water.

A more informal game can be played by allowing players to walk or swim with the ball in their court areas.

Watermelon Scramble.   A greased watermelon is tossed in the water. At a signal, swim for the melon and try to bring it ashore. This may be a team or individual event.

Tag Games.

Cross tag.   A single player is chased by "it" until another person dives or swims between the pursued and "it." When a person is tagged she selects someone to chase and play continues.

Chinese tag.   Free swimming tag which requires the player to hold one hand on part of the body where she was tagged until she touches someone else.

Relays.

Any number of relays may be devised. Divide group into teams and use 1. selected strokes; 2. arms only; 3. legs only. Relays which handicap a swimmer are thoroughly enjoyed by groups. These include pushing a ball, carrying a bag or pushing a peanut in a dog paddle.

OFFICIATING TECHNIQUES

Presently, girls compete in swimming and diving under rules printed in guides by Division for Girls and Women's Sports of the A.A.H.P.E.R. Although there is competitive synchronized swimming directed by the A.A.U., officiating techniques are omitted in the following discussion.

A swimming meet may require as many as 20 officials for proper administration. The number may be lowered by having properly trained officials double their responsibilities, i.e., serve as diving, form, and speed swimming officials.*

Officials are a referee, a diving referee, a form swimming referee, a clerk, one official scorer, three finish judges, three or five judges of form swimming, three or five judges of diving, three timekeepers, a starter, an announcer, and a turn and lane inspector.

The officials should be dressed in conservative swimming suits or white gymnasium costume with rubber-soled sandals. Equipment provided by the officials and meet manager includes:

1. Official Aquatics Guide
2. Clipboards and pencils
3. Whistles for starter and referee
4. Guns and cartridges
5. Stop watch for each time
6. Official forms for recording results
7. Working and master score sheets
8. Flash cards or special report forms for form swimming and diving judges

I. Speed Swimming
   The referee:
      1. Has full jurisdiction and decision over the meet
      2. Assigns duties to each judge
      3. Acts as chief judge
      4. Appoints a chief timekeeper and take-off judges and other needed officials
   The judges:
      1. Determine order of the contestants at the finish of the race
   The three timekeepers:
      1. Clock the time on the winning lane

---

* See *Aquatics Guide,* Official Rules and Technique for the Woman Official in Swimming, AAHPER, Washington, D.C.

Chief timekeeper:
1. Instructs timekeepers in use of watches
2. Reads all watches to determine official time
3. Examines and inspects watches frequently

The clerk of the course:
1. Notifies all participants five minutes prior to event
2. Supervises as contestants draw lots for starting position
3. Places contestants behind the starting line prior to each event

The starter:
1. Explains to contestants the signal to start and recall, the distance to be covered, and where race terminates
2. Gives the signal to start the race

The scorer:
1. Keeps an accurate record of the results of each race
2. Serves as an auditor of diving scores

The inspector of turns and lanes reports any infraction of the rules to the referee.

II. Diving Competition

The diving referee:
1. Manages the entire competition
2. Examines score sheets and confirms the final results

The diving judges:
1. Score each dive from their assigned location
2. Shall score dives in accordance with the table of values as established by D.G.W.S.

III. Form Swimming

The duties of the referee and judges of the form swimming contests are similar to those of diving officials, although their evaluation of selected skills is different.

It is necessary that officials for all events be thoroughly aware of the rules of each event. An alert official frequently reviews the *Guide* for rule interpretations and official's responsibilities.

EVALUATING THE RESULTS

Every swimmer should be tested on her understanding and skill of swimming and diving. The American Red Cross has established standards for beginners, intermediates, swimmers, and advanced swimmers. Individual skills tests have been established and are available to serve as measuring devices for skill attainment.[1]

Tests should be used sparingly. It is helpful to evaluate the skills of an individual when instruction begins and at least once more at the end of the instructional unit. An instructor finds it helpful to set skill goals upon which

[1] See *Instructor's Manual Swimming and Diving Courses*. The American National Red Cross, 1944.

to rate students and to equate improvement. For a beginner these might include:

1. Crawl stroke
2. Elementary back stroke
3. Back crawl
4. Breast stroke
5. Side stroke
6. Surface dive
7. Dive from pool deck
8. Treading water
9. Finning
10. Sculling

Intermediates might be evaluated on:

1. Performance of basic beginning strokes for a distance of 20 yards
2. Quarter mile swim within 10 minutes
3. Tread water three to five minutes
4. Execution of running dive from board
5. Surface dive and retrieve object in 10 to 12 feet of water

Advanced swimmers might be expected to:

1. Swim one-half mile
2. Swim 100 yards of each stroke proficiency
3. Show knowledge and skill in a racing dive as well as one back and one front dive from the springboard
4. Become qualified as a holder of Junior or Senior Life Saving Certificate

Measuring speed and distance is relatively simple. The former should be a concern for advanced and competitive swimmers.

Proper execution of dives and water stunts is more difficult to evaluate. It is advisable to explain the checkpoints very carefully. Discussion of dives and stunts, and officiating techniques helps students understand points upon which they are evaluated.

If grades are given they should be based upon written and oral tests and individual skill and achievement.

TERMINOLOGY

Aquatics—Water events of all kinds: swimming, diving, skiing, skin diving, water games, pageants, boating and sailing

Beat—A phase of the flutter kick, a downward movement of a leg. "Six beat kick" refers to six downward movements of the legs to one complete cycle of both arms

Bobbing—Process of raising the head from beneath the surface and then submerging again in a rhythmical pattern

Buoyancy—A natural tendency of the body to float

Coordination—Proper movements controlled accurately as to direction, force, and timing to produce efficient action

Cycle—When applied to the arms, means a completed stroke involving both arms

Dive—A descent into the water

Entry—A phase of the over arm stroke at which time the hand and arm enter the water at the completion of the recovery. In diving, refers to body entering the water

Extension—To reach or stretch out entire body or selected part, e.g., as arms

Float—To sustain the body position without movement

Recovery—The phase of arm or leg action which is without propelling force

Turn—A reversal of direction at end of pool, or course

Discussion Questions

1. Discuss the values of stressing beginning swimming skills at an early age. When should boys and girls learn to swim? Why?
2. Briefly explain what should be included in a complete school aquatic program. What pattern or progression would you follow in planning such a program?
3. Using the *Official Rules for Intramural, Interscholastic and Intercollegiate Swimming Meets* of the current DGWS *Aquatics Guide,* you and your classmates plan and conduct a class or intramural meet. Summarize the steps followed in planning, and make a critical evaluation of the outcome of the meet.
4. Plan a 10 lesson unit for a class of high school girls who are frightened non-swimmers.
5. Create a two or three minute solo routine using simple stunts and some form of rhythmical accompaniment.
6. Explain and demonstrate the progression in teaching the front jack knife.

Selected Audio-Visual Aids

Beginning Diving, 1957. (3 filmstrips) The Athletic Institute, 209 S. State Street, Chicago, Ill. (Purchase)

Diving, 1954, Nine Loop Film, AAHPER, 1201 16th Street, N.W., Washington 6, D.C. (Purchase)

Girls Springboard Diving from A One Meter Board, 1957. Nine Loop Films, AAHPER, 1201 16th Street, N.W., Washington 6, D.C. (Purchase)

Beginning Swimming, 1955. (11 min., 16 mm., b & w) Coronet Films, Coronet Bldg., Chicago, Ill. (Rental)

It's Fun to Swim, 1952. (11½ min., 16 mm., b & w) American Red Cross, Local Chapter. (Loan)

Learning To Swim Series. (crawl—12 min.; breast stroke—12 min.; back crawl—8 min., 16 mm.) International Film Bureau, 57 E. Jackson Boulevard, Chicago 4, Ill., or 20 W. 55th Street, N.Y. 17, N.Y. (Rental)

Swimming Synchronized, 1954. (14 min., 16 mm., sound, b & w) Visual Instruction Service, Iowa State College, Ames, Iowa. (Rental)

Synchronized Swimming: Basic Skills, 1952. (Silent, 30 min., 16 mm., b & w) Lillian MacKellar, 729 Galey Avenue, West Los Angeles 24, Calif. (Rental)

This is Synchronized Swimming, 1958. (3 reels: Basic reel—12 min., Intermediate reel—12 min., Advanced reel—16 min., 16 mm., sound, color.) Jole and Company, 1027 Camino Ricardo, San Jose 25, Calif.

Suggested Readings

I. *Swimming and Diving*

AAHPER, Division for Girls and Women's Sports, *Official Aquatics Guide,* Current Edition, 1201 16th St., N.W., Washington 6, D.C.

Armbruster, David A., and Morehouse, Laurence E.: *Swimming and Diving*, ed. 3, St. Louis, C. V. Mosby Co., 1958.

Barr, A. R., Grady, B. F., and Higgins, J. H.: *Swimming and Diving*, revised edition, Annapolis, U.S. Naval Institute, 1950.

Bourgaize, Ediola J.: *More Fun in the Water*, New York, Association Press, 1951.

Brown, Richard L.: *Teaching Progressions for the Swimming Instructor*, New York, A. S. Barnes, 1948.

Hazelton, Sidney C.: *Diving Manual for Instructors*, ed. 3, Hanover, N.H., S. C. Hazelton, 7 Dana Reed, 1950.

Kiphuth, Robert J., and Burke, Harry M.: *Basic Swimming*, New Haven, Yale University Press, 1950.

Lukens, Paul W.: *Teaching Swimming*, Minneapolis, Burgess Publishing Company, 1952.

Smith, Ann Avery: *Skillful Swimming*, Ann Arbor, J. W. Edwards, Inc., 1954.

Torney, John A.: *Swimming*, New York, McGraw-Hill Book Company, Inc., 1950.

II. *Synchronized Swimming, Water Skiing and Skin Diving*

Andersen, John H.: *Skiing on Water*, revised edition, New York, The Ronald Press, 1954.

Bronson, Howard G.: *Handbook for Skin Divers*, New York, Arco Publishing Company, 1956.

Conference for National Cooperation in Aquatics: *The Science of Skin and Scuba Diving: Adventuring with Safety Under Water*, New York, Association Press, 1957.

Dillon, Evelyn K.: *Synchronized Swimming Rules*, New York, Amateur Athletic Union of the United States, 223 Broadway, New York, N.Y.

Spears, Betty: *Beginning Synchronized Swimming*, Minneapolis, Burgess Publishing Company, 1950.

Yates, Fern, and Anderson, Theresa W.: *Synchronized Swimming*, New York, The Ronald Press, 1951.

PERIODICALS

Aquatic Artist, (monthly). Richard Dodson, 1512 South Boulevard, Evanston, Illinois.

Skin Diver, (monthly). P.O. Box 128, Lynwood, California.

Swimming Pool Age—Beach and Pool, (monthly). Hoffman-Harris, Inc., 425 Fourth Avenue, New York, N.Y.

11

Table Tennis

Table tennis is a year round recreational activity for all ages and abilities. The increased popularity of the game in the United States in the past 25 years is due largely to its adaptability to many skill levels and to its use as a family recreational sport. A ten year old child or a nonagenarian may find recreational pleasure in this game in his own basement or backyard with little previous skill, training, or physical conditioning. Highly skilled players find table tennis a vigorous game requiring adept footwork, stroking ability, and strategy. The hobbyist finds pleasure in helping the family construct their own table and rackets for indoor and outdoor use.

THE NATURE AND PURPOSE OF THE GAME

The name "table tennis" is descriptive of the game. Frequently called indoor tennis, gossima, or ping-pong, table tennis is a derivative of tennis with play restricted to a table surface. The confined area of play necessarily resulted in rule changes and equipment limitations.

Table tennis may be played by two (singles game) or four (doubles game). In singles, play begins with a serve and continues with the opponents

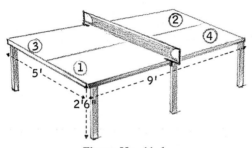

Figure No. 11–1.

alternately playing the ball until one player misses the ball, strikes it illegally, hits the ball into the net, or drives the ball over the net but not into the opponent's playing area.

Doubles play differs significantly from the singles game. In doubles, the service begins from the server's right-hand court and bounces in the opponent's right-hand court. After the service, partners alternate playing the ball until the rally ends and point is decided.

SCORING

A game is won by the individual or team that first gains 21 points and has at least a two point lead over the opponent. For example, if the score is tied at 20 points, play continues until one side wins two consecutive points. The winning score is 22–20, or if the score is tied at 21–21, the winner needs 23–21.

Complete rules are available from the United States Table Tennis Association;[1] however, rules basic to beginning play include:

1. The winner of a rally, coin toss, or other method of chance has option of serving or receiving, or court selection.
2. Each person serves until a total of five points is scored. The serve then passes to the opposing side.
3. When the score is tied at 20–20, service alternates between opponents after each point until game is completed.
4. At the completion of each game opponents change ends of the table for the next game of the match.
5. In doubles, the server must deliver from her right court diagonally to opponents' right court.
6. In doubles, players and partners must alternate returning the ball. That is, after the receiver returns the serve, the server's partner must return the ball, then the partner of the receiver shall play the ball and thereafter each player alternately returns the ball until the end of the rally.

Figure No. 11–2.

Points are scored by the side making the last good rally. Unsuccessful return and loss of point occur when:

1. Ball is missed by the racket
2. Ball is hit off the table on return
3. Ball is hit into the net

[1] United States Table Tennis Association, 333 N. Michigan Avenue, Chicago 1, Ill.

4. Player hits ball into her own half court (other than on service)
5. Player's racket or clothing touches the net or net supports while ball is in play
6. Player moves the playing surface while ball is in play
7. Player puts hand on playing surface when ball is in play

NEEDED FACILITIES AND EQUIPMENT

Table tennis lends itself to indoor and outdoor settings and utilizes a minimum of space and equipment. The table and rackets are easily made in home workshops or improvised in school or recreational settings. Standard equipment is readily available and within most school budgets.

Table and Net.   The United States Table Tennis Association establishes standards for official tables. The overall playing surface is 2½ feet from the floor. The playing surface may be of any material which allows an official ball an eight to nine inch bounce when dropped a foot above the surface. The usual surfacing is ¾ inch fir plywood, although more durable pressed woods and formica-type tops are gaining popularity. The surface should be dark and non-reflecting (dark green is desirable) with white end and sidelines ½ to ¾ inch, and white center line ⅛ inch in width.

The standard net is 6 feet long and 6 inches high. The net is supported by brackets outside the playing surface which pull it taut across the table, dividing the playing surface into two courts of equal size.

Racket.   Individual preference is of major importance in selecting the size, shape, and surfacing of rackets. The racket blade may not be white, pale in color, or have a reflecting surface. Institutions and recreation centers are increasingly selecting the durable rubber-faced rackets in preference to smooth wooden-faced or sandpaper covered rackets. Leather or composition wrapped handles assure a better grip.

Ball.   Regulation celluloid balls should be purchased from reputable manufacturers who conform to U.S.T.T.A. rules. The balls are fragile and easily damaged if stepped on or improperly stored. Balls are considered expendable equipment, as normal use causes eventual cracking and splitting.

Space.   All-purpose rooms, social-recreational areas, and gymnasiums are well suited for instructional and recreational games. Basements, garages, breezeways, and family room areas are popular home locations for tables. Six feet of unobstructed space on each side and 12 feet on each end of the table and a ceiling a minimum of 9½ feet above table surface is desirable. Non-reflecting finishes on all sidewalls aid in following the ball in flight.

Non-glare artificial illumination should provide 30 foot-candles of evenly distributed light on the table area. Two hundred watt frosted bulbs with a reflector shade installed over the table center are recommended.

Dress.   Dress is largely an individual or institutional decision. Clothes should be selected for comfort and freedom of movement. A gymnasium costume with tennis shoes or sneakers is appropriate for use in the instructional program. At all times avoid full skirts which might hinder a free arm stroke, and tight skirts which limit the range of body movement. Slippery soles and high heel shoes increase the hazard of falling.

TEACHING UNITS

Suggested course content for beginners and advanced students includes:

Unit for Beginners	*Unit for Advanced Students*
Brief history	Review fundamental skills
Selection and care of equipment	Review safety rules
Safety fundamentals	Advanced strokes
Fundamental skills	Forehand chop
Grip	Backhand chop
Stance	Drop shot
Footwork	Smash
Serve	Spins
Half volley	Advanced game strategy
Forehand drive	Official tournaments
Backhand drive	Singles
Scoring	Doubles
Basic game strategy	Novelty games
Singles	Evaluation
Doubles	
Official game	
Evaluation	

Suggestions for Expanded Activities
1. Repair or make additional equipment
2. Show films
3. Purchase personal equipment
4. Organize and conduct tournaments
5. Officiate games

BASIC SKILLS

Grip.   The "tennis grip" is superior for firm control of the racket and better for instructional purposes than unorthodox grips. Proper grasp of the racket results in the "handshake grip" with index finger and thumb bracing opposite sides of the blade. The handle of the racket is pulled firmly into the hand against the base of second, third, and fourth fingers. Unlike the common penholder grip (see below) the handshake grip allows maximum wrist flexibility and free movement of the racket to any position without changing the finger position.

Stance and Footwork.   The principles of stance and footwork are basically the same as in other court games. The more restricted area of movement and play makes the movement pattern less difficult for beginners.

In a singles game, the right-handed player faces the net, takes a relaxed position just left of the center and two or three feet from the end of the table. The feet are placed about 12 inches apart with the left foot slightly forward. Some experts prefer the center table position, but most players reach farther and hit more accurately with their forehand strokes and play "left" to protect their backhand. Body weight is equally distributed, knees slightly flexed with weight forward on the balls of the feet. This neutral position allows rapid movement forward, backward, and to either side of the table.

At all times the racket is held in front of the body, slightly to the forehand side, in preparation for a stroking position.

Playing the forehand, the right-handed player turns to the right with

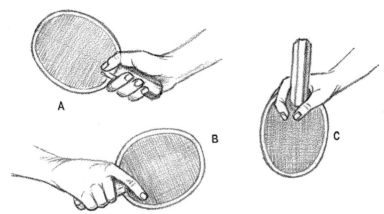

Figure No. 11–3.   A. Forehand Handshake Grip; B. Backhand Handshake Grip; C. Penholder Grip.

Figure No. 11–4.   Foot position.

Figure No. 11–5.   The Forehand Drive.

the left side of the body angled toward the net. In turning, the weight rests primarily on the right (rear) foot and shifts to the left (forward) foot in completion of the stroke.

As the right-handed player reaches for a backhand stroke, her body turns left with the right side angled toward the net. The weight shifts from back to forward foot as in the forehand return.

Getting into position to return a ball often means leaving the neutral position. If steps are taken forward, backward, or to either side, the player should return immediately to her neutral position to await the next play.

Footwork in doubles play is essentially the same as in singles, as partners alternate shots and are individually responsible for getting in position for their return. The novice may experience difficulty moving away from the playing area to allow room for her partner and yet staying near enough so she can prepare for her return stroke.

The Drives

The Forehand Drive.   Assuming the proper grip, the player watches the ball and places herself in position at right angles to the net. A ready position with a short backswing prepares her to contact the ball at the height of its bounce. Contact and follow-through with a swift, firm motion result in a shift of body weight (see p. 232, Stance and Footwork).

Variations in arm action and racket face cause different ball bounces. For example, a straight follow-through directed deep in the opponent's court results in a long powerful "smashing" drive with a direct bounce and an even rise; whereas a short follow-through in a downward direction puts underspin on the ball and results in a higher than normal bounce in opponent's court. Stroking the ball from left to right, or right to left, causes sidespin in flight and a bounce in the direction of the spin.

The Backhand Drive.   The backhand drive is similar to the tennis backhand. The arm extends across the body resulting in a shorter backswing than the forehand drive. Contact is made just before, or at, the height of the bounce and follow-through continues in a long arc as the player returns to a neutral position. Like the forehand drive, variations of arm and wrist action cause spins and bounces.

The Serve.   The serve is the initial action and an important offensive technique in winning table tennis. Once the serve is decided (see Scoring), play begins by lofting the ball in the air, or dropping the hand from the ball and stroking it with the racket. The ball must bounce in the server's court, travel diagonally across the net and land fairly in the receiver's court.

Execution of a legal serve is often difficult for beginners. The ball must not be hidden in a cupped hand and directly stroked; finger spins are not allowed; and rubbing the ball against the racket face while imparting power is illegal. The fingers must be straight and together and the thumb free as the ball is lofted or the hand dropped. At the moment of contact, both racket and ball must be behind the end line in the server's court and within imaginary sideline extensions of the table.

The most desirable serving position is approximately a foot from the end of the table with the body facing slightly to the right (right-handed

Figure No. 11–6.   The Backhand Drive.

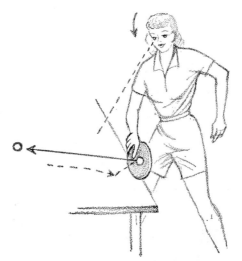

Figure No. 11–7.   The Half Volley.

player) and left foot slightly forward. Some skilled players prefer to stand squarely facing the net and twist to left or right, serving from both sides of the body. In either case, the ball should be struck close to the playing surface with sufficient force to drive it firmly and deeply into the opponent's court.

The Half Volley.   As in tennis and squash, use of the half volley is primarily defensive; however, it has merit for the skilled player as a deceptive offensive shot. The racket meets the ball just as it rises from the bounce, long before it reaches its rise height. Time does not allow for a deep backswing and contact results in a pushing stroke and a relatively weak return. A quick turn of the racket to either side adds spin to the shot.

Chop Strokes.   Chops are effective offensive strokes which should be mastered on both the forehand and backhand. With the racket held at shoulder height, wrist slightly flexed, the slightly open faced racket moves forward and downward rapidly contacting the ball. Impact behind the ball from the downward movement of the racket causes an underspin which results in a high bounce. As the stroke is completed, the arm is extended toward the front of the body.

Drop Shot.   The greatest value of the drop shot is deception, as it changes the pace of play. The stroke begins as a drive, but results in a fake as the forward stroking movement stops just before the racket hits the ball. The ball hits the stationary racket face and rebounds across the net to drop with little force and bounce.

Smash.   The smash is a hard hit, fast dropping return. The stroke is similar to the drive, but it is usually hit flat, imparting no spin to the ball. It is most effective on high bouncing shots as a point winner, for the additional ball speed makes it difficult to return.

Figure No. 11–8.   The Drop Shot.

Strategy.   As the player's skill increases consideration should be given to basic principles of strategy.

1. Enter every game with determination to win
2. Warm up prior to each match
3. Develop a sound defensive game so the ball will stay in play until the opponent's defense fails or offensive tactics win the point
4. Observe opponent's weaknesses and play them
5. Concentrate on the present shot, rather than the last or anticipated one
6. Vary style, speed, and type of return to keep opponent guessing
7. Generally keep returns low and deep in opponent's court, unless a "change-up" for deception is timely
8. Generally, keep the serve low
9. Learn to serve forehand and backhand and vary the spins applied
10. Serve to different parts of the table and avoid "telegraphing" placement with eyes or body position
11. In doubles get out of partner's way quickly
12. In doubles, it is generally sound to hit toward the opponent moving out of the way

CLASS ORGANIZATION

An adequate supply of tables, rackets, nets, and balls makes table tennis an ideal activity for any size class. The relatively small space required for tables permits use of gymnasiums, classrooms, corridors, or cafeteria. Art and science laboratory tables often substitute for official tables.

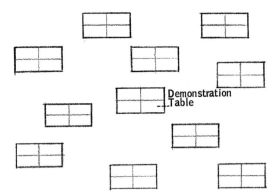

Figure No. 11–9.   Table arrangement in large class area.

Many instructors favor homogeneous grouping with a minimum of two basic skill groups. A large instructional area can usually accommodate 10 to 20 tables, so each basic skill group is organized in an instructional area. If possible, class size should be limited to four girls to a table with a racket for each player and a ball for each pair.

A suggested instructional plan is to place the demonstration table in the center of a staggered formation of student tables. Alternating the tables allows maximum play area and lessens the danger of collision.

When equipment supply is not large enough for the entire class, table tennis can be taught concurrently with other instructional units. On certain days or during a single class period squads can be assigned to table tennis as one of several activities.

The following suggestions are for the teacher with large classes and limited time.

1. Consider a change in dressing schedule if locker areas are crowded. Some groups would start playing prior to dressing (if dress and shoes allow) and dress for class after other groups.
2. Assign a minimum of four girls to each table, six if necessary. Have four work on game skills and play; two officiate and coach.
3. All equipment is set up and stored by the students assigned to each table.

TEACHING PROGRESSION

As soon as the class is introduced to the new instructional unit, student assignments should be made for setting up and storing equipment. The class should be instructed in care of equipment and basic safety rules early in the unit. The history of table tennis is interestingly combined with discussions of equipment, rules, and strategy.

Planned skill progression insures more rapid progress. The instructor introduces the proper grip, stance, and footwork after a game demonstration with another instructor or student. She should then work on individual and group instruction. After a new skill is introduced to the class the instructor explains and demonstrates its use, always relating the skill to rules, strategy, and play. Each time the class meets there should be a skill review and practice. Throughout the practice and game sessions the instructor moves to each table to assist in skill improvement, rule interpretation, and strategy. Allowing for differences in individual progress, the following suggested course outline is helpful:

Lesson I

1. Explanation of the objectives of the game
2. Demonstration of game
3. Explanation of use, care, and assembly of equipment
4. "Try out" play period for all
5. Demonstration and explanation of stance and forehand and backhand grip
6. Class practice of stance, grip, and "shadow," or mimetic, stroking without the ball

Lesson II

1. Review plan for setting up equipment
2. Review stance and grip
3. Introduce and demonstrate footwork for service
4. Teach rules and principles of service
5. Class practice session and short game

Lesson III

1. Review and practice acquired skills
2. Explanation of rules and scoring of doubles game
   (If adequate equipment, begin with single game)
3. Explain technique and use of half volley
4. Teach forehand drive
5. Practice session or short game

Lesson IV

1. Review serve, half volley, and forehand drive
2. Demonstrate and teach backhand drive
3. Review rules for singles and doubles game
4. Play official doubles game

LESSON V

1. Review
2. Student demonstration
3. Evaluation by teacher and pupils of class progress
4. Individual assistance for skill improvement
5. Informal skills test

LESSON VI

1. Review and practice
2. Reassignment to homogeneous groups
3. Discussion of doubles strategy and officiating techniques
4. Begin instruction of forehand chop

LESSON VII

1. Review of forehand chop
2. Teach backhand chop
3. Practice session or singles game

LESSON VIII

1. Review singles game rules and strategy
2. Teach smash
3. Explanation and demonstration of topspin, underspin, and side-spin
4. Single game with emphasis on strategy and use of all strokes

LESSON IX

1. Review
2. Novelty games
3. Teacher-student evaluation, with student's written evaluation of her progress with list of strengths and weaknesses of the class

LESSON X

1. Oral review of unit
2. Skill test

LESSON XI

1. Written test

SKILL DIFFICULTIES AND THEIR CORRECTION

Difficulty	*Correction*

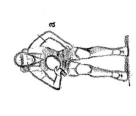

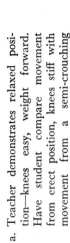

1. *Grip*

1.

a. Grasping racket as a pen or pencil

a. Change to more effective tennis grip

b. Holding racket stiff, so tense wrist and arm result

b. Teacher assists in placing fingers for proper tennis grip; stress relaxed wrist and elbow

c. Grasping the racket in palm of hand

c. Spread fingers comfortably and move index finger and thumb to opposite sides of blade

d. Racket head dropped with wrist stiff and high

d. Teacher stresses "ready position" with racket up and wrist firm for rapid movement in all directions

e. Racket turning in hand or slipping from hand

e. Stress firm, relaxed grip

2. *Stance and Footwork*

2.

a. Stiff knees and erect body position

a. Teacher demonstrates relaxed position—knees easy, weight forward. Have student compare movement from erect position, knees stiff with movement from a semi-crouching position

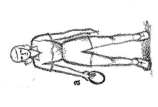

SKILL DIFFICULTIES AND THEIR CORRECTION (*Continued*)

Difficulty	*Correction*
	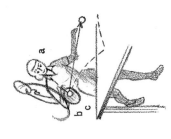
b. Failure to return to neutral position after each return	b. Emphasize neutral position by chalking footprints on floor
c. Failure to adjust body for best position to meet oncoming ball	c. Chalk positions on floor and ask student to practice moving to suggested positions for various returns

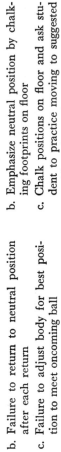

3. *Timing*

3.

a. Missing the ball

a. Stress concentration on the play. Watch ball, rather than opponent

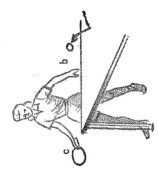

b. Hitting the ball into net

b. Concentrate on contacting ball at height of its bounce (see section on strokes)

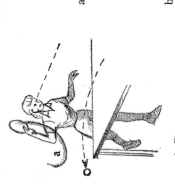

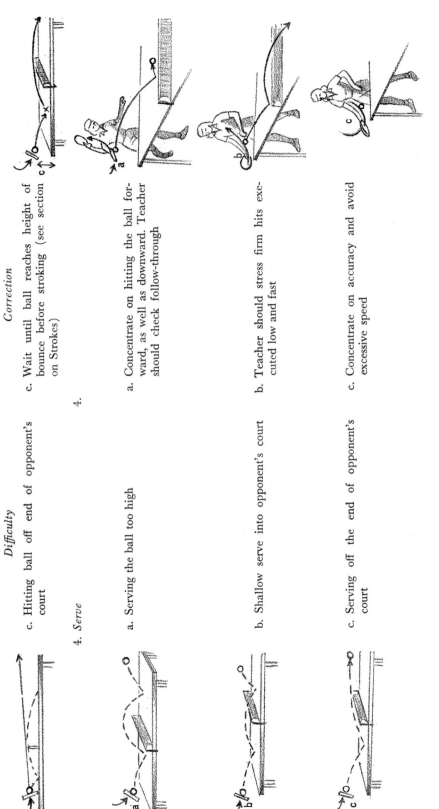

Difficulty

Correction

c. Hitting ball off end of opponent's court

c. Wait until ball reaches height of bounce before stroking (see section on Strokes)

4. *Serve*

4.

a. Serving the ball too high

a. Concentrate on hitting the ball forward, as well as downward. Teacher should check follow-through

b. Shallow serve into opponent's court

b. Teacher should stress firm hits executed low and fast

c. Serving off the end of opponent's court

c. Concentrate on accuracy and avoid excessive speed

243

SKILL DIFFICULTIES AND THEIR CORRECTION (*Continued*)

Difficulty	*Correction*
d. Serving into the net	d. Tip racket face forward and place the first bounce further from the net in the server's court. Teacher should check to see if contact with the ball should be higher for desired trajectory
e. Failure to use spins for deceptive serve	e. Teacher should demonstrate and check as student brings racket horizontally across ball while executing the serve
5. *Placement*	**5.**
a. Failure to place returns effectively	a. Concentrate on spot placement; play to opponent's weakness
b. "Telegraphing" ball placement	b. Avoid looking at intended spot. Use similar delivery style for all serves
6. *Drives*	**6.**
a. Hitting ball into net	a. Insist that stroke be made at height of the bounce. Avoid driving a dropping ball. Remind the student that a lifting stroke rather than a flat swing, is used on a low bouncing ball

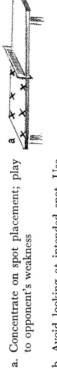

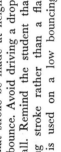

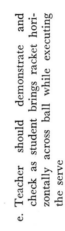

Difficulty	Correction
b. Hitting ball off end of table	b. Remind the student the ball is hit at the height of the bounce, not as it rises. Experiment by cutting down on upward follow-through and flatten the swing arc
c. Ineffective speed and power	c. Insist that follow-through is practiced. Review body motion and weight shift
d. Lack of control of backhand drive	d. Insist on concentrated practice, stressing body position and follow-through
7. Chop Strokes	**7.**
a. Hitting ball into net	a. Remind student to chop only high bouncing balls, and of the danger in returning chop strokes with a chop

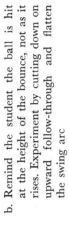

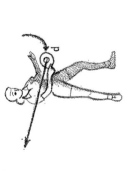

245

SKILL DIFFICULTIES AND THEIR CORRECTION (*Continued*)

Difficulty	*Correction*

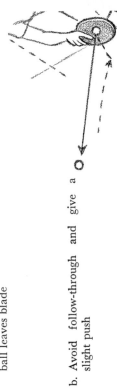

b. Ineffective placement of a high bouncing ball

    b. Insist upon follow-through in a downward motion

8. *Drop Shot*

a. Failure to disguise

8.

    a. Practice the drive, then concentrate on stopping racket movement before meeting the ball for a deceptive stroke

b. Loses deceptive effectiveness

    b. Avoid overuse. Play 11 point games in which the shot may be used only twice

c. High, ineffective return

    c. Explain that momentum of the ball hitting racket, rather than forceful racket contact, makes an effective return

9. *Half Volley*

a. Hitting into net

9.

    a. Open racket face for more rise as ball leaves blade

b. Driving ball out of court

    b. Avoid follow-through and give a slight push

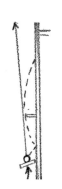

Difficulty	Correction

10. Smash

a. Smashing into net

b. Hitting off end of table

10.

a. Smash only those returns which bounce well above net level

b. Have student concentrate on relaxing the wrist and avoiding rushing a shot

247

NOVELTY EVENTS

The following novelty events increase student interest and offer pleasurable recreation.

Spin Around.   Played as a regular singles game except each player must make a complete turn, or spin, after each return before playing the next shot.

Two-Bat Doubles.   Played as a regular doubles game except doubles partners share a single racket. Players should return the ball, place racket on the table and move out of the playing area. The second partner picks up the racket, plays the ball and places the racket on the table as the first partner moves into play.

Weak Arm Doubles or Singles.   Played as a regular game of singles or doubles except all players must use their secondary hand to hold the racket, i.e., a right-handed person must use her left hand.

Elimination Table Tennis.   Played as singles by a group as large as 12. One half of the group stands on each side of the table. Play begins with a serve to opponent. After playing the ball, place the racket on the table and move to other end of the table. Players are eliminated when they make faulty returns. When only two competing players remain, they place racket on the table, spin around, and pick up racket between each returning stroke.

Team Table Tennis.   Played as a regular singles game with additional members on each side. Teams line up to the left side of their half court, player #1 serves, places the racket on the table and moves to the end of her team line. Teammate #2 picks up racket, returns ball, and goes to end of the line. Play continues until one team scores 21 points.

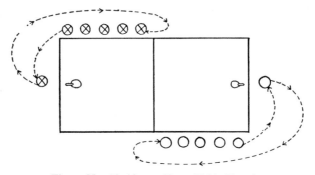

Figure No. 11–10.   Team Table Tennis.

OFFICIATING TECHNIQUES[2]

A thorough understanding of the official rules as published by the United States Table Tennis Association is necessary for every player and official.

[2] For thorough review see Mitchell, Elmer D., Editor: *Sports Officiating,* New York, A. S. Barnes, 1949.

Most players are their own officials; however, a table tennis tournament requires a chief referee, table umpires, and linesmen.

The chief referee is responsible for the total preparation and conduct of the tournament. Her duties include selecting officials, checking equipment and facilities, organizing schedules, and serving as arbitrator.

A table umpire conducts all play at her table. Her organizational duties include securing, adjusting and replacing equipment, and acting as judge in all table disputes. She is directly responsible for calling all points, faults, lets, and declaring the winner.

Linesmen are used primarily in semi-final and final matches. In the role of assistant to the table umpire, they check table and net specifications prior to each match. The two side linesmen call faults and hits on either side of the table, and the two end linesmen call faults in service, and rule on ball touches at the table ends.

EVALUATING THE RESULTS

Evaluation is a motivating factor for increasing interest, knowledge, and skill. The following tools are recommended for evaluation:

1. Written examination for understanding rules, strategy, safety, and history.
2. Tournament results (round robin, ladder, and double elimination in singles and doubles games). In the final analysis, the student's ability to win is a criterion of good skill development.
3. Subjective observation of student's form, strategy, and progress.
4. Skills tests including:
   a. Serve for accuracy. Mark a table area, assigning values to each area as pictured below. Score the player on five attempts on both forehand and backhand service.

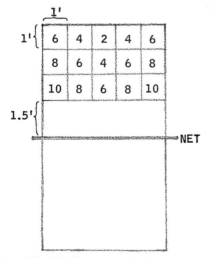

Figure No. 11–11. Serving for Accuracy.

b. Stroke demonstration and placement. Each student executes drive, chop, half volley, and smash at a table target area. Score from 0 to 10 for effectiveness and placement.

TERMINOLOGY

Angle Shot—Travels diagonally across the table from one half court to the other. Shot that legally strikes side of table

Backhand—Stroke played across the body, on the side opposite the racket hand

Backspin—Spinning motion of ball caused by hitting forward and downward, resulting in flight rotation toward the hitter, and high bounce

Blade—Racket's striking surface

Block—Meeting the ball with a firm, non-moving racket, so the ball rebounds across the net

Chop—Forward and downward stroking motion across the back of the ball, resulting in backspin

Drive—Forward and upward stroking motion of the ball, resulting in a fast return with topspin

Drop Shot—A faked drive resulting in little racket momentum, placing the ball low and close to the net

Flick—A modified drive using wrist and forearm action

Follow-through—Path of arm, hand, and body in last phase of stroke

Forehand—Stroke played on same side of the body as the racket hand

Gossima—Former name for table tennis

Half Volley—Playing the ball immediately after it bounces as it begins to rise

Let—"Call" for rule infractions requiring replay of the point. A served ball which hits the net before touching opponent's court

Neutral Position—A central position where player stands awaiting next return

Overspin—Same as topspin

Paddle—Name applied to racket

Placement—Intentional direction of a ball

Ping-Pong—Another name for table tennis devised from the sound of the game

Push—A soft hit placing the ball close to the net in opponent's court

Serve—Method of putting ball in play

Sidespin—A twisting motion of ball caused by stroking ball from left to right or right to left

Smash—A fast, hard return of a high bouncing ball

Topspin—Spinning motion of ball caused by hitting forward and upward, resulting in rotation in flight away from the hitter and a low bounce

Underspin—Same as backspin

DISCUSSION QUESTIONS

1. Explain and demonstrate the steps you would follow in teaching a beginner to play table tennis.
2. Explain and demonstrate the use of:
   a. Forehand drive; b. Backhand chop; c. Half volley; d. Smash.
3. Explain strategy and tactics of a doubles game.
4. What spins can be applied to a ball?
   a. Name each. b. How do you effect each spin? c. What is its effect on bounce?
5. Draw up a 15 lesson instructional unit for a class of 50 students. Show how you would objectively measure skill mastery in this sport.
6. Explain procedure and draw up plans for a double elimination tournament for 65 participants of varying skills and abilities.

Selected Audio-Visual Aids

Table Tennis. (10 min., 16 mm., sound) United World Films, R.C.A. Building, Rockefeller Center, New York 20, N.Y. (Rental)

Table Tennis. (12 min., 16 mm., sound) Teaching Films Custodians, Inc., 25 West 43rd Street, New York 18, N.Y. (Rental)

Table Tennis Techniques. (11 min., 16 mm., sound, color) Kenneth R. Davidson, c/o General Sportlight Company, 215 Fourth Avenue, New York 3, N.Y. (Loan)

Suggested Readings

A.A.H.P.E.R. *Recreation Games and Volleyball Guide,* Latest edition, Division for Girls and Women's Sports, 1201 16th Street, N.W., Washington 6, D.C.

Cartland, Douglas: *Table Tennis Illustrated,* New York, A. S. Barnes, 1953.

Clark, Coleman: *Table Tennis,* New York, Prentice-Hall Book Company, Inc., 1938.

DeWitt, R. T.: *Teaching Individual and Dual Sports,* New York, Prentice-Hall Book Company, Inc., 1953.

Gottlieb, William P.: *Table Tennis,* New York, Alfred A. Knopf, 1954.

Purves, Jay: *Table Tennis,* New York, A. S. Barnes, 1942.

Schiff, Sol: *Table Tennis Comes of Age,* New York, Henry Holt and Company, 1939.

United States Table Tennis Association: *Table Tennis for You,* U.S.T.T.A., 22 W. Monroe Street, Chicago, Ill., 1946.

12

Tennis

Although the French are often credited with originating tennis, actually it evolved from a game played by the ancient Greeks and Romans which is similar to modern handball. The English popularized an Irish version of the sport, and played it on a court bounded at the sides by two parallel nets staked down at the center, so that each was shaped like an hourglass. At first a hard leather, hair-stuffed ball was batted between partners back and forth across a rope by their bare hands; several years later by a gloved fist, then with a glove protected by leather thongs wrapped around it. Later, a parchment tambourine was used to swat a linen ball, then a crude short-handled paddle was devised, and finally a racket and ball simliar to those of today were used. It is believed that the word "tennis" is from the French "tenez" meaning "to play" or "to take."

Early scoring was complicated with fifteen "chases" given for one point from which arose the 15, 30, 40 game method of scoring. "Love," or nothing, which is symbolized by a zero or egg-shaped O, is from the French word "l'oeuf" for egg, pronounced by the English as "love."

King Louis X of France is responsible for tennis being called "The Sport of Kings." He jealously guarded the game for members of his court and banned the game for the masses when he found them playing it. In spite of the ban, the game became an activity for the "masses as well as the classes"

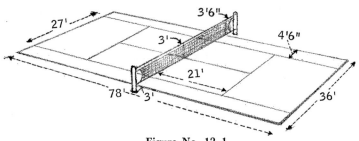

Figure No. 12–1.

252

and spread rapidly into England. It was during this period that a mesh net replaced the rope and the crude racket, the tambourine.

The popularity of tennis swept out from England into the world. Major Walter C. Wingfield, a British army officer, did much to give the game impetus at home and in the colonies. Mary Outerbridge, an American visitor in Bermuda, was intrigued with the sport and returned to the United States in 1874 well supplied with rackets and balls. Although delayed several hours by customs officers while they debated whether or not to permit her to bring such strange gadgets into the country, she not only succeeded in doing so, but with her brother successfully introduced the game to Americans. Largely due to their efforts and following among enthusiastic fans, the official governing body of this sport, The United States Lawn Tennis Association, was founded in 1881. By 1900 the Davis Cup Matches for international competition among men were established, followed shortly afterwards by the Wightman Cup Matches for women in the United States and England.

THE NATURE AND PURPOSE OF THE GAME

Tennis is a game played with racket and ball on an indoor or outdoor court by two or four players. In both singles and doubles play the object of the game is to score points while preventing opponents from scoring. Points are scored by effective service and ball placement which cause opponents to miss the ball, drive it into the net, or out of the court area. The skill of the game lies in mastering serving techniques, offensive and defensive strokes and footwork, and game strategy. In competition a player strives to win points, games, sets, and ultimately a match.

The singles game is played on a 27 by 78 foot court. The area is divided by a net strung tautly across the court and parallel to the base lines. The top of the net is three feet six inches at each net post, tapering to three feet in the center of the court. Each half of the court is divided into a back and fore court. The forecourt is further divided into the right and left serving or receiving areas. The doubles court is 4½ feet wider on each side. In a doubles game the additional "alley" area becomes valid playing space only *after* the service.

Play begins as the server delivers from behind the baseline and to the right of the center of the court. Serving from the right, she serves to her opponent's right court. Play between opponents continues until the winner of the point is determined. The server then moves to the left of center and behind the baseline to serve and begin play for the second point. Serving positions are alternated until the game winner is determined.

SCORING

The point progress of a game is 15, 30, 40 and game. When the score is tied 40–40 the score is called deuce and the tie must be broken and game won by winning two consecutive points. If the server wins the first point after deuce it is called *advantage in,* short for advantage in favor of the server. If the receiver wins the first point it is called *advantage out.* Players speak of it as "ad out" and "ad there." When a player has no score, it is referred to as "love." The server's score is called first during a game, whether officiated by tournament officials or by the players themselves. For example, the server's score would be love–30 if she has lost the first two game points, or 40–30 if she gains the next three. Singles and doubles are scored in the same way.

A set is won by the player or team who first wins six games, providing they have at least a two game lead over the opponents. A set can be won at 6–0, 6–1, 6–2, 6–3, and 6–4. It cannot be won at 6–5 but may terminate at 7–5 or in the case of a hard won battle may go as many as 15–13 games or more. A *match* is made up of the winner of two out of three sets for women and for mixed doubles. Men's competition requires the best three out of five sets. Players should change courts at the end of odd numbered games, i.e., after the first, third, fifth, etc., so that each side will compete under the same sun, wind, court, and spectator conditions.

Additional simplified information to be given students regarding scoring includes:

1. Each server serves a complete game
2. The first serve of each game must be from the right half of the court behind the baseline; the second points served from the left, and so on until the game is completed
3. Each player is allowed two tries to serve the ball correctly into her receiver's court, but she will not use the second ball if her first serve is good
4. Only on the serve must the ball be allowed to bounce before it can be returned
5. A point is lost by each person who misses the ball, or hits it out of bounds or into the net
6. Balls falling on boundary lines are scored as good ("liners are good")
7. In doubles play, either player may serve the first game. The order of service must be consistent throughout the set, but may change at the beginning of a new set
8. In doubles play either player may receive the first service in the first game. Thereafter, throughout the set, the partner receiving the first service in the first game will receive the first service in every odd numbered game

NEEDED FACILITIES AND EQUIPMENT

The *court* used out of doors has a surface of grass, clay, concrete, crushed stone, asphalt or other composition materials. Indoors play is on a wooden floor or on canvas covering. Markings on concrete and asphalt courts should be painted in white or bright yellow. Dry or wet lime is usually used to mark grass or clay courts, although cotton and plastic tapes stapled securely in the ground are favored in some sections of the country, especially for camp use.

The *net* may be made of steel or other metal, and of hemp or cotton cord twine. Although tarred nets are more expensive, they are almost a must for outdoor use and should be strung on a weather-resistant cable. The official net height is 3 feet 6 inches at the net posts and three feet at the court center. The net is held down at the center by a strap not more than two inches wide. The band covering the cord or metal cable should not be more than 2½ inches in depth at each side. The net for singles should be 33 feet long, for doubles 42 feet, and touch the ground along its entire length and come flush to the net posts at all points.

The recommended *costume* for this sport is an all white tennis dress, sneakers, a white or colored blazer, and white wool socks. White shorts and blouse are acceptable on most courts.

Other necessary personal equipment includes balls and a racket with a well fitting cover and press. The racket frames are made of wood, steel, aluminum, plastic or fiberglass, and strung with steel, aluminum, plastic, silk, nylon or gut. A maximum of 18 main strings crossed by 20 evenly spaced, lateral strings are standard and meet the specifications of the United States Lawn Tennis Association. Quality rackets have handles made of basswood or Malacca, covered with fine leather, whereas cheaper ones have "leather" grips made of rubber, plastic or imitation leather. The racket should weigh between 13 to 13½ ounces with a grip of 4½ to 4⅝ inches for women, and weigh between 11 to 13 ounces with a grip of 4 to 4½ inches for those between 9 and 12 years. Above all, the racket should not seem too heavy when swung vigorously back and forth for several minutes, and the grip should be small enough so that the hand fits comfortably around the handle.

Good balls are a must for all players, regardless of skill. Balls are manufactured under specifications of the United States Lawn Tennis Association, which requires that balls have a uniform outer surface, be more than two and a half inches and less than two and five-eights inches in diameter, and weigh more than two ounces but less than two and one-sixteenth ounces. Those meeting such specifications are packed and sealed in air-tight containers bearing the approval of USLTA. "Seconds" are not always marked, although some companies indicate that they are slightly defective by stamping out the letters USLTA. These cheaper balls are usually available at sporting goods shops upon request and are suggested for the use of beginners if one has a limited budget.

Instructors with more than adequate funds might well purchase an electric ball boy which "feeds" balls at various heights and angles across the net to players. This device can reduce teaching time by speeding stroke skill mastery. A hand robot machine is less expensive but not as satisfactory.

Driver, along with many other noted tennis instructors, believes that a backboard is best opponent a player can have because it usually returns the ball.[1] The best backboards are made of heavy beaverboard or pressboard in regulation half tennis court size, painted green with a white line three and one-half feet above the ground. They should be located at one end of each court. A line 39 feet from the backboard and parallel to it should be painted on the area to indicate a court baseline. Additional lines, 12 and 25 feet away, enable students to station themselves quickly for short and long rallying distances.

CARE AND REPAIR OF EQUIPMENT

Balls
1. Brush dirt from balls before putting them back into the can
2. Dry balls thoroughly before using them again
3. Store at normal room temperature, avoid extremes of heat or cold

Net
1. Take twine nets indoors nightly and fold, rather than roll, them
2. Repair broken threads, using the fisherman's knot
3. Slacken rope cables when nets are not in use
4. Dip cord nets in creosote before storing
5. Clean the steel cable with an oily rag, remove rust with emery cloth or heavy steel wool dipped in kerosene
6. Wipe metal nets with an oily rag at least once a month
7. Replace canvas bindings with ones purchased either from sporting goods suppliers or direct from the manufacturer

Rackets
Wood
1. Wipe the racket off with a dry cloth before putting it in a waterproof cover
2. Put it squarely in a press and tighten the four screws evenly
3. Alternate methods of hanging the racket in a storage room of even temperature, not to exceed 75° or 60 per cent humidity
4. Apply a thin coat of shellac over the strings at the end of the season, and a thin coat of wax over the entire frame
5. Have broken strings repaired at a local sporting goods shop or by the manufacturer

Metal
1. Occasionally wipe off the racket with a good cleanser which has a wax base to prevent rusting
2. Although broken shafts and heads can be welded in local machine shops inexpensively, this can often be done better by the manufacturer

[1] Driver, Helen: *Tennis For Teachers*, Enlarged Edition, Printed and distributed by the author, 803 Moygara Road, Frost Woods, Madison 4, Wisconsin.

Fiberglass and Plastic
1. Wipe off carefully before storing
2. A press or cover is not necessary for these rackets
3. Return to the manufacturer for restringing or other repairs

TEACHING UNITS

Unit for Beginners	*Unit for Advanced Students*
Brief discussion of history and game purpose	Review of entire unit for beginners
Selection and care of equipment	Advanced skills
Fundamentals	Smash
Grip	Lob
Footwork	Chop
Forehand	Advanced strategy for singles and doubles
Backhand	Individual skill development
Serve	Elimination and ladder tournament
Volley	Evaluation
Rules and scoring	
Strategy for singles and doubles	
Round robin tournament	
Evaluation	

Rainy Day Materials

Films and filmstrips
Chalk talks on game strategy for singles and doubles
Care and repair of equipment
Discussion and illustrated talk on tennis champions

BASIC SKILLS

Footwork. The ability to get around the court quickly, moving forward or back, to either side, as well as to shift body weight and position, is the prerequisite to successful play. The knees should be kept relaxed and slightly bent with body weight carried forward. Players should be taught to shift their weight to the forward foot (usually the one opposite the hand holding the racket) and to *move into* each stroke with full power, as well as to move quickly around the court in order to play the ball in *front of the body*.

Jump rope drills are ideal for teaching students to push off from the balls of the feet as they start each movement, as well as for general warm up purposes. Suggested patterns include:

Figure No. 12–2.   The Grip.

1. Skip in place 25 times on both feet, 10 hopping from the left foot, 10 from the right.
2. Skip forward 10 times, 10 backward, 10 to the left, 10 to the right.
3. Skip on both feet in place facing forward, turn to the left and hop twice, return to place, hop twice turned to the right, return to place.
4. Move forward with fast running steps, skip backward, round in a circle, to both sides, changing directions suddenly upon command.
5. Repeat all four patterns mimetically swinging a racket, then with an actual racket.

The Grip.   Three standard grips are the Eastern, Western, and a modification of the two, or the Continental. Although there are certain values found in all three, the one most commonly and most successfully used is the Eastern, for it permits easy, free ball stroking.

The Eastern Grip.   Shake hands with a racket held perpendicular to the ground, holding the first two fingers directly behind and well around the handle, with the heel of the hand at the end and the index finger spread slightly apart, thumb extended.

The Serve.   A correct serve results from a combination of the correct stance, ball toss, proper swing, and footwork. In movement it is similar to the overhand baseball throw. The student stands sideways to the baseline with feet spread comfortably apart and weight equally distributed, with the forward shoulder pointed in the direction the ball is to go. The racket is held in the Continental grip (similar to the Eastern backhand with the racket shifted from one-sixteenth to one-eighth of a turn toward the forehand grip). Since the higher the ball is tossed when contacted the greater chance it has of being a good serve, it should be thrown straight up into the air as high as the fully extended arm and racket can reach above the head over the forward foot, and contacted at its maximum height when

Figure No. 12–3. The Serve.

practically motionless and just before it comes back down toward the ground. As the ball is tossed into the air, the weight shifts to the rear foot. When the ball starts down, the racket is swung back behind the head and the whole body weight shifts to the forward foot as the ball is contacted above the serving shoulder. On the natural follow-through the racket is brought down and across the body. The amount of spin put into the contacted ball is determined by the angle of the racket, and is largely a matter of individual experimentation and discovery. Although this spin-type serve is often both difficult to learn and teach, it has so many advantages to the player who masters it, that it is especially recommended to be taught to those students who are highly coordinated.

The straight, or flat, serve, in which the same footwork, ball toss, and arm motion patterns are used as in the foregoing spin, or slice, serve, is best for those beginners who have below or average coordination. In this serve, the Western grip, (that is, holding the racket as though it were a hammer and being used to drive a nail into a board above one's head in front of the

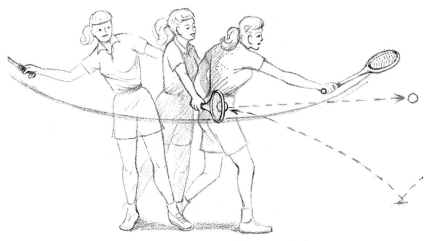

Figure No. 12–4.   The Forehand Drive.

body) is suggested. To get this grip place the racket flat on the ground, reach and pick it up without changing hand or racket position.

The Forehand Drive.   Used most often in game play, this stroke is usually the most easily mastered. Stand sideways to the net, feet in a forward-back position, hold the racket in the shaking hands grip, and hit the ball with a fully extended arm and racket, holding the elbow well out and away from the body. Shift the entire body weight forward as the ball is contacted.

The wrist should be kept firm and one should *move into the stroke,* hitting the ball in the center or "sweet part" of the racket so that it travels swiftly in a straight line and barely clears the net. The follow-through should also be in a straight line pattern, and will be if the ball is contacted at an imaginary 9 o'clock position and the racket swept on through to 3 o'clock without the racket head dropping lower than the wrist.

The Backhand Drive.   Although similar to the forehand stroke, the backhand drive is often more difficult for right-handed players to master, whereas many left-handed ones will develop a backhand superior to their forehand. Hold the racket in the Eastern grip modified by slightly moving it one quarter turn forward, and hold the thumb behind the handle for additional support. Stand facing sidewards, feet in a forward and back stride, knees relaxed, and bend forward at the waist so that the racket arm can swing freely back and then across the body at waist height. Hold the racket head perpendicular to the ground, contact the ball, shift body weight forward, and follow-through in a straight line pattern.

Students who have great difficulty learning the forehand and backhand strokes can often be helped by the use of a portable stroke developer, a device in which a ball is suspended from an iron pipe.[2] Any ingenious in-

[2] Williamson, Jane: Improved Tennis Aids, *Official Tennis-Badminton Guide.* DGWS, 1952–1954.

structor can improvise a similar gadget using adhesive tape, a fishing pole, and a wire hook.[3] Similar equipment is excellent for assisting those having problems hitting the ball, or getting the feel of a full, powerful but relaxed swing.

The Volley.   Used primarily at the net and in the forecourt, a volleyed ball is hit either forehand or backhand before it bounces. The best grip is that used for the serve (the Continental) with the hand holding the racket moved up about three inches from the end in a shortened grip. The stroke is a short, sharp, chopping motion which causes the ball to spin. The ball should be well above the top of the net when volleyed, and the stroke used as an aggressive, sudden attack. The footwork and stroking fundamentals are the same as for the forehand and backhand, but the swing is shorter and the ball rebounds off the racket face more than it is stroked. The half volley, in which the ball is "picked up" just as it bounces, is hit like the regular volley and is used to return a ball when in a tight spot at an unfavorable court position.

The Smash.   Similar to the serve, this stroke can be a forceful attacking shot of great speed. It is done using the same grip, footwork, and timing as the serve and is most effective when used on a high, weak return at the net or in midcourt. The player watches and waits relaxed, until the ball drops toward the court. Contact is powerful with a firm follow-through.

The Lob.   The purpose of the lob is to move the opponent around

Figure No. 12–5.   The Backhand Drive.

[3] Browne, Mary K.: *Streamline Tennis,* New York, American Sports Publishing Company, 1940.

Figure No. 12–6.   The Volley.

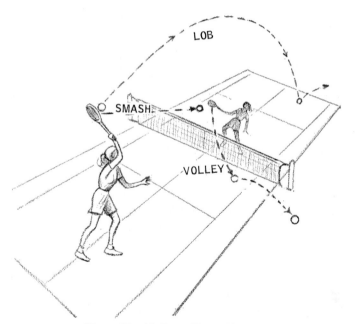

Figure No. 12–7.   Types of Strokes.

the court or send the ball over her head. It is a defensive time-gainer and should be placed strategically on the court. Played either on the forehand or backhand side, it is done by shortening and slowing down the back swing and lifting the ball with a forward upswing and follow-through as the racket, with the face tilted back, contacts the ball. This often effective, but delicate, stroke can send an aimed high and flatly hit ball into an unguarded area, and thus often becomes a sure point winner.

GAME STRATEGY

The attacking style is usually played at the net with the defensive players moving back to baseline positions. Although most players "beat themselves" through their own errors, this may be avoided by carefully analyzing all mistakes made and not repeating them. Consistent, steady play is more fruitful than taking unwise chances, or trying to "kill" as many shots as possible. Beginners especially should be trained (1) to hit the ball *away* from their opponents and, (2) to *anticipate* where the returned ball will land on the court and *be ready* to receive it, and (3) to *outsmart their opponents* by placing returned shots to their weakness (this may be one of the doubles partners, the backhand of one, or the inability of both to move quickly around the court). Other aspects of general strategy include:

1. Return to home base or the center line at midcourt position after each stroke
2. Conserve strength by letting impossible shots go past and going after those you can get
3. Take your time and get into proper position before hitting the ball and *play it in front of your forward foot*
4. It is not how *hard* you hit the ball, but *where* you hit it
5. Always win your own serve and vary its speed and placement
6. A deep cross court shot is usually much more effective than a baseline drive
7. Disguise your intended return as long as possible

DOUBLES STRATEGY

Teamwork is necessary for success in doubles. Although advanced players prefer to play side by side, beginners should be taught the up and back method, the side by side, and a fast shift to either one. Since the most advantageous court spot is at the net, this position should be gained and held as long as possible. Other suggestions include:

1. Keep the ball in the opponents' backcourt as much as possible
2. Make the opponents hit the ball up to you on their returns by placing it at their feet
3. Play the ball so that it lands halfway along the baseline until an open spot appears, then shoot quickly for this hole
4. The server should come to the net after most serves if both partners are especially good net players
5. Smash, volley, and lob as often as possible and keep the ball back into the far court
6. Keep your opponent guessing and on the move

Key phrases to use to teach strategy are (a) play through *your strength* to your opponent's *weaknesses,* (b) anticipate, (c) keep your opponent moving, (d) change the pace, and (e) always change a losing game.

Ball Spins

ANALYTICAL CHART OF SPINS

Kind of Spin	How to Impart to Ball	Action of Ball on Bounce	How to Play
1. Topspin	Stroke forward and upward	Ball rotates away from striker in flight; as ball hits court it will dive down	1. Impart the opposite spin which is underspin 2. Half-volley
2. Underspin	Stroke forward and downward	Ball rotates toward striker in flight; as it hits court it will "bite" and bounce higher than normal	1. Impart the opposite spin which is topspin 2. Drop shot 3. Half volley
3. Sidespin to left	Stroke across ball from right to left	Ball rotates about its oblique axis from right to left in flight; as ball hits court it will hop right on opponent's court	Aim ball to side of court—the side from which opponent's racket started in its stroking
4. Sidespin to right	Stroke across ball from left to right	Ball rotates as above, only left to right—hops left on opponent's court	Same as above, only aim left of opponent

CLASS ORGANIZATION

Although every teaching situation differs in time length, class size, available facilities, and other factors, there are certain essentials to keep in mind when teaching the tennis unit. These are to:

1. Follow a clearly given demonstration (explained as briefly as possible) with student activity as soon as possible. Explain by using key phrases and terms and remember that students learn largely by *doing*, not watching or listening.
2. Give enough time for students to experiment and explore stroke movements until they get the "feel" of what they are doing and *why* they are doing it.
3. Use a variety of teaching methods, remembering that some people are more quickly motivated by their own movement experimentation, while others may be motivated by watching a demonstration of a skillfully played game.

4. Group the students homogeneously but change the grouping frequently enough so that those showing the greatest improvement are reclassified. The Dyer Tennis Test may be used for an initial grouping, for it is simply administered, does not take up much precious class time, and is quickly scored. (See p. 283 for the directions for giving this test.)

Careful planning coupled with good teaching is necessary if each class is to be an educational experience wherein all students will gain in skill mastery or learn many new things during that period. Driver and Hillas and LeFevre have splendid and specific suggestions for organizing classes for each tennis lesson. (See the suggested reading list at the end of the chapter for a complete bibliography of these books.) Although their methods must be tailored to fit each instructor's unique situation, they will serve as an excellent pattern. Regardless of which of the many techniques given below for grouping students are used, class members should develop their own rotation system so that all receive the same amount of time in each assigned role, such as a ball tosser, hitter, coach, or retriever, as shown in the following illustration.

Suggested formations for teaching the forehand and backhand drives are:

1. The teacher should face the class which is in a single or staggered line so that all can see and hear well. Explain briefly how the strokes are done, demonstrate them, and have the class repeat them mimetically, without a ball or racket, copying her movements as she, with back turned to the group, performs each stroke. Repeat, using the racket.
2. Have one group of four demonstrate stroking backhand and forehand shots while the rest watch.
3. Have the class work in partners hitting the ball back and forth.

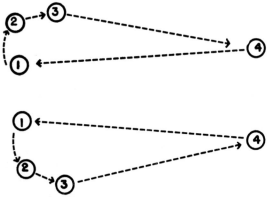

Figure No. 12–8.   1 strokes the ball; 2 drops the ball so that it bounces waist high for 1, 3 analyzes the form and makes suggestions for improvement, and 4 retrieves the ball. (From Vannier and Fait: Teaching Physical Education in Secondary Schools.)

4. Have partners count one each time the ball is hit successfully across the net by a player and count two as it is returned, etc. Have each couple begin again if the ball is missed. Play until one group reaches 10 points first, then 15, then 25.
5. Have groups of four work in assigned roles as shown in figure 12–9. Have the one who is coach award one point each on a checksheet to the hitter when she uses the correct grip, stance, footwork, backswing, and follow-through of the forehand and backhand.
6. After players have learned placement fairly well, award one point for each time they succeed in making the opponent move around the court in order to get the ball, and one point for the hitter who succeeds in returning each well placed ball.
7. Award three points for a ball correctly returned cross court, two points for one in the back court, and one point for a ball correctly returned at midcourt.

Suggested group formations for teaching the serve are:

1. Teacher demonstration and brief explanation followed first by mimetic movements done to counts, and then by using the ball and racket.
2. Use the following diagram. A serves to B who then serves to A, C to D, followed by D to C. (Additional students can be assigned to coach each server, then to become the server and her partner, her coach.)

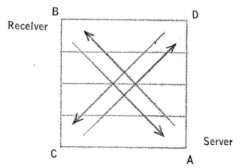

Figure No. 12–9.   Suggested Group Formation for Teaching the Serve.

Suggested group formations for teaching the smash and lob are:

1. Have students work in couples. A throws the ball to B first near the net, and then at midcourt for the smash. Partners change roles.
2. Repeat formation for practicing the lob. A throws to B for a midcourt, then backcourt lob, first on forehand side, then backhand. Partners change roles.
3. Have students lob back and forth to each other using their rackets each time instead of throwing the ball.

Suggested group formations for teaching the volley are:

1. Have students in couples with two, four, or six on a court. Those at baseline drive to their partners who volley ball back. Partners change roles.

2. Arrange six players as illustrated below. F drives the ball to A, B, or C who volleys back to anyone on the baseline. Play continues until all are eliminated for missing the ball or using the wrong stroke. Players change roles.

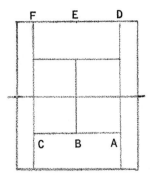

Figure No. 12–10.   Suggested Group Formation for Teaching the Volley.

Suggested group formations for working at a backboard include:

1. Have players stand 20 feet from the board,* feet together and strike the ball from a bounce, hitting each rebounded ball by stepping into the shot, using either forehand or backhand stroke.

2. Place two, four, or six players in a file. The first in each line rallys against the board, then the second, and so forth. The one hitting the ball above the tennis net line the greatest number of consecutive hits for a given time period wins.

3. Have players work in partners. Two, four, six, or eight can be in each line. The first two, working together, keep the ball in play alternating shots, trying to do so longer than any other couple.

4. Same couple formation. First two in each line compete to see which one can out-rally the other. One point is scored for each person doing so, and all compete to win for their line or team.

5. Players working singly hit first one forehand stroke, then one backhand, two of each, three, four, etc.

6. Practice serves from behind a 39 foot line. Score one point for each correctly placed ball which lands in a target area above the net line and below the ten foot top line. Have each person serve 10 balls.

TEACHING PROGRESSION

Although some instructors favor starting a class unit with the volley, the majority of experts claim that most students will learn other strokes

---

* A line, the exact tennis net height, should be drawn on the board, a target area, and a ten foot line from the floor to show where the ball should not land. Players should always aim at the target, playing the ball between the two lines.

more readily after they have mastered the grip, footwork, timing, and rhythmic feel of the forehand. Regardless of how the class is started, throughout the unit each student should receive as much individual coaching from the teacher as possible, and be encouraged to develop her own style of playing, as long as it is done in good form. Little time should be spent in the initial lesson discussing the history of the sport or explaining how a stroke is done, game strategy, or rules. Rather, the group should begin practicing and experimenting with the basic movements of each stroke after they are demonstrated by the teacher. The forehand and backhand drives can be taught in a single lesson, especially to skilled students. The serve, usually more difficult to master, should be taught early in the unit, too, so that by the third lesson the group can start playing a game. Rules can be more easily learned as the class progresses and can be taught in conjunction with strokes, such as the rules relative to serving and the serve itself. Usually a rainy day is the best time to catch up on scoring rules, or game strategy, and these can best be taught through films or filmstrips, followed by a class discussion.

Since the use of backboard practice for at least 15 minutes at a time is far superior to working with a poorly skilled partner, each player should be assigned a backboard practice time, whether it be during the class or after school hours. Students should be encouraged to *think through their mistakes* and to analyze for themselves when they fail to hit the ball correctly, or send it out of bounds. The teacher, through the repetition of key words such as "stroke the ball," or "hit in the *sweet part* of your racket," can help each person grasp the meaning of these phrases more quickly. Since many girls need to develop back and shoulder girdle strength, a certain portion of each class period should be spent doing specific exercises which will do this. Emphasis should be placed in each lesson upon mastering good form and the rhythmic movement of the body, for accurate ball placement and speed are dependent upon these two factors.

Since the whole-part-whole method of teaching is most productive in helping students learn quickly, early in the unit the class should watch a demonstration game of both singles and doubles played by experts. Likewise, when teaching each stroke, the teacher should demonstrate the correct way of doing it, followed by pupil experimentation before the class begins to work on each single aspect of the stroke, such as the proper ball toss in learning the serve, or the basic footwork of the forehand. Above all, each class member should have a pleasurable learning experience each period, and go away from the lesson with a feeling of having accomplished something of real value from her investment of time, energy, and much hard work. The instructor should stress positive actions such as "do this" instead of "don't do that." With encouragement, a motivated drive to learn to play tennis correctly and skillfully will spurt student effort until this desired goal is obtained.

A suggested unit consisting of ten lessons for beginners-intermediates follows. Skills at lob, volley, smash and chop may not be appropriate for all groups.

Lesson I

1. Warm up exercises
2. Brief discussion of the history and basic idea of a tennis game
3. The three grips (Eastern, Western, Continental)
4. Ball bounce up from the "sweet part" of the racket for 50 times without moving the feet; down for the same number of times
5. Basic footwork patterns
6. The forehand stroke
7. The backhand stroke
8. Backboard practice

Lesson II

1. Warm up exercises
2. Review of previous lesson
3. Brief illustrated chalk talk on ball spins
4. Supervised backboard and court practice of forehand and backhand strokes
5. Watch a singles and doubles game demonstration and explain simplified game rules for singles and doubles as students watch the game

Lesson III

1. Warm up exercises
2. Review of previous lessons
3. The serve
4. Supervised backboard and court practice of the serve
5. Play the best two out of three games of doubles

Lesson IV

1. Warm up exercises
2. Review of previous lessons
3. Supervised backboard and court practice of the serve, forehand, and backhand
4. Play the best three out of four games of singles

Lesson V

1. Warm up exercises
2. Review of scoring
3. Supervised backboard and court practice
4. Volleys at the net and midcourt

Lesson VI

1. Warm up exercises
2. Assign backboard practice for after class
3. Teach the lob (to those ready for new skills)
4. Practice the volley
5. Play the best two out of three doubles games

Lesson VII

1. Warm up exercises
2. Review the lob and volley (where appropriate)
3. Play any ball placement games (see suggested novelty games on page 280)

Lesson VIII

1. Warm up exercises
2. Review the serve, volley, forehand, and backhand strokes
3. Discuss briefly game strategy for singles
4. Start a round robin, one set tournament in singles and doubles (the rest of the games to be played during after school hours)
5. Teach the smash

Lesson IX

1. Warm up exercises
2. Discuss briefly game strategy for doubles
3. Play two out of three doubles games as teacher observes, giving individual coaching hints

Lesson X

1. Warm up exercises
2. Teach the chop (but only if the students have learned other strokes well)
3. Play singles or doubles
4. Review of entire unit

Rainy Day Plans

Discuss history more in detail
Show films and filmstrips
Discuss the purchase and care of equipment
Repair or learn how rackets are repaired
Learn about the tennis "greats"
Inside wall practice

SKILL DIFFICULTIES AND THEIR CORRECTION

Difficulty

Correction

1. *The Forehand and Backhand Drives*

1.

Grip

a. Forefinger extended

a. Remind student to curl all fingers around the racket

b. Too tight and tense a grip, or holding the racket too loosely

b. Say "relax" repeatedly to the student during the period

c. Racket face tilted back or forward too far

c. Demonstrate correct position; have student re-grasp the racket several times and check the face position with her then and later several times during the period

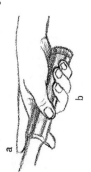

d. Awkward, incomplete swing; swinging the racket too close to the body

d. Instructor places her hand over student's hand and they do the stroke together until the latter gets the "feel" of the stroke

SKILL DIFFICULTIES AND THEIR CORRECTION (*Continued*)

Difficulty	Correction
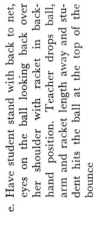  e. Body gets in the way for the back-hand stroke	 e. Have student stand with back to net, eyes on the ball looking back over her shoulder with racket in back-hand position. Teacher drops ball, arm and racket length away and student hits the ball at the top of the bounce

Footwork

f. Wrong foot forward	f. Demonstrate law of opposition in movement
 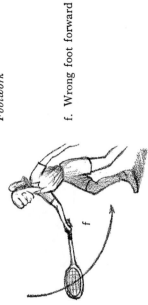	

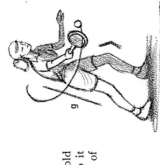

g. Weight shifted at wrong time

g. Demonstrate weight shift. Take hold of student's hand and have her do it with you until she gets the feel of the movement

The Swing

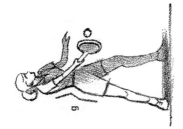

h. Unrhythmic movement, "punching at" the ball

h. Demonstrate a rhythmic stroke, have student copy it without, then with, a racket; stress a full swing each time the ball is hit

SKILL DIFFICULTIES AND THEIR CORRECTION (*Continued*)

Difficulty	*Correction*
i. Swinging racket up or down too far instead of in a straight line in a faulty follow-through; turning the racket face too far forward or back	i. Demonstrate the 9 o'clock past 3 o'clock stroke. Check and remind student to check position of the racket face
j. Wrist and racket head dropping during the stroke	j. Demonstrate correct form for stroking and have student copy the movement.
k. Incorrect wrist action	k. Keep wrist in a more locked, restricted movement
l. Improper timing	l. Start backswing sooner. Start forward swing before the ball bounces in front of the body

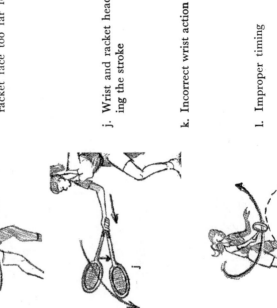

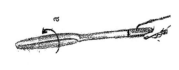

Difficulty *Correction*

Dropping the Ball

m. Too near body, or too close, or at side of body

m. Stress dropping the ball in front of forward foot and moving into the stroke. Practice ball drop repeatedly

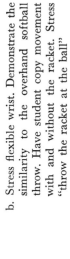

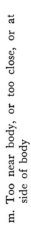

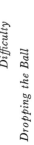

2. *The Serve*

2.

a. Incorrect grip

a. Check grip and have student do it correctly for you several times

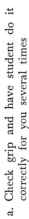

b. Incorrect wrist action

b. Stress flexible wrist. Demonstrate the similarity to the overhand softball throw. Have student copy movement with and without the racket. Stress "throw the racket at the ball"

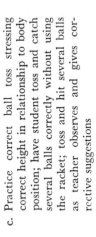

SKILL DIFFICULTIES AND THEIR CORRECTION (*Continued*)

Difficulty	*Correction*
c. Ball toss too far in front of, or behind; too far left or right; too low, or too high	c. Practice correct ball toss stressing correct height in relationship to body position; have student toss and catch several balls correctly without using the racket; toss and hit several balls as teacher observes and gives corrective suggestions
d. Hitting the ball with the wood of the racket; failure to connect ball with the racket	d. Re-stress hitting the ball on the "sweet part"; observe and correct timing of ball toss and swing
e. Incorrect backswing; serving too early or too late; too far back of head; too far right; too far left	e. Re-teach by demonstrating whole serve; work on individual part of the serve; reemphasize correct timing of swing to the ball toss

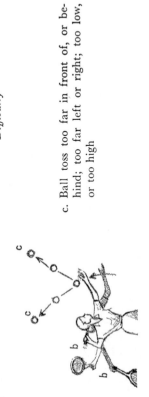

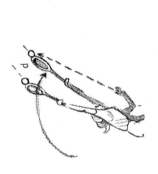

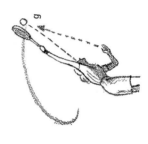

Difficulty	*Correction*
f. Hitting the ball into the net	f. Toss ball higher, hit it above the head instead of at eye level
g. Missing the ball entirely	g. Stress "watch the ball." Have student repeat ball bounce drills; work individually with the player against the backboard. Suggest devices suggested on page 268.

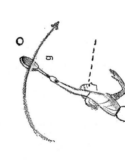

SKILL DIFFICULTIES AND THEIR CORRECTION (*Continued*)

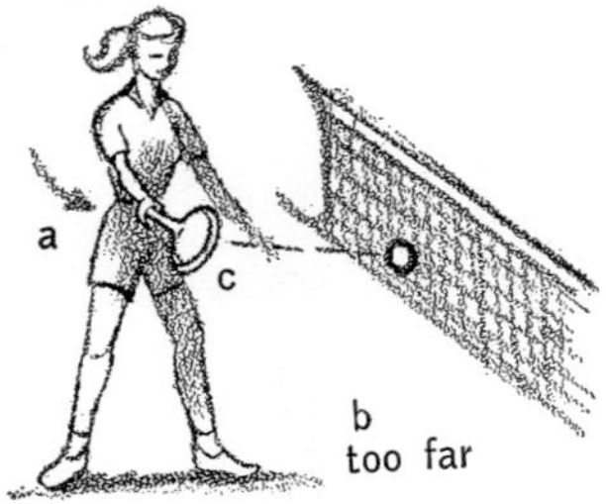

Difficulty	*Correction*

3.

3. *The Volley*

a. Player too tense

a. Stress a relaxed, easy body position with knees slightly bent

b. Standing too near or too far from the net

b. Show again the correct court area from which the volley can best be played

c. Dropping the head of the racket

c. Have student do the stroke in slow motion several times and point out each time this error is made. Be sure student knows what this mistake causes the ball to do

d. Wobbly wrist action

d. Stress tightening grip slightly before stroking the ball

e. Missing the ball entirely

e. Stress "watch the ball" until it becomes automatic to do so

Difficulty	Correction

4. *The Lob*

4.

a. Not hitting the ball high enough into the air; hitting it too much like a line drive

b. Inability to fool opponent whether a lob, forehand, or backhand drive is to be used

a. Demonstrate correct lob again; show what the opponent can do to an incorrectly played lob

b. Discuss and demonstrate the defensive and offensive lob; demonstrate and stress modifying the stroke at the last minute so as not to give the opponent enough time to be prepared for it

5. *The Smash*

5.

a. Missing the ball entirely, or failing to hit it squarely

b. Hitting the ball into the net

a. Stress relaxation and watching the ball at all times

b. Correct hitting the ball too low and too far out from the body

NOVELTY EVENTS

Tether Ball.   The game object is to hit the ball either with one's bare hand, paddle, or tennis racket so that it will wind around the pole. One player may hit it in one direction and her opponent in the other. Players alternate turns hitting the ball. Award one point for winding the ball around the pole. Play for 5 to 10 points. (Younger and beginning players.)

Bounce Ball.   This game is played on a doubles deck tennis area (40' × 18' with a 3' high net). One, two, three, or four players can be on each side. The server, who has only one try each serve, stands anywhere behind the rear line and hits the ball across the net from the bounce with one or both hands to any player. Hitting the ball into the net, out of bounds, or into any obstruction causes a "side out." Each team before serving rotates one position clockwise. Only the serving side scores. Play 15 points with winner two points ahead. (Beginners and intermediate players.)

Eight Player Tennis.   Played on a regulation tennis court using a ball and rackets. Four players per side are stationed with two at the net and two in the backcourt. Each player covers her own position with those in the backcourt returning the ball over the net players. The ball is rallied until a point is won and the game scored as in tennis. Teams alternate serves and players rotate positions after each game. (Intermediate players.)

Tenikoit.   Played on a court 17 feet by 40 feet with a five foot high net, and a rubber ring (often referred to as a deck tennis ring), this is an ideal game, but only for two or four players. One underhand serve is given each person and the game can be scored as tennis. The ring must always be thrown with only one hand. If caught by either hand, it must be thrown from that hand, and must travel parallel to the group. (Beginners and intermediate players.)

Squad Tennis.   Four players per side play on a regulation court with each group having only one racket. The first player hits the ball and gives

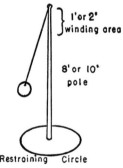

Figure No. 12-11.   Tether Ball. (From Vannier and Foster: Teaching Physical Education in Elementary Schools.)

the racket to another, etc. The game is scored and played as regular tennis. A variation of the same idea of one person using the racket, then the next, etc., can be played at the backboard, with one point given to each player who succeeds in causing her opponent to miss the ball. (Intermediate and advanced players.)

Placement Game. Two players try to outrally each other, using the entire court, scoring one point each time they can do so. Variations: (a) play only within the alley boundaries, (b) only in the backcourt, (c) only in the forecourt, (d) cross court each shot. (Intermediate and advanced players.)

Call Your Shot. Two or four players; score one point each time the person to whom the ball is hit does not return it using the shot she is told to use. Begin the game with either the serve or a courtesy stroke. (Advanced players.)

OFFICIATING TECHNIQUES

Although players usually call their own games except in final tournament play or official matches, game officials have specific duties they should perform at matches. These include:

The Duties of the Umpire

Before the Match

1. Have score card, pencils, and official rule book with you
2. Check the tennis net height and correct it if necessary
3. Check the umpire's chair so all spectators can best hear the decisions called

During the Match

1. Mark the score card before announcing the score after each point is made
2. Call the server's score first
3. Repeat the decisions of the linesmen
4. Have players change sides at each odd game in each set
5. Say "correction" then give the revised score, if it is necessary to do so
6. Give a rest period between each set
7. Announce the set score at the end of each game
8. Call game, set, and match point at the proper time
9. Announce the final winners and record the game results

The Duties of the Net Umpire

1. Sit close to the net post on the umpire's side of the court
2. Make a decision and tell it to the umpire on service "lets"
3. Keep each game score as a means of assisting the umpire

The Duties of the Linesman

1. Sit facing the line you are checking
2. Watch the line rather than the ball
3. Call only "outs" or "faults," never "good"

4. Announce to the umpire by holding both hands over your eyes if you were unable to see, so that she can make and call the needed decision

The Duties of the Ball Boy

1. Keep the server supplied with balls
2. Do not touch or move a ball until the umpire's decision has been given
3. Avoid getting in the player's way at all times

EVALUATING THE RESULTS

Experts are generally agreed that a player's skill can be evaluated by means of (a) a form rating scale, (b) tournament standing, (c) recording of rallying accuracy against a backboard, and (d) checking one's ability to place the ball accurately into certain court areas. But as Driver states:

> "Unfortunately there is no proof that a player's *form* rating, or her *rallying* ability, or her *placing* ability correlate satisfactorily with her playing ability. Moreover, when we look at the records of nationally ranked tennis stars, we find tournament results are not always reliable. A player, eliminated one week in a tournament by an inferior opponent, may win the next week over a player ranked far above herself.
>
> "Tennis tests, however invalid and unreliable, are worthwhile for two reasons: (1) they measure ability to rally, place the ball, use correct form, and show the amount of improvement the student has made, and (2) they are an incentive for practice, for they establish tangible goals."*

A Form Rating Scale.   Since the mastery of good form is imperative if one wishes to become a skilled tennis player, the instructor should use a form rating scale for each student at least twice during a unit, observing and rating her during game play as well as at practice against a backboard. Such a rating scale might well include the items shown on page 283.

Accuracy Test.   The Broer-Miller Tennis Test is recommended for discovering the strengths and weaknesses in both the forehand and backhand strokes, as well as placement ability. For this test a rope is stretched four feet above the net top and the court is marked off in areas for scoring as shown in Figure No. 12–12. In order to score the value shown, the ball must go between the rope and net top and land in the area or on a boundary line of that area. Those which go over and land into an area score only one-half of that valued area. A trial is counted if the ball is missed, but let balls may be taken over. Each player has 14 balls for forehand tries, and 14 for the backhand. A curved scale for rating all in the group can be made and

* Driver, Helen: *Tennis for Teachers,* Enlarged Edition, 803 Moygara Road, Frost Woods, Madison 4, Wisconsin.

TENNIS FORM RATING SCALE

Name_____ Class_____
Circle—Beginner   Intermediate   Advanced
Dates_____; _____

Rate 1—far above average; 2—average; 3—below average

Forehand	*Serve*	*Lob*
Grip	Grip..........—|—	Footwork.......—|—
Stance.........—|—	Ball Toss........—|—	Swing...........—|—
Swing.........—|—	Weight Shift.....—|—	Placement.......—|—
Follow-through.....—|—	Placement.......—|—	*Strategy*
Placement.......—|—		Placement.......—|—
	Volley	Anticipation......—|—
Backhand	Stance..........—|—	Wins own
Grip	Footwork........—|—	serve.........—|—
Stance.........—|—	Stroke..........—|—	Wins by place-
Swing.........—|—	Placement.......—|—	ment rather
Weight shift......—|—		than oppo-
Follow-through.....—|—		nent's errors....—|—
Placement.......—|—		Shows knowl-
		edge of
		game
		strategy.......—|—

the test, although time-consuming to give, does motivate players to work harder on both their strokes and placement skill.

Tournament Standing.   A ladder, round robin, or a double elimination tournament is suggested for obtaining a more accurate knowledge of a player's ability to compete. Although it is time-consuming to use any of these, games can be played outside of, as well as in, class time.

Rallying Against a Backboard.   The Dyer Tennis Test is recommended for this purpose. A line three inches wide and three feet from the

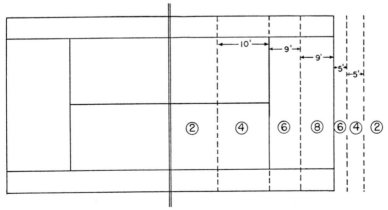

Figure No. 12–12.   Court Markings for the Broer-Miller Tennis Test. (From Mathews: Measurement in Physical Education.)

floor is drawn on a backboard or smooth wall area to represent a net. A restraining line is drawn five feet from the wall base. Each student, tested one at a time, has two balls in one hand, access to a box of extra balls placed nearby, and a racket. The object of the test is to hit the ball so it will strike above the wall net line as many times as possible in 32 seconds. The ball is put in play by a hit from a single bounce. All balls hit while the player is over the restraining line do not count. If control is lost over any ball, another one may be put in play. A point is counted for each ball correctly hit and the best score from three tries is recorded. Score tables for this test can be obtained from the March, 1938 *Research Quarterly*. The instructor can also devise her own curved scale for rating each group.

TERMINOLOGY

Ace—A skillfully placed serve which the receiver cannot return and usually cannot touch with her racket

Chop Stroke—A sharp hack-like stroke which causes the ball to backspin and bounce low

Drop Shot—A deceptive shot which barely clears the net

Fault—A served ball which goes out of bounds, or not into the proper service court

Foot Fault—Moving the feet, failure to keep contact with the ground, or stepping over the baseline while serving

Lob—Upward ball flight sending it far over the head of an opponent

Slice Stroke—Similar to the chop, this aggressive stroke is used to hit the ball downward and off to one side

Smash—Hitting the ball down at an opponent's feet with great force

Volley—Playing the ball before it bounces

DISCUSSION QUESTIONS

1. Devise a tennis unit of eight lessons each for (a) beginners, (b) intermediates, and (c) advanced players, giving the objectives, course content, and means of evaluating each one.
2. Plan the organization for a four hour tennis clinic for teachers along the lines suggested by Hillas and LeFevre in their book, *Tennis, A Manual for Teachers.* If possible, present the clinic to a group of teachers in your community. Evaluate what you have learned from this experience.
3. Observe a set of singles and doubles. Score one point each time each player uses good game strategy. Discuss your findings with them.
4. Read and summarize the chapter, "The Use of Rhythm in Tennis Coaching" from the book, *Tennis For Teachers* by Helen Driver. Try teaching the serve to a beginner using the rhythmic method suggested. Evaluate your findings from this experiment.
5. Demonstrate the correct footwork for the (a) serve, (b) forehand drive, (c) backhand drive, (d) volley, (e) lob.
6. Write a short, one page paper on any of the world's tennis greats, giving reasons why this person became a champion.

SELECTED AUDIO-VISUAL AIDS

Basic Tennis Strokes. (14 min., sound, b & w). Capitol Film Company, Box 791, East Lansing, Michigan. (Rental)

Beginning Tennis Series. (5 slide films). Athletic Institute, 209 S. State Street, Chicago 4, Illinois. (Purchase and Rental)

Don Budge Instructional Films. United States Lawn Tennis Association, 120 Broadway, New York, N.Y. (Rental—special reduced rate for educational institutions)

Tennis Tactics. (11 min., sound, b & w). Association Films. Branch Offices in Chicago, Dallas, San Francisco. (Rental)

Slow Motion Long Films for Tennis Instruction. United States Lawn Tennis Association, 120 Broadway, New York, N.Y. (Sale only—$12.00 complete)

SUGGESTED READINGS

Agutter, George: *Lessons in Tennis,* American Sports Publishing Company, 45 Rose Street, New York, N.Y., 1957.

Connolly, Maureen: *Power Tennis,* A. S. Barnes, New York, 1954.

Cummings, Parke: *American Tennis, The Story of the Game,* Little, Brown and Company, Boston, 1957.

Driver, Helen: *Tennis for Teachers,* Enlarged Edition, Helen Driver, 803 Moygara Road, Frost Woods, Madison 4, Wisconsin, 1956.

Hewitt, Jack: Comprehensive Tennis Knowledge Test, *Research Quarterly, Vol.* VIII, No. 3, October, 1934, p. 74.

Hillas, Marjorie, and LeFevre, John: *Tennis, A Manual for Teachers,* W. C. Brown Company, Dubuque, 1955.

Moss, T.: *Lawn Tennis for Teachers and Players,* New York, The Macmillan Company, 1949.

Murphy, William E.: *Tennis for Beginners,* The Ronald Press, New York, 1958.

Scanlon, Marion: A Tennis Stroke Developer, Journal of Health and Physical Education, 15:149, March 1, 1944.

Scott, Gladys: Achievement Examinations for Elementary and Intermediate Tennis Classes, *Research Quarterly,* Vol. XII, No. 1, March, 1941, p. 40.

Unit on Tennis; Six Pamphlets for the School Coach and Advanced Player, United States Lawn Tennis Association, 120 Broadway, New York, N. Y.

PERIODICALS

Sports Illustrated, 540 North Michigan Avenue, Chicago, Illinois.

World Tennis, Box 3, Gracie Station, New York, N Y.

13

Track and Field

Track and field includes activities as old as basic human movements. The competitive events of today undoubtedly grew from the first men who gained pleasure in running, leaping over streams and fallen trees, and throwing rocks and spears. These survival skills turned to sport as man became less dependent on them for existence.

During the Golden Age of Greece the pattern for modern track and field events developed. The Olympic Festival of 776 B.C. included broad jumping, discus and javelin throwing in much the same form as the Olympic Games of today. Many other peoples contributed and refined events. For example, the shot put and hammer throw originated with the Celts, while hurdling is attributed to the cross country fence hoppers of England. Pole vaulting, an exciting event for men, was a practical method of crossing moats and streams in feudal England and Germany.

Competitive track was not popular until brief enthusiasm for it grew in England in the middle of the nineteenth century. The real emphasis came with the revival of the modern Olympic Games in 1896. Since that time American men have been enthusiastic competitors and have dominated track and field events, whereas our women have neither responded as well nor have been as successful in this competitive event as the European and Asian women.

Interest in running, jumping, and throwing revives before each Olympic Game Year and then a relapse occurs for several years. The present concern for youth fitness and the potential of track and field in developing this fitness is stimulating interest and increased instruction in some sections of the country.

NATURE AND PURPOSE OF THE SPORT

Track and field events are divided into the three major groups: running, jumping, and throwing. Many forms of competition use a combination of these skills. Performance is individual but a group may combine and participate in selected team events. Track competition recognizes individual skill as well as team score. The variety of events assures everyone an activity in which she can develop speed, skill, agility, and endurance. Although many people do not look to track and field for social or recreational values found in other sports, skills developed in this area can be of life-long benefit and are important lead-ups to the many other sports using running, jumping, and throwing.

Women participate in events modified and designed for their age and ability levels. The track events include the dashes, relays, and hurdles. Field events are hop, step and jump, running high jump, broad jump, shot put, discus throw, basketball, softball and baseball throw, and javelin throw. These activities have the greatest appeal to elementary and high school girls who are interested in self-testing and individualized competition.

NEEDED FACILITIES AND EQUIPMENT

One of the advantages of track and field in the instructional program is the small amount of equipment necessary for large groups. The facilities should be laid out in one central area so a single teacher can supervise all the activities. No dangers are hidden in the events and no unusual safety precautions are necessary if the field events are practiced where a careless hurler will not endanger other students.

Track Area. The track is an oval of one-quarter or one-half mile in length with curves of from 80 to 110 feet radius. The outdoor track has a hard level sub-surface covered with cinders. It must be smooth and properly graded for drainage. The indoor track is wood, clay or dirt. One side of it is known as the straightaway and is measured for dash events. It should be a minimum of 22 feet wide to allow for six lanes of 42 inch hurdles. The curves and backside should be 18 feet, allowing a minimum of 3 feet for each of six lanes.

Field Area. Field events are generally held inside the running track. If they are properly placed and conducted, there is no safety hazard. The

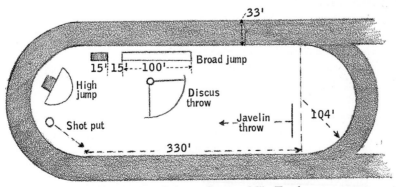

Figure No. 13–1. Quarter Mile Track.

jumping pits should be filled with sawdust, or sawdust and sand to aid drainage. These are spaded and raked frequently to maintain softness.

The throwing events begin near a track curve so the hurler has the greatest diagonal distance across the field. Throwing events should not be conducted simultaneously with other field events.

General Equipment.   Each event has specific equipment necessary in teaching or competitive meets. (The quantity needed depends on class size and teaching procedure.)

Running Events
Dashes
a. Well marked and properly measured track
b. Starting pistol and cartridges or whistle
c. Starting blocks
d. Stop watches
e. Finish posts and wool yarn
Pursuit and Shuttle Relays
a. All equipment for dashes
b. Batons
c. Twenty yard area marked as passing zone. Lines are drawn ten yards each side of starting line
Hurdles
a. Same equipment as dashes
b. Four 2 foot hurdles for each lane
   (1½ foot for elementary age)
c. Four 2½ foot hurdles for each lane for advanced college girls.
Jumping Events
Running Broad Jump
a. Jumping pit at least 5 by 20 feet
b. Take-off board not less than two feet nor more than three feet square, covered with powdered resin
c. Steel tape for measurement
d. Rake
Standing Broad Jump
a. Same as running broad jump
b. A trench dug in front of take-off board to a depth of three inches
Running and Standing Hop, Step and Jump
a. Take-off board moved farther away from pit than in broad jump
b. Steel tape, rake
c. Jumping pit
Running High Jump
a. Jump standards with bamboo cross bar resting on pegs which extend not more than three inches beyond the standards
b. Jumping pit at least 8 by 14 feet
c. Tape or wooden measuring rod
d. Rake and shovel

Throwing Events
Shot Put
a. Six pound shot for high school girls and eight pound shot for college women
b. Marking stick
c. Steel tape 100 feet long
d. Line two inches wide and ten feet long at delivery point
Discus
a. Discus weighing two pounds, three and a quarter ounces and 7.56 inches in diameter
b. Same as b, c, and d needed for shot put
Javelin
a. A 6 foot 8 inch javelin weighing one pound for high school age; a 7 foot 2 inch javelin weighing one pound, five ounces for college age
b. Throwing line same as shot put
c. Marking stick
d. Steel tape
Baseball, Softball, and Basketball Throw
a. "Official" basketball and "league" baseball or softball
b. Take-off line identical to other throwing events
c. Marking stick
d. Steel tape

Costume.   Since there is great variation in dress, students and instructors should be governed in their selection by safety, comfort, and attractiveness. Shirts should have sleeves of some sort and a tail that does not fly out or drag over the bar when jumping. Shorts should fit the leg snugly and comfortably. Elastic in the undergarment or outer shorts is desirable. Tennis shoes and sneakers are satisfactory for class work and may be used in competitive meets, providing all persons wear similar type shoes. Spikes are unquestionably valuable and may be used for interscholastic competition. Thin white socks or pushers (half-socks) may be worn with track and field shoes. A warm up suit should be worn before and after all events.

TEACHING UNITS

The beginners unit should aim to introduce a student to many events of track and field. The advance unit is developed around specialized techniques and individual skill development in selected events. A suggested unit for beginning and advanced students includes:

Unit for Beginners	*Advanced Unit*
Purpose and value of track and field	Intensive review
Explanation of events	Competitive strategy

Unit for Beginners	*Advanced Unit*
Brief history: Women in track	Advanced techniques of
Warm up and conditioning activities	Shot put
Fundamental techniques of running	Discus throw
Sprinting	Javelin
Starts	High Jump—Straddle Roll
Techniques of running dashes	Specialize in two or three events,
Techniques of middle distance	train and compete
running	Advanced meet
Techniques of throwing	Evaluation
Holding object	
Preliminary swings	
Footwork and delivery	
Release and follow-through	
Techniques of jumping	
Take-off and run	
Jump	
Landing	
Specific skills	
Hurdling	
Relays and baton passing	
Shot put	
Discus	
Baseball, softball throws	
Basketball throw	
Javelin	
Running and standing broad jump	
Running and standing hop, step and jump	
Running high jump—Western Roll	
Officiating a meet	
Evaluation	

BASIC SKILLS

Warm up and Conditioning Activities.   Warm up activities are important for all events. Jogging is an excellent way to begin. Jog high on the toes, feet straight, at a tempo slightly faster than a walk. Swing arms freely and increase jogging pace. Light calisthenic exercises which stretch and relax the muscles are beneficial in preparing the body for increased movement and preventing strains and pulls. Bicycling, leg stretches, reaches, and torso bends should be included in the 10 to 20 minute warm up.

RUNNING EVENTS

Some skills are basic to all or part of every dash or relay.

The Start.   The runner begins from starting blocks or holes dug for the feet to aid in drive and speed at the take-off. There are two general types of starts: the bunched start and standard (elongated) start. The height of the sprinter usually determines starting style with smaller girls preferring bunched starts.

A runner can determine her block position in the following way: stand with both heels near the starting line, back to the finish line. Place left foot directly ahead of right with heel to toe. Mark a spot at the middle of the left foot. Move the right foot ahead of left and mark the toe point. The marks represent where the front of each starting block is placed. Minor adjustments can be made if the feet seem too close or too far apart. At the official's signal "on your mark" the runner backs into the blocks and places the stronger leg (usually the left) in the front block with her toe on the ground and ball of the foot pushing. The rear leg touches the block and the knee drops to the ground. In a bunched start the back knee is even with the forward foot. The thumb and index finger are placed parallel to the starting line as the other fingers extend to the ground, forming a firm triangular base beneath the shoulders and extended arms. Body weight is on the thumb and fingers, the rear knee, and foot of forward left leg. Eyes look down the track eight to ten yards.

On the signal "get set" the hips are raised. If using a bunch start with feet close together, the hips rise more than in an elongated start with feet spread. The hips are at least level with the back. Hold the position for two seconds.

The gunshot is the signal for both legs to drive. The back leg immediately leaves the block as the knee comes forward with foot low to the ground. The front leg pushes forcefully against the block and arms and hands begin a powerful thrust as the body pulls out at a 45-degree angle.

Figure No. 13–2.   The Start.

Figure No. 13–3.   The Standing Start.

The arms work in opposition—the left one swings upward as the right foot swings through. Shoulders move forward and slightly up as the head and chest rise with the first strides until the runner is at proper sprinting angle in six or seven steps.

The standing start is used when the runner does not want to take a lead position at the beginning of the race. She leans slightly forward with feet comfortably spread, arms in opposition to legs. The initial push is from the forward leg as the back leg steps out; arms continue coordinated opposition movements.

Sprinting.   As the runner reaches full stride, the body is angled about 20 or 25 degrees to benefit from the pushing power of the kick. On each stride the rear leg just completing the drive is brought forward with heel under the hip as knee moves toward the front. Weight lands on the ball of the foot, knee straightens and pressure is applied through the foot as heels almost touch the ground. The arms swing at right angles with elbows bent and close to the side, directly front and back as the hands swing to shoulder level.

Breathing should be as normal as possible. Take a breath on "go" and at least two or three while running if natural breathing is too tiring.

Regular running form should be continued to the finish line. The head is forward and eyes straight ahead. It is not advisable to jump, lunge, throw head back, or raise arms to throw the chest out when crossing the line.

Middle and Long Distance Running.   Although long distance running is not a competitive event under DGWS[1], many women are interested in developing their individual skills. In longer distances the knee lift is not as great and the runner is more erect taking shorter strides and using more of the foot. The arc of the hand and arm swing is reduced accordingly. When running 200 yards learn to "float" or coast for part of the distance.

[1] AAHPER: *Official Rules for Track and Field Events and Meets.* Jan. 1958–Jan. 1960.

Sprint the first 60 to 75 yards, lessen the stride and let down for 90 yards then return to full stride.

Relays.   Relays are an American innovation which require running skill and ability to receive and exchange a baton. The team event is run in "legs" with each member running a section of the race and receiving and/or passing the baton within a 20 yard transfer area. If the baton is not successfully exchanged in the area the team is handicapped by time lost.

All of the techniques of starting and sprinting apply in the short distance pursuit and shuttle relays. A shuttle relay involves a team traveling over and back across the same ground. In a pursuit relay an awaiting runner is followed by her teammate and contacted as both run to continue the course in the same direction.

The baton is passed in a nonvisual or blind exchange, or a visual or sight exchange. The visual exchange is the safest, but also the slowest method. The condition of the incoming runner determines the type of pass. If she has come only a short distance and is not too tired to control the placement of the baton, a blind exchange is made. Use a sight exchange if the runner is obviously too fatigued to control the baton. This is the most popular pass for beginners.

The first runner starts from a crouched position with the baton in the middle of her left hand held by the last three fingers. Thumb and index finger are by the starting line.

Preparing for a *blind exchange* in a pursuit relay the "leg" runner is in a standing start position with the heel of the back foot just inside the passing zone. She turns to observe the approaching teammate and leans forward and shifts her back foot and brings leg halfway forward. As the teammate reaches a guide mark, the receiver moves forward into a sprint using both arms to accelerate. She then places her right hand to receive the baton by:

Basket Pass.   The receiving runner places fingertips on hips, elbow out at the side. The baton is placed in the open palm by a downward motion.

Inverted Basket Pass.   The receiver's thumb is on the hip, palm open, fingers spread out and down. Baton is placed in the palm by an upward swing.

Figure No. 13–4.   Starting with the Baton.

Figure No. 13–5.   The Basket Pass.

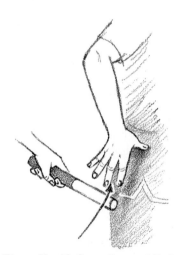

Figure No. 13–6.   Inverted Basket Pass.

Figure No. 13-7.   Underarm Extension Palm up Pass.

Underarm Extension Palm up Pass.   The arm is extended to the rear, palm up. The baton is placed by a downward motion.

Underarm Extension Palm Backward Pass.   The arm and hand extend to the rear with thumb and fingers spread so the palm is toward the oncoming runner. The baton is placed in the "V" of thumb and forefinger on upward swing.

Visual exchanges with the receiver facing the approaching runner are:

Overarm Extension Palm up Pass.   Arm of the receiver is palm up reaching back as the runner places the baton with a downward swing.

Overarm Extension Palm Outward.   The receiving thumb and fingers are extended with palm out to receive the baton passed perpendicular to the ground.

Underarm Extension Palm Backward Pass.   Executed just as the blind underarm extension. This is an excellent pass for beginners as the movements are simple and familiar.

After grasping the baton securely, the runner transfers it to her left hand if she is to pass to another runner.

Baton passing is more difficult in shuttle relays and beginners should use a hand touch in preference to a baton. The runner is in standing position with right arm extended parallel to the starting line awaiting a touch from the oncoming runner. When using a baton, the right hand of the receiver should be raised above the shoulder, palm upward and forward. The incoming runner slaps the baton across the palm of the receiver between the thumb and forefinger.

Figure No. 13-8.   Overarm Extension Palm up Pass.

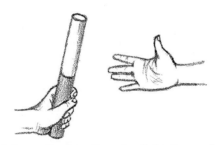

Figure No. 13–9.   Overarm Extension Palm Outward Pass.

Figure No. 13–10.   Hurdle Stride.

Hurdling.   The techniques of the start, sprint, and finish as previously described apply to hurdles plus the additional skill of hurdling. Hurdling is divided into the phases of approach, hurdle stride, and sprint between hurdles.

Approach.   A runner defines her strongest leg as the take-off or trailing leg.

The first hurdle is 15 or 22 yards from the starting line. The runner counts her strides to the take-off point in front of the hurdle. If she uses nine strides her take-off leg is placed on the rear starting block; if eight strides the take-off leg is on the front block with lead leg behind. Timing and consistent starts are important. If adjustments must be made they should be at the block rather than at the hurdle. Watch the hurdle bar rather than predetermined marks on the track.

In 50 yard events for *high school* and *college girls* the hurdles are 2 feet in height and the first is placed 15 yards from the starting line. In 60 yard events for *college women* the first 2 foot 6 inch hurdle is placed 15 yards from the start. The hurdles in 65 yard events for *high school* and *college students* are two feet in height and the first is 22 yards from the start.*

Hurdle Stride.   As the stride begins to clear the two, or two and a half foot bar, the lead leg is brought straight forward with a high knee lift. The toe is pointing upward and the knee remains flexed. The body bends forward with a definite thrust of the shoulders and chest to keep the body horizontal and ease the lift of the take-off leg. In *sprint hurdling* the lead arm swings in opposition to the lead leg and extends with the body thrust. In a *double arm thrust* both arms move forward with the step and reach of the lead leg. Simultaneous movement of both arms gives more leverage and force across the hurdle, but places the arms out of position for the thrusting force on the first step from the hurdle. A modified double arm style is often used.

---

* See section on Officiating and Scoring for placement of hurdles for all events.

The trailing leg should push the center of gravity forward and upward for the body to clear the barrier. The leg extends fully so the hurdler "runs over" rather than jumps up and down. As the leg rises to a position parallel to the ground, the knee rotates so the toes are pointing away from the body with the knee and ankle flexed. The eyes focus on the next hurdle.

Sprint.   The lead leg comes to the track forcefully and close to the barrier so a sprint push can begin. The ball of the foot is beneath or behind the body to insure a balanced landing. Assume a sprint position and stride toward the next hurdle. The distance between hurdles is measured so an odd number of strides is taken and take-off and lead legs are consistent over each barrier.

FIELD EVENTS

The field events include all jumping and throwing skills.

Running High Jump.   The jump is preceded by a running approach which develops momentum to get across the bar. To determine the spot to begin the approach, go to the front of the bar and find a spot where one foot can swing upward without knocking off the bar while standing on the other leg. Turn and angle off at approximately 45 degrees, taking a seven step approach. Mark the spot; that will be the starting position.

The Jump.   The western roll and barrel (straddle) roll have replaced the "scissors" form of clearing the bar in a sitting position with legs scissoring.

Western Roll.   As the jumper reaches the take-off point her left shoulder is toward the bar. The right leg swings forward and up over it as the left leg straightens and rises off the toe. It tucks by the side of the right leg as it passes over the bar. As the feet clear, the left leg touches the ground first with the hands following quickly. As the body turns on the front, the right leg is extended behind.

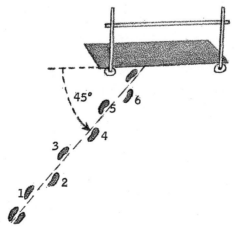

Figure No. 13–11.   Running High Jump—the Approach.

Straddle Roll.   Approach the bar and push off as in the Western roll with the leg farthest from the bar as the lead leg. As the right (lead) leg swings up and over the bar, the left leg leaves the ground and rolls in behind the right leg. The body is face down as it passes the bar with right leg reaching over to touch the ground as left leg stays up and extended. The landing is on the right leg and both hands.

Running Broad Jump.   The total jump includes a short, speedy approach, the jump, and landing.

The Approach.   The runner finds the starting position by standing on the take-off board with both feet and stepping out with the foot opposite the desired take-off foot. Run 16 to 20 full strides while someone counts the sixth, twelfth and sixteenth strides. Mark these check points and use them to standardize the stride and determine speed and take-off position. Begin the approach on the take-off foot, sprint forward and hit the take-off board with the heel first. The leg straightens and the body rocks over the foot as the toe and ankle aid the drive of the take-off leg. The jump must be high.

Flight in the Air.   There are two basic methods of flight—the *hitch kick* and the *tuck jump*. To execute the powerful hitch kick, the legs begin

Figure No. 13–12.   The "Western Roll."

Figure No. 13–13.   The Straddle Roll.

Figure No. 13–14.   The Running Broad Jump.

a cycling action as soon as the jumper is in the air. At least two relaxed smooth kicks are done before the feet come together for a landing.

The take-off is the same for the tuck or sailing jump. The lead leg swings upward and both knees come toward the body as if sitting in a chair.

Landing.   In preparation for landing the legs extend and the arms swing behind the body. The heels contact the pit as the arms are thrust forcibly forward and the body falls forward.

Running Hop, Step and Jump.   A short sprinting approach brings the runner to the take-off board on the foot opposite the regular take-off foot. The foot hits the board and does a low hop covering as much distance as possible. The opposite leg swings forward then back in preparation for a step as the hop ends with the body balanced over the foot and bent knee. Body balance is important as the step is taken and total length should be sacrificed for a balanced push off into the jump. The flight and landing are like the running broad jump.

Standing Hop, Step and Jump.   This event uses the skills of the running hop, step and jump except there is no approach and the hop begins from a standing position on the take-off board.

Standing Broad Jump.   The jumper stands with both feet on the take-off board. With toes over the edge, the body rocks from forward and back. The take-off is made by simultaneous drive and spring from both legs as the arms swing upward lifting the body. At the height of the jump the arms are forward, heels near hip height as the upper part of the body leans forward. Legs swing forward as the arms remain extended to assure a forward or sideward fall.

Throwing Events

Shot Put.   The following description is for a right-handed delivery. Grasp the shot so it rests against the closely cupped fingers of the right hand supported in front by the thumb. Weight shifts to the rear right foot with

Figure No. 13–15.   The Shot Put.

the shot tucked against the neck or front of the shoulder. The right elbow is bent and pointing back from the body. The left arm is extended forward and upward for balance.

The left leg lifts and swings forward and back in anticipation of forward momentum. As it swings forward for the last time a quick, gliding hop brings the right foot (still carrying the weight) forward and the left foot to the edge of the delivery line. Without hesitation the body turns, so the right side of the body faces the direction of the put. Simultaneously the right arm straightens and pushes upward and forward. The shot leaves the hand with a final finger push. Body weight is behind the put as the right foot reverses. The left leg is extended and the left arm pulls back to help the body rotation away from the foul line.

Discus Throw.   Place the discus on the palm of the right hand barely hooking the end joints of the fingers over the rim, and extend the thumb across the center with the back rim resting against the inside of the wrist. Hand positions are modified for larger hands by placing more of the fingers over the rim with palm behind the center.

Beginners should master the standing throw first. Turn the left side of the body toward the direction of the throw. Feet are comfortably spread. Transferring the weight alternately, the right arm swings backward with palm up and forward across the body with the left hand holding the discus in the parallel swing. With bent relaxed knees, the weight shifts to the right foot as hips and shoulders twist right. Head and chest are up. With a quick swing of the body left and an easy arm swing, the discus is released as the legs push the body to an erect position. The throwing arm continues up and around in a follow-through. In a vigorous throw, the hurler may be carried into a half turn so her right foot ends where the left one was at the start.

To get more power in the throw, shift weight from right to left foot, step across in a semi-crouched position so right foot comes in front of the left. The left foot snaps around in front toward the line. The feet and legs are braced as the arm whips through, and the wrist snaps releasing the discus slightly ahead of the shoulder with a clockwise spin. As the throw is made the left arm whips back and the chest is lifted. The reverse follows the release.

Basketball Throw.   The hurler stands with feet apart and body at right angles to the delivery line. An official basketball is held by the right hand and supported by the wrist and fingers. As the body bends backward the left leg and arm extend and the right knee bends. The body weight transfers to the left foot before the right arm and wrist whip through. Reverse follows. Steps may be taken in the delivery.

Baseball and Softball Throws.   These throws may be done with any form and from a stand, run, or step-hop. The preferred overarm throw begins by facing the throwing line with the left foot slightly in front. Both hands grasp the ball at chest or chin level. The hands pass overhead as the left leg lifts. The body leans backward, rotating slightly to the right. The right knee flexes as the bent right arm comes back to a position parallel to the ground. The left arm is up for balance. The body braces against a firm left leg and the right arm follows with a whip-like motion and a flick of the wrist and fingers.

Javelin Throw.   The throw may be taken with or without a run, but the beginner should practice it from a standstill before coordinating all movements for a running delivery.

Grips.   There are three common grips. For the *Finnish grip* grasp the shaft at the rear edge of the corded binding with the thumb and second

Figure No. 13–16.   The Discus Throw.

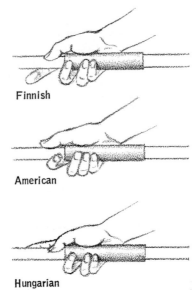

Finnish

American

Hungarian

Figure No. 13–17.   The Javelin Grips.

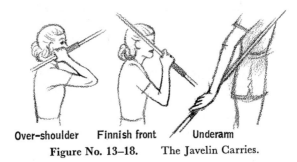

Over-shoulder   Finnish front   Underarm

Figure No. 13–18.   The Javelin Carries.

finger. The index finger extends under and around the shaft, the third and fourth fingers hold the binding.

The *American grip* is more natural as it is similar to the tennis hand-shake with the arm extended. The thumb and index finger grasp the shaft at the rear edge of the binding as the other fingers close around it.

The *Hungarian grip* is similar to the Finnish. The index finger extends directly underneath the shaft. As in the Finnish grip, the pull is made by the thumb and second finger.

Carry.   The carry is an important phase in the preparation for delivery. In the *Finnish carry* the elbow is bent and the hand is over the shoulder with palm up. The javelin points down in the front carry and the arm moves easily with the run.

In the *over the shoulder carry* the elbow is bent and pointing forward to the delivery line with the point upward.

The *underarm carry* is more difficult for beginners. As in the other

carries, any grip may be used. The point of the javelin is up with the carrying arm outside and extended behind the body. The javelin comes under the
arm next to the body.

Run.   Measure the distance of the run as in preparation for a running
broad jump. Begin at the take-off line and run approximately 90 feet marking three check points, the first five strides from the line, then eight strides,
and another eight strides. Begin the run passing the 2, eight-stride check
points. As the runner strikes the last mark she begins the preparation for
the throw and reverse by one of the following methods:

1. *Finnish Cross Step.*   As the left foot touches the check point the
right foot strikes the ground straight ahead as the javelin point is leveled.
The left foot comes into the path of the right foot as the body turns slightly
with the left side toward the line. The javelin arm moves backward. The
right leg crosses left with body still turned and feet parallel to the delivery
line. The left moves forward with toes toward the line as the body whips into
the throw with the arm following. Body momentum brings the right leg
through in a reverse.

2. *Rear Cross Step.*   After the left foot reaches the check point the
right foot moves forward, the left foot moves into the path, turning left side
toward line. The right foot moves up and *behind* the left, then the left foot
moves forward and to the right. After the throw the right foot reverses.

3. *Hop-step.*   After the left foot hits the check point, the right one
moves forward going right. On the second count the right foot hops with
foot parallel to the line. On count three the left foot moves forward and the
throw and reverse follow.

The throw is made with the body turned forward, eyes focused on the
direction of the throw and left arm extended. The throw is straight over-

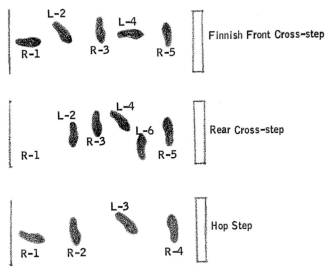

Figure No. 13–19.   Approach Runs.

head, pulling with body and shoulder muscles first and finishing with a strong wrist snap. It is made an instant before the reverse.

CLASS ORGANIZATION

One teacher can instruct a large class with proper equipment and facilities. She should determine what activities are appropriate for the age level. Ideally, all girls should participate in each track and field activity suggested by DGWS by the end of high school. Intramural and interscholastic events should be sponsored. The teacher gives a general introduction and instruction in the basic skills of running events. Using student assistants, the class can be divided into squads for practice, as the instructor roams and teaches jumping and throwing events to single squads, thus making the best use of facilities.

Heats should be lined up for the fastest use of the track where lanes are limited.

To prevent boredom and fatigue in the early instructional periods, the squads should have a plan of rotation from sprinting to discus or baseball throw, to broad jump, to javelin and so on through the events. As the students progress, keep time trials and distance records to encourage individual improvement.

Class members should be introduced to conditioning and warm up exercise and be encouraged to "loosen up" by themselves before instructor begins. Some teachers prefer that class leaders conduct warm ups at the beginning of each lesson.

Many basic skills can be taught indoors during inclement weather. Starting, baton passing, throwing form, hurdling, running, and even the hitch kick while swinging on a rope can be practiced. Relays, selected films, and officiating techniques are part of the indoor program.

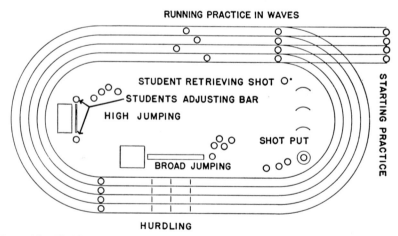

Figure No. 13–20.   Organization of the class for the teaching of track and field events.

TEACHING PROGRESSION

As previously mentioned, teaching progression is largely dependent on the teacher's choice of presentation and the available facilities. If progression is from one activity to another after basic skill development, begin with known skills and move to the more complex. The progression within the events is:

Running Events	Jumping Events	Throwing Events
Dash	Standing Broad Jump	Basketball
Relays	Running Broad Jump	Softball
Hurdles	Standing Hop, Step and Jump	Baseball
	Running Hop, Step and Jump	Shot Put
	Running High Jump	Discus
		Javelin

A teaching unit of 15 lessons for beginners might include:

Lesson I

1. Explanation of the nature and value of track and field
2. Brief history and "women in track"
3. Use of warm up exercises
4. The crouch start

Lesson II

1. Warm up
2. Review start
3. Demonstrate and practice sprinting
4. Explain and demonstrate techniques of throwing

Lesson III

1. Warm up
2. Review start and sprint
3. Practice basketball throw
4. Demonstrate and teach the standing broad jump

Lesson IV

1. Warm up
2. Time 50 yard dash
3. Softball and baseball throws
4. Practice standing broad jump

Lesson V

1. Warm up
2. Select relay teams on basis of 50 yard times and demonstrate and practice baton passing
3. Running broad jump
4. Measurement of basketball, softball, and baseball throws

Lesson VI

1. Warm up
2. Relay practice
3. Demonstrate and explain shot put and discus
4. Practice shot put and discus

Lesson VII

1. Warm up
2. General review
3. Individual practice session with teacher assisting

Lesson VIII

1. Warm up
2. Begin low hurdle practice
3. Standing and running hop, step and jump

Lesson IX

1. Warm up
2. Review discus and shot put
3. Informal meet of 50 yard dash, 100 yard pursuit relay, 50 yard hurdle, running broad jump, and standing hop, step and jump

Lesson X

1. Warm up
2. Running high jump
3. Javelin demonstration and practice

Lessons XI and XII

1. Warm up
2. Individual practice and skill improvement
3. Rules and officiating

Lessons XIII and XIV

1. Conduct official class meet

Lesson XV

1. Written examination
2. Student-teacher evaluation of the unit

SKILL DIFFICULTIES AND THEIR CORRECTION

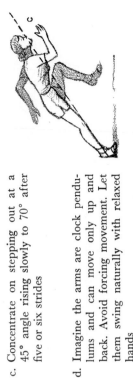

Difficulty	*Correction*
1. *Dashes*	1.
a. Spreading feet too far in blocks resulting in loss of power and push	a. Review technique of setting distance in block. Remember the strong foot is forward. Try several distances and have teacher check speed leaving blocks
b. Shoulder low and head down	b. Be sure the elbows are firm and arms are directly below the shoulders, chin up and look down the track
c. Rising too quickly when leaving the blocks, or leaning too far forward during the dash	c. Concentrate on stepping out at a 45° angle rising slowly to 70° after five or six strides
d. Swinging arms across the body causing shoulder and body sway. Fists clenched tightly	d. Imagine the arms are clock pendulums and can move only up and back. Avoid forcing movement. Let them swing naturally with relaxed hands
e. Slowing before crossing finish line	e. Continue speed for five yards beyond the finish, then slow gradually

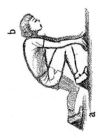
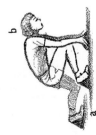

SKILL DIFFICULTIES AND THEIR CORRECTION (*Continued*)

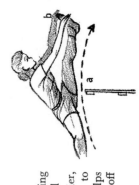

Difficulty	*Correction*

2. Relays

2.

a. Dropping the baton on the pass

a. Practice solves this problem. As the baton touches the hand, the passer exerts pressure as the receiver firmly grasps it

b. Failing to pass the baton in the 20 yard zone

b. Check mark which incoming runner crosses to signal take-off for receiver. If receiver runs out of zone before getting baton, move the guide mark closer to the zone line. If the incoming person overruns the receiver, move the mark further away

3. Hurdles

3.

a. Jumping up and down, thereby losing forward momentum

a. Run over the barrier by extending take-off leg and pushing forward

b. Failure to use arms for balance and pull across the hurdle

b. As the lead leg crosses the barrier, reach as if trying to grasp a bar to pull the body over. The reach helps keep the body straight on take-off and landing

Difficulty	Correction

c. Trailing leg drags over barrier	c. As the body bends the trailing leg "snaps up" close to body with toe parallel to the ground
d. Loss of stride between hurdles	d. The landing leg comes close to the barrier for a push. Keep stride consistent

4. *Running High Jump*

4.

a. Using inaccurate acceleration and poorly gauging check points	a. Review approach and practice without the jump
b. Taking-off on wrong foot	b. Take-off on inside foot (except in scissors) leading with outside leg

SKILL DIFFICULTIES AND THEIR CORRECTION (*Continued*)

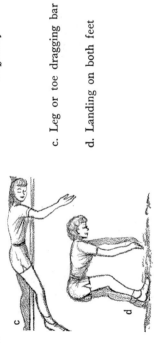

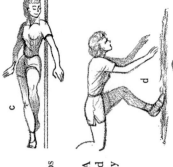

Difficulty	*Correction*
c. Leg or toe dragging bar	c. Keep body close to bar and hips high, so legs are easily raised
d. Landing on both feet	d. Land on one foot and both arms. A two foot landing turns the body and forces a straightening of the body too soon

5. *Running and Standing Broad Jump*

a. Inaccurate acceleration and poorly gauging check **points**	a. See 4a
b. Failure to use the entire foot in take-off	b. Practice a heel-to-toe roll from the block with an upward push
c. Loss of balance in flight	c. Review the flight of both jumps concentrating on arm action

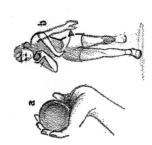

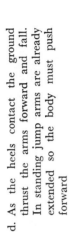

Difficulty	*Correction*

d. Falling backwards on landing

d. As the heels contact the ground thrust the arms forward and fall. In standing jump arms are already extended so the body must push forward

6. *Running and Standing Hop, Step and Jump* (In addition to approach mentioned above)

6.

a. Hopping too high and stepping too far resulting in poor balance

a. Keep the hop low and step short enough so the body is balanced for the greatest effort of the jump

b. Falling on landing

b. Keep arms extended and roll body forward

7. *Shot Put*

7.

a. Holding shot too far in the palm of hand

a. Place it at base of fingers. Teacher reminds student the shot is pushed

b. Failure to get balanced before approach begins

b. Lift the forward leg and extend the left arm. Be comfortable before starting footwork

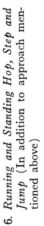

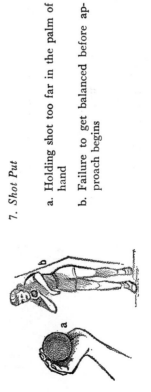

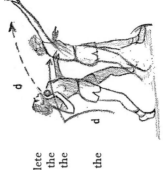

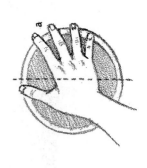

SKILL DIFFICULTIES AND THEIR CORRECTION (*Continued*)

Difficulty	*Correction*
c. Hesitating between steps resulting in loss of power	c. Develop a smooth delivery. Practice form mimetically
d. Failure to use whole body in the push	d. Teacher should review complete throwing sequence emphasizing the importance of a body braced as the throw begins
e. Stepping over line on follow-through	e. Practice the reverse *following* the shot delivery
8. *Discus Throw* (See common errors of shot put)	8.
a. Placing the fingers too far over the rim	a. Review grip and place hand so the palm is behind the center of the discus weight

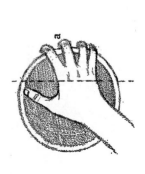

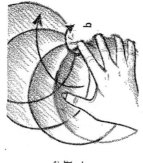

Difficulty

b. Throwing the discus with a counter-clockwise motion

Correction

b. Without a full approach, practice sailing the discus and releasing it off the index finger in a clockwise rotation

9. *Baseball, Softball, Basketball Throw*

a. Failure to wind-up

b. Throwing without body thrust

9.

a. Review wind-up technique and practice mimetically

b. The body unwinds and moves through and the arm whips through last

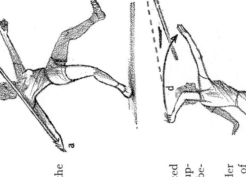

SKILL DIFFICULTIES AND THEIR CORRECTION (*Continued*)

Difficulty	*Correction*
10. *Javelin Throw*	10.
(In addition to approach problems as mentioned previously)	
a. Failure to bring arm back far enough for wind-up power	a. Arm moves back in the run as the body winds-up for delivery
b. Releasing the javelin too soon, losing proper arc in flight	b. The release should be practiced from the run. It is released upward and forward on the count before the reverse
c. Releasing from a sidearm swing	c. The arm comes over the shoulder to release the javelin at an angle of approximately 35 degrees with the ground
d. Javelin lands with back end first	d. Release sooner

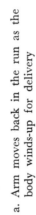

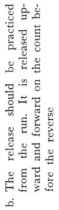

NOVELTY EVENTS

Since there are many events and skills involved in track and field, the need for stimulation from novelty events is not as great as in some activities. However, all events chosen should improve basic track and field skills.

Running Races or Relays

Sack Race.   Each team has a "gunny sack" which the runner must climb into, hop to the goal, return and give to the next runner.

Three Legged Race.   The team is divided into pairs. At the "go" the first pair ties their inside legs together, runs to the goal and back, unties their legs and gives the rope to the next pair. The race continues with next couple in each line competing until one team is declared winner.

Baserunning Contest.   Each person runs the bases of a softball (baseball) diamond trying to establish the best time on a stop watch. If a team event, the "team time" is the average of all runners' times.

Backward Race.   The contestants run backward to the goal and forward to the next runner.

Throwing Events

Tin Plate Toss.   Hurl tin plates as a discus for distance. Indoors, paper plates may be used.

Broomstick Hurl.   Throw broomstick as a javelin for distance.

Quoit Quirk.   Throw rubber ring for distance.

Jumping Events

Standing Backward Jump.   With back to pit, jump backwards from both feet.

Cross the Brook.   A "brook" of varying width is marked on the field. On signal everyone must run and cross the brook. If successful, the runner must cross it at a wider point and so on. If unsuccessful, try a narrow spot and begin again. For variation, one person can be "it" and control where a person crosses by chasing her toward the brook.

Height Jumps.   Jump against the wall and touch. Try to gain height.

OFFICIATING AND SCORING

Track and field officials include a referee, inspectors, judges, field judges, timekeepers, starter, course clerk, scorers and assistants, and an announcer. The first obligation of each official is to be familiar with the conduct of the events. These are available in the *Official Track and Field Guide.*[2]

The dash, relay, and hurdle events are measured by the timekeeper at the finish line. Time is taken from the pistol flash or handkerchief drop to the moment the finish line is crossed. The suggested dash, relay, and hurdle distance are:

[2] AAHPER, Division for Girls and Women's Sports. 1201 16th St., N.W., Washington 6, D.C.

Running Events *Dashes*	*Pursuit and Shuttle* *Relays*	*Hurdles*
Suggested distances		Suggested distances
25-30-40 yd—Elementary	30-40 yd.—Elementary School	High School—50 yd. three, 2 ft. hurdles, 15 yd. at start and finish, 10 yd. between hurdles.
40-50-60 yd.—Jr. High School	50-60-75 yd.—Jr. High School	College—(a) less advanced 50 yd. four, 2 ft. hurdles, 15 yd. at start, 7 yd. between hurdles, 14 yd. at finish. (b) more advanced 60 yd. four, 2 ft. 6 in. hurdles, 15 yd. at start and finish, 10 yd. between hurdles.
50-60-75 yd.—Sr. High School	60-75-100-220 yd.—Sr. High School	
60-75-100 yd.—College	75-100-220 yd.—College	
		High School and College—65 yd. four, 2 ft. hurdles 22 yd. at start and finish, 7 yd. between hurdles.

False starts are penalized by loss of one, then two yards. The third violation results in disqualification. Loss of time is the only penalty for a poor baton pass. Knocking over more than one hurdle or failing to take both feet over the hurdle results in disqualification.

The jumping events are measured by the field judges to discover distance covered. All lateral jumps are measured perpendicularly from the nearest break in the pit (it may be a hand if the jumper falls backward) to the board. The running jumps measure to the outer edge and the standing to the near edge of the board from the pit. Measurement in the high jump is from the ground to the upper edge of the crossbar at the center.

All of the jumping events allow three trials and the running jumps permit unlimited approaches.

The throwing events are measured from the nearest mark made by the object thrown to the inner side of the toe board or line. Three trials are allowed with the best measurement counting.

Scoring.   The times and distances determine the places. Points are awarded to the first three places: First place—five points, second place—

three points, and third place—one point. Team scores are the total of individual and relay event points.

EVALUATING THE RESULTS

There is little need for additional evaluative devices if periodic records are taken on every student. The real purpose of evaluating—for self-improvement—is served as the student sees her skill progress. The results of the meet at the end of the unit are further indications of a student's growth. Student understanding and ability in conducting a meet should be included in evaluation when grades are given.

TERMINOLOGY

Anchor Leg—Last section of a relay race
Barrier—A hurdle
Box—Position of competitors to front and side of runner impeding her change of position
Curb—Inside border of the track
Free Track—Indicates the runners will not be confined to lanes
Heat—One race with a portion of the total race entries
Line—A two inch line 10 feet long which serves as a restraining and foul board in throwing events
Reverse—The interchange of feet after release in a throwing event. Also called recovery, it serves to maintain balance
Sprint—Fast run
Wind Sprint—Short bursts of speed between easy jogging of equal distance

DISCUSSION QUESTIONS

1. What are the values of warm ups for both track and field events according to your knowledge of physiology?
2. Explain a few of the skills common to all throwing events.
3. Select one track or field event to demonstrate and review with your team.
4. Plan a ten lesson track and field unit for sixth grade girls.
5. Select a committee to plan a class meet. Explain how class members can serve as officials *and* competitors in the informal meet.

SELECTED AUDIO-VISUAL AIDS

Beginning Track and Field 1956. (Five filmstrips) The Athletic Institute, 209 S. State Street, Chicago 4, Ill. (Purchase, Rental)
Track and Field Events for Women. (still prints) Dean-Brunson Studio, 139 N. Main Street, Logan, Utah. (Purchase)
United World Track and Field Series 1947. (16 mm., sound, 11 reels) United World Productions, 1445 Park Avenue, N. Y. 29, N. Y. (Purchase and Rental)

SUGGESTED READINGS

A.A.H.P.E.R., *Softball—Track and Field Guide.* Current edition, Division for Girls and Women's Sports, 1201 16th Street, N. W., Washington 6, D.C.
Bresnahan, George T., and Tuttle, W. W.: *Track and Field Athletics,* ed. 3, St. Louis, C. V. Mosby Co., 1950.

Canham, Don, and Micoleau, Tyler: *Track Techniques Illustrated,* New York, The Ronald Press, 1955.

Doherty, J. Kenneth: *Modern Track and Field,* Englewood Cliffs, N.J., Prentice-Hall Book Company, Inc., 1953.

Gauthier, George E., and Haney, George E.: *Fundamentals of Track and Field Athletics,* Minneapolis, Burgess Publishing Company, 1951.

Mayer, E., and Haverstick, Martha: On Your Mark, Get Set, Go! Journal AAHPER, Vol. 28, No. 4, April, 1957.

Miller, Donna Mae, and Ley, Katherine L.: *Individual and Team Sports for Women,* New York, Prentice-Hall Book Company, Inc., 1955.

Miller, Richard I.: *Fundamentals of Track and Field Coaching,* New York, McGraw-Hill Book Company, Inc., 1952.

Moulton, Gertrude E.: Track and Field in a Program of Physical Education for Girls, Journal of Health and Physical Education, Vol. 13, No. 2, February, 1942.

PERIODICALS

Sports Illustrated, 540 North Michigan Avenue, Chicago, Illinois.

Scholastic Coach, Scholastic Magazines, Inc., 33 W. 42nd Street, New York 36, N.Y.

III

Team Sports

"THE GREAT AIM OF EDUCATION IS NOT KNOWLEDGE BUT ACTIONS". . . . SPENCER

14

Basketball

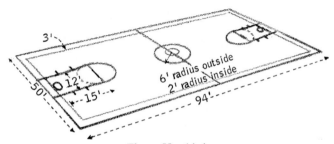

Figure No. 14–1.

Basketball is truly the "All-American game." Created by Dr. James Naismith to fulfill a class assignment, basketball has grown into the most popular participating and spectator team sport in the country. The game as originally played in Y.M.C.A. class at Springfield, Massachusetts, was a simple, 13 rule indoor winter sport that served the same team purposes as football during the fall and baseball in the spring. Originally, a large number of men composed two teams and were allowed to bat, pass, and throw in an attempt to get the ball into peach basket goals nailed to each end of the gymnasium balcony.

Although women were not in Dr. Naismith's original plans, they quickly saw the value of the game. A short two weeks after the game was introduced, a group of women teachers asked to play. The game spread rapidly, but misinterpretations and misunderstandings of the rules led to confusion across the nation. A rule misinterpretation by Miss Clara Baer in 1893 at Newcomb College in New Orleans ultimately developed the three division court game. The first rules committee met in 1899 and accepted the three court game. It was not until 1936 that the two division game was recognized by the basketball rules committee.

Through the years the sport has had a history of multiple and differing rules. In 1899 some players and teachers refused to accept modification of the men's rules. Today a limited number of teams play modified boy's rules rather than rules designed for women.

Since 1905, there has been an active and permanent basketball committee that plans and revises rules. This committee remains as the most active on team sports in the Division for Girls and Women's Sports of the American Association for Health, Physical Education, and Recreation in its effort to revise and introduce rules to make the game more interesting and to protect the health and safety of players.

THE NATURE AND PURPOSE OF THE GAME

Basketball is played by two teams of six players each (three forwards and three guards), on a rectangular court no larger than 94 by 50 feet. The court is divided into two equal areas so that the forwards and guards of one team are in separate playing areas at the beginning of the game. The forwards of one team oppose the guards of the other team in each court as the game proceeds.

Play begins with one forward of a selected team receiving the ball from the referee in the center circle and thereafter teams alternate receiving to begin each quarter. The visiting team has option of choice of basket or privilege of receiving the ball in the center at the start of the first and third or second and fourth quarters. The captain of the opposing team has the remaining choice. If both teams are "home" the option is decided by a toss of a coin. As the ball is put in play by the forward, each team tries to get the ball and move it by throwing, bouncing, rolling, dribbling, or juggling so a forward may shoot into the basket in her end of the court and score a goal. The team not in possession of the ball tries to keep the opposing team from scoring as it tries to intercept the ball so it can make a scoring attempt. Whenever a team scores a field goal the opposing team receives a center throw to resume play.

An official game consists of four, eight minute quarters. There is a two minute time interval between the first and second, and third and fourth quarters and a ten minute time at the half. When the ball is "dead" and time is out, a team may make any number of substitutions with individual players entering any number of times. When a team has no eligible substitutes and one player is disqualified, the team may continue to play with five players. If the team loses two or more players, either by injury or disqualification, the game is awarded to the opponents by default.

During play as opposing teams vie, tie balls, violations, fouls, and out of bounds balls occur. A tie ball is called when two opposing players place one or both hands on the ball simultaneously; or when a player places two hands firmly around a ball already held by an opponent. A tie ball is put in play by a jump between opposing players in a nearby restraining circle.

When a ball goes out of the court boundary it is put in play from outside the court by a member of the team opposing the player who last contacted the ball in bounds. If opposing players touch the ball simultaneously, it is put in play by a jump ball from the nearest restraining circle.

A violation is a minor offense, such as traveling with the ball, stepping on or over the side or center line when in possession or playing the ball, or holding the ball longer than three seconds in bounds, five seconds out of bounds or 10 seconds on a free throw. Violations result in the opposing team being awarded the ball out of bounds. Double violations require a jump ball between opponents.

Fouls are rule infringements resulting in a penalty for the fouling individual or team, and one or more unguarded free throw attempts for the team fouled. Individual fouls are charged against an individual player responsible for personal contact, overguarding the ball or player, threatening the eyes of an opponent, boxing-up, delaying the game, or using unsportsmanlike tactics. A player must leave the game when she commits five fouls or a single disqualifying foul. Fouls charged to a team occur in the conduct of the game by the team, coaches or spectators. The team is disqualified when five team fouls are committed. One free throw is awarded unless the player fouled was in the act of shooting for a goal. If the player fouled was shooting and the goal was made in spite of the foul, the goal is scored and one free throw is awarded. If the goal attempt was unsuccessful, two free throws are awarded. If one free throw is awarded and the unguarded throw is made the ball is put in play from out of bounds on the sideline opposite the free throw line by the forward taking the free throw. If the throw is missed the ball is in play. If two or more free throws are awarded the ball is dead after all but the last one when procedure of the single foul is followed.

SCORING

The score of a team is the total of its field goals and free throws. Each field goal counts two points and each free throw, one point. The team with the largest score at the end of the official playing time or overtime period is declared the winner. If the score is tied at the end of the playing time, the game is continued for one or more extra periods until (1) a team is ahead by one point at the end of any two minute extra period, or (2) a team scores a total of two points after the first extra period. When a game is discontinued, the score is recorded as 0-0. A defaulted game score remains *unchanged* if the defaulting team had the *lesser* score. If the defaulting team was leading, the score is recorded as 2-0.

Scorers keep official records of the position, names, and numbers of players and substitutes, individual scoring, individual and team fouls, and time out periods. A sample score sheet for one competing team illustrates scoring method.

METHOD OF SCORING BASKETBALL

NAME OF TEAM ___Seniors___   BALL IN CENTER   [1-3]   [2-4]

	NAMES OF PLAYERS	NUMBER IN GAME	GOALS FIRST HALF		INDIVIDUAL FOULS					GOALS SECOND HALF	
FORWARDS	Jean Smith (a)	4̸ 4	2 ⊙⊙2		X̸ 2 3 4 5						
	Gwen Brown	2̸			1 2 3 4 5						
	Laura Miller	3̸	⊙⊗	⊗⊗	1 2 3 4 5						
	Alice Smith	5			X̸ 2 3 4 5						
	Mary Jones	14	⊙	2	1 2 3 4 5						
	Anna Thomas				1 2 3 4 5						
					1 2 3 4 5						
					1 2 3 4 5						
					1 2 3 4 5						
					1 2 3 4 5						
GUARDS	Grace Watson (c)	10			1 2 3 4 5						
	Florence Osburn	11			1 2 3 4 5						
	Sylvia Shaw	1̸2̸			X̸ 2 3 4 5						
	Betty Rowan	1̸8̸			X̸ 2 3 4 5						
	Lillian Walton				1 2 3 4 5						
	Doris Walsh F	15			1 2 3 4 5						
					1 2 3 4 5						
					1 2 3 4 5						
					1 2 3 4 5						
					1 2 3 4 5						

	TEAM TIME OUTS				TEAM FOULS					
	X̸ 2̸ 3 4				1̸ 2 3 4 5					

WON BY: _____
SCORE: _____
DATE: December 8, 1959
PLACE: Center State H. S.

RUNNING SCORE	1̸ 2̸ 3̸ 4̸ 5̸ 6̸ 7̸ 8̸ 9̸ 1̸0̸ 11 12 13 14 15 16 17 18 19 20 21 22 23 24 25 26 27 28 29 30 31 32 33 34 35 36 37
	38 39 40 41 42 43 44 45 46 47 48 49 50 51 52 53 54 55 56 57 58 59 60 61 62 63 64 65 66 67 68 69 70 71 72 73 74

Figure No. 14–2.   Official Score Sheet.

1. Names of all team members are entered in their positions. A "C" indicates the team captain.
2. Numbers are recorded for players in the game. As a substitute enters the game, her number is recorded and the number of the player leaving the game is scratched. If a player changes to another division, indicate the change to a guard position (G) or forward (F) after her name.
3. Score a field goal in proper column beside scoring player's name, by making a figure 2. When the player is awarded a free throw, draw a circle. If two free throws are awarded, connect the two circles by a line. When free throws are made, mark an (x) in the circle.
4. Keep the running score by marking through one point for each free throw and two points for a field goal.
5. Mark individual and team fouls.
6. Record team time outs.
7. Cross out the "ball in center square" which does *not* apply to the team listed.

NEEDED FACILITIES AND EQUIPMENT

The Court.   Basketball is played in and out of doors with leather and rubber balls in many informal settings; however, an official game is played on a rectangular court at least 74 feet long and 42 feet wide and no larger than 94 by 50 feet. There should be at least 22 feet of overhead clearance. The outer court boundary line and center division line across the court width are two inches wide. A narrow broken line three feet inside the boundary indicates guarding distance on throw-ins. Two, two inch lines mark the inner center circle with a two foot radius and the concentric outer circle with a six foot radius. The free throw line, one inch wide, is marked from a spot 15 feet from the center of the face of the backboard and extending six feet in either direction, parallel to the end line. A free throw circle six feet in radius is drawn from the center of the free throw line. The half of the circle within the free throw lane is marked in dotted lines. Lines two inches wide from the free throw line to the end line enclose the 12 foot wide free throw lane. Two lines, eight inches long and two inches wide are placed perpendicular to each of the lane lines at a distance of seven and ten feet from the end line of the court.

Backboards.   Rectangular or fan shaped backboards are made of plate glass, wood, metal, or other flat rigid material. The white or transparent boards (with white marking) hang 4 feet inside the court parallel to the end line.

Orange colored metal basket rings with nets attached hang in the center of the board with the rim ten feet above the floor.

Ball.   The leather or composition covered round ball is between 29½ and 30 inches in circumference, and weighs between 20 and 22 ounces. Balls of reputable manufacturers meet official specifications. Each team of six should have at least two balls for practice.

Costume.   The official gymnasium costume is satisfactory for most game situations. Attractive shorts and shirts which allow freedom are desirable for interscholastic games. Footwear is an important safety feature. Each player should wear one or two pairs of light socks that cushion the feet and prevent blisters. Basketball shoes with cupped soles are generally preferred over the tennis-type shoe.

TEACHING UNITS

Suggested units for beginning and advanced students follow:

Unit for Beginners	*Unit for Advanced Players*
History and purpose of basketball	Complete review
Fundamental ball handling skills	Individual techniques
Catching	Passing with either hand
One hand underarm pass	Hook pass
Two-handed underarm pass	Hook shot
Chest pass	Jump shot
Bounce pass	Feint and pass, dribble or shoot
One hand overarm pass	Reverse pivot

Unit for Beginners	*Unit for Advanced Players*

Unit for Beginners

Basic individual tactics
    Bounce and limited dribble
    Feints
    Dodging
    Stopping
    Pivoting
    Jumping for tie ball and re-
        bound
    Guarding opponent
    Intercepting passes
Basic goal shooting
    Two-handed chest shot
    Foul shooting (two hand under-
        hand)
    Two-handed overhead shot
    One hand push shot
    Lay-up shot
Novelty games
Team strategy—offensive
    Leading passes
    Simple set plays from sidelines
        or center throw
Team strategy—defensive
    Player to player defense
    Area zone—triangular form
Beginning officiating
Evaluation
    Skills tests for passing, receiv-
        ing, shooting
    Team play
    Written test on rules and of-
        ficiating

Unit for Advanced Players

Screening
Team tactics—offensive
    Rebounding
    Spot passing
    Line and zigzag pass
    Figure eight
    Play development
Team tactics—defensive
    Defense against dribble
        and out of bounds play
    Shifting zone defense
    Combination zone and player
        to player defense
Tournament play
    Officiating
    Scoring, timing, refereeing and
        umpiring
    Conduct a class tournament
Evaluation
    Skills tests
    Written test
    Rating test for official's rating

BASIC SKILLS

Footwork, body balance, and ball handling are the foundation skills of basketball. A review of basic sports skills is helpful in preparation for game play.

Stance.   A player preparing to move or receive a pass is in a slightly crouched position with the knees well bent and head and chin up; shoulders are slightly forward. The arms are relaxed and elbows bent with fingers spread comfortably at waist level. One foot is slightly ahead of the other so the body is comfortable with weight equally distributed.

Running.   In running the body leans forward as the knees rise to medium height. The arm action is natural and relaxed, and the arms swing forward to near shoulder height and back behind the hip.

Jumping.   Development of leg swing for high and accurate jumping is necessary for playing rebounds, tie balls, and jump shots. A basic jump is made with flexed knees and relaxed arms. The arms thrust upward as the legs straighten and the body extends as high as possible.

Catching.   The type of catch used depends upon the position of the ball, the position of opposing players, and the anticipated move to follow. In preparation the arms are relaxed with elbows away from the body and hands at waist level. The fingers are relaxed and spread upward in the direction of the ball. With the receiver facing the oncoming ball, she steps forward to meet the ball with arms extended, elbows in, and hands extended. As the ball reaches the fingertips it is cushioned into the fingers as the arms pull back slightly to "give" to ball momentum. The ball is caught by the fingers, thumb, and heel of the thumb, *not the palm.*

Figure No. 14–3.   Catching.

The hands are on the sides and to the back of the ball for all catches. When catching a high pass (above the waist) the thumbs point toward each other with fingers pointing upward. On a low pass (below the waist) the fingers point downward, little fingers pointing toward an imaginary spot to the rear and bottom of the ball, thumbs are directed to back and top of the ball.

Passing.   A skillful basketball game hinges on effective passing to maintain possession of the ball. There are numerous ways of passing with the type used by a player dependent upon the position of the body and hands of the passer and intended receiver.

Chest Pass.   The two-handed chest pass is the most widely used because it can be caught at chest height and lead to a speedy and accurate shot or return pass. The body may be almost erect or crouched with the ball at chest level close to the body. Both hands hold the ball with fingers spread from the rear to the side, and pointing slightly upward. Thumbs are behind the ball with palms near, but not touching. Elbows are flexed and close to the body. The arms push forward from the shoulders as the elbows extend and the wrists snap as the ball is released in a straight line. As the ball leaves the hands, the thumbs give a simultaneous push and the palms turn toward the line of ball flight. The hands rotate inward

Figure No. 14–4.   The Chest Pass.

on the follow-through as thumbs point downward and fingers extend in the direction of the pass. If it is not a deceptive pass, body weight should be transferred to the forward foot to give additional power.

Two-Handed Underhand Pass.   The "flip" pass is not popular among girls except as a hand-off to a forward in a pivot play, or as a short pass when unguarded in front.

The pass may be made off the front of the body or from either hip. In any case, the cupped hands grasp the ball with fingers behind and on the side pointing downward; thumbs are on top pointing toward line of flight. When passed off the front of the body, the elbows are flexed and point away from the body more than in the chest pass. Feet are in side stride position. The arms extend forward as the elbows straighten, and wrists snap upward as the ball is released at waist height. The arms follow-through to shoulder height with thumbs pointing up and fingers toward the path of the ball.

When the ball is passed off either hip, body position varies slightly. To pass from the right hip the body is in forward stride position with the left foot forward. The hands draw the ball to the right hip so the right elbow is bent, pointing outward from the body, and the left elbow is across the body with the back of the left hand resting on the hip. The ball moves forward with an arm extension and wrist snap as the body weight transfers to the forward left foot. The release and follow-through are the same as the "flip" from the middle of the body.

Two-Handed Shoulder Pass.   The two-handed shoulder, or sidearm, pass is useful at the completion of a pivot, or as a deceptive pass when the ball moves one direction and the body another. The pass may be made from either shoulder. The ball is held in both hands so the fingers and thumbs point upward and back and cover the sides and rear of the ball. The elbows are flexed so the right arm is close to the side and the left is across the front of the body. Feet are in forward or side stride position with the body rotated to the right from the hips and waist. The arms extend and wrists snap in a rapid movement as the weight shifts to the left leg. The body follows the ball as the arms and the hands extend and rotate inward as in the chest pass.

Two-Handed Overhead Pass. This is a successful pass for skillful, tall players who are closely guarded or who want to release the ball quickly after catching a high pass. The ball is raised above and behind the head with the fingers at side and rear, and thumbs beneath the ball. The elbows are slightly bent and the wrists flexed. The body inclines forward and weight shifts forward as the arms extend and wrists and fingers snap to add thrust to arm and shoulder power. The ball is released at a point in front of the body about head level as the hands follow the ball to eye level and turn inward, palms down and thumbs toward one another.

One Hand Underhand Pass. The underhand pass is effective from both sides of the body as a short, deceptive pass and a "feeder" to a forward cutting to the basket. The pass resembles the underarm softball pitch. In executing a pass from the right side, the left foot is forward and body is comfortably crouched. The right hand is spread over the back of the ball and the right wrist and lower arm support the ball. The right elbow bends and leads the arm and ball past the hip as the left hand is placed on the ball as a guide. As the right arm starts forward the left hand

Figure No. 14–5. The Two-Handed Underhand Pass.

Figure No. 14–6. The Two-Handed Shoulder Pass.

Figure No. 14–7.   Two-Handed Overhead Pass.

Figure No. 14–8.   One Hand Underhand Pass.

moves away. The arm swings by the body and parallel to it, the arm extends and weight transfers to the forward foot. The ball is released at waist height as the fingertips, hand (palm up), and arm follow the ball flight.

One Hand Shoulder Pass.   The pass is much like an overarm softball throw and is effective as a well controlled long or medium distance pass. To execute the pass the feet are comfortably spread and body weight equally distributed. The right hand is spread behind the ball so that it is supported by the fingers and thumbs. It is brought back to the right shoulder by bending the elbow back and away from the body. The left hand comes across the body to serve as a steadying guide as the body rotates to the right. As the body weight shifts to the left foot, the left hand leaves the ball. The right arm brings the ball forward passing close to the ear. The right elbow extends and the wrist snaps as the fingers thrust forward and pass under the ball causing a slight reverse spin. The throwing hand and arm follow-through in the direction of the ball and end with palm down and fingers extended forward.

Bounce Passes.   One hand and two-handed bounce passes are used for short passes in the scoring area, or any other place on the court when an opponent is between the passer and receiver, or when a slow pass cannot be used.

For the one hand bounce pass the preliminary movements are similar to the shoulder or push pass, except the ball is brought between the shoulder and waist on the right side of the body. The left hand may balance the ball as the right hand is behind and toward the top with fingers extending upward. The right elbow is flexed and close to the side. The ball is pushed to the floor so it will bounce and rise at a level where the receiver can get it easily. The arm follows-through toward the floor with palms down. If a waist level rebound is desired the ball should bounce three or four feet from the receiver. If a lower rebound is necessary, bounce farther from the receiver.

The two-handed bounce is executed much like the two-handed chest pass except the action begins about waist height. The fingers are spread to the sides with the thumbs behind the ball. The elbows are close to the sides as the ball is pushed toward the floor with an arm extension downward. The arms rotate outward as the wrists and fingers thrust the ball away at waist level. At certain times a spin is valuable with the bounce pass. On a long pass or when the ball must rebound close to the receiver with considerable momentum, top spin can be added by cocking the wrists back and then uncocking them vigorously on the release. The ball leaves the small fingers first and the index fingers last. The hands follow-through so the fingers point toward the floor.

Backspin is used on short, relatively fast passes where a rebound up and away from the receiver is desired. The ball is released by a cocking wrist action and release by the fingers first and thumbs last. As the ball leaves the hands of the passer it is spinning toward her as the palms of the hands follow-through facing the spot where the ball strikes the floor.

Side spins are applied when it is necessary for the ball to bounce right or left on the rebound. To spin the ball so it bounces to the receiver's right

Figure No. 14–9.   One Hand Shoulder Pass.

Figure No. 14–10.   The Hook Pass.

side, bring the left hand to the right (under the ball) while pulling the
right hand forcefully to the left (on top of the ball). At the moment of
release, the ball is spinning in a counterclockwise direction. As the ball hits
the floor it "jumps" to the passer's left. A reverse hand action results in a
clockwise spin and a bounce to the left of the receiver.

Shove Pass.   The shove pass is an effective way of clearing the ball
from under the basket or controlling a rebound without really gaining possession of the ball. As the ball comes toward the receiver, she pushes the
ball toward a teammate with one or both hands. The hands and fingers
are firm and extended, elbows flexed. The wrists are flexed as the hands
meet the ball. The arms extend and the wrists snap giving direction to the
ball. The palms and firm arms follow-through in the direction of the pass.

Hook Pass.   The hook pass is an advanced technique used effectively
to return a ball to an inside court position when the player is held along
the sidelines. For a right-handed hook pass, the body is in forward stride
position, left foot forward. Initially the ball is held firmly by both hands
at waist level. The body turns so the left shoulder is toward the receiver as
the left hand moves toward the left side leaving the right hand, fingers
spread and pointing upward, and right forearm supporting the ball. As the
passer jumps upward, the right arm is raised sideward so it crosses the right
shoulder and passes overhead where the ball is released by a forceful wrist
and finger snap. The left arm remains extended for balance while the right
hand pulls under the ball as it rolls off the fingertips. The hand, palm down,
and fingers follow the path of the ball as far as possible.

Evading and Maneuvering Techniques.   There are many skills involving ball handling and body control which are important to all offensive
and defensive playing positions.

Bounce and Limited Dribble. The bounce and limited dribble are legal ways by which a player may advance while keeping possession of the ball. In the execution of a bounce a player pushes the ball to the floor with one or both hands so it rebounds into her possession. The player may stand or move in any direction as long as she gives the ball only one impetus.

A limited dribble allows a player a second contact with the ball. The second impetus must be given with only one hand and must be successive without allowing the ball to rest in one or both hands after the first bounce. In both the bounce and the dribble the ball is pushed to the floor by wrist and finger action at an angle determined by the distance the player will cover.

Juggle. When executing a juggle a player tosses the ball in the air and moves to regain it before another player touches it or it touches the floor. For a right-handed toss over an opponent's head, the player should run left to recover the ball behind her opponent.

Jumping for Tie Balls. The player crouches in a forward stride position with both feet flat on the floor. The weight is forward on the toes as the body weight is down through flexed hips and knees. The first push-off comes from the rear foot (right when players have left shoulders together) while the final push-off comes from an extension of ankles, knees, and hips. Simultaneously, the arms swing forward and upward with the right tapping hand extended, fingers cupped, wrist flexed. The tap is timed so the ball is touched and directed to a teammate or open area at the height of the jump.

Stops. There are two common methods of stopping body momentum —the stride and jump stop. The stride stop is considered the superior as it leaves the player in a stance suitable for passing, shooting, or bouncing and dribbling. It is a lead-up for footwork in the lay-up shot. The stride stop is simply described as a skip coming to a sudden stop. The player hops off her right foot, grasps the ball, lands on her right foot and steps forward on the left foot. At the end of the stop the feet are in a running stride posi-

Figure No. 14–11. Jumping for Tie Balls.

tion, 12 to 15 inches apart. The body weight is low and the rear foot serves as the pivot foot.

In the jump stop both feet touch the floor simultaneously and either foot may be used as the pivot foot. The player anticipates the ball, pushes off the floor to catch the ball and then brings the feet down together.

Pivoting.   Pivots are used when a player has possession of the ball and wants to change or reverse body direction to elude an opponent. Throughout the pivot one foot must remain in contact with the floor. Whether the pivot is made from a forward or side stride position, the knees are relaxed and the body weight is low. The ball is kept close to the body as a pivot of a few inches or a quarter, half, three-quarter or whole turn is made.

The body weight is on the ball of the stationary foot as the free foot pushes off. In a side stride position the body backs away or moves forward with either foot remaining on the floor. In a forward stride position if the left foot is forward, the body turns left and backward or the left leg crosses forward and in front of the right pivot foot.

The Reverse Turn.   This is used when the player is in forward stride position and confronted by an opponent. The knees are bent and the body crouched. The body turns, as if to a command of "to the rear, march," in the direction of the rear foot and away from the forward foot. The body spins on the balls of both feet as the toes of the front foot push off. The "new" rear foot may be lifted into a step after the turn is completed.

Feints.   Feints, or fakes, are movements of the ball, body, or eyes designed to mislead an opponent and draw her out of position. Usually, it is a movement contrary to the intended final movement of the player. Feints are done very quickly from either a stationary position or while moving. Feints (fakes) include:

1. *The ball fake.* Accomplished by moving the ball in one direction and shooting, passing, bouncing, or dribbling in another.
2. *Foot fake.* Placing the foot in one direction and then moving the body or ball in another. This is used by offensive and defensive players.
3. *Eye feint.* Looking one way and passing another.
4. *Head fake.* The head and upper part of the body make a movement in one direction and then suddenly turn and bounce, dribble, pass, or shoot in another.
5. *Arm fake.* Thrusting the arm upward or sideward to raise the opponent's defense and then passing below the defense.

Cutting and Dodging.   These are techniques designed to get a player free so she may receive a pass or shoot. The techniques include changing running pace, stopping, pivoting, body fakes and combinations of these skills. To be effective the player must "break" smoothly and rapidly and avoid a set pattern of movements.

Goal Shooting. Shooting incorporates all the skills of stance, body balance, finger control, and follow-through. The type of shot a player makes depends upon her position on the court. The following diagram gives an indication of when a player should use a rim shot or a bank or angle shot off the backboard.

The Two-Handed Chest Shot. This is used from a set position anywhere in the offensive court when the forward is not too closely threatened by a defender. The feet may be in forward or side stride position. The body is relaxed in a semi-crouch, weight equally distributed, and eyes focused on the rim where the shooter will generally aim. The ball is extended in front of the body at chest level, or lower for a very long shot, by the fingers grasping behind and to the sides of the ball. Fingers point upwards and thumbs toward each other. The relaxed shoulders help keep the elbows comfortably close to the body. The force of the shot begins as the knees flex and the wrists "cock" allowing the ball to drop back toward the shooter.

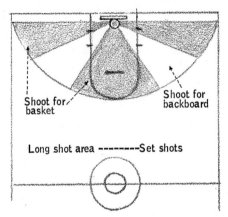

Figure No. 14–12.   Goal Shooting.

Figure No. 14–13.   The Two-Handed Chest Shot.

Figure No. 14–14.   The Two-Handed Overhead Shot.

As the arms extend the ball upward in front of the chest, the body extends upward and forward and the wrists straighten as the fingers direct the ball in an upward arc. The palms of the hands follow-through to face the basket, and the fingers maintain extension as the shooter moves forward for a possible rebound.

The Two-Handed Overhead Shot.   This is used for a short or medium distance set shot. Proper execution requires strong arm and finger action. The body is erect, head up, and eyes on the target. The knees flex slightly as the ball is raised overhead by easily bent elbows and held by the thumbs behind and underneath, with the fingers pointing outward on the sides and rear half of the ball. The arms and knees extend as the body weight shifts to the toes. The wrists extend and the fingers and thumbs drive the ball toward the basket.

The One Hand Shoulder (Push) *Shot.*   This shot can be used effectively when the shooter is closely guarded in a set position, or following a bounce or dribble. The shot is similar to the lay-up in hand position and take-off. The right-handed player takes-off on the left foot with the guiding left hand leaving the ball. As the body rises away from the defender, the right arm extends upward and forward. The ball is released well above the shoulder with a finger push at the height of the jump.

Lay-up Shot.   Often called an angle or under the basket shot, it is made from a position close to the basket, from the front or either side. An angle shot from the side is banked off the backboard. A player moving in from the right cuts for the basket, receives the ball and may bounce, dribble, or move directly to the shot. The ball is carried with the left hand to the front and underneath, and the right hand on top and slightly behind. Both hands carry the ball to shoulder or head height as the left foot pushes off.

The right knee rises to lift the body, the guiding hand leaves the ball as the right arm and wrist straighten and direct the ball to the backboard. The palm of the right hand follows in the direction of the backboard as the fingertips "guide" the ball. The player turns as she lands from the jump so she partially faces the court, ready to play for a rebound.

Figure No. 14–15.   The One Hand Shoulder (Push) Shot.

Figure No. 14–16.   The Lay-up Shot.

When laying-up from the front of the basket use either hand to lay the ball over the rim.

Two-Handed Spin Shot. The loop shot is made when the shooter has her back toward the goal and is closely guarded. It is a highly skilled shot that is used as a "change of pace" when no other forward is in a position for a safer shot. The ball is held below the waist near the body with the fingers pointing downward and thumbs on top pointing forward. With her back to the basket, the forward steps left on her left foot so she moves parallel to the basket. The ball is carried to the left and directed to the basket by a forward and upward motion of the arms as the elbows extend, wrists snap, and the body turns. The wrist and finger action upward causes the ball to spin toward the shooter. The palms and fingers follow-through upward with palms facing.

The Hook Shot. This is executed from both the right and left sides when the shooter is facing away from the basket and is closely guarded from the rear, or when the shooter is moving away from the basket. The ball is held by the fingers and supported by the heel of the right hand. The shot is preceded by a forward or sideward step (left quarter turn) and immediately followed by a left shoulder turn toward the basket. Simultaneously, the right arm swings upward in an overhead arc and toward and above the left shoulder. The fingertips and wrists guide the arcing ball over the rim (if shot is from the front) or to the backboard. On the follow-through, the hand pulls under the ball, palm down, and fingers extend toward the target.

Figure No. 14–17.   The Hook Shot.

Figure No. 14–18.   Foul Shooting.

Foul Shooting.   Several types of shots are successfully used in the attempt for a free throw. The frequently used two-handed chest and one hand shoulder shot (described previously) are believed less accurate than the two-handed underhand loop. The forward taking a free throw stands directly in front of the basket with toes behind and near the foul line.

To execute an underhand loop shot the feet are spread and toe out from the body to insure balance. A side stride offers the best balanced position. The fingers are spread over the sides of the ball pointing downward, and the thumbs are on top and forward. The arms hang comfortably down as the eyes focus on the forward rim of the basket. The body remains erect as it sinks with a knee bend and the heels rise from the floor.

The force of the throw begins as the body straightens naturally, and the arms and hands extend upward and forward toward the basket. The hands release the ball at the closest point to the basket without applying a deliberate spin. At the completion of the shot the weight is forward and the body is balanced and erect. The arms and hands are outstretched to the basket.

GAME STRATEGY

Basketball is a game of offensive and defensive tactics with the ultimate team objective of scoring goals and preventing opponents from scoring. A team in possession of the ball is the offensive team. The system of play used by the offensive team depends on the type of defense used by opponents.

DEFENSIVE PLAY

Every player on a team becomes a defensive player when a member of the opposing team gains possession of the ball. Although both guards and forwards have defensive duties, there are differences in the types of guarding. Forwards strive for interception of passes, bounces, and dribbles. This is done by close, aggressive guarding or setting up a blockade to keep the ball from passing the center line.

Guards must concentrate on defending the goal and must stay between the goal and the ball to prevent a forward from penetrating to a position of a "sure shot." When forwards are outside of the scoring zone (any area within 15 to 18 feet of the basket), the guards stay several feet away and toward the goal. Shooting accuracy is lessened outside this area and the possibility of pass interception, bounce or dribble interception is greater. If the forward attempts a shot there is usually indication and the guard can move closer to cover the ball.

Defensive Team Play.   There are two systems of team defense: 1. player to player, and 2. zone—with variations on each form. The skill and endurance of guards, the type of offensive game played, and the skill of opponents are the major factors which determine the system used.

When player to player defense is used each guard is responsible for her own particular forward. No matter where the forward moves in the court the guard is responsible for defending against her actions and shots. The guards continue to work as a team and cover for one another when a forward maneuvers free, evading her guard. Guards return to cover their own forwards when the ball crosses the center line or when it moves out of the dangerous scoring area.

There are many types of *zone defense,* ranging from a set zone in which each guard has personal responsibility for an area of the court, to the shifting zone which involves both zone and player to player defense.

Set Zone.   This stationary defense requires each guard to defend her area whenever an offensive player enters. The following illustrations indicate how court responsibility is divided:

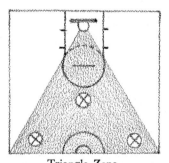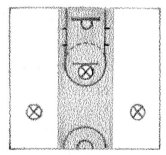

Triangle Zone   Set Zone
Figure No. 14–19.

In play, the real "set" of the area zone must be changed when two forwards overload a zone in the scoring area. The guard from the next zone moves over to guard a player, or all guards move into a single zone if the forwards cluster.

Triangle Zone. (See Figure No. 14–19.)   As the name indicates, the guards form a triangle with (a) one up, two back, or (b) two up and one

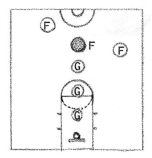 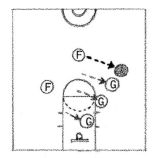

Figure No. 14–20.   Straight Line Zone.

back. The guards shift in relation to the ball and one another. The triangle remains spread to keep the forwards out of shooting range. When the ball is passed into the scoring area, each guard picks the forward in, or entering, her zone and shifts to player to player defense until the goal is made, or the ball is passed from the scoring area.

Straight Line Zone. (See Figure No. 14–20.)   The guards form a straight line, three deep, and maintain this formation keeping between the ball and the goal as long as the ball is outside the scoring area. When the ball is passed or moved into the scoring area, defending players shift to player to player defense.

The Shifting Zone.   This is used primarily to keep forwards away from the basket area. Its success depends on guards' skill in anticipating and intercepting passes. It resembles zone defense in that no restrictions are placed on the forward a defending player guards. However, it differs from an area zone in that the zoning pattern is set by a guard as she moves in anticipation of a pass and interception while her two teammates, alert to her move, shift to maintain a basic zone pattern.

The Blockade.   The blockade is a zone formation used by the defending forwards when the opposing guards gain possession of the ball. It is an advanced strategy requiring the three forwards to run to the center line and form a wall over two-thirds of the court. This formation encourages a high pass from the guards in possession to their forwards. Two guards of the defending team move toward the center line to intercept the pass and one guard remains in the backcourt to slow or intercept the ball if the blockade attempt is unsuccessful.

Offensive Play

At the beginning of a game, offensive play will be determined by the type of defense faced. Generally, when player to player defense is used by the opponent, the offensive team players attempt to break by eluding their defense quickly and making a direct attack on the goal. This is best accomplished by keeping the forwards spread, to prevent an umbrella grouping of the guards, and to pass rapidly so there is only one defensive player between the passer and receiver. The zone defense is penetrated best by playing away from the scoring area in an attempt to pull the guards out by drawing the attention to one side or the front of the court, and then moving the ball to an open area and shooting. The most skillful tactic in beating the zone is to pass the ball faster than the guards can move to protect their zones. An offense with an effective standing or running screen combined with a long shot will probably cause the defense to shift to player to player defense.

A team should encourage forwards to develop screen plays against all types of defense. In a screen play, a player passes to her teammate and moves to a position where her body protects the teammate's possession of the ball from the defending player. In a *moving screen,* the protecting team- mate moves alongside of the player who bounces or dribbles unguarded. The stationary screen usually protects a player shooting near the goal. A player pivots and passes to a teammate behind her, then remains in a protective position in front of her until she shoots.

An offensive team gains confidence if it has a few simple plays as a basis for a plan of attack when it gains possession of the ball. These plays should not stifle initiative, or be confusing by numerous maneuvers. Simple plays from center or out of bounds require accurate timing and passing. The triangular return is a quick, two pass series which can lead to a shot or a pass to a teammate in better shooting position. Forward A puts the ball in play by a short pass to Forward B moving toward the sideline. Forward B returns quickly to Forward A who moves toward the basket for a shot or a pass to a cutting teammate. (See Figure 14–21.)

A *center play* may begin with Forward 1 in the center circle. Forwards 2 and 3 move down court together from opposite sides, then F_2 cuts for the center of the court to receive the pass as F_3 is moving toward free throw line. F_3 receives second pass and shoots. F_1 moves down right side toward the basket for a rebound. F_2 moves left to receive a pass if F_3's shot is blocked or to rebound. (See Figure 14–22.)

An alternate beginning play from center starts with F_2 and F_3 on the same side of the court. Both move down court with F_2 receiving the pass as F_3 cuts behind F_2, receives the second pass while F_1 runs down the court to receive a pass in the shooting area. F_1 shoots or dribbles and shoots. If the

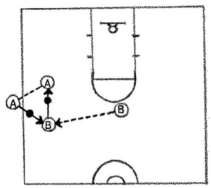

Figure No. 14–21.   Out of Bounds Triangular Play.

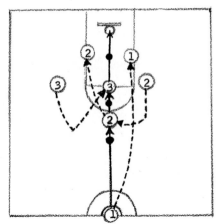

Figure No. 14-22.   Center Play.

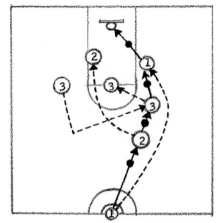

Figure No. 14–23.   Alternate Center Play.

shot is blocked, F_2 and F_3 who are moving in for a rebound, pull out for a pass and setup from scrimmage. (See Figure 14–23.)

DUTIES AND SPECIFIC SKILLS OF EACH PLAYER

All players should be skilled in ball handling, passing, maneuvering, and guarding. Specific skills include:

FORWARDS

1. Several consistent shots for scoring
2. Ability to move in and recover rebounds
3. Ability to maneuver against player to player and zone defense
4. Ability to vary style and speed of play, avoiding "set plays"
5. Ability to "feel out" style and weaknesses of a single guard and of total defense
6. Ability to pass to a spot so moving player receives the ball
7. Ability to regain composure and shoot quickly

GUARDS
1. Ability to "feel out" strengths and weaknesses of opposing forwards. To look for patterns of movement repeated frequently
2. Ability to anticipate movements of the opposing forwards without being drawn out by feints
3. Alertness to signals used by opponent
4. Ability to cover a teammate's position, if necessary
5. Ability to play the ball, rather than an opponent
6. Ability to "tie-up" ball
7. Ability to change defensive team pattern and individual guarding style when the situation requires it
8. Ability to rebound and change to offensive play

CLASS ORGANIZATION

All players, whether they will eventually be forwards or guards, should develop fundamental skills—including shooting—and experience play at both positions. Drills should be conducted so all available floor space and baskets are utilized at all times. Ten or 12 players can usually participate in each drill. If stations are set up, squads can rotate during the drill sessions and larger numbers can be handled. Half court play is advisable when classes are large and the players are not conditioned to a full court; however, full court, official games should be important in the unit. Officiating and observing should be planned and evaluated as part of the unit.

The following drill formations are helpful in developing specific skills:
1. *Bounce and pivot drill.* Number 1 bounces, stops, pivots and passes back to #2 who moves to meet the pass. Repeat until all players have a turn. May be varied with dribble and pivot.

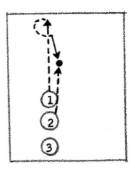

2. *Catching and passing drill.* Number 1 in each line runs forward to meet pass and return the ball to A. Players should be encouraged to meet the ball on the move. The ball should be received without crossing the center line. Passes should be delivered from the catching position. Player A is changed after the complete squad has practiced.

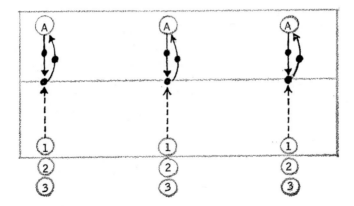

3. *Dribble-pivot drill.* Player #1 has possession of the ball. She takes a dribble which must carry her across second line before she recovers it on the rebound. She then takes a rear pivot or reverse turn and passes the ball to player #2.

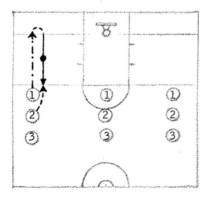

4. *Dribble-scoring-shooting.* Player #1 dribbles to the left of a stationary guard trailed by teammate #2, and screens as #2 shoots.

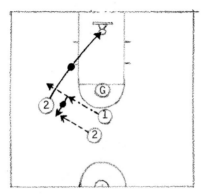

5. *Drill for shooting and ball recovery.* Player in line 3 has the ball and dribbles across in front of line 2 and passes to line 1 player who is running toward the basket and shoots. Player in line 2 recovers the ball and passes it to line 3 for a repeat drill. Player from line 1 goes to the end of line 2, line 2 goes to line 3, line 3 goes to line 1.

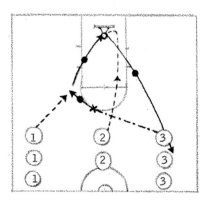

6. *Drill involving passing, catching, guarding, and shooting.* Player #1 receives the pass from #2. Number 2 immediately runs in and simulates a guard on defense. Number 1 dribbles either right or left and shoots. Number 2 takes the position of #1; #3 takes the position of #2 and #1 goes to the end of the line. Accurate form and skill in passing and shooting are the goals of the drill.

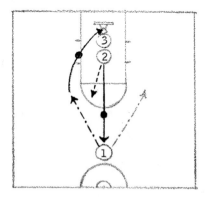

7. *Feint and pivot drill.* B bounces or dribbles as A comes out to guard her. B feints to one side, pivots to the other side and passes back to the next player, C, who comes to meet the pass.

C and D repeat the drill as players A and B go to the ends of the opposite lines.

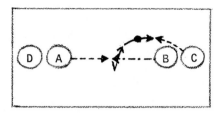

8. *Passing drill.* Three girls line up in the following manner:

All players start to run an even, natural stride in the same direction. Number 1 passes the ball diagonally ahead to #2 and then #1 runs behind #2 who is moving toward the center position. Number 2 passes to #3 who has advanced and then #2 runs behind #3. The passing and changing continue as players move down and back the length of the floor.

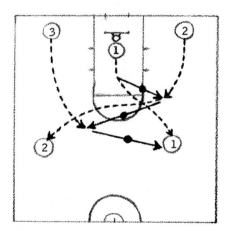

9. *Set shot drill.* Two lines, one on either side of the basket. Number 1 shoots and goes to end of line B. Number 2 recovers the ball, passes to #3 and goes to end of line A. Continue until all players have shot and recovered from *both sides* several times. A variation can be a drill for the lay-up if the lines move far-

ther from the basket. Practice the lay-up from a run, and preceded by a dribble.

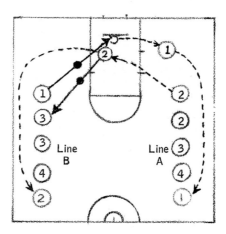

10. *Triangular shooting drill.* Player #1 is at the free throw line.
    Player #2 pivots and passes to #1 who is moving toward the
    basket. Player #1 shoots, recovers and passes to #3. Player #2
    has moved to the free throw line in preparation for a break for
    the basket.

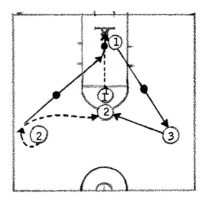

TEACHING PROGRESSION

Most players have some background and skill in catching, passing, and
shooting a ball before beginning basketball game skills. On the first day of
the basketball unit students should become familiar with the court area
and general purpose of the game. One of the best ways to demonstrate the
need for skill development is to play a basketball-type game, suited to the
student's skill level, during the first lesson. Throughout the unit, encourage
game play frequently to point up skill development and rules.

A teaching unit for beginners or intermediates might be planned as follows:

Lesson I

1. Nature and purpose of the game
2. Keep away or "captain ball"
3. Demonstration, drills, and games using:
   One hand underarm and overarm pass
   Chest pass
4. Combine passing and guarding

Lesson II

1. History of basketball
2. Review catching, passing, guarding skills
3. Demonstrate and practice two-handed chest shot, one hand push shot
4. Novelty events using shooting skills
5. Bounce pass
6. Novelty game stressing new skills

Lesson III

1. Review
2. Two-handed underhand shot
3. Explain basic rules
4. Practice feints, dodges while being guarded
5. Informal game (stop play only when necessary to explain rules, etc.)

Lesson IV

1. Review with student question period
2. Two-handed overhead passes and shots
3. Lay-up shots
4. Dribble
5. Relays stressing dribbling, stopping, and passing
6. Brief game

Lesson V

1. Chalk talk on offensive team play, and player to player defense
2. Practice set plays from center
3. Jump for tie ball

4. Practice rebounding
5. Game situation

Lesson VI

1. Review of rules
2. Official game—changing players' positions at half time
3. Students evaluation of their progress

Lesson VII

1. Review skills, simple offensive and defensive tactics
2. Hook pass and shot
3. Chalk talk on zone guarding
4. Practice both forward and guard system of zone guarding

Lessons VIII and IX

1. General review—skills and rules
2. Regulation game
3. Beginning officiating skills

Lesson X

1. Stress offense play with moving passes, evasive tactics, and play development
2. Encourage team cooperation in zone defense

Lesson XI

1. Skills tests and rating scales
2. Begin class tournament with substitutes keeping incidence charts on teammates

Lesson XII

1. Written examination
2. Continue class tournament

Subsequent Lessons for More Advanced Players

1. Stress shifting zone defense
2. Deceptive offensive action using fast, accurate passing, feinting, pivoting, and screening
3. Encourage development of students' officiating skills

SKILL DIFFICULTIES AND THEIR CORRECTION

Difficulty	*Correction*

I ERRORS IN INDIVIDUAL TECHNIQUES
1. Catching

1.

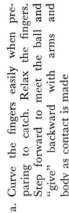

a. Ball hits hands and bounces free due to tense hands and arms

a. Curve the fingers easily when preparing to catch. Relax the fingers. Step forward to meet the ball and "give" backward with arms and body as contact is made

b. The catcher slaps at the ball to avoid catching and "hurting the fingers"

b. Use two relaxed hands and point the fingers up or down, depending on ball height, but *never* directly toward the ball

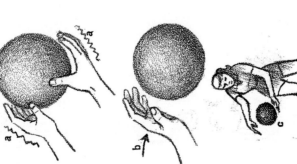

c. Ball gets by a player who is attempting to catch on the side of the body

c. Place one hand behind the ball, the other on the side when catching on the side of the body

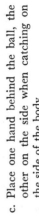
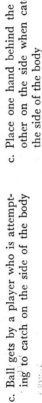

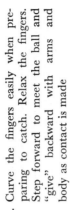

SKILL DIFFICULTIES AND THEIR CORRECTION (*Continued*)

Difficulty	*Correction*
2. Passing	2.
a. Errors committed on all passes	a.
(1) Ball is pushed with palm of the hand resulting in loss of control and force	(1) Control the ball's path and momentum with fingers and wrists
(2) Pass is slow and looping allowing opponent time to intercept	(2) Pass directly to target by snapping wrists and extending fingers. Step behind the pass whenever possible to add momentum and direction
(3) Ball begins flight and suddenly drops short of target as arms pull back instead of following-through	(3) Follow-through with palms turning toward the line of ball flight and extend the arms and wrists. The body moves forward when possible
b. Chest Pass	b.
(1) Loss of power and direction as hands push from the sides with elbows away from the body	(1) Teacher demonstrates how important body force is to the accuracy of the pass. Stress elbows close to the body and hands will fall more naturally on the rear of the ball

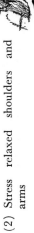

(2) Stress relaxed shoulders and arms

(2) Body erect and stiff slowing the entire pass motion

c. Underhand Passes

c.

(1) Ball loops high due to delayed release

(1) On two-handed pass release ball about waist level with a wrist snap *in the direction* of ball flight. On side passes be certain the passing elbow is away from the body. On one hand pass step forward to flatten the swing arc, and let the ball roll off straightened fingers at waist level. The teacher may mark a wall target for student to throw toward in practicing the release

(2) Ball is fumbled or lost as a player attempts to tie it

(2) Keep both hands on the ball until the release. Use the underhand passes cautiously when opponent is guarding closely

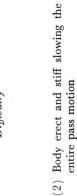

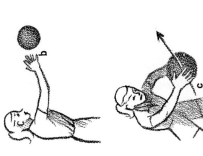

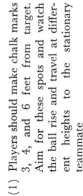

SKILL DIFFICULTIES AND THEIR CORRECTION (*Continued*)

Difficulty	*Correction*

d. Shoulder Passes

(1) Ball is fumbled or tied as the beginning passer brings the ball back on one hand

d.

(1) Teacher reviews technique of pass, stressing the importance of the free hand as a steadying guide

e. Two-Handed Overhead Pass

(1) Pass is over used causing slow game and encourages charging when guarded closely

(2) Pass loops high as ball drops behind the passer's head before delivered

e.

(1) and (2) Use the pass sparingly and quickly when a high pass is received. Practice passing to a teammate, avoiding the drop behind the head. Step forward to flatten the flight even more

f. Bounce Pass

(1) Players bounce the ball too close or too far from teammate so she has trouble gaining possession

f.

(1) Players should make chalk marks 3, 4, and 6 feet from target. Aim for these spots and watch the ball rise and travel at different heights to the stationary teammate

(2) Ball is brought high over the shoulder and thrown straight down, resulting in a high bounding vertical pass easily intercepted

(2) Keep the ball close to the shoulder. See (1) above. Follow-through with the arm in the direction of the ball flight to the floor

(3) Goal Shooting

Many errors of shooting due to loss of power, direction, and momentum are caused by poor hand and wrist action, follow-through, and body position as described in passing difficulty and correction. See the preceding section. Errors common to all shots are:

a. Failure to arch the ball due to stiff wrists, a palm push, or loss of power by elbows extended to the side

a. Teacher should review common principles in chest and shoulder shots, and underarm loop shot. Elbows are in toward body, fingers and wrists release the ball upward as the arm(s) and hand(s) follow-through [See (b) below.]

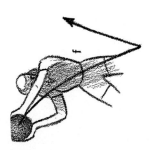

355

SKILL DIFFICULTIES AND THEIR CORRECTION (*Continued*)

Difficulty	*Correction*
b. Releasing the ball and lunging with the body result in a hard rebounding ball	b. Stress the importance of a medium arch. Demonstrate and explain that a low, flat arch cannot enter the basket from above, and a very high arch is difficult to control and slow, allowing the opponents time to get set for a rebound
c. Failure to spot and deliver to selected lay-up spot	c. Suggest that student stands by the basket, selects a spot and an angle and *watches* the spot and ball as she delivers. Repeat several times, then trot and run in—"always get as close to the spot as possible by running and jumping and keep watching the spot until delivery"
d. Taking-off from the right foot for a lay-up (right-handed) resulting in improper balance and awkward landing	d. Teachers reviews mechanics of opposition movement. Demonstrate how the body turns toward the court so the shooter is ready to rebound

II ERRORS IN TEAM STRATEGY

1. Committed by guard when forwards attack

a. Guarding too close allowing forward to feint and pivot so she gets between the guard and the basket

b. Playing the forward and not the ball often results in defensive play only

c. Playing a "watching" game as forward recovers her own shot or play is under the basket

d. Failing to shift and cover for a teammate whose forward slipped by

2. Committed by guards when they gain the ball

a. Delaying action to their forwards giving opponents an opportunity to regain or tie ball

1.

a. Maintain enough distance, depending on player's agility and skill at anticipating moves, to keep the forward away from the basket

b. Watch the ball as well as the player and be aggressive in intercepting passes. Anticipate a pass to your forward and move in

c. Stay alert and play for the ball

d. Stay alert and aware of all players in own half court and position of the ball. Teacher should emphasize that guards have more than a one person responsibility even in player to player defense pattern

2.

a. If the ball is being brought in from out of bounds, move quickly before opponents get set. If the ball is in the court move it down the sideline if necessary, taking the safest path

SKILL DIFFICULTIES AND THEIR CORRECTION (*Continued*)

Difficulty	*Correction*
b. Throwing long looping passes to their forwards	b. To avoid interception, use short, fast, accurate passes to work the ball across the center. Long passes are used only when time is short or there is a forward clear to receive the pass
3. Committed by forwards when attacking and guarding	3.
a. Standing still awaiting or calling for a pass until a guard has time to cover	a. Forward should keep moving and receive most passes at a spot and jumping in the air
b. Holding the ball too long or faking long enough for the defense to get set	b. Keep the ball moving and players moving
c. Bunching under the basket making rebounds and shooting difficult	c. See (b) above
d. Bouncing under the basket allowing guards time to intercept	d. Teacher points out the bounce is time consuming and poorly controlled. Player should shoot or move the ball out to a teammate
e. Consistently cut and break in the same pattern, or use unperfected and complicated plays	e. Use three or four simple, perfected plays and change to a spontaneous form when it seems possible or necessary to score
f. Failing to try and recover ball when guards gain possession	f. Use player to player defense or blockade zone

NOVELTY EVENTS

Horse. A goal shooting contest where participants follow the leader. The first player shoots from any place on the court using any style of shot. If the shot is missed the next player may select type and place of shot. If the first shooter makes the goal, the second player must attempt the same type shot from the same position. If she makes the shot, the player following must attempt the same shot. The first player to miss gains an "H." The player following the "H," may set a new style and position. As players miss they add "H," "O," "R," "S," and "E," and when a "horse" is determined, the game is over.

Spot Shot. Spots are placed on the floor in front of the basket at 5, 10 and 15 feet and at any angle from the basket. Players have three shots from each spot. The goals score a point each. The winning team or player has the greatest number of points.

Circle the Globe. Mark 6 spots in a semi-circle around the goal area. A player begins at the first number and progresses as far as she can without missing a shot. When a player misses she stays by her spot, passes the ball to the next player who progresses as far as possible without missing. The winner is the first player to complete the trip "around the globe."

Variation: *Ladder Climb*. Mark lines at 45° angles to left and right of the basket. Players begin at the rung farthest from the goal and move up the ladder.

Dare You. Mark and number ten spots anywhere on the halfcourt. (Beginners should be closer to the basket than advanced players.) Players begin from spot #1. When a shot is made, the player progresses to the next spot for another shot immediately. If she misses, her competitors call "dare you" to which she must reply "take it" or "stay." If she "takes it," she takes another turn from the spot where the last shot was missed. If she makes the shot, she continues until she misses and must again hear "dare you." If she misses she goes to the number one spot to await her turn and begin again.

If she "stays," she remains at the spot where she missed until her next turn.

The winner is the first player who shoots successfully for the tenth spot.

Twenty-One. Players shoot in sequence. The first shot, a long one, is taken outside of the free throw circle. Whether the basket is made or missed the player rebounds and takes a short shot close to the basket. Long shots score two points, short shots one point. The person making 21 points first is the winner.

Arch Goal Ball. Two teams, lined up one behind the other, stand facing the basket 15 or 20 feet away from it. At signal, the ball is passed over the heads of the players. When the last player in line gets the ball, she dribbles forward and shoots for the basket, continuing until she is successful. She then takes her place at the head of the line and the game continues until one team finishes and is declared the winner.

Variation: Each player shoots only once for the basket, scoring one point for her team if successful. Five points are scored for the team finishing first. The team with the highest number of points wins.

Beginning players may benefit from the numerous novelty games. These include: Sudden Death Basketball, One Goal Basketball, Sideline Basketball, Scramble Basketball, Bucket Ball, Captain Ball, and Endball.[1]

OFFICIATING TECHNIQUES

Officials are a necessary part of basketball. The teacher and students, acting as referees and umpires may call practice games and intramural games. It is desirable that interscholastic games be officiated by persons holding ratings of the Women's National Officials Rating Committee.[2] The umpire and referee are assisted by one or two timers and one or two scorers.

The floor officials should wear a comfortable skirt, blouse, and blazer with appropriate shoes. Both officials have whistles. Rated officials should wear the official uniform—a navy blue and white tailored cotton blouse with the WNORC emblem.

At the beginning of a game one official is designated as official-in-charge and she begins as the referee. The referee takes a position on the side opposite the timers and scorers and the umpire begins on the side opposite the referee. Each official has approximately one half of the floor as the leading official and the other half as the trailing official. Each is responsible for the side nearest her and the end and goal area to her right. The arbitrary court division does not restrict an official in calling fouls and violations anywhere on or off the court. The leading official moves with the ball so she is always in a position to see a play in her own territory. In order to be in a better position to see rule infringements, the leading official stations herself near the end line during close play at the basket.

A summary of the duties of the officials follows:

Both Officials
1. Must be aware of "before game procedures," review signals for scoring and timekeeping, and check equipment used for timing, scoring, and during game play.
2. Must call fouls, violations, tie balls, out of bounds, and goals and know the procedure following each for executing free throws, throw-ins, jump balls, and center throws.

Referee's Specific Duties
1. Starts the game and each quarter with a center throw.
2. Signals goal scored and indicates team and person scoring when score is in own half of court.

---

[1] For detailed descriptions of these games see Donnelly, R. J., Helms, W. G., and Mitchell, E. D.: *Active Games and Contests,* New York, The Ronald Press, 1958.

[2] Information on securing ratings and detailed techniques of officiating are available in *Basketball Guide,* current edition, The Division for Girls and Women's Sports, 1201 16th Street, N.W., Washington 6, D.C.

3. Tosses all balls when the jump is taken in the center restraining circle.

4. Recognizes timer's whistle at end of quarters, half, or complete game and signals end of playing period.

5. Sees that a disqualified player leaves the court before a free throw is taken.

6. At the end of the game checks score book and announces the results.

Umpire's Specific Duties

1. Starts the center throw after field goals when the ball is closer to her than to the referee.

2. Signals and announces the goals scored in the basket to her right.

3. Informs scorers when necessary.

4. Checks with scorers concerning substitutes.

5. Warns players and notifies them when they are disqualified. Notifies the referee of disqualifications.

6. Notifies captains and scorers if time for substitution is exceeded.

EVALUATING THE RESULTS

Evaluation should show an adequate measure of the student's knowledge, skill, and ability as an individual player and team member. The following evaluative techniques are suggested.

1. Use of an incident chart by the teacher to see the number of times during a game a player passes and shoots successfully, fumbles the ball, intercepts a pass, rebounds, travels, fouls, etc.

2. Use of student evaluation of herself and fellow classmates as cooperating team members.

3. Observation of student's use of skill and strategy in a game.

4. Written test of rules, safety precautions, and game strategy.

5. Observation of officiating skill.

6. Simple skills tests of ball handling, shooting, maneuvering, and jumping. The following are three examples of self-testing activities which can be administered with student help.

   a. *One minute goal shoot.* The first shot is taken at the foul line thereafter the student recovers the ball and shoots as quickly and accurately as possible. Score the number of shots attempted and the number made.

   b. *Jump and reach.* The player stands facing a wall with toes touching. She reaches as high as possible, feet remaining flat on the ground. She then turns and jumps without running, touching as high as possible above her first mark. Allow four trials, counting the highest. Record the difference between her reach and the highest jump.

   c. *Speed and accuracy passing.* A circle of 36 inches in diameter is drawn on the wall. The center of the circle is three and a half feet from the floor. The student stands on a line 12 feet from the wall. Each pass must be made behind the line, although she may go forward to recover the ball. Using selected passes, score the number of successful hits made in the circle in 30 seconds. Allow two 30 second trials for the chest, shoulder, and underarm passes scoring only the better results in each case.

TERMINOLOGY

Blocking—Personal contact which impedes the progress of an opponent not in possession of the ball

Boxing-up—A player with the ball is guarded between two opponents so she cannot pass or shoot successfully. It results in a foul

Center Throw—Method of beginning play at each period and after each goal. The official throws to an unobstructed forward in the center circle

Charging—A foul committed by the player in possession of the ball as she moves the ball or her body to make contact with an opponent

Foul—A rule infraction by a team or individual which results in one or more free throws for the opponent

Free Throw—An unguarded attempt for a basket taken behind the free throw line and awarded to a player as a penalty for opponent's foul

Holding the Ball—A violation for possession of the ball more than three seconds in the court, 5 seconds out of bounds or 10 seconds taking a foul shot

Juggle—Playing the ball so one person gives impetus to the ball into the air and gains possession of it again before it is touched by another player or hits the floor

Jump Ball—A ball tossed between two opponents in one of the three restraining circles. Players attempt to tap the ball to their respective teammates

Obstruction—A foul involving personal contact with an opponent who is in the act of bouncing, dribbling, passing, shooting, juggling, or pivoting

Pivoting—Moving the body around in a circle, or part of a circle, while one foot remains in contact with the floor

Tie Ball—Opposing players gain possession, with one or two hands, of the ball simultaneously; or one player places both hands securely on a ball already held by an opponent

Traveling—Progression, such as jumping or walking while maintaining possession of the ball

Violation—A rule infraction which results in a throw-in from out of bounds by the opposing team. When both teams have simultaneous violations, play is resumed by a jump ball

DISCUSSION QUESTIONS

1. What qualifications do you look for in selecting guards and forwards for membership on your intramural teams?
2. Plan a basketball clinic for 25 of your classmates who wish to develop skills in officiating.
3. Plan a ten lesson unit for a. beginning players, b. advanced players.
4. Using a chalk board or magnetic board, demonstrate and explain the comparative values and use of a. player to player defense, b. area zone defense, and c. shifting zone defense.

5. Explain procedure and draw up plans for a high school round robin tournament for seven teams. As the person in charge of the tournament, what suggestions will you make concerning eligibility, officiating, and awards?

Selected Audio-Visual Aids

Basketball Coaching Kit. (24" × 36" steel playing court and magnetic pieces). The Program Aids Company, Inc., 550 Fifth Avenue, New York, N. Y.

Basketball Rules for Girls, 1954. (6 unit filmstrip), 1955 Supplement (1 unit). Teaching Aids Service, 31 Union Square West, New York 3, N. Y. (Purchase)

Basketball Strategy for Girls, 1955. (10 min., 16 mm. film and loop film, sound, b & w). Young America Films, Inc., 18 E. 41st Street, New York 17, N. Y. (Purchase)

Basketball Techniques for Girls, 1955. (10 min., 16 mm. film and loop film, sound, b & w). Young America Films, Inc., 18 E. 41st Street, New York 17, N. Y. (Purchase)

Defensive Footwork in Basketball (boy's film). (9 min., 16 mm., sound, b & w). Encyclopedia Britannica Films, 1150 Wilmette Avenue, Wilmette, Illinois. (Purchase and Rental)

Illustrated Sports Charts, 1951. (Packet of eight 11" × 17" wall charts). University of Colorado Book Store, Boulder, Colorado.

Observing Girls' Basketball Skills, 1955. (30 min., 16 mm., sound, b & w). Bureau of Audio-Visual Instruction, State University of Iowa, Iowa City, Iowa. (Purchase and Rental)

Shooting in Basketball (boy's film). (10 min., sound, b & w). Encyclopedia Britannica Films, 1150 Wilmette Avenue, Wilmette, Illinois. (Purchase and Rental)

Suggested Readings

Anderson, Forrest: *Basketball Techniques Illustrated,* New York, Ronald Press, 1952.

Basketball Guide, Current Edition, DGWS, 1201 16th Street, N.W., Washington 6, D.C.

Kennard, R.: *Tips on Girls' Basketball,* Sports Tips and Teaching Aid, Marion, Indiana, 1941.

Lawrence, Helen B., and Fox, Grace I.: *Basketball for Girls and Women,* New York, McGraw-Hill Book Co., Inc., 1954.

Meissner, Wilhelmine, and Myers, Elizabeth: *Basketball for Girls,* revised edition, New York, The Ronald Press, 1950.

Meyer, Margaret H., and Schwarz, Marguerite M.: *Team Sports for Women,* ed. 3, Philadelphia, W. B. Saunders Company, 1957.

Miller, Donna Mae, and Ley, Katherine L.: *Individual and Team Sports for Women,* ed. 3, Philadelphia, W. B. Saunders Company, 1955.

Paterson, Ann, editor: *Team Sports for Girls,* New York. The Ronald Press, 1958.

Redin, Harley J.: *The Queens Fly High,* 2011 W. 10th Street, Plainview, Texas, 1958.

Selected Basketball Articles, Division for Girls and Women's Sports of the American Association for Health, Physical Education, and Recreation, 1201 16th Street, N.W., Washington 6, D.C.

Periodicals

Athletic Journal, Athletic Journal Publishing Co., 1719 Howard Street, Evanston, Ill.

Journal of the American Association for Health, Physical Education, and Recreation, 1201 16th Street, N.W., Washington 6, D.C.

Scholastic Coach, Scholastic Magazine, Inc., 33 W. 42nd Street, New York 36, N.Y.

15

Field Hockey

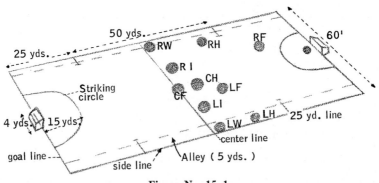

50 yds.
25 yds.
60'
RW RH RF
R I
CH
Striking circle
LF
CF LI
4 yds. 15 yds.
LW LH 25 yd. line
goal line
center line
side line Alley (5 yds.)

Figure No. 15–1.

Hockey is one of our oldest team games. Early Greek art and Egyptian hieroglyphics show figures playing the sport with sticks similar to those used today. The word "hockey" comes from the French "hoguet." In Ireland the game has been called "hurley," "shinty" in Scotland, and "bandy" in Wales. Originally, it was an activity for men, but now it is played almost exclusively by girls and women.

Field hockey was brought to the United States from England in 1901 and introduced to the college women at Vassar, Bryn Mawr, Smith, Wellesley, and Mount Holyoke by Constance Applebee. "The Apple" as she is affectionately known throughout the country by her many admirers, still advises and coaches. It is largely through her efforts that hockey has been so enthusiastically received and has grown in popularity in America. In 1922, the United States Field Hockey Association was organized to promote the best interests of the game. Girls and women who enjoy playing may join the local hockey clubs which form this association. Since 1927, when the International Federation of Women's Hockey Associations was formed, teams

364

from England, Scotland, Wales, Australia, New Zealand, South Africa and the United States have enjoyed competing against each other. An All-American team, composed of outstanding players from sectional and national tournaments, plays throughout this country as well as in Europe, Australia, and South Africa, demonstrating games and taking part in hockey clinics.

NATURE, PURPOSE AND SCORING OF THE GAME

Hockey is a field sport in which two teams of eleven players each try to score goals, using a wooden stick and a hard ball. Players move the ball by dribbling and passing.

Scoring.   For a goal to count at least one member of the attacking team must contact the ball within the defenders' striking circle. Goals count one point and are scored only if the whole ball passes over the goal line into the goal cage.

Players.   A hockey team is composed of five forwards (a center forward, two inners, and two wings), and six defensive players (three halfbacks, two fullbacks and a goalkeeper). "Right" or "left" precedes the position names of inners, wings and fullbacks. Halfbacks are called "right," "left," or "center," e.g., right wing or center halfback. Every player (except the goalkeeper) must carry a stick during the game and use it to move the ball. The ball may be stopped with the stick, with the hand or with the foot, but the goalkeeper is the only player who may advance the ball with her body, legs, or hands.

The Game.   An official game is played in two 30 minute halves with a ten minute half time. Time outs may only be called by an umpire and are taken for injury, damaged equipment, or game interference. Games for less experienced players are usually shortened to 25 or 15 minute halves. The ball is put into play with a center bully at the beginning of each half, and after a goal has been scored.

NEEDED FACILITIES AND EQUIPMENT

The following items represent a minimum list of necessary equipment and facilities which should be available. They are discussed in more detail below.

1. A well marked, turfed, and smooth field
2. A stick for each player
3. At least one ball for every 8 to 10 players
4. Shin guards for each person
5. Two pairs of goalie pads
6. Distinguishing team pinnies
7. Whistles, official rule guide, score book
8. First aid kit
9. Protective glasses guards

Field.   The playing field is a turf covered rectangle 90 to 100 yards long by 50 to 60 yards wide. (The turf should be as smooth as possible with all lines clearly marked with 2 inch white lines.) At the center of each goal line is a goal four yards wide. Two 7 foot goal posts, four yards apart and joined by a crossbar seven feet from the ground mark the goal mouth. Six feet behind the goal line are two 6 foot posts. The sides, back, and top are enclosed by netting or wire mesh.

The field is divided into two equal halves by a *center line* parallel to the goal lines. Two lines at either end of the field, at right angles to the sideline and extending onto the field seven yards indicate the *25 yard lines.* Parallel to, and five yards in from each sideline is a broken *five yard line.* The space between side and five yard lines is called the *alley.* At each end of the field is a *striking circle.* The "circle" is actually two quarter circles, measured 15 yards from the corresponding goal post, and joined in front of the goal by a 4 yard line parallel to the goal line.

Equipment

Stick.   The hockey stick has two major parts, a shaft-like handle, and a curved head. The left side of the head is the flat, hitting surface, the right side is rounded. Only the flat side may be used to contact the ball. There are no left-handed hockey sticks, right and left-handed players use the same stick and grip.

Hockey sticks vary in weight, height, and hand grip, and should be selected to fit the individual player. Sticks, as in other sports equipment, vary in quality. The head is made of ash and the grain of the wood should follow the curve of the blade. The handle, or shaft, is cane with rubber insertions, bound with string and encased in a rubber grip.

Selection of a stick depends on the player's height, arm length, playing

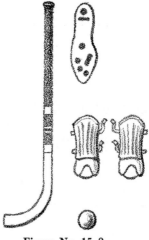

Figure No. 15–2.

position, and preference. To determine the length of stick needed, hold the stick vertically with both hands at the top of the handle—the blade should just clear the ground. Weight and size of blade should also be considered. Forward line players may prefer lighter sticks with thinner blades, backfield players may choose sticks with heavier heads.

Balls. Official hockey balls are made of cork and string, covered with leather or plastic and painted white. Composition cork balls are less expensive and are used for practice.

Costume. The player's gymnasium costume is satisfactory for instructional purposes but for school or club games a tunic is recommended. Freedom of motion and appropriateness are the chief determiners. Socks and rubber-soled shoes are essential. Rubber-cleated shoes are helpful on wet or muddy fields. Shin guards should be worn to protect the lower legs.

The goalkeeper wears white hockey leg pads and heavy shoes. The leg pads are much larger than shin guards, extending from ankle to thigh. They should be buckled to the outside of the player's legs. Cleated, square toed, padded shoes protect the goalkeeper when kicking the ball. Squares of sponge rubber inserted over the instep increase protection for the foot.

Care of Equipment

Stick. During the season the stick should be carefully wiped and stored. After each session all dirt is removed, rough places are sanded smooth and linseed oil or wax is applied to the head. If worn, rubber grips will need replacing, and the decorative stringing holding the grip in place re-tied. Sticks should be stored in a cool, dry place.

Ball. Match balls probably will need repainting after each match. Practice balls, depending on amount of use, should be repainted two or three times during the season. A ball rack makes painting easier and holds freshly painted balls.

Shin Guards. Straps and rubber pieces should be kept in repair. Buckling shin guards in pairs after use is a time saver.

Goal Keeping Equipment. Goal pads should be brushed, straps checked and buckled in pairs and then stored in a dry, well ventilated place.

Goal shoes collect mud and often require scraping. Neat's foot oil is used to protect the leather.

TEACHING UNITS

A hockey teaching unit may be built around the following suggested topics. The flick, left hand lunge and circular tackle may not be appropriate for all groups.

Unit for Beginners	*Unit for Advanced Students*
Brief history	Review of all basic skills and rules
Nature and purpose of the game	Advanced skills
Safety measures	Scoop

Unit for Beginners	*Unit for Advanced Students*

Unit for Beginners

Basic stickwork
Passing
    Drive
    Push pass
    Flick
    Fielding
Tackles
    Straight tackle
    Left hand lunge
    Circular tackle
Goalkeeping
The roll-in
The bully
Rules
Simple game strategy

Unit for Advanced Students

Left job or jab
Right cut
Right hand lunge
Advanced strategy
Officiating
Evaluation

Rainy Day Suggestions

Indoor practice of the bully, tackles, push and flick passes
Films and filmstrips of games and rules
Discussion of rules, player positions, and duties
Game strategy—chalk talk or magnetized board
Care and repair of equipment

BASIC SKILLS

To play field hockey well, one must master the following skills:

Holding the Stick. Put the head of the stick on the ground, toe pointing forward and handle against player's leg. Place the left hand at the top of the stick and grip easily. Raise the stick to a vertical position, toe pointing back over player's head. The right hand is placed directly below the left, fingers curled around the handle. A "V" formed by the thumb and index finger of each hand is in line with the toe of the stick. Lower the stick to a perpendicular position, so the head is slightly to the right and in front of the right foot. The flat (hitting surface) is facing forward. The left forearm is straight and in line with the stick, and hands and wrists are relaxed. This is the basic grip position. The left hand maintains this position, but for some strokes, the right hand moves farther down the stick.

The Dribble. This is a series of short taps on the ball so a player can "carry" the ball. The right hand is placed about four inches down the stick. The back of the left hand should be facing forward. In this position the elbows are away from the body, the left elbow pointing diagonally forward. With the stick nearly perpendicular, the wrists move the stick forward and back so the ball is advanced by a series of short, sharp taps. The ball is dribbled in front and slightly to the right of the right foot. The body faces

Figure No. 15–3. The Dribble.

Figure No. 15–4. Carrying the Stick while Moving.

forward, the left shoulder slightly ahead of the right, in good running position. The ball should be tapped hard enough to allow rapid running between taps, but not so hard an opponent will intercept.

Carrying the Stick. The stick is carried in a comfortable position for running and so it may be quickly used for play. The left hand is at the top of the handle, the right halfway down, with the stick parallel to the ground in front of the player.

Drive

Figure No. 15–5.   A. The Stationary Drive; B. The Running Drive.

Drives.   Drives are powerful strokes used for passing and shooting. The hands are together and the stick perpendicular to the ground. The stick swings with a pendulum-like motion in line with the intended path of the ball.

Stationary Drive.   The stance is open, from 1½ to 2 feet apart, and the body turned sideways to the direction of the intended hit. The ball should be slightly nearer the left foot, about 18 inches from the toes. A quick backswing followed by a forward swing should meet the ball squarely as weight shifts from right to left and arms straighten in the follow-through of the stick below shoulder level. Wrists should stiffen in order to prevent swinging the stick above the shoulders, or making "sticks."

The Moving Drive.   The right foot is forward with the ball outside and a little behind it. The left shoulder should be in line with the direction of the intended pass. As the stroke is made, the body twists from the waist, the stick swings backward then forward in the direction the ball is aimed.

The Push Pass.   This is a wrist stroke used to pass quickly to a nearby teammate. The grip is the same as for the dribble. The weight is on the forward foot. With the blade directly behind the ball, the right hand pushes sharply forward simultaneously with a slight pull back with the left. The follow-through continues until the right arm is straight and toe of the stick faces up.

The Scoop.   This is used for short passes, goal shooting, and as a dodge. Lay the stick back so that the blade slants upward. Separate hands, with the left at the top and the right midway down. The ball should be in front and slightly to the right of the forward foot. Place the stick toe under the ball, scoop up and shove forward by pulling upward and forward with the right hand, simultaneously with a downward thrust of the left.

The Flick.   Accurate and hard to intercept, the flick is similar to the push pass (see above) except the ball is lifted slightly off the ground. As the stick contacts the ball both wrists and the left arm twist quickly to the left. The hitting surface should be turned toward the ground at the completion of the stroke. Emphasis is placed on a low follow-through.

Figure No. 15–6.   The Push Pass.

Figure No. 15–7.   The Scoop.

Figure No. 15–8.   The Flick.

The Jab or Job.   A one-handed spoil stroke used when maximum reach is needed. *Either hand* may be at the top of the stick and the jab is made from either side of the opponent. The bottom edge of the blade jabs the ball. The stick arm is extended and the reach increased by a step toward the ball. This is a "last resort" stroke and several jabs may be needed to contact the ball.

Stopping the Ball.   The ball may be stopped with the stick, hand, or foot.

Figure No. 15–9. Stopping the Ball.

Figure No. 15–10. The Left Hand Lunge.

With the Stick. Give with the ball (the dead stick method), or meet the ball by moving the stick up and forward so that it will rebound off the ball (the loose stick method).

With the Hand. Stop ball with upheld hand so it will fall directly to the ground.

With the Foot. Step on it at the instep by trapping it with the foot in a quick, decisive movement.

Tackles. These are used when a player wants to get the ball from an opponent, or force a pass. Tackles should be made when the ball is away from the opponent's stick.

The Straight Tackle. The straight tackle is made from the front. Hold the stick in dribbling position. The weight should be on the forward foot, the body bent slightly forward. The tackler is facing and slightly to the stick side of her opponent. The stick head is put firmly on the ground, ahead of the oncoming ball. As the ball hits the tackler's stick, she starts to dribble.

The Left Hand Lunge. The tackler is on the opponent's stick side running in the same direction. The stick is in the carrying position. As the lunge is made the weight is on the left foot, the stick held only in the left hand. The stick head is "thrown down" just in front of the ball. The tackler quickly turns to her left, places her right hand on the stick, and begins dribbling.

The Circular Tackle. This is used by a player tackling on the opponent's left side. Both players are running in the same direction, or the tackler is coming diagonally from the left of the dribbler. The tackler moves slightly ahead of her opponent and circles in front. The ball is contacted when off the opponent's stick. The tackler dribbles the ball away.

Dodges. There are ways the player with the ball avoids an opponent. The element of surprise is important in all dodges. In executing the *right dodge,* send the ball to the tackler's *non-stick* side with a short pass so it rolls behind the opponent. The dodger runs past the stick side of the

Figure No. 15–11. The Circular Tackle.

Figure No. 15–12.   The Bully.

opponent. Sometimes called "push right, run left," this dodge is easily intercepted if the ball is sent too far or there is an opponent nearby. The left-
dodge may be equally effective. Just before the player expects to be tackled,
she pulls the ball a few inches to her own left and immediately continues
to dribble. (Sometimes called an "L," because the ball is pulled left and
tapped forward.) The dodger keeps the ball well under control while dribbling so she is able to execute the dodge when tackled.

Scoop. (See scoop stroke, p. 371.) As in the scoop stroke, the ball is
lifted and pushed forward. When the player tackling reaches her stick for
the ball, the dodger scoops over the opponent's stick and continues dribbling.
Control of the ball is essential.

The Bully.   This is used by two opposing players to put the ball in
play at the beginning of each half, after each goal, and after some fouls.
The players taking the bully, stand facing each other, and opposite sidelines. The players' feet are apart, knees bent, and weight forward. The
right hand should be halfway down the handle to give support. The
players tap the ground, then their opponent's stick. Repeat three times.
Sticks are tapped on the ground on either side of the ball and they tap
each other above the ball. (Saying "ground-sticks, ground-sticks, ground-
sticks" may help beginners keep track of the taps.) After the third tap of
the sticks either player may play the ball. All the other players must
be at least five yards away until the bully is completed.

The Roll-in.   A method used to put the ball in play after it has gone
out of bounds over the sideline, unless put out by two opposing players.
Usually taken by a wing, wing halfback, or fullback, the ball is rolled by
a player outside the field to a teammate. All players must be outside the
alley until the ball has been released. The player making the roll-in must
have feet and stick outside the field, and have stick in one hand. The ball

Figure No. 15–13.   The Roll-in.

is rolled along the ground into the field, not bounced or thrown. It is important to be able to take roll-ins with either hand. The player crouches in a forward stride position, getting low to the ground, and uses an underhand swing. She immediately reenters the field.

GAME STRATEGY

Offense Tactics.   All forward players should be fast runners skilled in dribbling the ball quickly downfield, passing, dodging an attacker, and goal shooting. Each player should stay in her own area of the field, passing to teammates rather than dribbling out of position. Team play depends on carefully directed passes and constant awareness by each player of her teammates' positions.

The forwards should play in a line 10 or 12 yards apart with the player dribbling the ball slightly ahead. A pass usually should be ahead of the intended receiver and be perfectly timed for her to pick up and dribble forward. The line must vary its attack in order to deceive the defense, and work together as a strong unit when doing so.

Suggested tactics for free hits and roll-ins are:[1]

1. The forwards must create a space by pulling away from the ball to deceive the defense.
2. If the defense moves with the forward, the ball must be rolled or hit to the space.
3. If the defense does not move with the forward, the ball is rolled or hit directly to the forward's stick.
4. All forwards should be moving on free hits and roll-ins to outwit the opponent.

[1] Volp, Ann: *Coaching Forwards*, Selected Field Hockey and Lacrosse Articles, DGWS, AAHPER, 1955, Washington, D.C.

5. On roll-ins and free hits, the forwards should think of moving away from the opponents, as in man to man guarding in basketball.
6. Vary play on free hits and roll-ins.

In shooting for goals the following suggestions will prove helpful:

1. Learn to shoot from any position and in any direction while on the run.
2. When alone and far ahead of the rest of the forwards, dribble in close and shoot quickly using a push, scoop, or flick.
3. Usually, the inner goal post is the best point of aim when shooting.
4. Follow-up the shot by rushing toward the goalie, trying to outwit her.
5. Vary shots, making some hard, some easy, causing the goalie to mis-time her kicks.

Defense Tactics

Marking. Each back should guard a forward line player, staying close in order to intercept her passes or to tackle. The right halfback should mark the left wing; the right fullback, the left inner; the center halfback, the center forward; the left fullback, the right inner; and the left halfback, the right wing.

Interchanging. On the bully, the center halfback should be about five yards away in order to intercept an opponent's pass or gain control of the ball. Although beginners should learn to play their own position well, advanced players should master the techniques of interchanging and covering, i.e., the defense players change positions as safety players or as hastily-shifted defensive blocks set up to catch an unguarded, rapidly advancing player with the ball. This is used largely when the forwards have moved down to, or behind, the 25 yard line as the remaining defensive players cover to stop the advance.

Covering. To facilitate the interception of long passes and to cover their own half of the field more adequately, fullbacks, and sometimes wing halfbacks, may play in a deeper defensive position. For example, if the ball is on the 50 yard line on the left side of the field, the left fullback will play up the field, closer to the action of play. The right fullback "covers" in a deeper position, closer to the center of the field. Should the ball be passed to the right side of the field, the right fullback moves up and the left fullback shifts back to a "covering" position closer to her own goal line and near the center of the field.

Intercepting. Timing is vitally important in gaining possession of a ball being dribbled or passed to others. Team members must quickly move into position to receive the pass or change the direction of the ball going up or downfield. In order to be adept at such interception, players must watch the ball closely at all times and be ready to move quickly into free space through which a pass might be attempted.

Goalkeeping. The goalkeeper should stand about a yard in front of

Figure No. 15–14.   Goalkeeper and Attackers' Positions When Various Goals are Attempted.

the cage. Unless she is sure she can get the ball away, she should not rush out alone to tackle. As the ball approaches, she should turn toward it with legs and feet close together and be ready and able to shift her position when necessary. She should know where to kick the oncoming ball, or drive it with her stick to the right or left. Although it is safer to stop the ball before clearing, often there is not enough time to do so. She should come out of her position when (1) she can reach the ball before an opponent does, or (2) to meet a lone forward if the goalkeeper is the only defense player in the striking circle. She should never come out when two forwards are free in the circle, for they are too apt to shoot the ball around her. Above all the goalkeeper should be aware that although it is the backs' job to keep the forwards from shooting, her duty is to stop the shot if they do break through and get into scoring position.

DUTIES AND SPECIFIC SKILLS OF PLAYERS

The Attackers.   All forwards should be fast runners, skilled in basic stickwork and be able to play in a united line. Teamwork should be built around the center forward. The wings should be the speediest of the line and be well skilled in driving the ball to the center of the field, or taking it down the alleys. They should be able to work effectively with the inners on the triangular pass and score from either the right or left. On the long or short corners, the wings should center the drive and then move quickly onto the playing field. The right and left inners must work as connectors between the center forward and the wings. Both should be skilled at shooting, and the left inner (and left wing) should master the trick of turning her shoulders and passing to the right, while running. The real job of the forward line is to score points as often as it can.

The Defense.   The halfbacks should be fast, steady, and versatile players whose task it is to back up, mark, and cover the offense. They must be able to feed the ball up to the forward line. The right halfbacks should be skilled in executing the left drive and the left hand lunge, whereas the left halfback should be especially adept at using her right hand on the roll-in and the circular tackle. The center halfback must mark the opposing forward and back up her own forward line, intercept passes, and prevent shooting. As an offensive player, she must be quick to size up situations, know when and where to pass, how to draw an opponent out of position, and be able to score.

The fullbacks should work as a pair, each aware of the other's position on the field and be able to change quickly from offensive to defensive play. Each backs up inner bullies on her side of the field. The right fullback backs up the center bully, behind and to the right of the center half. Both must be skilled tacklers and possess good, accurate driving ability. Offensively they should be fast runners and know when to go to the goalkeeper's assistance.

The goalkeeper must have speed, quick reaction time, agility, endurance, and stability. Above all, she should be a fine team player aware of her relationship to the others on the field. She must be both an attacking and defending player. Preventing the opponents from scoring is only part of her task, for she must also get the ball away, clearing it to her teammates. The player must be highly skilled at kicking, and her mind as well as her body must be ready to meet any quickly changing game situation.

SIMPLIFIED GAME RULES*

OUT OF BOUNDS

If a ball goes over the sideline:	*The ball is put in play by:*
1. From the stick(s) of player(s) on the same team	1. Roll-in for opponents
2. From the sticks of opponents	2. Wing bully on alley line
3. From body(ies) of player(s) on the same team	3. Free hit for opponents on spot where ball was touched

* For complete rules see the current *Field-Hockey Lacrosse Guide*, published by DGWS. Rules given are adapted from Cooper, Elizabeth F.: Simply Worded Field Hockey Rules, Field Hockey-Lacrosse Guide, 1958–1960.

If a ball goes over the endline:	*The ball is put in play by:*
1. From the stick of the attacking team	1. 25 yard line bully
2. From the sticks of opponents	2. 25 yard line bully
3. From the stick of the defense unintentionally	3. Corner (long)
4. From the stick of the defense intentionally	4. Penalty (short) corner
5. From the body of the defense	5. Penalty (short) corner
6. From the body of the attack	6. Free hit for defense anywhere in striking circle

Roll-in. When the ball passes completely over the sideline after being hit by a player, an opponent rolls it in by hand.

Regulations:	*Penalty for failure to follow:*
The ball must be rolled and must touch the ground within three feet of the point where it left the field. The roller must have both feet and her stick outside the sideline. She may not play the ball again until someone else has touched it.	Opponents take roll-in
All other players must be out of the alley (and within the playing field) until the ball has left the roller's hand	Roll-in taken over by same team
Roller must have her stick in one hand (It is a foul to participate in the game without a stick)	Free hit for opponents just inside sideline

Corners. *Long Corners.* This is taken when the defending team from inside the striking circle unintentionally sends the ball over the endline, not scoring a goal. Both teams "line up" for the corner. Six defending players must stand with feet and sticks behind their own goal line and at least five yards from the ball. Usually these players are the goalkeeper, two fullbacks and three halfbacks. The other five defending players must remain beyond the 25 yard line until the ball is touched by a player other than the wing taking the corner, or until the ball is out of the striking circle.

The wing on the side of the goal where the ball went out, stands on the goal or sideline five yards from the corner. (She may straddle the line.) She hits the ball to any member of her team, who must have feet and sticks outside the striking circle until the ball is hit by the wing. Attacking players usually line up with four forwards around the outside of the circle, and three halfbacks slightly behind and covering the spaces.

The forward receiving the ball must control it before shooting for a goal. The ball may be deflected or passed, but a goal must not be attempted until it has been controlled or stopped by a member of the attacking team other than the wing taking the corner, or has been touched by an opponent.

Penalty for failure to follow regulations:

By attacking team: Free hit for defending team anywhere in circle.

By defending team: Take the corner again.

Penalty (Short) Corner. This is taken when the defending team intentionally hits the ball over the goal line (not scoring a goal), or when the defending team makes a foul in the striking circle (except in case of deliberate or repeated fouling in which case a penalty bully is given). (See also substitute rule.)

Teams line up as for long corner but the attacking wing takes the hit on the endline at a point not less than ten yards from the nearer goal post. The attacking team decides on which side of the goal to take the penalty corner. Procedure and penalties are the same as for long corner.

FOULS

Sticks: raising any part of the stick above shoulder level while playing ball.

Dangerous hitting: undercutting the ball so that it goes into the air in a manner dangerous to an opponent, or hitting the ball directly into an opponent.

Advancing: permitting the ball to rebound off any part of the player's feet, hands, or body *in any direction* that gives an advantage to that player or her team. The ball may be stopped with the hand or foot provided the ball is stopped completely. If stopped in the air, it must be dropped *directly* to the ground. An exception to this rule is made in the case of the goalkeeper who may kick the ball, and who may let the ball rebound from her hand as long as she does not place or throw it. (The goalkeeper loses these privileges when outside the circle.)

Wrong side of stick: touching the ball with rounded side of stick.

Hitting the ball between own feet.

Slashing sticks, or any other interference with opponent's stick.

Personal contact: tripping, pushing, shoving, or striking opponent.

Obstruction: putting any part of the body between an opponent and the ball (referred to as *turning on the ball*), or running between an opponent and the ball so as to break her stride.

Playing without a stick in hand.

Delaying the game.

Offside: getting ahead of the ball (in the opponent's half of the field) with less than three of the opposing team between you and the goal. To avoid this foul, forwards should stay on a line with each other and not get ahead of the ball when one of their own forwards has it.

Substituting illegally.

Penalties for Fouls

Foul outside the striking circle	*Penalty*
1. By member of one team	1. Free hit on the spot for opponent
2. By members of opposing teams at the same time	2. On the spot bully except if foul occurred in the alley when bully is taken on the alley line

Foul inside striking circle	
1. By attacking team	1. Free hit anywhere in circle for defense
2. By defending team	2. Penalty corner (except deliberate or repeated fouling in which case a penalty bully is given)

For illegal substitution	
1. By one team	1. Penalty corner
2. By both teams at the same time	2. Bully on spot designated by umpire

Free Hit.   A free hit is taken on the spot where the foul occurred (except in the case of a foul by the attack in the striking circle, in which case the defense may take the hit anywhere in the circle). All other players must be at least five yards away. The ball must be motionless when hit. Any legal stroke may be used. The player taking the hit (usually the nearest halfback) may not play the ball again until it has been touched by another player.

Penalty for failure to follow regulations is a free hit for the opposing team (unless committed by the defense in the striking circle, in which case a penalty corner would be awarded).

Penalty Bully.   A penalty bully is called when a member of the defending team deliberately fouls, a defender fouls repeatedly, or by fouling prevents an otherwise "sure goal." The bully is taken five yards in front of the center of the goal, by the player who committed the foul and any member of the opposing team. If the goalkeeper is taking the bully, she may not remove her pads or use her goalie privileges.

All other players must be beyond the nearer 25 yard line until the bully is completed.

The two players taking the bully continue to play the ball until:

a. *A goal is awarded* because the ball goes through the goal off the stick of the attacker, *or* off the stick or body of defender, *or* the defender fouls.

b. *The bully is over with no score* because the defender sends the ball out of the striking circle onto the playing field, *or* the attacker sends the ball over the goal line (not scoring a goal), *or* the attacker fouls.

c. *The bully is taken over* because the defender hits the ball over the goal (not scoring a goal), *or* there is a double foul, *or* an improper bully, *or* any other player interferes.

If a goal is made, the ball is restarted with a center bully.

If a goal is not made, the ball is restarted with a 25 yard bully.

Rough Play and Misconduct. The umpire may warn or suspend a player for either.

Accidents and Interference with the Game

The umpire may stop the game for not more than five minutes in case of injury to a player, or long enough for a player to replace a broken stick, or to take care of any matter which may be interfering with the progress of the game. The ball should be restarted with an on the spot bully unless the preceding play calls for some other method.

Substitutes

Officially, substitutes may be put in only at half time or in case of injury or disqualification. However, in high school and college games the coaches may agree on also allowing substitution at corners and bullies. The substitutes must report to the scorers and umpire.

Once a substitute replaces a teammate, that girl may not reenter the game. However, a player who is winded may drop out of the game and return to it if her team has played short and no one has substituted for her.

Penalty

a. For illegal substitution by one team, a penalty corner is awarded the opponents.

b. For illegal substitution by both teams at the same time, a bully is given on a spot designated by the umpire.

TEACHING UNITS

A suggested field hockey unit of ten lessons for beginning players might follow this pattern:

Lesson I

1. Brief history, nature, and purpose of the game
2. Dribble

3. Push pass
4. Partner relay using dribble and push pass

Lesson II

1. Film of game or watching part of an actual game
2. Review dribble and push pass
3. Drive
4. Stick stop
5. Relay or novelty game using drive and stick stop

Lesson III

1. Chalk or magnetized board talk on positions and basic rules
2. Review of skills
3. Straight tackle
4. Simplified game

Lesson IV

1. Discussion of positioning
2. Relay passing across five man line and shooting for goal
3. Bully
4. Roll-in
5. Short game

Lesson V

1. Review of skills
2. Left hand lunge
3. Discussion of team play—responsibilities of each position
4. Game

Lesson VI

1. Review straight tackle, left hand lunge
2. Right dodge
3. Game—interrupted when appropriate for explanation of
      corners
      roll-ins
      free hits
      bullies
   as situations within an actual game

Lesson VII

1. Circular tackle
2. Forward line shooting

3. Goalkeeping
4. Backfield—defending goal
5. Game

Lesson VIII

1. Game play all period, stress:
    positioning
    marking
    covering
    \backing up
2. Players not in game practice:
    skills necessary for their positions
    two, three, and five-man relays

Lesson IX

1. Tournament started or regulation game played
2. Players not in game work on skills
3. Oral or written examination

Lesson X

1. Tournament completed or regulation game
2. Evaluation by students and instructor

CLASS ORGANIZATION

Since students learn mostly by doing, the class meetings in the units should be active ones. Begin with dribbling relays, followed by hitting, first from a stationary, then a running position. Stickwork relays and simple novelty games will make the learning of basic techniques easier, faster, and more enjoyable. Straight, zigzag, stopping and starting, circling to the right then left are formations suggested.

Passing relays, to both the right and left, done on the run and receiving the ball from the right and left should follow the dribbling relays. Players should work in pairs for this, changing positions as they move up and then downfield.

Early in the unit the class should watch a game played by experts or see one in a film in order to gain a basic understanding of what the game is all about. After viewing the film, the class should review the skills taught before learning the various tackling and intercepting techniques. Here the instructor should again stress the duties of the forward line players and those of their defensive teammates. As shown in the following

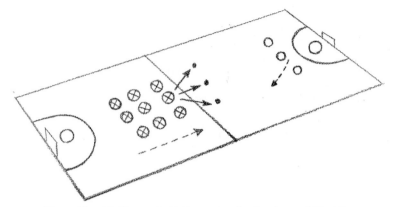

Figure No. 15–15.   Drill Formation for Passing and Tackling.

diagram, two squads should drill together on passing and tackling techniques.

Both the O's and the three X's move as a unit. If the former retain possession of the ball, they are to shoot for a goal when in the striking circle, or the latter are to do so if they gain and can successfully dribble the ball downfield, passing it back and forth, then shooting for a goal when in the striking circle.

Player positions and their duties should be stressed before actual play begins. This can be done following a chalk or magnetized board talk by having each team member stand in her chosen player position. The five forwards of one team stand on their side of the line facing the opposing forward line team. Next the defensive players from each team take their positions. It is a good idea to start the game with a bully, first by the wings on one side of the field, then the other, next by the inners, and finally by the centers. Beginners bunch too much and this tactic will help them grasp an understanding of the importance of playing in their own positions.[2] Stop the game every time they get into a muddle, re-stress positioning, and have each one stand where she is to check her own position, or see for herself if her team really is bunched together. Teach marking as soon as the class gains skill in moving the ball successfully up and downfield. A round robin class tournament is recommended if there is enough time and players for it to be conducted during the regular class period.

Those not playing in the game should be practicing skills on the sidelines so that they might gain mastery of the many techniques of the game. Skill and knowledge tests, although time consuming, do serve as a means of motivating students, as well as a help to the teacher in evaluating their learning progress or her own teaching ability.

[2] Powell, Agneta: For the Beginning Coach With Beginner Hockeyists. *Official Field Hockey-Lacrosse Guide,* September 1956–1958, N.S.G.W.S., AAHPER, Washington, D.C.

SKILL DIFFICULTIES AND THEIR CORRECTION

Difficulty | *Correction*

1. *The Drive* | 1.

a. Stick is raised too high above the shoulder

a. Emphasize the "sticks" rule. To avoid sticks behind the body, bend right elbow more in front of the body, lock wrists at the end of the stroke, and reach stick toward ball

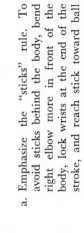

b. Right hand not close to the left one

b. Keep hands together at the top of the stick

SKILL DIFFICULTIES AND THEIR CORRECTION (*Continued*)

Difficulty	*Correction*
c. Wrong foot forward on the drive to the right	c. The right foot should be forward and the ball just back of the heel
2. The Dribble	**2.**
a. Hitting the ball too far forward	a. Stress barely tapping the ball and keeping it close to the stick
b. Wrists too stiff	b. Keep wrists flexible
c. Elbows stiff and kept too close to the body	c. The left elbow should lead and be held more away from the body than the right
d. Stick held incorrectly and with wrong hand on top; too much in a straight up and down position	d. The left hand should be at the top of the handle with the right slightly below it; the stick held ahead and slightly to the right of the player with the top and blade inclined forward

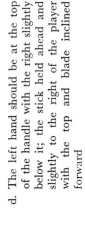

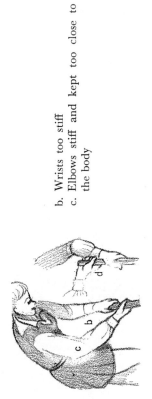

3. *Carrying the Stick*

    a. Carrying it with only one hand

    b. Carrying it with blade pointed up toward the sky like an Indian with an upraised tomahawk

3.

    a. Use both hands

    b. The stick should be carried across the body, hands widely spaced, blade upward

4. *Push Pass*

    a. Inflexible wrists; hands together

    b. Backswing, wrong foot forward, and poorly timed shift of body weight

    c. Both hands not working together properly; one pushing too much

4.

    a. Stress pliable wrists for force and direction; keep hands apart

    b. Since there is *no* backswing, body weight must be shifted accurately as one steps into the shot. The pass to the right should be outside of the right foot with body twisted right and toes pointed straight ahead; for a backward pass the ball is behind the right foot, body twists far back to the right and toes point straight ahead

    c. Push forward with the right hand and pull back equally with the left and *step* into the stroke in the direction of the pass

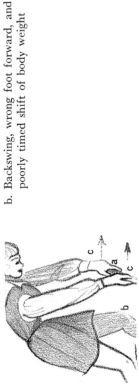

SKILL DIFFICULTIES AND THEIR CORRECTION (*Continued*)

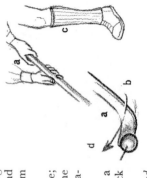

Difficulty	*Correction*
5. Flick	**5.**
a. Wrists too stiff, stick not turned enough to put a good spin on the ball	a. Start as in the Push Pass and follow with a quick turnover of the stick to put a spin on the ball with hitting surface turning from right to left toward the ground as the stroke is completed
b. The ball back, or at the side, of player's foot	b. The ball should be slightly ahead and outside the right foot
c. Incorrect hand positions on the stick	c. The back of the left hand and palm of the right should face in the direction of the stroke
6. The Scoop	**6.**
a. Handle held against the body; right hand not down the handle far enough and all fingers wrapped around the handle	a. Hold stick well in front at sharp angle to the ground with hitting surface upward; move right hand down with thumb on top and palm of right hand up
b. Stick blade up too much; too much wrist action resulting in the ball being raised too high	b. Lay the stick blade back more; raise the ball only slightly off the ground. Practice slowly with a stationary ball
c. Weight not moved forward	c. Shift weight forward and make a short follow-through with the stick in the direction of the scoop
d. Pushing the stick forward too much so that the ball rolls back over the stick	d. Push the stick forward *and upward* at the same time

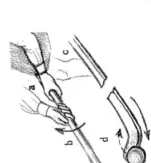

Correction

7.

a. Give with the stick more in order to absorb the ball impact; get the feeling of catching the ball and keeping it near the stick

b. Separate hands 6 to 8 inches, rest the entire blade on the ground, pull left hand back and move the stick forward to meet the ball, watch the ball more closely

8.

a. The tackler should be on the opponent's right

b. Stick path should be diagonally toward the ground with the left hand throwing the stick down to the left and in front of the opponent's ball

c. Tackle from slightly behind, bending and reaching far forward with the whole body

d. Keep the arc of the stick low and straighten the elbows some; there should be no follow-through

e. The stick should contact the ball just after it leaves the opponent's stick on the dribble

Difficulty

7. Stopping the Ball

a. Not giving with the stick enough as the ball is contacted

b. Missing the ball by holding the stick incorrectly; taking the eyes off the ball

8. Left Hand Lunge

a. Tackler on the wrong side

b. Path of the stick directly toward ground

c. Tackler not reaching enough or using whole body; arms and body are held too rigidly

d. Making "sticks" before the downswing or as the tackle is completed

e. Improper timing, going for the ball too late or too soon

SKILL DIFFICULTIES AND THEIR CORRECTION (*Continued*)

Difficulty	*Correction*
9. *Jab or Job*	9.
a. Stick hitting surface faced incorrectly	a. The hitting surface should be upward
b. Hitting the ball in one continuous stroke	b. Jab at the ball in a fast series of quick, sharp movements
c. Arms bent too much	c. Keep the arms straight and firm
10. *Circular Tackle*	10.
a. Being too close to the opponent and running into her on the tackle	a. Get well ahead before tackling; turn the stick back before starting the run and allow yourself enough time to do so
b. Starting the tackle too soon	b. Begin just before the ball leaves the opponent's stick
c. Losing control of the ball after getting it away from the opponent	c. Dribble the ball out more in a larger circle beyond the opponent's reach

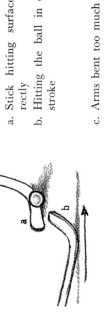

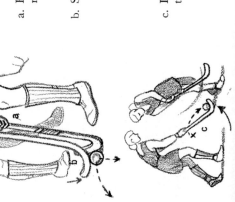

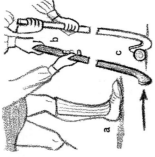
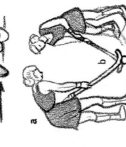

Difficulty	Correction

11. Straight Tackle

11.

a. Tackler in wrong position

a. Tackler should be slightly to the stick side and facing her opponent

b. Hands held too close together on the stick

b. Keep hands well apart

c. Wrong stick position with stick too near player's body

c. The stick should be held approximately at right angles to the ground with the handle slightly farther from the player than the head

12. Bully

12.

a. Body held too rigidly upward

a. Bend closer to the ball

b. Raising the stick too far off the ground

b. Since speed is vital, barely raise the stick off the ground

13. The Roll-in

13.

a. Rolling the ball in directly to the advancing player

a. Roll the ball in front of the advancing players so it can be quickly picked up and dribbled forward

b. Stick held improperly so that part of it is over the line

b. Hold the stick in either hand, well outside the sideline

c. Letting the opponents know which direction the ball will be rolled by tell-tale body position

c. Practice and perfect looking and facing one way and rolling-in ball into the field in another

NOVELTY GAMES

Hockey Keep Ball (Beginners and Intermediates).   Divide two teams as in regular hockey. Play on only one-half of the field. Either team can score using the same goal. Begin with a center bully.

Hockey Ten Passes (Intermediates and Advanced).   Played as Hockey Keep Ball on the entire field, the object is for each team to get and keep possession of the ball. Each successful pass to a teammate counts one, the second player passes it on for count two, etc. The other team tries to get possession of the ball and start passing it for their own series of ten successful passes. The winning team completes the ten consecutive moves first.

. **Hockey Snatch Ball** (Beginners and Intermediates).   Divide players into two teams facing each other 40 to 50 feet apart. Number each so that two opponents with the same number (or actual team playing positions as in regular hockey) stand diagonally opposite each other. On the center line place two sticks and one hockey ball. When any number is called by the leader, two opposing players run to gain possession of the ball and dribble it back successfully (as the other attempts to gain possession of it) across her own line. Play for time or points with each ball going across the line counting one point.

Shiney. (Novelty Event).   Played on almost any outside area, using hockey sticks, crooked sticks from trees, or broomhandles and a hockey ball, tin can, or block of wood. The object of this game is for each team to score one point each time the ball crosses over the opponent's goal line.

Variations: (1) Play the game on roller or ice skates using the larger end of a broom, a volleyball, or an ice hockey puck. (2) Play the game indoors with a softball or tennis ball, brooms, or regular hockey sticks.

Deck Hockey (Beginners and Intermediates).   Played indoors using as many of the regular hockey rules as possible, the object of the game is for a team member to throw a deck tennis ring and catch it in the air, advancing it successfully across the opponent's goal line in order to score 1 point. Play for time or 10 points.

Variation: Catch the ring and throw it to teammates using a short stick 10 to 12 inches long.

Hockey Skill Contests and Relays (Beginners, Intermediates, and Advanced).   These can be used successfully as a means of motivating interest and for fun. Although practically all of hockey skills can be utilized for this purpose, the following ones are suggested:

Circle dribbling, using the flick, scoop, push pass, drive and fielding	Drive for distance; for accuracy
	Shooting for goals against a skilled goalkeeper
Dribble, pass	Passing and tackling games
Dribbling around objects	

Driving around objects
Shuttle relays for driving and field-
   ing; dribbling, dodging
Dribbling and push pass

Mass Hockey (Intermediates).   Using many players divided equally into two teams, this game is played in 10 minute or less quarters. Regular hockey rules are used except that (1) one is eliminated if she fouls, (2) the ball is put in play where the foul occurred by a bully, (3) there are no side boundary lines or offside penalty.

OFFICIATING TECHNIQUES

Two umpires are needed for officiating with each taking one end of the field, as in soccer. The one on the side nearest the timers and scorers takes all center bullies during the first half and at the start of the second half and recognizes substitutes. Both officials should wear costumes which are easily distinguished from those worn by the players, skirts which allow freedom of movement, low heeled shoes, and white blazers. They should have sunglasses, if needed, and a rule book.

Before the game the umpires should:

1. See that the lineups are in the score books correctly and that the timers and scorers know their duties.
2. Introduce the captains; chat with the players.
3. Toss a coin for goal choice.
4. Set length of halves and length of in-between rest period.
5. Check players' sticks and uniforms.
6. Explain signals they will use and how players must react to them.
7. Discuss how some of the common fouls can be avoided and ask if captains wish fouls named when called during a game.

Each umpire should officiate along the sideline and is responsible for the half of the field to her right. She should be careful not to interfere with the game's progress by getting in the players' way. She should keep on a line with the ball and only enter the field near the striking circle when it is necessary that she do so in order to see the play there clearly. When the ball is on the other half of the field, she should stand near the center line and be ready to follow the game closely when it returns to her side of the field.

Arm signals should be used to show (1) *a free hit,* by raising one arm sideways at shoulder height in the direction the hit is to be taken, and (2) *a roll-in,* by first announcing, after the whistle is blown, which team is to take it and then signaling with one arm in the direction the roll-in is to be taken.

The whistle should be blown:

1. To start the game and at all center bullies
2. When a foul occurs
3. For time out; time in
4. To start and finish a penalty bully
5. To resume play with a 25 yard bully after the penalty bully
6. To recall play on an incomplete bully, free hit, penalty corner, corner, roll-in, or if a bully should be repeated
7. When the ball goes out of bounds
8. At the end of each playing period
9. When a goal is scored

It should not be blown to start a corner hit, penalty corner hit, free hit, roll-in, or any bully on the field except for the center and penalty bully. Since it is difficult for all players to hear, the voice should be used sparingly. All decisions should be called quickly and in a decisive manner.

Each umpire should watch particularly:

1. On the bully to see that the feet are not moved until the play is completed
2. The wings for being offside
3. Players kicking or advancing the ball illegally
4. During the corner plays for fouls deliberately committed

At the end of the game the officials should check and sign the score book, and talk with players or coaches who wish to discuss any point of the game with them.

EVALUATING THE RESULTS

The use of incidence charts during game play, rating scales to evaluate individual performances, progress charts, tests on specific skills, tournament standing or results, and knowledge tests on rules, strategy, and other aspects of the game are all recommended as means of evaluating players.

Kelly and Brown have developed a 106 item objective test designed particularly for major students.[3] Perhaps the best skill test for college women is that devised by Schmithals and French.[4] This test is usable also for high school girls. For this ball control test the field is marked as shown in Figure 15–16.

On a signal, each player dribbles forward to the left of the foul line until she reaches the restraining line where she shoots the ball to the right of the first obstacle and runs around to the left of it to recover the ball.

[3] A sample copy of this test may be obtained from Dr. Ellen Kelly, Illinois State Normal University, Bloomington, Illinois.

[4] Schmithals, Margaret, and French, Esther: Achievement Tests in Field Hockey for College Women, *Research Quarterly,* 11:33, December, 1940.

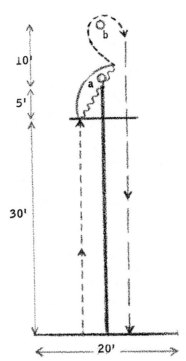

Figure No. 15–16.   Field Markings for the Ball Control Skill Test.

She then dribbles around the second obstacle, turns to the right to recover the ball and then drives it back over the starting line. Six trials are given and the final test score is their average. A trial does not count if the ball or player crosses over the foul line before coming to the restraining line, or if at the first obstacle, the ball is not sent from the left side of the foul line.

TERMINOLOGY

Advancing—Moving the ball to one's advantage with any part of the body

Backing up—The assistance rendered by the backs to their own forwards

Bully—The technique used to put the ball in play whenever both teams are to have equal opportunity to get it. Two players face each other squarely, touch first the ground then the opponent's stick (with their stick) three times, and then play the ball

Corner—The method of putting the ball back in play after the defending team has hit the ball over the endline, or made a foul in the circle

Dangerous Hitting—Undercutting the ball (hitting it with the stick blade facing up) so that it goes into the air, or hitting the ball into another player even though it may remain on the ground

Dodge—Technique used by a player with the ball to evade an opponent and still retain possession of the ball

Drawing an Opponent—Forcing one's opponent to mark closely or attempt a tackle so space will be left clear for a pass to one's teammate

Dribble—A series of short strokes used to move the ball downfield

Drive—A forceful stroke used for shooting, clearing, and passing

Fielding—Receiving a pass and controlling it close to the stick so it may be played immediately

Flick—A stroke in which the ball is pushed with a strong twist of the wrists putting spin and loft on the ball

Free Hit—A chance to hit the ball with no one nearer than five yards—awarded to a team fouled against and usually taken by the nearest back

Interception—Taking possession of the ball as it is passed from an opponent to another opponent

Interchange—A temporary exchange of positions between teammates

Marking—Keeping oneself in position in relation to a specific opponent so that one can either intercept the ball intended for her, or tackle her once she has it

Obstruction—Going between an opponent and the ball in such a manner that her playing of the ball is hindered. It is possible to obstruct with just the stick or shoulder

Reverse Stick—Use of the stick so that the toe points down

Roll-in—Technique used to put the ball back in play after it has gone out of bounds over the sideline

Sticks—A foul caused by raising the stick above shoulder level

Tackle—An attempt to take possession of the ball when it is in the possession of an opponent

Tackle-back—Trying to regain the ball from one who has successfully tackled you

DISCUSSION QUESTIONS

1. Describe and demonstrate three types of tackles. When would you use each one in a game?
2. Draw a suggested team play for a long and a short corner.
3. Explain (a) backing up, (b) marking, (c) interchanging, (d) obstruction, (e) covering.
4. Where is the best place for a goalie to stand for a shot (1) coming to her *non-stick* side, (2) stick side, (3) directly in front of the cage?
5. Make a list of 25 coaching hints you would wish to pass on to a team.

SELECTED AUDIO-VISUAL AIDS

Filmstrips compiled by Marjorie Pollard. (25 frames, 35 mm.). SportShelf, 10 Overbrook Terrace, New York 33, N. Y. (Rental)

Field Hockey Filmstrips by Dorothy Yanisch and Jean Landis, 1952. Available from authors, State Teachers College, West Chester, Pa. (Purchase)

Field Hockey Rules Filmstrips. Teaching Aids Service, 31 Union Square West, New York 3, N. Y. (Purchase and Rental)

Hockey Basic Strokes 1956. (18 min., silent, b & w). Marjorie Pollard Publications Ltd., The Deanery, Bampton, Oxford, England.

Magnetic Bulletin Board Field Hockey Coaching Kit, No. PM-600, The Program Aids Company, Inc., 550 Fifth Avenue, New York, N. Y. (Purchase)

Wall Charts: Set No. 1—Position of Hands, Drive, Dribble, Push
            Set No. 2—Goalkeeping, Three Methods of Tackling
            Set No. 3—Dodging

Available from Marjorie Pollard. Marjorie Pollard Publications, Ltd., The Deanery, Bampton, Oxford, England, or Gertrude Hooper, 242 Highland Street, Milton 86, Massachusetts. (Purchase)

Suggested Readings

Armbruster, David A.: *Basic Skills in Sports for Men and Women*, St. Louis, C. V. Mosby Company, 1953.

Burger, Elizabeth: Women's Hockey at Home and Abroad, *Journal of Health, Physical Education, and Recreation*, Vol. 22, No. 7, September 1951, p. 22.

Deitz, Dorothea, and Frech, Beryl: Hockey Knowledge Tests for Girls, *Journal of Health and Physical Education*, Vol. 11, No. 6, June 1940, p. 366.

Dyer, Joanna, White, Ruth, and Adair, Ellen: Lead-up Games to Field Hockey, *Journal of Health and Physical Education*, Vol. 6, No. 7, September 1935, p. 38.

Ebeling, Alma: Charting Field Hockey Rules, *Journal of Health and Physical Education*, Vol. 9, No. 8, October 1938, p. 504.

Kjellstrom, Louise, and Turnbull, Jenny: Hockey for Beginners, A Motion Picture Project, *Journal of Health and Physical Education*, Vol. 11, No. 8, October 1940, p. 486.

Lees, Josephine T., and Shellenberger, Betty: *Field Hockey for Players, Coaches, and Umpires*, New York, The Ronald Press, 1957.

Palfrey, Sarah: Mother Stands at Guard, *Sports Illustrated*, December 1954, p. 51.

Papatsos, Cal: The Lure of Field Hockey, *Journal of Health, Physical Education, and Recreation*, Vol. 24, No. 8, October 1953, p. 12.

Pollard, Marjorie: *Hockey For All*, New York, Thomas Nelson and Sons, Ltd., 1957.

Potter, Arthur M.: Field Hockey for Boys and Men, *Journal of Health, Physical Education, and Recreation*, Vol. 28, No. 7, October 1957, p. 8.

Taylor, Maurie: Six-Player Hockey for the Small School, *Journal of Health and Physical Education*, Vol. 11, No. 8, October 1940, p. 484.

Periodicals

The Eagle. Official publication of the United States Field Hockey Association, Circulation Manager Agnes Stegmuller, 30 Lamont Avenue, Glenolden, Pa.

16

Lacrosse

Lacrosse was played on the North American continent long before white men arrived, for the American Indian played the game "baggataway" as a method of conditioning for war, and a ritual to gain favor with the Great Spirit. The rough and dangerous game drew entire tribes into competition on areas with no boundaries where goals were often several miles apart. The Indians used a light, strong stick with a hoop, or hook, at one end. A net of rawhide strips hung from the end to carry the wooden or rawhide ball. The stick also served to beat off opponents in the heated battle of gaining possession of the ball.

French missionaries in Canada renamed the game Lacrosse for the stick which resembled a bishop's crozier. Canadians developed rules and safer techniques of play and lacrosse became the national game of that country. Introduced in England about 1865, it was spread to all parts of the British Commonwealth and to the United States by Canadian enthusiasts.

The American women's game came directly from England rather than from the American men's game. The All-England Ladies Lacrosse Association modified rules, eliminated the rough element, and sent players and coaches to introduce the game in the United States. By 1931 lacrosse was played in isolated spots in the northeast section of the country resulting in the formation of the United States Women's Lacrosse Association. The popularity of the sport has grown with the exchange of British and American touring teams, annual national tournaments, and clinics. Lacrosse has not had the rapid growth it deserves as a team activity. The game for women must overcome the prejudice against the men's rougher version, and be accepted by the hundreds of physical educators who are unfamiliar with it and fearful of introducing it into their programs.

400

NATURE, PURPOSE, AND SCORING OF THE GAME

Lacrosse is a field game played by two opposing teams of 12 members each. It is an extremely fast game in which each team advances the ball by catching and throwing, or running to a position to score a goal by shooting between and under the goal posts.

Before play begins, field boundaries are established by the team captains. Unlike all other field games, no rules govern the total playing area, although goals must be placed at least 90 yards apart and no further than 110 yards. An official game has two periods of 25 minutes each (unless shortened by mutual agreement) with no time outs other than those called by an umpire. A ten minute rest may be taken between halves.

At the beginning of both periods and after each goal, play begins with a center draw by the opposing center players. All players carry a crosse and use this net-like implement to begin their offensive or defensive responsibilities. The small sponge rubber ball is advanced by the use of the crosse in running, passing, catching, picking up, or shooting. Each team attempts to defend its goal and score against its opponents.

When the ball passes out of the established boundaries, the umpire stops play and awards it to the player who was nearest to it as it went out. Whenever play is suspended by an official's whistle, all players must stand and hold their positions until directed by an official, or play resumes.

If two players of opposing teams were equally close to the ball as it went out of bounds, the umpire awards a throw-in between them.

Whenever a foul occurs play is suspended and the person fouled is given the ball and five unobstructed yards for a free position.

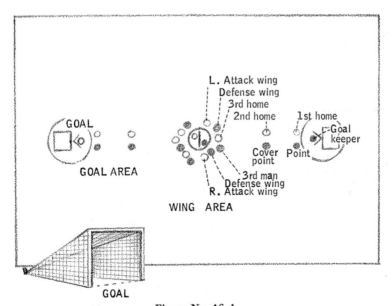

Figure No. 16–1.

Players.   Each team of 12 members has five attacking players, six defensive players and one center who plays both attack and defense. The attack positions, in order of their field positions, are: first home, second home, third home, right attack wing, and left attack wing. The center position stands alone. The defense positions are: right and left defense wing, third man, cover point, point, and goalkeeper. Distribution of players is not compulsory and all players actually have offensive and defensive responsibilities and may move to any part of the playing area. Substitutes are available and may enter the game in case of injury and at halftime.

Scoring.   The winning team scores the greatest number of points. A goal counts one point and is recorded when the entire ball crosses the goal line from the front and stays beneath the 6 foot crossbar. A legal goal must be propelled by a crosse of the attacking player or the crosse, or body of a defending player. Tied games are recorded as a draw.

NEEDED FACILITIES AND EQUIPMENT

One of the advantages of lacrosse is that the field area does not require extensive maintenance and the necessary equipment is limited and inexpensive. With proper care equipment lasts many years.

Field Area.   The field is the approximate size of a hockey or football field. A smooth surface is not as necessary as it is in hockey or soccer for true ball roll.

The field has no definite boundary markings, but within the established area are two goals between 90 and 110 yards apart. Each *goal* consists of two square posts 6 feet high, 6 feet apart and joined by a crossbar 6 feet from the ground. The goal line is drawn from post to post, and with the 2″ × 2″ wooden frame, forms a square with inside measurements of 6 feet. The wooden posts and crossbar are painted white. Netting, not more than 1½ inch mesh, is attached to the posts and bar and pegged to the ground six feet behind the center of the goal line.

The *goal crease* is formed by drawing a circle with a radius of 8½ feet from the center of the goal line.

A center circle with a radius of 10 yards is drawn in the center of the field. Lines are drawn, from the circle center, 2 yards on each side and parallel with the goal line.

Ball.   The ball used in women's lacrosse is made of black, white, or yellow sponge rubber. It weighs no less than 4½ ounces and no more than 5 ounces, and is between 7¾ and 8 inches in circumference.

Crosse.   The crosse is a stick with a net-like section on the end for carrying and controlling the ball. It may be any length but may not be more than 12 inches at its widest part or weigh more than 24 ounces. "The wood must be on the right-hand side of the bridge, i.e., left-handed crosses are illegal. A string must be brought through a hole at the side of the tip of the turn to prevent the point of the stick catching an op-

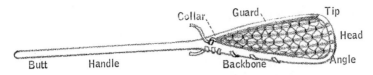

Figure No. 16–2.   The Crosse.

ponent's crosse. The leather thongs (lengthwise strings) must be woven
to within two inches of their termination and tightened sufficiently to
prevent a ball from catching in the meshes or resting in a pocket formed
by loose lengthwise strings. No metal of any kind shall be allowed upon
the crosse."[1]

The crosse is composed of the following parts:

Handle—usually 25 to 27 inches long. It is used to control the entire
　　　　crosse.
Butt and Grip—end of the handle where one hand is placed.
Throat—the upper end of the handle just below the crosse face.
Wood Wall—Wooden section or backbone of the face.
Angle—curved section between backbone and tip. Should be at least a
　　　　90° angle. It is the weakest part of the crosse.
Guard—a heavy mesh of gut approximately two and one-half to three
　　　　inches in width. This strong upright runs opposite the backbone.
Tip—bent portion and end of wood nearest the guard.
Bridge—thick gut that is placed several inches above the collar and
　　　　attached to the guard and backbone to prevent the ball from
　　　　lodging in the crosse.
Collar—point of attachment for the thongs of the gut wall and length-
　　　　wise strings.
Strings—leather, lines, or hide thongs running lengthwise and crosswise
　　　　to form the netting for controlling the ball.

Care of the crosse insures a long life. A few rules should be followed:

1. Wipe the stick after playing.
2. Treat the strings with leather conditioner; the wooden frame with
   linseed oil.
3. Tie the lead string before playing and always untie it after playing
   to relieve strain on the angle.
4. Hang the stick by the wood.
5. Never grease the guard and bridge.
6. Mend and repair the stick as soon as possible. Store away from heat
   and dampness.

[1] *Field Hockey-Lacrosse Guide.* Sept. 1958–Sept. 1960, Division for Girls and
Women's Sports, 1201 16th Street, N.W., Washington 6, D.C.

Costume. The official gymnasium costume with socks and tennis shoes or sneakers is satisfactory for instructional purposes. For school or club game tunics are recommended. The short sleeved shirt and a pleated one piece dress are comfortable and attractive. Rubber-soled shoes are required and rubber cleats and spikes are permissible. The goalkeeper is the only player who needs additional equipment in the form of hockey goalkeeper's leg pads, chest and thigh protector, a face mask, and gloves (if desired).

TEACHING UNITS

The following unit for beginners aims at introducing the player to a game as quickly as possible. Skill drills are important but are appreciated more where the ultimate use is understood by students. The advanced unit is centered around improving attack and defense and learning to officiate.

Unit for Beginners	*Unit for Advanced Players*
Brief history	Intensive review of purpose
Object and purpose of the game	and basic game skills
Field dimensions	Intensive explanation of
Equipment: care and use	rules of play
Brief overview of fundamental skills	Officiating
Beginners game	Advanced strategy
Demonstration and practice of skills	Attack
Grip of the crosse	Defense
Cradling	Interchange
Catching	Goalkeeping
Picking up	Intramural and interscholastic
Throwing	play
Center draw	Evaluation
Marking	
Body checking	
Crosse checking	
Tackling	
Game play and simple strategy	
Explanation of rules	
Stand	
Free position	
Throw-in	
Evaluation	

BASIC SKILLS

The Grip. The crosse is held with both hands, the left at the butt and the right at the collar. Place the stick in front of the body with the stick head on the ground and the butt leaning against the player. The player grasps the butt end firmly with the thumb and fingers of the left hand, knuckles on top.

The left, or power, hand lifts the stick to a vertical position as the right hand forms a loose ring around the collar. The knuckles are under the stick as the thumb and fingers remain loose to allow the crosse to swing unhampered. When held vertically the "V" of the thumb and fore-finger of the right hand is between the player's face and the stick. The arms remain relaxed and the right elbow drops toward the stick handle. The right is the guiding hand, the left the power hand.

Cradling.   Cradling action serves to keep the ball under control in the crosse when running or preparing to pass or shoot. Natural teaching progression moves from horizontal cradling position to the vertical position to facilitate game play. With the crosse almost horizontal, the head slightly higher than the butt and the wood turned toward the player and the ground, begin walking and running to get used to the rhythmic move-ment of the crosse. In this position arms are bent upward with approxi-mately a 90-degree elbow angle. The up and down cradling results from relaxed arms and powerful left wrist as the crosse arcs forward and up-ward and downward and inward from the original position. Cradling is a coordinated action of shoulders, hips, and ankles with the stick re-sponding to the body movements.

As skill develops the player will cradle from a more vertical position in order to protect the crosse from opponents and to be prepared to pass and shoot quickly. Swing the stick to the left extending the left wrist as the right knee bends inward with heel off the ground. As the body turns left, the right elbow drops until it almost touches the shaft and the left elbow drops downward and close to the side of the body. The left forearm

Figure No. 16–3.   Cradling.

is directed away from the body. On the swing back to the right, the left knee bends inward with heel off the ground, right knee relaxed.

Whether walking, trotting, or running the bottom hand rotates the stick. Both hands are on the same side of the body as the crosse moves from hip to hip. The bottom hand stays approximately at waist height as the top hand moves from shoulder to shoulder.

When the cradling motion reaches either side of the body the open side is away from the body so the ball can be caught. On the right, the wood is nearest the body, on the left the guard is nearest. As the crosse passes in front of the body, the open side is toward the face.

Picking Up the Ball.   When the ball is lying or rolling on the ground it should be picked up with the crosse, so passing, running, or shooting can continue. Beginning players find this an important skill because so many balls get free on poor passes and unskilled catches.

The player lowers her body as she approaches the ball. As the knees bend the crosse is carried toward the ball, low on the side of the body. If the left hand is the bottom or lower hand, the crosse is on the left side. The hands remain apart, at the butt and collar, as in the basic grip. The front foot (usually the right) is directly alongside the ball as the pickup is made. As the head of the crosse approaches the ball a sharp, vigorous push from the bottom hand with knuckles almost scraping the ground scoops under as the runner increases speed to escape her opponents. The stick is raised to the cradling position.

Picking up a ball moving toward or away from the player requires additional skills. When it is moving away, the same techniques of a near horizontal crosse, vigorous push, and a move through the ball apply. Those rolling toward a player should be considered an "upside down" catch. The crosse is raised to a near vertical position at the side of the body so there is room for the crosse to "give" as the ball enters. Continue to run and begin cradling immediately.

Catching.   Catching is an important skill which gives a beginning player confidence to control a ball approaching from any angle. Begin with

Figure No. 16–4.   Picking up.

Figure No. 16–5.   Catching.

the crosse in a near vertical position on the right side of the body. As the ball approaches from the front, the top arm extends as the crosse goes to meet the ball. When the ball meets the net the arms give gently with the impact, and cradling to the left begins. With balls approaching directly to the left side of the receiver, the crosse is moved across the body, face forward. As the ball is caught cradling begins to the right side. The beginner should toss up her own ball, on both the right and left sides while walking, trotting and running. Later she catches balls thrown from the hand and the crosse.

The snap catch is used on balls approaching from an angle, or when an opponent vies for the ball. Simply, this catch is an attempt to wrap the stick around the ball very gently and divert its momentum rather than giving to it. The crosse is closer to the body and as the ball approaches from the right the body turns easily from left to right to meet it with relaxed knees, arms and shoulders. If the ball is traveling from the left the stick swings from right to left.

Passing.   Passing must be developed so the ball travels with both speed and accuracy. The two basic passes—overarm and underarm—are necessary for beginners while advanced players use a sidearm pass successfully.

Overarm Pass.   This imitates the action of an overarm throw. The crosse is in position as it swings to the right of the body in a nearly vertical position. The lower hand is across the body at waist level and the

Figure No. 16–6.   The Overarm Pass.

upper hand is to the right and away from the body. The right shoulder
is drawn back and the right arm extends upward. The right arm bends
slightly, the elbow drops and the crosse head dips backward. The left hand
pulls forcefully and the top hand thrusts forward and upward with a
loose wrist. The right shoulder turns forward as the weight shifts toward
the left foot. The head of the stick follows-through to point to the spot
the ball is intended, and the butt hand and stick finish under the right
armpit.

Underarm Pass.   This is used when an overhead pass is hampered by
an opponent. (The stick swings around to the left, down across the body
and up in one motion.) The lower hand lifts the butt of the stick so the
head swings toward the ground with a circular movement. As the body
turns left the stick is nearly parallel to the body reaching beyond the
back leg. The head of the stick swings by the body and forward as the
weight transfers and shoulders come forward. The head of the crosse
finishes in front of the body with arms straight. The higher the head of the
stick at the finish, the higher and slower the pass.

Sidearm Pass.   This pass is similar to the overarm pass except that the
path of the crosse in delivering is in a forward and outward arc, parallel
to the ground with the face open and away from the body. The follow-
through moves the head of the stick across the body and the butt end
under the right armpit.

Shooting.   Effective goal shooting is the secret to winning lacrosse,
for the only way to win is to score. The majority of shots are made from
passing plays around the goal area rather than from a play where one

person runs downfield and shoots. Once basic passing skills are mastered, shooting should be practiced from a catch to an immediate shot. The overhand, sidearm, underarm, and overhand pivot shots should be basic skills of attack players.

Overhand Shot. The technique of this shot is similar to the overhand pass. It is used in a long distance goal attempt or when the attacking player has dodged her defense for a right side shot. The left hand is the force of the lever action as the right hand guides and directs the shot.

Underarm (Shovel) Shot. On this shot the player is usually running with her right side angled toward the goal. As in an underarm pass, the crosse is on the left of the body. The shot is made off the right foot as the player moves across the goal. It is an effective shot when the attack has moved from behind her defense and moved across with her right side between her opponent and the goal.

Sidearm Shot. This is effective on a short play when the attack has dodged to the right of her defense. As in the sidearm pass, the left elbow is out and away from the body and the right arm is back with elbow close to the right side. The ball is thrown as the left arm pulls toward the body and the right arm extends in the direction of delivery.

Overarm Pivot. This is similar to the overhand pivot shot in basketball. It is difficult to master but an effective scoring shot. With an attacking player looking toward center, her teammate moves downfield to the left of the attack. The attack moves left toward the goal, receives a pass directly in front of her and pivots away from the goal, shifting weight to the right foot and then shoots low to the far corner.

Center Draw. The center draw is the method of beginning play at each half and after every goal. Opposing centers stand with one foot

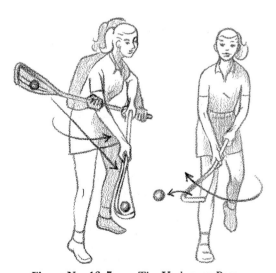

Figure No. 16–7. The Underarm Pass.

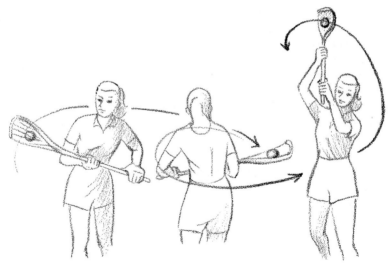

Figure No. 16–8.   Overhand on a Pivot.

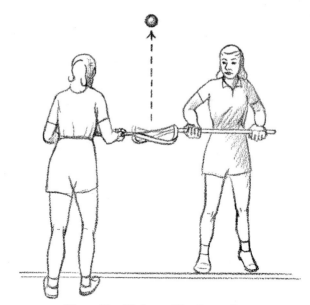

Figure No. 16–9.   The Center Draw.

toeing the center line. If each player holds the collar with the right hand, each faces the goal she is attacking. If the left hand is at the collar the player's back is to the goal she is attacking. The crosses are held at hip level above and parallel to the center line with the backs of the crosses together. The umpire places the ball between the backs of the crosses and on signal the players lift their crosses up and apart so the ball rises in the air. Each center tries to catch the ball to begin attacking action.

Body Checking. The object of body checking is to impede the course of an opposing player carrying the ball, and force her into a hurried and poorly executed pass or shot. No body contact is permitted. The player checking places herself between the attacking player and her intended goal. The "checker" is on the balls of her feet with relaxed knees and ankles so the body weight can change quickly as the attacker moves. The defender travels in the same direction with her crosse up to cover an attempted pass as she forces the attack to slow down, change course, or pass.

Crosse Checking. A defending player may tap an opponent's crosse in an attempt to dislodge the ball. Beginners should learn this difficult skill by tapping downwards *only* when the crosse is unprotected by the attacker's body. More advanced players may up-check, dislodging the ball so it may be caught in the air.

Dodging. This is the simplest way an attacking player can get around the person marking (guarding) her. If dodging when in possession of the ball, cradle on the side of the body away from the opponent. There are three basic dodges: the power dodge, pivot (roll) dodge, and face dodge.

Power Dodge. This is accomplished by drawing the defending player far out to the side of the field then suddenly changing pace and running by her.

Pivot Dodge. This dodge is similar to the pivot in basketball. As the defense commits herself or comes in off-balance for a crosse check or rushes too quickly, roll to the weak side and in for a shot.

Face Dodge. This is the most difficult and most useful dodge. As the defending player moves toward the attacking player, the attack puts her right foot forward, turns quickly to the left and pushes off with the right foot for a sudden sprint downfield.

GAME STRATEGY

The rules of lacrosse permit each player to roam anywhere on the field; consequently it is the individual's responsibility to fulfill her duties if a team is to have an effective attack and defense.

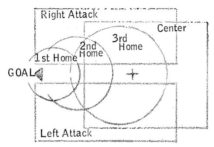

Figure No. 16–10.   Attack Players' Territory.

The Attack.   Attack play is a creative movement initiated by one individual and responded to by the other players. In most games the ease of play and cooperation give the impression that the team is executing a well rehearsed play. This is not true in lacrosse. The smooth operation is the result of perfect stickwork, a sense of timing adapted to the speed and skill of teammates, and total game sense.

A defense player usually begins the attack by passing to an attack person—usually the wings or center. As an attacking player receives a pass she should start immediately for the goal until checked. A pass to third home might follow, then to second home, and then to first home for a shot. For example, center passes to an attack wing, as she should not penetrate too deeply too often. Second home takes the next pass as first home makes a quick dash in front of the goal to shoot as she receives the ball. Second home pulls to one side so first home will have space in front of the goal.

In order to receive a pass successfully an attack player must leave her opponent behind and maneuver to a position to help in the attack. Whether a pass or a shot follows, accuracy is important. The homes should have excellent stickwork and be able to shoot as soon as they receive the ball.

Some additional guides for the attack are:

1. Attack players should avoid crowding in front of the goal because each attack player draws a defending player into a position to defend the goal.

2. Attack players should pass to a free teammate in a more advantageous position.

3. Attack players need a variety of shots, especially a long low, bouncing shot which is difficult to defend against.

The following attacks show how alert players use passing skill and field positioning to score.[2]

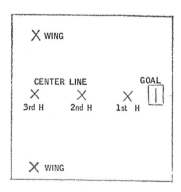

[2] *Official Field Hockey-Lacrosse Guide,* 1946–1948, pp. 112–113. National Section on Women's Athletics of the AAHPER.

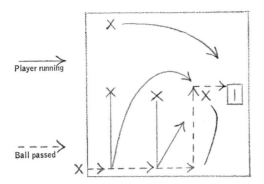

Goal is shot by 3rd H who cuts in an arc. Play—Wing to 3rd to 2nd to 1st to 3rd. *Other possibilities:* 1. Wing to 3rd to 2nd to 1st and back to 2nd on "give and go" around defense. 2. Wing to 3rd to 2nd to 1st and a high pass over the defense to the opposite wing who has run downfield and cut into a scoring position.

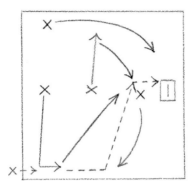

Goal scored by 2nd H who pulls out to the opposite side of the field from the ball to draw her defense and then cuts into scoring position. *Play*—Wing to 3rd to 1st to 2nd. *Other possibilities:* 1. Wing to 3rd to 1st and back to 3rd on "give and go." 2. Wing to 3rd to 1st to opposite wing as in other possibilities (2) above.

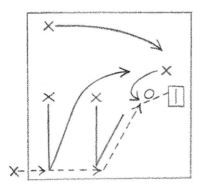

1st H scores goal on pivot shot as she moves from the right of the goal in front of her defense. *Play*—Wing to 3rd to 2nd to 1st. *Other possibility:* Wing to 3rd to 2nd to 1st to 3rd on shovel pass.

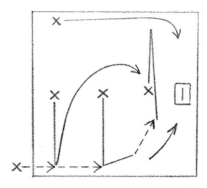

Goal scored by 1st H who moves to opposite side of field and cuts back in front of defense. *Play*—Wing to 3rd to 2nd to 1st. *Other possibilities:* 1. Wing to 3rd to 2nd to 1st and back to 2nd. On this play, 1st blocks out defense and gives pass to 2nd who follows ball to goal. 2. Wing to 3rd to 2nd to 1st to 3rd who cuts in arc to scoring position.

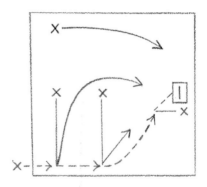

Goal by 1st H on shovel shot from left side of goal. *Play*—Wing to 3rd to 2nd to 1st. *Other possibility:* Wing to 3rd to 2nd to 1st and back to 2nd or 3rd as 1st screens out defense by moving in front of her. The opposite wing could be used also.

(All of these plays may be used on the other side of the field when the ball is brought up there.)

Defense.   The defense player should have sound stickwork and the ability to move rapidly and adapt to any movement of her opponent. The object of defense play is to prevent opposing players from gaining or keeping possession of the ball, or moving the ball close to the goal.

Individual defense players mark their own opponents, tackle and body check, crosse check and intercept the ball whenever possible, pass quickly and accurately, and interchange with each other whenever necessary. Close man to man marking enables the defender to have an equal chance of intercepting a pass. Follow the opponent wherever she goes, making certain not to be left behind when she maneuvers and changes directions. The defender stays between the goal and the attacker following her crosse with a hope of checking if she dodges, passes, or shoots.

A defending player makes decisive tackles without hesitation. The defense is approximately parallel with the attack before tackling, allowing time for a defense to cover a free player.

When a defending player intercepts a ball she passes it if a player is free, or runs upfield until a safe pass is possible. Help defending teammates by getting free for a pass when no forwards are available.

Interchange is the process by which a free attacking player is intercepted. It requires cooperation, speed, and timing. Third Man usually stays with Third Home, unless she is passed and then she recovers to the nearest loose player. Cover point usually starts the interchange as a free opponent is headed toward the goal with the ball. One of the Wing Defenses would come in to cover Second Home. Point marks First Home closely but watches the action of Cover Point. If Cover Point goes to tackle, Point may move to Second Home leaving First Home to be looked after by a Wing Defense. After the threat passes, players return to mark their own opponent.

DUTIES AND SPECIFIC SKILLS OF EACH PLAYER

Members of a lacrosse team must be proficient in stickwork, move well, think rapidly, and understand team work. Although the rules permit a player to roam anywhere on the field, each player should know her territory and her responsibilities.

Goalkeeper should
1. have leg and body pads, padded gloves, and face mask
2. be able to catch in limited space in all positions
3. be able to give long accurate passes to her attacks
4. try to cover every shot with her body or crosse
5. anticipate the attacks and find out from which side they usually shoot
6. obey the rules by clearing at once or running out of the crease
7. never clear in front of the goal
8. pass quickly and return to her goal
9. watch first home in order to intercept passes to her
10. never leave crease to attack if first home has the ball

Point should
1. be primarily responsible for marking first home
2. be outstanding at body checking
3. be able and ready to attack a player who is moving toward the goal
4. be able to move into the crease when the goalkeeper goes out and work in a limited space
5. be able to start and stop quickly and give long passes

Cover Point should
1. be good at body checking
2. be a steady player with skill at anticipating attacking movements
3. stop center when she runs through

4. mark her second home but go to attack an oncoming player making for the goal
5. never hold the ball but clear to an attack in good position
6. act decisively in defense interchange so wing defenses will know when to come in against second home

Third Man should

1. have speed, good footwork, and knowledge and ability to intercept play
2. never go downfield even when her team is attacking
3. interchange with center if center is drawn back

Wing Defenses should

1. be exceptionally fast players
2. be defense and attack players
3. cover second home when cover point has gone out
4. mark their opponents closely at the draw

Center should

1. mark opposing center closely
2. go back to help in defense
3. be available to shoot if there is an opening, without crowding her homes
4. intercept and relay passes
5. be ready to interchange with third home and act as an extra attack

Wing Attacks should

1. have speed and endurance
2. combine in attacking movements
3. serve as links between defense and attack
4. pass quickly or run rapidly toward goal
5. pass accurately to their homes
6. play out at their wing positions
7. shoot well at long and close range

Third Home must

1. work in limited space
2. take a position that will give her working space yet draw her third man from the oncoming player
3. rush for goal and pass to a free attack
4. be prepared to interchange with second home or center
5. be able to use players on both sides of the field

Second Home should

1. be an excellent shot from every angle, close and long, and in small spaces
2. have deceptive body movements to divert her cover point
3. be able to interchange with first home and wing attacks

First Home should

1. be deceptive in body and carrying action
2. have exceptional skill in shooting and handling catches and converting them into shots immediately

3. be ready to tackle goal out of the crease
4. tackle any defense near who gets the ball
5. field balls behind the goal

CLASS ORGANIZATION

A fairly high degree of proficiency in handling the crosse and ball is necessary before this game is enjoyable. To eliminate discouragement at her lack of skill and to minimize rough tactics, initial instruction should give the player satisfaction at being able to catch and throw. If the outdoor season is limited, start beginners indoors on cradling, catching, throwing, and picking up so actual games can begin quickly outdoors.

All lacrosse skills should be learned while moving; at first walking in place, walking forward, sideward, jogging, and then running. The following drills are suggested for indoor practice:

I. Cradling
    A. One group is seated on the floor in a circle practicing cradling; a second group is running around the outside cradling away from the inner circle. Reverse the groups.

    B. Players stand with backs against the wall and cradle to left and right. Knuckles of both hands touch the wall and prevent improper elbow movement.

II. Picking up, Cradling
    A. Teams of equal numbers place a ball on the floor about six feet ahead of each team. Each member runs forward, picks up the ball, cradles, turns at the end of the gymnasium, and replaces the ball.
    B. Roll the ball away from self, repeating the above formation.
    C. Teammate rolls the ball to a player who picks it up, cradles, and returns.

III. Tossing and Catching
    A. Players walk and cradle, tossing the ball up in front and ahead.
    B. With players in single file, the teacher throws a ball to each player who catches, cradles, and runs around the gymnasium.
    C. Four players, one at each corner of the gymnasium. On signal they begin cradling, then throw to the person diagonally opposite. She catches and returns the throw. Practice continues with walk increasing to a trot and then to a run.

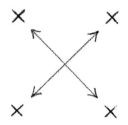

IV. Shooting

Hang gymnasium mats on the wall or move portable goal inside. Players are in two lines—one to the front and one to the side. They alternate approaching, shoot, and move to the other line.

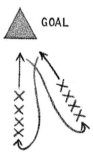

V. Dodging and Body Checking

Four players are on the floor. Each couple has half of the floor. One partner body checks the length of the floor as the other partner attempts to dodge. Reverse actions as the couples return to starting position.

```
Waiting turn
┌─────────────────────────────────────┐
│  3    4        ──────►   ──────►)    │
│  X    X        ◄──────   ◄──         │
│ ─ ─ ─ ─ ─ ─ ─ ─ ─ ─ ─ ─ ─ ─ ─ ─ ─ ─ │
│  1    2        ──────►   ──────►)    │
│  X    X        ◄──────   ◄──         │
└─────────────────────────────────────┘
```

TEACHING PROGRESSION

The following unit is suggested for beginning lacrosse players:

LESSON I

1. Nature and purpose of the game
2. Brief history and comparison with men's game
3. Film of game techniques

Lesson II

1. Equipment and its care
2. Field, players, and positions
3. Cradling and grip
4. Picking up
5. Drills and relays (indoors)

Lesson III

1. Review
2. Cradling and pickup combined
3. Catching
4. Marking and body checking
5. Shooting
6. Selected novelty games

Lesson IV

1. Review
2. Catching and throwing
3. Basic rules—stand, throw-in, free position
4. Indoor or outdoor game

Lesson V

1. Review positioning
2. Simplified game
3. Drill on game weaknesses—stress shooting

Lesson VI

1. Strategy of attack and defense
2. Game

Lesson VII

1. General review
2. Film of advanced play

Lesson VIII

1. Techniques of goalkeeping
2. Game

Lesson IX

1. Officiating
2. Oral evaluation and question and answer period

Lessons X and XI

1. Class tournament
2. Team evaluation

Lesson XII

1. Written evaluation
2. Rules
3. Strategy

SKILL DIFFICULTIES AND THEIR CORRECTION

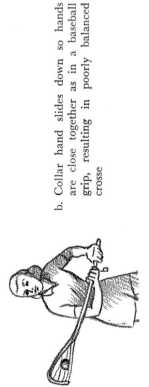

Difficulty	*Correction*
1. The Grip	1.
a. Both hands slide up the handle so balance and distance of reach are lost	a. The teacher demonstrates the loss of distance by extending arms and crosse against the wall with correct and in-correct grip
b. Collar hand slides down so hands are close together as in a baseball grip, resulting in poorly balanced crosse	b. Emphasize the need to keep the stick head up in a position not tiring to the arms
c. Failure to place "V" of right hand between stick and player's face when stick is in vertical position making cradling difficult	c. Review entire procedure for proper placement of hands

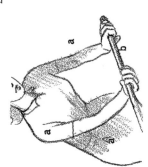

Difficulty	*Correction*

2. Cradling

Difficulty

a. Arms are stiff and shoulder immobile preventing a smooth running style

b. Bottom hand grip slips to the front so the wrist cannot extend enough to turn the stick head and ball falls

c. Failure to turn body when tackled

3. Pickup

a. Player fails to bend to pick up the ball

b. Player scoops the ball with butt hand high so it rolls out as player rises, or head of stick catches on the ground

Correction

2.

a. Have the student overswing and exaggerate arm movements until the shoulders relax. Later suggest practice with back against the wall to get proper arm movement

b. Review grip and emphasize the importance of the butt hand in controlling crosse movement

c. Practice twisting from the waist, putting the right or left shoulder forward and move the butt hand around to right or left so swing continues in a rhythmical pattern

3.

a. Stress flexion in the knees and body lowering

b. Practice the scoop so the knuckles of the lower hand almost touch the ground

421

SKILL DIFFICULTIES AND THEIR CORRECTION (*Continued*)

Difficulty	*Correction*

c. Loss of speed and momentum as the pickup is completed leaving the crosse and player vulnerable to a body check

d. Stick is too flat to catch ball rolling toward a player

c. The teacher tackles the player completing a pickup to show the importance of speed in avoiding opponents

d. Remind the student this pickup is like an "upside down" catch with the crosse head down on contact. Do not reach in front of the feet for the ball

4. *Catching*

4.

a. Grip changes when catching, thus hands are in poor position for cradling or passing

b. Failure to cradle or pass after catching, thereby inviting a tackle

a. Insist that beginner meets the ball with the movement of her body, rather than hands. Run to a position for a proper catch

b. In drills, the catch should be followed immediately by a pass or by cradling—both while running

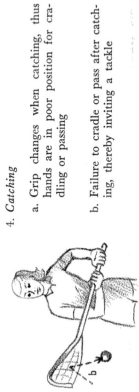

5. *Passing and Shooting*

5.

a. Passing with the upper arm resulting in little power and follow-through

b. Consistently inaccurate passes

a. Review the overarm pass making certain that the butt hand pulls and collar hand pushes. The butt hand finishes under the collar hand armpit

b. Teacher should explain that all accurate passes must run along the wood and off at the angle with the whole stick directing flight

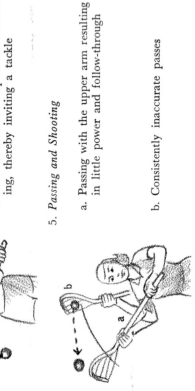

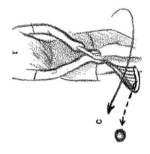

c. Student should experiment with a lower finish and more forward, rather than upward, follow-through

a. Practice guarding techniques of basketball. Pick up a crosse and continue the same technique until body movement becomes more natural and easy, then follow the opponent's crosse with your own as body stays between the goal and opponent

b. Control is important. Teacher can demonstrate that a player off balance or unable to control her crosse is ineffective in a pickup, run, and pass, even if she dislodges the ball with a crosse check

c. High, slow, ineffective underarm passes caused by high finish of the head

6. *Marking, Body, and Crosse Checking*

a. Failure to move effectively with an opponent

b. Slipping top hand down to extend for a crosse check often results in a foul or dangerous hit

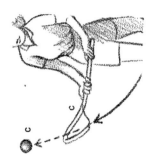

NOVELTY GAMES

Many soccer, hockey, and basketball novelty games are valuable and fun for teaching field position, dodging, and body checking. The unique skills of stickwork deserve emphasis as the key to pleasurable play.

Relays

Pivot Pickup.   Two teams of an equal number of partners. On the teacher's signal a couple from each team runs downfield toward two balls lying on the ground. A member of each couple picks up a ball, cradles it to a goal line, passes it to her partner who carries it back to its spot. The couples return and two more couples run out.

Cradle Relay.   Two or more teams in single file. First player puts ball in crosse, runs to goal line cradling, returns and drops the ball in next person's crosse (crosses should not touch). The cradle relay continues until all members of one team have crossed the finish line.

Zigzag Race.   Two teams of an equal number of players. Teams are in single file standing two crosse-lengths apart. First player in each line with a ball. On signal she turns and runs, weaving in and out of teammates. At the end of the line the ball is passed to first person in the line (by crosses). The dodging relay continues.

Keep Away (Advanced Players).   Players select an opponent whom they mark. One "team" is given the ball to keep as long as possible. As a competitive event, start the game with a draw and time the possession by each team. The winning team holds it the longest total time.

Ball Snatch.   Two teams line up in "Indian Snatch Club" formation about 20 yards apart. Each team member is given a number corresponding to an opponent. As the teacher rolls a ball between the two lines she calls a number. The two players run forward and try to pick up the ball and cradle it over their team line. A point is scored by the successful player.

Lacrosse Softball.   Played like softball. The pitcher delivers the ball with her crosse, the batter catches it and then throws, as if batting. Baserunners should keep outside of the bases and need touch home plate only.

OFFICIATING TECHNIQUES[3]

An official game requires one field umpire and two goal umpires. The field umpire enforces all rules and gives all decisions on goals. She observes any rule infringements and awards penalties. She is responsible for checking on all field markings and equipment and generally overseeing the conduct of the game.

Each goal umpire observes the action concerning the crease, signals her decision when a goal is made, and observes infringements of the rules con-

---

[3] For an excellent guide to efficient umpiring see, Delano, Anne Lee: The Umpiring of Women's Lacrosse, *Field Hockey-Lacrosse Guide,* Sept. 1958–Sept. 1960.

cerning the crease. She may stop play for an infringement but the field umpire awards the penalty.

EVALUATING THE RESULTS

General skills in lacrosse can be measured, but the individual's ability as a team member is difficult to evaluate. The following suggestions are helpful in understanding the total class progress:

1. Keep progress charts to record scores on skills tests including cradling, pickups, catching, passing, shooting, marking, and dodging.

2. Use rating scales, by teacher and pupils, to evaluate an individual's team ability, understanding, and skill as an offensive and defensive player.

3. Give written tests to evaluate knowledge of rules, officiating, and strategy.

4. Use an incident chart to record the skills successfully performed and the errors committed during a game.

Terminology

Body Checking—Placing one's body in the way of an opponent so that the opponent's progress is impeded

Cradling—Action of the body and crosse which keeps the ball under control in the netting

Crease—A circle eight and one-half feet in radius surrounding each goal. It serves as a restraining line when shooting for a goal

Crosse Checking—Tapping the crosse of an opponent in an attempt to dislodge the ball

Draw—The method of beginning play between opposing centers at each period and after each goal

Free Position—A position awarded a player when an opponent has fouled. The player is given the ball in her crosse and may run, shoot, or pass. All other players must be at least five yards away

Holding Down—Holding an opponent's crosse by one's own crosse—either in the air or on the ground. Unlike legal tapping, holding is a foul

Marking—Guarding an opponent by staying close by and moving as she moves

Stand—A stationary position all players must hold, unless otherwise directed by the umpire, when the umpire suspends play

Stick—Another name for the crosse

Tackle—Approaching an opponent for the purpose of body checking

Throw-in—Putting the ball in play as the umpire throws between opposing players. Used when both players were equidistant from the ball as it went out of bounds

Discussion Questions

1. What are the major contributions of lacrosse to the team sport program for girls and women?
2. Explain attack and defense strategy. What is the value of interchange? Illustrate.

3. Name three or four fundamental skills all players should develop. Demonstrate each of these.
4. Lacrosse is a growing team activity and needs skilled teachers. Outline a unit for a clinic for teachers who are anxious to learn and teach the activity.

SUGGESTED AUDIO-VISUAL AIDS

Lacrosse 1952. (25 min., 16mm., sound) United States Women's Lacrosse Association, Film Service Chairman: Mary E. Lick, Middleburg College, Middleburg, Virginia. (Rental)

Lacrosse Techniques 1952. (9 film loops, color) USWLA. Film Service Chairman Mary E. Lick for Rental. Mrs. Marian Mooers Tietz, Newton Road, Newtonville, N.Y. for purchase.

Lacrosse Bulletin Board Materials. Official publications of USWLA. Includes skills, coaching notes, etc. Secretary USWLA, Roberta Brennan, 215 Auburn Street, Auburndale 66, Massachusetts.

SUGGESTED READINGS

Burbeck, Louise G., and Wheeler, Helena: *Lacrosse for Girls,* L. G. Burbeck, Skidmore College, Saratoga Spring, N.Y., or H. Wheeler, 9 Shadow Lane, Larchmont, N.Y.

Field Hockey-Lacrosse Guide with Official Rules and Standards. Current edition, DGWS, 1201 16th Street, N.W., Washington 6, D.C.

Newhof, Carol, editor: *Selected Field Hockey-Lacrosse Articles,* DGWS, 1201 16th Street, N.W., Washington 6, D.C.

Paterson, Ann, editor: *Team Sports for Girls,* New York, The Ronald Press, 1958, Chapter 5.

Physical Education for High School Students, AAHPER, 1201 16th Street, N.W., Washington 6, D.C., 1955, Chapter 13.

PERIODICALS

Lacrosse for Girls published several times yearly by All-England Ladies' Lacrosse Association. Write Gertrude Hooper, 242 Highland Street, Milton 86, Massachusetts.

Crosse Checks yearly publication United States Women's Lacrosse Association, Doris Cholerton, 239 Rector Street, Philadelphia 28, Pa.

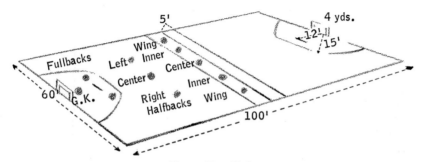

17

Soccer

Figure No. 17–1.

Since the origin of soccer is attributed to widely separated places such as Sparta, Ireland, Greece, England, and Rome, it is likely that the game developed in several localities at about the same time. The ancient sport of "Harpastrum," in which a crudely shaped ball was either hit with the hands or kicked, later became "feetballe," a rough and rugged kicking game played as a mob sport. An inflated animal bladder organ covered with leather was moved by sheer force through the alleys, streets, and out into vacant fields between goals often located miles apart. Although many English monarchs, including King Edward II, Queen Elizabeth, and James I, passed edicts forbidding their subjects to play this bloody, brawling sport because of the many complaints of damaged property from shopkeepers, somehow the game survived through the centuries. Even if the nobility looked down upon this degrading contest played by the lowly, rugged commoners, it was an Englishman from the upper class, J. C. Thring, who drew up the rules, giving the game respectability by making soccer safer to play, and by introducing it into the private schools and adult clubs of England.

Even though the game was played in America during early colonial times, it did not gain in popularity until after World War I. The first intercollegiate match for men was played in 1869 between Princeton and Rutgers, and a modified game for women was first introduced at Bryn Mawr College in 1919. Since then soccer for both sexes has become increasingly favored in our school and college programs, and has grown as a popular recreation sport for varying ages. As an international game played and enjoyed by millions throughout the world, soccer has no equal for it is the national sport of 53 countries.

THE NATURE AND PURPOSE OF THE GAME*

Soccer is a running and kicking game played with an inflated leather or rubber ball which has a circumference of 28 inches and which cannot be touched with the hands, except by the goalkeeper. It is a team game of speed, endurance, body and ball control. The object of the game is to advance the ball down a field no larger than 100 yards long and 60 yards wide, or smaller than 80 × 40 yards, by using the body and feet, and to score points by sending it between the goal posts and under the crossbar. Goal posts at each end of the field are eight feet high and six yards apart.

A team is made up of 11 players: a goalie (who is the only player who can handle the ball), a right and left fullback, a right, left, and center halfback, and five forwards known as the center forward, right inner, right wing, left inner, and left wing.

The game for girls is made up of four 8 minute quarters with a rest period of two minutes between each, and 10 minutes between halves. Play is begun by a kick-off by the center forward at the center line and the ball is thus put in play at the start of each quarter and after each scored goal. On the kick-off the ball must be rolled at least the distance of its circumference toward the opponent's territory. No player from the offensive team can cross the center line nor can an opponent cross the restraining line, until the ball is kicked. The center forward, who starts the game, cannot again kick the ball until it has been touched by another person.

The ball is moved by players up and down the field, or passed to teammates by dribbling or kicking it with the feet. When it goes out of bounds on the side, it is placed on the line and kicked back into the playing area by one from the opposite team to that which sent it out. When it is sent out of bounds over the end line or over the crossbar by any member of the defending team, a *corner kick* is given to an attacking player from the nearest corner. If the ball goes over the crossbar or over the goal line outside of the goal posts when kicked by an attacking team player, it is kicked by any defending team member from anywhere on the quarter circle marking the penalty area. This is a *Defense Kick*. A *roll-in* by the official is taken when two players simultaneously commit a foul, or two opposing players simul-

* See current DGWS Guide for complete rules.

taneously cause the ball to go out of bounds. The two stand 5 yards in from the line facing each other, ready to kick the ball while all other players stand at least 5 yards from the ball.

A *foul* is called when a player is tripped, pushed, charged into, kicked, held by another player, or has touched the ball with her hands. If the foul occurs outside the penalty area by either team, or in the penalty area by the attacking team, a free kick is awarded to the opposing team. All other players stand at least 5 yards away until the player place kicks.

A *penalty kick* is given when any defending team member commits a foul in the penalty area. The official places the ball on the penalty mark 12 yards from the goal, and all players except the goalkeeper and player taking the kick must stand outside the penalty area. After the ball is kicked (usually by the center forward of the attacking team) all rush in to make or prevent a goal. A field goal, made by successfully kicking the ball under and between the goal posts, counts two points, while a penalty kick counts one.

NEEDED FACILITIES AND EQUIPMENT

Because only a minimum of equipment is needed for this activity and it can accommodate 22 players or more, soccer is ideal for those many teachers faced with a limited budget and large classes. There should be a minimum of one regulation ball for every five to seven players. The field should be level, free of holes, turfed, and be well marked. Each player should wear shorts and a blouse, a tunic, or any other kind of regulation gymnasium costume. Rubber-cleated shoes are recommended. The goalkeeper (and other players, if they desire to do so) should wear shin guards and other protective equipment. Pinnies, used to distinguish teams, should be numbered and be in bright contrasting colors. Eyeglass guards should be worn by those needing them. A first aid kit should be taken to the playing field, if it is located several blocks from the gymnasium or a first aid station.

TEACHING UNITS

Suggested topics for a soccer unit include:

Unit for Beginners	*Unit for Advanced Players*
Short history and purpose of the game	Review of safety rules
Safety rules	Review of fundamental skills
Dribbling	Variation of body trapping
Kicking	Leg trapping
Inside and outside of foot	Heading
Top of instep	Kicking
Heel	Game strategy
Toe	Attacking; evading
	Advanced game strategy

BASIC SKILLS

The Dribble.   Done by moving the ball with the inside and instep of the feet, the dribble is a series of short taps performed by using alternate feet. The ball should not move more than ten inches away from the body. Advanced players may use the outside of the foot or the toe.

Figure No. 17–2.   The Dribble.

Blocking.   This is done by using any part of the body, except the arms and hands, to stop the ball. If the arms are used, they must be kept folded against the chest. The body should "give" as it contacts the ball, by caving in and moving slightly backwards. The thighs and abdomen can also be used to block ball progress.

The Chest-High Block.   Hold the arms close to the body, bend forward when contacting the ball and "give" as the contact is made.

The Thigh-High Block.   Meet the ball on the inside of the leg above the knee. Extend arms sideways for balance and "give" as the ball meets the body.

Heading.   Keep eyes on the ball, jump into the air and contact the ball at the hairline in front of the head. To send the ball sideways, use the side of the head.

Figure No. 17–3.   Blocking. A. The Chest-High Block; B. The Thigh-High Block; C. Heading.

Shouldering.   Watch the ball, jump into the air and move the shoulder back then forward as the ball is contacted by the top of the shoulders.

Figure No. 17–4.   The Instep Kick.

The Instep Kick.   The ball is kicked by swinging the right, slightly bent leg forward, shifting body weight from right to left, extending the foot and leg, and lifting the ball up and away from the body with the top of the foot.

Figure No. 17–5.   The Inside Foot Kick

The Inside Foot Kick.   This can be used to pass the ball diagonally to the right or left, depending upon which foot is used. The right leg is swung diagonally across the body as the knee straightens, weight is supported on the left foot, and the ball swept out and away from the body by the right foot.

The Outside Foot Kick. The ball is kicked diagonally ahead by swinging the left leg forward to the left, supporting body weight on the right foot and sweeping the ball out and away from the body with the fore part of the left foot.

Figure No. 17–6.   The Outside Foot Kick.

The Place Kick. Done by kicking the ball from a stationary place with either the in- or outside of the foot, heel, or toe, this skill may be preceded by running steps. Body weight shifts from the right to left foot as the ball is contacted and lifted up and away from the body by the extended right leg and foot.

The Punt. The ball is dropped from one or both hands an extended

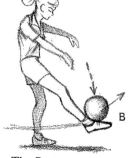

Figure No. 17–7.   The Punt.

arm's length in front of the body and kicked behind and under it with either fully extended leg and foot before it touches the ground. Only the goalkeeper, in the penalty area, may punt.

Trapping with the Sole of the Foot. As the ball comes toward the player in a slow roll, she stops it with the sole of her foot, heel pointed downward. Correct timing is necessary.

Figure No. 17–8.   Trapping with the Sole of the Foot.

The Drop Kick (Permitted only by the goalkeeper within her penalty area). The ball is kicked as it rebounds from the ground after dropping from both extended hands held forward at waist level. The body weight shifts from right to left, and as the ball is dropped the right leg swings forward, straightens, and the ball is kicked on the outside and top of the foot. Two steps may precede the kick.

Trapping with One Leg. The player prepares to stop the ball by lining up directly in its path. For a right leg trap the left leg moves forward, flexes and carries the body weight down and slightly forward. The right knee bends and the shin contacts the ball forcing it to a stop against the ground.

Two Leg Trap. Hold feet close together and deeply bend knees, lean body slightly forward, keeping arms out to the side. Stop the ball until good control of it is gained before passing or dribbling it to another player.

Shooting. Kicking for a goal requires quick, accurate movements. Get within the penalty area and kick the ball hard and straight, catching the goalkeeper off guard.

Tackling. Made either directly in front of an oncoming player or to the side, a tackle requires correct timing and accuracy. Put one foot on the side of the ball and quickly move it away from the player. For a side tackle, shift body weight to one foot and hold that leg in a deep bent position. Hook the ball with the opposite leg (it should be the one nearest the opponent) and draw the ball sharply away from the dribbler.

Figure No. 17–9. Tackling.

GAME STRATEGY

The factors necessary for successful and winning strategy are the skills of each individual player blended into united team effort. If this is to be accomplished, position play is a must. This seems to be the hardest concept for girls and women players to grasp, for the problem of players bunching is one most common to teachers. A good team is made up of skillful individuals who can play as a team dependent upon and receiving the unique contribution each makes to the unified whole. Such teamwork, accurate kicking, skillful blocking, quick passing, and agility in dodging an attacker are all essential parts of good strategy. Other aspects of offensive and defensive play are:

The Offense

1. Pass ahead of an intended receiver and out to the sidelines until nearing the opponent's goal.
2. Play your own position. When interchanging with a teammate do so quickly, endeavoring to throw the opponent off guard.
3. Play in your own area of the field and avoid bunching.
4. Keep the ball low and near the ground for better control.
5. Look for weaknesses in the opponent's strategy and skill and capitalize upon them.
6. Help the forward line score as often as possible.
7. Master the skills of playing a *long passing game* out to fast forwards (this is good especially when the field is wet); a *short passing game* quickly, endeavoring to throw the opponent off guard.
   triangle passing game using any three players (usually a wing halfback and two forwards) to zigzag the ball downfield quickly. Change from one style of attack to another often enough to keep the opponent guessing.
8. Conserve energy whenever possible and take advantage of "breathers" when the ball is elsewhere on the field and playing it is someone else's responsibility.
9. Be sure all forward line players *know* to whom the ball will be kicked and the opponent does *not know* this for certain.
10. Take free kicks quickly before the defensive team can get organized.
11. Rush for a goal in the penalty area.
12. Have the wing take a corner kick with her forward line teammates forming a semicircle between her and the far side of the goal. The receiver should get the ball directly in front of the goal and kick for it quickly.
13. On a free kick or roll-in, it is best to have the forward line ahead of the ball, and for a right or left halfback to kick or roll the ball in.
14. Take advantage of wind and all other environmental playing conditions.

The Defense

1. The player with the ball should always be tackled by the nearest defender.
2. Work out beforehand a plan for interchanging positions.
3. Always keep two strong lines of defensive players plus the goalkeeper between the oncoming attackers and the goal.
4. Each player should play her own position, and tackle successfully any offensive player who comes into that area.
5. The main job of the halfbacks as defensive players is not to allow the ball to get past them, if they can help it; of the fullbacks, never to let the ball go past them; and the goalkeeper, never to let the opponent score. If the halfbacks fail, the fullbacks must come to the rescue, and the goalkeeper comes to the rescue of them all if, and when, they fail.

6. Back up a teammate when an opponent evades a tackler.

7. Always anticipate what a play will be before it becomes a reality.

8. On the kick-off, the fullback should move up to the halfback line and mark each approaching forward.

9. On a penalty kick the halfbacks, who should stand next to the forwards they are marking, should rush to the goalkeeper's assistance when the ball is kicked. The fullbacks should stand at the outer edge of the penalty area and on each side of the goal posts.

10. On the corner kick the two fullbacks should be in the goalkeeper's cage. Two halfbacks should be on the same side of the goal as the ball, with the third in the opposite area. The forward line should be halfway down the same side of the field.

11. On the kick-in, one halfback should mark a wing, the center halfback the inner, and the other halfback the center forward.

12. The goalkeeper must always keep her eye on the ball, and usually stand about six feet in front of the goal, slightly left to the center of the goal.

DUTIES AND SPECIAL SKILLS OF PLAYERS

The Goalkeeper

1. Keep the opponent from scoring by anticipating movements.

2. Possess the ability to move quickly at all space levels and in all directions.

3. Be able to kick the ball far down the sidelines of the field.

4. Must be one not easily upset or panicked.

The Fullbacks

1. Must be able to kick accurately, anticipate actions, and have the ability to move quickly.

2. Must clearly realize that their main task is to keep the opponent from getting the ball past the fullback area into scoring position, and to be able to get it back up to their teammates if and when it does.

3. Must mark the inner on their side of the field.

The Halfbacks

1. Must be able to run fast, have much endurance, be able to dribble, tackle, and pass accurately.

2. Must have working knowledge of their duties and know when to change from offensive to defensive players, how to intercept passes, and the correct playing position to take at all times.

3. The right and left halfbacks should mark the opposing right and left forwards.

The Forward Line

1. Must be fast runners, accurate dribblers, and aggressive players, skilled in passing, blocking, and trapping.

2. Must be skilled in taking advantage of, as well as creating, opportunities for moving the ball downfield and scoring points.

CLASS ORGANIZATION

After each skill has been explained and demonstrated, the class should have ample opportunity to practice it until they are polished enough for team play. Squad drills, carefully planned and organized, as well as competitive novelty games in which these skills are utilized, are recommended. Suggested class organizations for drilling purposes are:

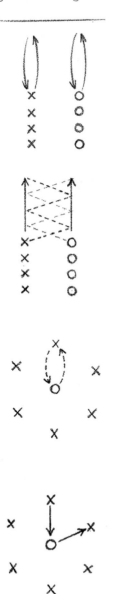

The Dribble. Arrange group in two or more lines. Dribble from the center of the field to the end line and back, using the feet alternately.

Dribble Pass. Two lines, players in each line working as partners, dribble the ball passing it diagonally in front of each other, from the center of the field to the end line and back.

Have players in each squad weave in and out of players stationed five yards apart.

Heading. Circle formation with one player in the center. The ball is tossed by each one into this player who heads it back to her. Each one takes her turn in the center.

Player in the center throws the ball clockwise to each person to head it back to her.

Trapping. Circle formation with one player in the center. Each outside player kicks the ball into the center, who traps it, then kicks it back to the next player, who traps it before kicking it back to her. Each takes her turn in the center. Practice one foot trap, lower leg trap, upper leg trap, and body trap.

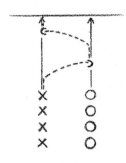

Dribble, Pass, Trap, Dribble, and Pass. Arrange two lines with players in each line working as partners, starting 30 or more feet from the center of the field. First player in line one dribbles the ball, passes it out diagonally to first player in the second line who traps it, dribbles it, then passes it diagonally to the first player as they both progress up the field, turn at end of line and dribble back.

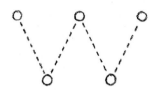

Pass, Trap. Progression for teaching: inside of one leg, with both legs, with the inside of both legs, with the heel.

Dribble and Shoot. X's try to dribble through to shoot. The O's as defensive players, clear the ball. X's halfbacks feed the ball up to the forward line.

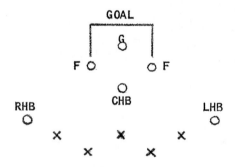

Passing and Tackling. Two lines 10 feet apart. The first two in each line advance dribbling and passing the ball toward a player who is stationed about 15 feet out. She attempts to tackle while the two try to avoid being tackled.

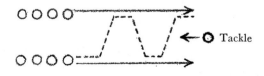

Tackling. Double line formation 15 feet apart. One player in line A slowly dribbles the ball to opposite player in line B who tackles her. Next have one couple in line A advance to tackle as their passes go from one to the other. Rotate positions.

Punting, Drop Kicking.   Double line of players 20 or more yards apart. Punt to each other. Combine punting or drop kicking with trapping, dribbling, and passing.

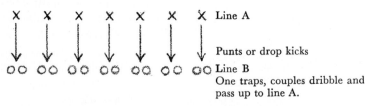

Position Play.   Station players as they should be on the field. Walk through a play in slow motion taking the ball downfield. Repeat in normal motion.

TEACHING PROGRESSION

A suggested unit of 10 lessons for beginners includes:

Lesson I

1. Short history of the game
2. Safety precautions
3. Warm up exercises
4. Dribbling
5. Kicking—Inside of foot (stationary circle practice)
     Outside of foot
     Top of instep
     Heel
     Toe
6. Relays, drills

Lesson II

1. Watching a game of one quarter played by skilled players, or in a movie
2. Warm up exercises
3. Review of the five ways to kick
4. Review of dribbling relay
5. Dribble, pass
6. Trapping with both legs

Lesson III

1. Warm up exercises
2. Review of dribbling, passing, trapping with both legs, one leg trap, sole of foot trap, body trap

3. Relays and drills of skills taught
4. Novelty game—soccer keep away

Lesson IV

1. Warm up exercises
2. Review of previous lesson
3. Heading
4. Punting
5. Front tackle
6. Line Soccer
7. Brief discussion of rules. Positions and duties of players (blackboard or magnetized board talk)

Lesson V

1. Warm up exercises
2. Review of previous lesson
3. Side, hook, and split tackle
4. Relays and drills of skills taught
5. Four minute soccer game with rules discussed at teachable moments during game play

Lesson VI

1. Warm up exercises
2. Review of previous materials
3. Ten minute game
4. Discussion of rules
5. Punting

Lesson VII

1. Warm up exercises
2. Review drills of dribbling, passing, tackling, and punting
3. Simple playing strategy, stressing offensive play
4. Ten minute game

Lesson VIII

1. Warm up exercises
2. Review drills of heading, blocking, punting
3. Shooting for goals
4. Simple playing strategy, stressing defensive play
5. Ten minute game

Lesson IX

1. Warm up exercises
2. Play most of the period with rules stressed at teachable moments

Lesson X

1. Evaluation: short pencil-paper test, skill tests

In teaching soccer, emphasis should be placed first upon developing individual skills and secondly, upon using these mastered skills during team play. After the demonstration and explanation of each technique, the teacher should watch and correct the movement patterns of each learner as she experiments with the separate parts of the intricate skill pattern she is teaching herself. Although ideally, there should be one ball for every small group of students, as many as ten can use the same one, if an effort is made to keep each person as active as possible in all drills used. Kicking can best be taught in a double line formation. Skilled squad leaders, who have been given some additional instruction during after school hours, can work as the instructor's helper in correcting movement faults as they occur. This assistance enables the teacher to keep an eye on the whole class and be on the lookout for those in the group who most need help. It is suggested that a short game of five minutes be played when the class is ready for this experience. It should be stopped at teachable moments, for this is the best time and way to teach rules. Position play, the duties of each player, offensive and defensive strategy can often be grasped more readily by beginners if a magnetized board or an illustrated blackboard talk is used. Each person should learn to play several positions before choosing the one on which to concentrate. Homogeneous grouping is best for teaching offensive and defensive teamwork, and those with superior skills should play against a team made up of players equally adept.

Beginners, especially, need almost constant reminding to play on their own half of the field and to stay in their own position. Each should have a clear understanding of just what her job is before she attempts to assume her assigned team role.

Many of the isolated game skills can be practiced in the gymnasium on rainy days. Tackling, marking opponents, heading, trapping, dribbling, and all forms of kicking can be learned and perfected inside. Novelty games, drills, and competitive relays can be used to help maintain interest in the game when inclement weather keeps the class indoors for several days and it is impossible to play a regular game. Care should be taken, however, not to have too many players in action on the floor at one time, else confusion and accidents result.

Advanced players will enjoy learning the intricate techniques of good game strategy, as well as perfecting their timing, coordination, developing speed, and their ability to use their minds and bodies in order to win games played against equally skilled opponents.

SKILL DIFFICULTIES AND THEIR CORRECTION

Difficulty	*Correction*

1. *Dribbling*

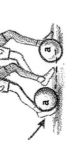

1.

a. Kicking the ball too far in front; using the feet incorrectly

    a. Stress keeping the ball close to the body by *tapping* it with the inside of the foot; walk through a dribble in slow motion using alternate feet, repeat movements while running

b. Dribbling when it would be better to pass

    b. Be sure player understands *why* and *when* to dribble or pass

2. *Kicking*

2.

a. Missing the approaching ball

    a. Have the player watch the spin of the ball as it comes toward her

441

SKILL DIFFICULTIES AND THEIR CORRECTION (*Continued*)

Difficulty	*Correction*
b. Kicking with the toe; throwing the ball in the air for a punt instead of bending over it as it drops from the hands	b. Have student kick with toe, then kick correctly in order to get the "feel" of doing it right and to gain insight on *why* the instep is better to use. Demonstrate how to get closer to the ball, dropping it and kicking it mimetically. Do this to counts. Next use the counts and the ball
c. Lack of control before kicking the ball	c. Combine kicking, passing, and trapping drills. Say "trap, control, then kick" until student knows the meaning of the phrase and can put it into practice
d. Ability to kick or dribble well with only one foot	d. Practice to develop the weaker foot

3. Trapping

3.

a. Practice without opposition. Stress "watch the spin of the ball." Practice with opposition first in slow, then in normal speed

b. Be sure student masters simple traps before going on to more advanced ones. **Start** with the two leg trap. Demonstrate how one "gives" when attacking a ball; show how this also occurs in trapping and stress why

a. Missing the ball

b. "Tensing up" and "fighting" the ball instead of "giving" with it

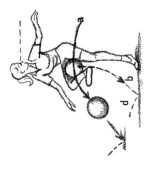

443

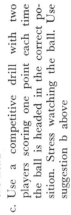

c. Using the wrong trap in a game situation

  c. Develop equally ability to do all kinds of trapping through drills without, and then with competition between squads or teams

d. Letting the ball get too far away from the body after trapping

  d. Practice keeping control of the ball until it can be passed off to another player. Show ways the body can bend and twist for doing so

4. *Heading*

  a. Toss easy balls at close range until player gets the idea that heading cannot hurt her

a. Fear of heading

  b. Stress keeping the eyes on the ball until it meets the hairline in front of the head

b. Closing the eyes

  c. Use a competitive drill with two players scoring one point each time the ball is headed in the correct position. Stress watching the ball. Use suggestion b above

c. The ball hitting the top of the head, or too low on the head

  d. Have student jump to head. Be sure she understands the advantage for doing so

d. Heading with both feet on the ground

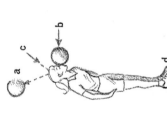

5. Tackling

a. Unnecessary roughness; tripping

b. Playing the person instead of the ball

6. Game Strategy

a. The show off who wants to "star"

b. Bunching

c. Trying to use too many set plays which fail

d. Fighting hard to gain or regain the ball only to lose it by using foolish strategy

5.

a. Stress the agile art of tackling without touching the player. Praise player for using this tactic, reprimand in front of the team when she uses unnecessary roughness

b. Teach that the object is to get the ball *away from the player* and not to get the player

6.

a. Stress the value of team play. Avoid praising just one player or letting the team or spectators do so

b. Use a magnetized board and chalk talks to stress correct position play. Have a person assigned to watch each player and record the number of times each quarter the player was offside or bunched

c. Use the M or W forward line formation mostly when in scrimmage

d. Coach all to keep any opposite team player from getting the ball. Stress *"get the ball, control the ball, keep the ball, and Score!"*

445

NOVELTY GAMES

Line Soccer (Beginners).   A field 30 feet square is used with seven to ten players per team. One or two players on each side are stationed near their sidelines, all the rest behind their own end line. As the referee drops the ball in the center, one from each extreme right end rushes to kick the ball over the opponent's goal at the opposite end (this scores two points). Only these two players may kick the ball, but the end players may use their hands to stop it. Fouls are called if (a) any runner pushes or blocks another, (b) any other than the end players touch it with their hands, or (c) the ball is kicked over the opposing side or end line. Penalty for fouls: a free kick (scores one point) to the opposing side's runner from the center field. A ball kicked over the line by anyone other than the runner does not count. The next player in each line then becomes the runner.

Variation: Have two or more players come out from each side with one as the forward player and the others as backs.

Gymnasium Soccer (Beginners and Intermediates).   This game is played as much like the outdoor game as possible. Use a basketball court, with goals of two jumping standards at the end lines placed nine feet apart and connected by a crossbar six feet high. This goal is placed equidistant from the sidelines. Use six to nine players on a side, and an old basketball or regulation soccer ball. The game is scored as in soccer and starts with the ball being dropped between two centers in the jump circle. A penalty kick is given for roughness, kicking, holding, tripping, hitting, and for any player touching the ball with her hands inside her own goal area. The ball is given to an opponent out of bounds for touching it outside of the player's own penalty area. Follow-up play is given when any defensive player commits a foul in her own penalty area. Otherwise the ball is centered after a penalty kick or when a penalty kick is given both teams.

Out of Bounds: The sidelines are used for the throw-in. A corner kick is given when a ball goes over the end line if it is last touched by a defending player. If it is last touched by an attacking player, the goalkeeper puts it in play with a place kick taken within 6 feet of the goal line as the opponents stand 15 feet away until the ball is kicked.

The ball is centered if the official does not know which side kicked it out of bounds. Regular soccer rules are observed.

Circle Soccer Keep Away (Beginners).   Two teams with one player in the center as in dodge-ball. The outside team kicks and butts the ball, attempting to hit the inside players. The ball may not be touched with the hands. If it stops inside the circle, an outside player must recover it and dribble it back out to the outer circle. One is out when hit by the ball. Teams change places and the one eliminating the other in the shortest time wins.

Soccer Center Ball (Beginners).   "It" is in the center with all others in a circle kicking the ball back and forth across the area as "it" attempts to touch it. If she does, she exchanges places with the last person who kicked it. Circle players may not touch the ball with their hands. One becomes "it" if she kicks the ball over the center's head. A ball going out of the circle area must be dribbled back, and "it" and any others may go after it.

Dribble Tag (Beginners and Intermediates).   Players scatter as "it" dribbles and attempts to hit any player. If she is successful, the new "it" is the one tagged with the ball.

Soccer Ten Kicks (Beginners and Intermediates).   Two teams try to get possession of the ball, after which using soccer skills, one player kicks it to another on her side, counting "one" as she does. Then if it goes to another teammate the count is "two," etc. Each side tries to get up to ten kicks first. As a play is broken up by the opposing team, begin counting "one" again.

Long Ball Soccer (Intermediates and Advanced).   Two teams play in a limited space in which a starting line is drawn. At right angles to the starting line and 100 feet into the playing area, a base one foot square is drawn. As one team takes any position in the field, the other stands near the starting line. The batter places the ball on the base and kicks the ball into the field, then runs to the base and back, as fielders try to put her out by trapping the ball, heading it, or blocking it with both feet off of the ground, or by kicking the ball so that it will hit the runner. Play until three on each side are out for an inning, and play as many innings as desired.

OFFICIATING TECHNIQUES

Two umpires, or one umpire and two linesmen, are used for officiating a soccer game. If there are two umpires, they decide which part of the field is to be taken by each as shown in the diagram below. It is the duty of each on her part of the field to call and watch kick-ins

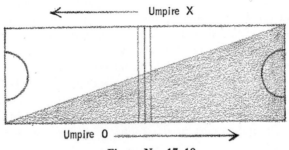

Figure No. 17–10.

and fouls. One acts as the main official and starts the game and each succeeding quarter. She explains to players the signals used, and describes to them how they should react to these signals. She avoids errors, and expresses a willingness to explain any interpretation of a called decision between halves and the end of the game.

The timekeepers and scorekeepers are then given their instructions for calling time, methods of keeping score, and notifying the umpire when a player enters the game without reporting.

As in all sports officiating, the umpires should refrain from calling fouls if they feel that the rule enforcement would give the offending team the advantage, or if the infraction is a minor one. Since game rules are devised for the protection of the player, beginners who compete should be carefully watched and fouls called frequently enough for safe play, with the officials making split second decisions whether or not to stop play, realizing that too frequent interruptions will deaden a budding enthusiasm for the sport. It is wise, except in tournament play, for the officials to stop the game in order to be sure players do understand why fouls are called on them, so that the offenders can avoid repeating infractions of rules.

A corner is called when the defense sends the ball over its own goal line at any point outside of the goal posts. It is important that the umpire stand near the kicker taking the awarded corner play and be alert, from this vantage station, for a possible score resulting from the play. In all free kicks and corner kicks, she should insist that the rule, when infractions occur all other players except the kicker must stand at least five yards away, be observed, for some crafty players will deliberately stand closer so that during the called delay, their teammates can gain added time for marking opponents or calling a proposed play.

The officials must be alert to a player who is offsides, simply, one who is in her opponent's half of the field without possession of the ball when fewer than three opponents stand between her and the goal.

When a goal is scored, she should be certain that the entire ball has crossed over the line and that the goalkeeper takes only two steps while holding or bouncing the ball in her hands. The goalkeeper may however, take any number of steps when bouncing it on the ground.

Above all, the umpire should not be "whistle happy" during the game. She can avoid this by not blowing the whistle on a kick-in, goal kick, free kick, or corner play. She should blow her whistle sharply when an attacker fouls inside the opponent's penalty area, but should hold her whistle briefly if a defender fouls, for a goal might result on following play. She should blow her whistle in a short, sharp, commanding way, tell her decision promptly, stick to it, and call time out if, and when, player dissension occurs as a result of the foul being called. Ideally, the official should be a person fully cognizant that her part in the contest is to see that the game runs smoothly and safely.

EVALUATING THE RESULTS

Each player should be tested for her knowledge of the background, rules, and strategy of the game and the results of this written examination should be coupled with those of a skill test, if a final grade is to be given for the soccer unit.

Rating scales for subjectively classifying players during game play can be devised based upon the criteria established for players of average, below, or above average ability.

Skill tests which might be used are:

The Soccer Dribble Test.   Set four posts in a straight line 20 feet apart, as pictured. On "go" the player dribbles the ball from the starting line interweaving around the posts as shown. When passing post number 1 coming back, she kicks the ball across the starting line. If she loses control of the ball, she must regain it and complete her dribble. Record the amount of time taken from the word "go" to the ball's crossing the starting line. Record the best of three trials and award a grade from those curved recorded times of the best scores made by each in the group.

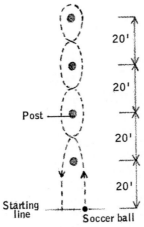

Figure No. 17–11.   Field Arrangement for Soccer Dribble Test.

Soccer Dribble for Speed and Left Foot Pass for Accuracy.   Mark the area as shown in Figure 17–12. On a signal, the player dribbles the ball placed on point B along line AB until it reaches any point between X and Y, when it is then kicked through the goal with the left foot.

Time is taken from the word "go" until the ball crosses the goal line, and should be recorded in seconds and tenths.

The contestant must kick the ball toward the goal from some point between X and Y, and not nearer to the goal than the 6 yard line when the kick is made; if this rule is violated, no score is recorded. The player may try until she scores. Three trials are recorded and the best of the three is curved along with those other best recorded tries by each in the class.

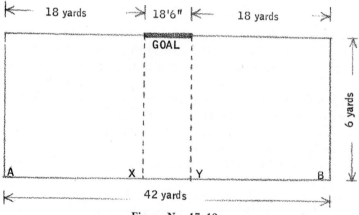

Figure No. 17–12.

Soccer Dribble for Speed and Right Foot Pass for Accuracy. Use the same diagram and directions given above except that in this test the player starts from point A and kicks with the right foot.

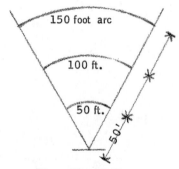

Figure No. 17–13.

Soccer Punt for Distance. Equipment needed includes several balls, three pointed marking sticks, a 100 foot tape, and timer. The area should be marked as shown. Each player has three trials. Without stepping over the line she takes several steps and punts the ball as far as she can. One student places a marker where the ball first lands and returns all balls to the kicking line, while two others measure and mark the distance, having the zero end of the tape in the field. The instructor should read and record all measurements made, as well as supervise the placement of the markers.

Distances should be measured from the markers to the midpoint of the kicking line and be recorded to the nearest foot. They may also be measured from the markers to the nearest arc and these added to arc distances from the midpoint of the kicking line. Another try is given if the ball goes outside the landing area, and this turn does not count. The best score is recorded and a grade awarded from those curved best scores made by all other class members.

Trapping Test. The instructor kicks the ball or passes it to the player, and the number of times she successfully traps it out of 10 tries is recorded. A variety of traps should be used, or the test can be run 10 times for each type of trap.

Kicking for Accuracy. The player stands 30 yards away from five concentric circles and attempts in five tries to kick the ball into the center circle. She receives 10 points if the ball hits on the line or in the center circle, eight for the next, etc., with the last circle worth two points. No point is scored if all circles are missed. The total number of points made in the five attempts is totaled. Curve the scores of the class and award a letter grade for each student.

TERMINOLOGY

Blocking—Using any part of the body except the arms and hands to stop the ball

Corner Kick—Place kick taken on the goal line, five yards from the nearer corner when the ball is sent over the end line or crossbar by a defending player

Defense Kick—Place kick awarded when the attacking team sends the ball out of bounds over the end line not between the goal posts

Dribble—Short series of foot taps used to move the ball

Drop Kick—Dropping the ball and kicking it as it bounces up from the ground

Free Kick—Awarded to the opposing team when a foul is committed anywhere except in the penalty area by the defending team

Kick-in—A ball kicked back into the field at the sidelines by a member of the opposing team when the ball has been kicked out of bounds

Kick-off—Taken by the center forward, who kicks the ball forward or to the sides, at the beginning of the game, at each quarter, or after each goal is scored

Marking—A back remains sufficiently close to the opposing forward for whom she is responsible in order to intercept a pass, to tackle—should the forward gain possession of the ball—or to prevent the execution of a pass

Penalty Kick—A place kick taken on the penalty kick mark 12 yards from the center of the goal that is awarded when any member of the defending team fouls in the penalty area

Place Kick—Kicking the ball from a stationary ground position without touching or picking it up with the hands

Punt—Dropping the ball and kicking it with the top of the foot before it touches the ground

Tackle—Method of getting the ball away from an opponent without any body contact

Trapping—Stopping and gaining control of the ball by use of a foot or one or both legs.

DISCUSSION QUESTIONS

1. Discuss the values of stressing soccer in the junior and senior high school program rather than on the college level.
2. Explain, demonstrate, and teach trapping, punting, dribbling, and tackling. Which skill is easiest for you to teach to others? Why?
3. Officiate a soccer game played between two beginning teams. Which fouls were hardest for you to see and call? What were the mistakes in strategy made by both sides?

4. A sprained ankle and a charley horse are two of the most common soccer injuries. Consult an American Red Cross First Aid textbook and summarize in a brief paragraph the suggested treatment given therein for each.
5. Draw sketches to show your coaching suggestions for (a) penalty kick formation, (b) a wise kick-off play, and (c) the lineup of players for a corner kick.
6. Some girls are reluctant to play goalkeeper. How would you go about "selling" them on the advantages of playing this position?

Selected Audio-Visual Aids

Official Soccer-Speedball Guide, Soccer Technique Chart: National Section for Girls and Women's Sports, 1201 16th Street, N.W., Washington 6, D.C.

The Great Game: British Information Service, 30 Rockefeller Plaza, New York, N.Y. (Rental)

King Soccer: Teaching Films Custodians, Inc., 25 West 43rd Street, New York 18, N.Y. (Rental)

Physical Education Instructor, (Soccer and Speedball): Commonwealth of Virginia, State Board of Education, Richmond 6, Va. (Rental)

Soccer for Girls: (10 min., sound, b & w). Coronet Instructional Films, 65 East South Water Street, Chicago, Illinois.

Suggested Readings

AAHPER, Division for Girls and Women's Sports, *Official Soccer, Speedball and Fieldball Guide,* Current Edition, Washington 6, D.C.

DiClements, C. L.: *Soccer Illustrated,* New York, A. S. Barnes, 1955.

Frymir, A. S., and Hillas, Marjorie: *Team Sports for Women,* New York, A. S. Barnes, 1935.

Hewlett, J. M., and Bennett, B. L.: Fundamental Kicking in Soccer, *Athletic Journal,* November, 1951.

Hupprick, Florence: *Soccer and Speedball for Girls,* New York, A. S. Barnes, 1942.

Official NCAA Soccer Guide, Current Edition, National Collegiate Athletic Association.

Meyer, Margaret H., and Schwarz, Marguerite M.: *Team Sports for Women,* ed. 3, Philadelphia, W. B. Saunders Company, 1957.

Paterson, Ann, editor: *Team Sports for Girls,* New York, The Ronald Press, 1958.

Periodicals

The Journal of Health, Physical Education and Recreation, AAHPER, 1201 16th St., N.W., Washington 6, D.C.

The Athletic Journal, The Athletic Journal Publishing Company, 1719 Howard Street, Evanston, Ill.

18

Softball

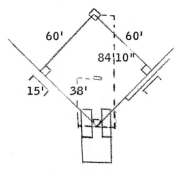

Figure No. 18–1.

Like other truly American sports events softball just "growed" like Topsy. Softball, so popular with youth and adults in the schools and playgrounds, is a direct descendent of Abner Doubleday's game of baseball. A game of indoor baseball was originated in 1887 by George W. Hancock of the Farragut Boat Club in Chicago. Originally played with a broom as a bat and a boxing glove ball, the game drew on the skills of Rounders, Barn Ball, and One Old Cat. As the game attracted enthusiastic followers, Hancock devised rules and provided a large softball and a small-headed bat.

Variations of the game were played under the names of mush ball, pumpkin ball, and kitten ball. Recreation groups moved the sport outdoors under the title of playground ball, and here it gained its greatest popularity as a sport suitable for men and women in an area smaller than that required for baseball.

Softball was officially adopted in 1933 after the first national tournament in Chicago. Walter A. Hakanson of the Denver YMCA is credited with naming the present-day game. Since 1927 when the American Physical

Education Association adopted softball rules for girls as drawn up by Gladys Palmer, the National Section for Girls and Women's Sports and presently, the Division for Girls and Women's Sports, has continued its interest in rule development. The Division publishes the rules and strives to insure playing standards for the pleasure and safety of the participants.

Softball is one of the few team games that readily lends itself to informal, co-recreational settings. Played at picnics, playdays, backyard gatherings, and in competitive leagues, the game is satisfying to both men and women of all skill and experience levels. The small area needed for play, the flexible rules, and carryover value make it the "ideal" team sport for girls and women.

NATURE AND PURPOSE OF THE GAME

Like baseball, softball is a game using throwing, batting, catching and running skills by two opposing teams on a diamond-shaped field. Each team of nine players alternates turns at bat and in the field throughout a regulation game of seven innings. Teams may remain in the offensive (batting) position until the defending (fielding) team succeeds in getting three of the team members out. Each team member has a specific position to play when on the defense. They are catcher, pitcher, first baseman, second baseman, third baseman, shortstop, rightfielder, centerfielder, and leftfielder. Each position is primarily responsible for covering a specific area of the field.

Game play begins with one team in fielding position and the other team at "home" with one team member preparing to bat. The pitcher, in preparation for delivering the ball, stands squarely facing the batter. She

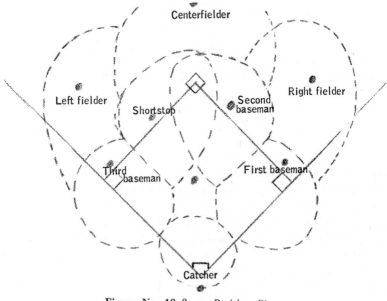

Figure No. 18–2.   Position Play.

has both feet in contact with the pitcher's plate and holds the ball in front of the body in both hands. The ball is delivered toward the batting area with an underhanded motion, so that the hand is below the hip and the wrist no farther from the body than the elbow. The pitcher may take one step toward the batter during the delivery.

The batter of the opposing team attempts to hit the pitched ball with the bat so that the ball travels into the fair territory of the diamond and outfield area. The pitcher attempts to throw the ball so that it is difficult to hit, or if hit, is easily fielded by her defending teammates. They are positioned in the field to catch the ball on the fly, bounce, or roll and get the batter out.

A player in batting position is "out" if she swings and misses three times, fails to hit after three called strikes, bunts foul on the third strike, hits a fair or foul ball that is caught, or is put out at first base.

When the ball is hit foul (and is not caught), the batter may remain at bat. If the batter is successful in hitting the ball into fair territory, she attempts to run to first, second, third base and home to score a run. She does not have to run all the bases on her own hit, but may stop safely at any of the first three bases and await a teammate's hit to drive her forward. The defensive team tries to get the ball to a base ahead of the runner in order to force her out. Players who advance around the bases score runs and further the real team object—to win the game by gaining more runs than the opposing team.

SIMPLIFIED RULES

Strike. This may occur in any one of the following:
1. Batter swings at the pitched ball and misses.
2. A pitched ball is called a strike when it is delivered over home plate between the knees and shoulders of the batter.
3. A fly ball which goes foul and which is not caught (except on the third strike).
4. A foul tip that remains lower than the batter's head and is caught by the catcher.

Ball
1. A pitched ball that does not go over the plate between the batter's knees and shoulders and at which the batter does not swing.
2. When the pitcher goes through the preliminary motions of pitching but fails to deliver.

Fair Hit Ball. A legally batted ball that:
1. Lands and remains in the infield between home and first and home and third.
2. Touches or goes over first or third base.
3. Lands in the outfield in fair territory between the extended lines from home to first and home to third.

Foul Ball.   A batted ball which:
1. Lands fair and rolls foul in the infield.
2. Hits foul in the outfield.

Batter Out.   Batter is out when:
1. She swings at and misses the third strike.
2. She bunts foul on the third strike.
3. A foul tip is caught on the third strike.
4. A fair or foul fly is caught.
5. She interferes with the catcher.
6. She is hit by her own batted ball in fair territory before it has been played by a fielder.
7. The ball reaches first base and is caught before the runner reaches first base.
8. She is tagged with the ball before reaching first base.

Baserunner Out.   The baserunner is out when she:
1. Leaves her base before the ball leaves the pitcher's hand.
2. Is tagged when off base.
3. Fails to return to her base before the ball reaches the baseman following a fair fly that is caught.
4. Interferes with a fielder trying to field the ball.
5. Is forced out at base.
6. Passes a baserunner.
7. Is hit by a batted ball.

For complete rules, see *Official Softball-Track and Field Guide*. Division for Girls and Women's Sports, Current Edition.

SCORING

The Official Scorer has a unique responsibility in softball. She has the authority to make all decisions involving judgment on a play as long as there is no conflict with the Official Playing Rules or the umpire's decision.

The *box score* is the summary of all action of a player in a game. It is helpful to understand this chart as it is often used by newspapermen to report the results of baseball and softball games.

Player	P	AB	R	H	PO	A	E	RBI

P   Position of the player indicated by numbers

1. catcher	5. third baseman
2. pitcher	6. shortstop
3. first baseman	7. leftfielder
4. second baseman	8. centerfielder

9. rightfielder

Figure No. 18–3.   Box Score.

The score is kept in the following manner:

1. Each player's name and position are listed in the order in which she bats or is supposed to bat.
2. First column (AB) indicates the number of times player is at bat. No turn at bat is charged to player if she hits a sacrifice bunt or fly; is awarded a base on four balls, or on interference or obstruction; or is hit by a pitched ball.
3. Second column (R) indicates the number of runs player scores.
4. Third column (H) number of safe hits.
5. (PO) number of putouts made by player.
6. (A) number of assists for putouts by player.
7. (E) number of errors made.
8. (RBI) number of runs batted in by player.

Summary information which must be tabulated after every game includes the score by innings, and final score; runs batted in, and by whom; two and three base hits and home runs; stolen bases and by whom; sacrifice bunts and flies and by whom; players and number of double and triple plays; number of persons left on base; number of bases on balls, batters struck out, and hits and runs given or allowed by the pitcher; winning and losing pitchers; number of wild pitches and passed balls; players hit by pitched balls; the length of the game and the number of innings pitched by each pitcher; and the names of the umpire and scorers.*

NEEDED FACILITIES AND EQUIPMENT

Field.   A softball game requires a level, unobstructed field area "within a radius of 200 feet from home plate between the foul lines."[1] There should be at least 25 unobstructed feet between home plate and the backstop and outside the foul lines. The diamond has 60 foot baselines with a pitching distance of 38 feet (46 feet for men). The field should be free from rocks and holes and the diamond should be placed so that the players do not have to look directly into the sun.

The following figure shows the basic layout of the diamond with:

1. Three foot lines parallel to first base.
2. The batter's box, each side measuring three by seven feet.
3. The 10 by 8 feet, 5 inches catcher's box.
4. The two 15 foot coaches' boxes.

Balls.   Although 14 to 16 inch balls are used indoors, the official softball must measure between $11\frac{7}{8}$ and $12\frac{1}{8}$ inches in circumference. It may weigh between 6 and $6\frac{3}{4}$ ounces. The exterior is smooth or cowhide

---

* See *Official Softball-Track and Field Guide*. Division for Girls and Women's Sports, current edition, for complete scoring information.
[1] Division of Girls and Women's Sports, *Softball-Track and Field Guide*, January 1958–1960, p. 51.

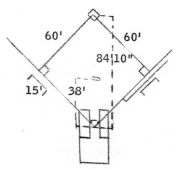

Figure No. 18–4.   Diamond Layout.

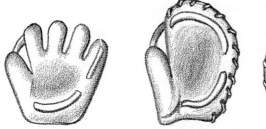

Figure No. 18–5.   Gloves.

leather smoothly seamed with stitches concealed. The center is kapok, or cork and rubber, covered with yarn. The hide cover is glued over the round ball. Rubber covered balls are ideal for play on damp ground in early morning classes.

Bats.   These are made of hardwood and must be no longer than 34 inches or more than $2\frac{1}{8}$ inches in diameter at the largest part. Weight is a matter of player preference. A safety grip, at least 10 inches long, of cork or composition material, is a necessary part of "Official" bats.

Gloves and Mitts.   Protective hand covering which aids in skill development is recommended for all defensive players. Only the catcher and first baseman are allowed to wear mitts—gloves without separated fingers. The catcher's mitt is heavily padded with a deep pocket, while the first baseman's mitt (often called the *claw*) is less padded and more flexible. Fingered gloves worn by all other players should be of soft horse, cow, or elk hide.

Masks and Body Protectors.   These must be worn by the catcher and plate umpire. Wire masks are padded with sponge rubber or hair and are adjustable for all players. Body protectors are usually kapok, covered with a dark canvas or check so the ball is visible against the background.

Plate and Bases.   Home plate is a five sided figure, 17 inches across the edge facing the pitcher. When laid, the $8\frac{1}{2}$ inch sides are parallel to the inside lines of the batter's box.

The pitcher's plate is a 24 x 6 inch section of wood or rubber which is

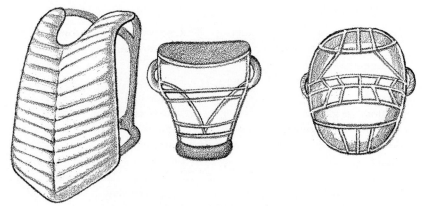

Figure No. 18–6.   Protective Equipment.

placed level with the top of the ground. The front of the plate is 38 feet from the outside point of home plate.

First, second, and third base are 15 inch padded squares of hair or felt covered by heavy canvas. Each base has a strap underneath to hold it securely to the ground.

Care of Equipment.   Softball equipment is easily maintained and stored. Bats should be wiped, rough edges sanded, and treated with linseed oil prior to storage. Grips should be repaired or replaced with leather or cork. Store in a dry room at constant temperature.

Leather balls should not be used on damp ground as they absorb water and become misshapen when hit. Both rubber and leather covered balls should be stitched immediately when split.

Gloves, masks, and body protectors should be hung for rapid drying. All leather surfaces should be cleaned and treated with neat's-foot oil to prevent hardening and cracking.

The pitcher's and home plate should be pulled from the ground and stored in a cool place. Canvas covered bases should be removed after every game to prevent water damage. After brushing and reshaping they should be stored flat to insure longer life.

TEACHING UNITS

The following suggested units assume that players have some skill and experience in throwing, catching, and batting. In all cases, a brief review of the basic skills is helpful for improving team play.

Unit for Beginners	*Advanced Unit*
Nature and value of softball	Complete review
Review of basic skills	Game situation
Throwing: underhand and	Individual skills
overhand	Sidearm throw

Unit for Beginners

Catching: flies and grounders
  (thrown and batted)
Batting
Novelty games and throwing
  relays
Brief history of game
Care and use of equipment
Individual skill development of:
  Pitching
  Bunting
  Throwing to bases
  Base running
  Fielding
Knowledge and rule understanding
  of:
  Pitching
  Fair and foul balls
  Batting
  Strikes and balls
  Outs and force out
  Infield fly rule
  Third strike rule
Game situation
Beginning game strategy
  Placing hits
  Pitching strategy
  Hit and run
  Backing up and covering
  Positioning fielders and relaying
Beginning officiating and team man-
  agement
Evaluation
  Skills tests
  Written and demonstrated
    knowledge and skill, and team
    and individual strategy
  Officiating and scoring
  Class tournament

Advanced Unit

Underarm whip throw
Base stealing
Sliding
Pitching
  Fast ball
  Curves
  Slants
Team strategy
  Offensive: hitting, bunting,
    signals, double steal, and
    squeeze play
  Defensive: Player placement on
    field
Tournament play
Perfect scoring techniques
Develop umpiring skill and get
  WNORC rating
Evaluation
  Individual skills test
  Written test of rules, tactics,
    officiating, and scoring
  Demonstration of officiating
    ability
  Observation of playing skill

BASIC SKILLS

Catching.   As in throwing, each team member needs skill in catching. The following principles apply regardless of the kind of catch that is being made. The player should be ready to receive the ball, both mentally and physically alert, so she can move quickly into position in line with the ball. Use the total body for the catch, not just the hands and arms. Know ahead what play will follow the catch. The catching position depends both on the height and speed of the ball and the throw the fielder wants to make.

The catching player moves to meet an approaching ball. If the ball is going over the fielder's head, she turns and runs with her back to the ball, looking over her shoulder. (This is faster than running backwards.) The height at which the catch is made determines the direction of the fingers. Both hands reach for the ball with fingers and arms relaxed and hands slightly cupped. As the ball hits the glove hand the fingers squeeze, and the free hand closes on the top so that the ball is trapped. The ball is caught in the glove pocket, slightly to the thumb side. The hands and arms "give" with the impact of the ball, cushioning the catch.

If possible, the ball should be caught above the waist to facilitate throwing. The fingers point upward and the thumbs are together. For catches below the waist, fingers point downward and the little fingers are together.

Throwing.   Throwing is one of the essential skills for a softball player.

Overarm Throw.   This should be a basic skill of all players as it is the fastest, most accurate of all ball propulsion. The ball is held in the right hand with the first two fingers on top of the ball, the third and fourth fingers spread comfortably to the side with the thumb supporting under the ball.

With the feet in stride position, weight equally distributed, and left foot forward, the left shoulder turns toward the target moving the body at right angles away from the target. As the right arm moves back to a position behind the head about ear level, the weight shifts to the rear leg. The elbow points away from the body with the upper arm parallel to the ground. The wrist is cocked backward. On the release the forward leg extends in the direction of the target, the shoulders turn parallel to the target as the body rotates and the arm is brought forward in a semicircular motion. The hand passes forward past the ear, the elbow straightens, wrist uncocks, and the ball rolls off the first two fingers. The power of the swing carries the arm down and

Figure No. 18–7.   The Overarm Throw.

across the body, rotating the body so that the shoulder of the throwing arm points toward the target.

Underarm Whip Throw. The underarm throw is used for a quick throw when there is little time to stand or to take a full backswing after fielding a grounder. The ball is held with the thumb on top, the first and second fingers under, and the third and fourth fingers on the side of the ball. The body is crouching more than for the overarm throw with the ball held below shoulder level. The arm swings back, bent elbow restricting backswing, parallel to the ground, wrist cocked. The forward foot extends and the arm swings across the body at waist level as the body follows around.

Pitching. The well controlled delivery of a ball into the strike zone is one of the highly individualized skills of softball. The pitcher stands on the plate squarely, facing the batter with the ball held in both hands. She must remain motionless for a minimum of one and not over 20 seconds before removing one hand.

The Basic Pitch. The ball is held in a tripod; the tips of the thumb, index, and middle fingers over the seams. It is pushed forward above waist level as the trunk rotates to the right to allow a full backswing and the arm circles downward and backward. While delivering the ball the pitcher may take only one step, which must be toward the batter, and taken as the delivery is made. The ball must be delivered with an underhanded motion, the release and follow-through forward, beyond the straight line of the body. "The hand shall be below the hip and the wrist not farther from the body than the elbow."[2]

On the delivery, the right arm swings forward as a step is taken with the left foot. The arm follows-through in line with the pitch, elbow straight, and the ball rolling off the ends of the fingers. On the follow-through, the right foot moves parallel with the left in a side stride position. Power is

Figure No. 18–8.   The Basic Pitch.

[2] *Op. cit.*, p. 58.

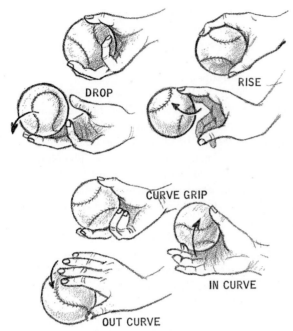

Figure No. 18–9.   Hand Positions for Deliveries.

gained from a full arm swing, elbow extension and wrist snap, and from body rotation.

Once this straight, fast pitch is mastered, pitchers should learn a drop ball and a rise ball, an outcurve and incurve. The grip and the type and amount of spin the pitcher gives the ball determines the curve, rise, or drop.

Drop Ball.   The ball is held with the thumb to the right, first three fingers to the left and the little finger back. The palm faces the batter on the delivery and the ball is released with an upward motion of the hand. The ball rolls off the three fingers with a forward spin.

Rise Ball.   The ball is held with the thumb underneath, first and second fingers on top, and third and fourth fingers slightly to the left. On the delivery the knuckles are forward. The wrist snaps upward, the fingers pull and the thumb pushes, resulting in a backspin on the ball. When properly executed the ball rises near the plate.

Outcurve.   The palm is turned toward the left as the ball is held in a triangle formed by the thumb, first and second fingers. On the release the second finger is away from the ball. The wrist is snapped sharply to the left thrusting the ball out of the little finger side of the hand. The ball curves from right to left—away from a right-handed hitter.

Incurve.   This pitch curves toward a right-handed batter. The ball is gripped between the thumb and first two fingers. On the release the wrist is snapped from left to right.

Fielding.   Fielding involves the basic skills of catching and throwing. As the ball is hit, the fielder moves from a waiting position to a ready position to receive it. She positions herself after watching the ball in flight and awaits with feet in a side stride, weight evenly distributed on the balls of the feet and the knees and hips slightly bent.

Fielding Ground Balls.   With the upper body nearly erect, the fielder bends the knees to get down to the ball. The hips are low and the weight over the feet until the ball is scooped up by the fingers and wrists. If the ball is bouncing the catch is made as it rises. The finger tips should be touching the ground ready to rise with the bounce. The palm of the left hand is at right angles to the path of the ball, the right hand next to it with little fingers together. The right hand snaps over the left to hold the caught ball and the natural "give" of the fielding action starts the backswing for a whip or sidearm throw.

Catching Fly Balls.   Whenever possible flies should be caught at shoulder level. A catch at this level prevents the fielder from blocking her own vision and puts her in a position for a rapid throw. The fielder tries to position herself so she will be *standing* (not running) when the catch is made. The fingers are pointed up, thumbs together with the palm of the glove hand facing the ball. If the fly is caught at the right shoulder, the hands, arms, and body give backward and are the beginning motion of the backswing preceding the throw. While awaiting the fly, the feet point in the direction of ball flight and as the ball is caught the trunk turns to the right and the right leg moves back to take the impact. The weight shifts through to the forward left foot as the throw is made.

Batting.   This is one of the most important offensive skills an individual or a team possesses. Every player may eventually develop her own style, but basic principles of grip, stance, stride, and swing may be taught.

Grip.   The standard grip is used by most players. The left hand is placed around the bat several inches above the end. The right hand is placed above the left and touching it. The natural grip is firm, but not

Figure No. 18–10.   Hand Alignment.

Figure No. 18–11.   Stance and Swing.

tense. The second joints of the fingers of the top hand are aligned with the
knuckles of the lower hand. Batters attempting to power hit often use the
end grip, bringing the hands as far down on the bat as possible. For more
accurate and less powerful hits a player may move her hands up the handle
of the bat. This is particularly useful to a player who swings late because
of weak arm and shoulder strength.

Stance.   A comfortable, natural stance is taken in the batter's box.
The distance from the plate is gauged by the individual's reach and swing.
Feet are comfortably spread, knees relaxed to support the upright trunk
facing the plate. The bat is held up and back by an almost straight left arm
and a bent right arm. The elbow of the right arm is pointing toward the
ground and away from the batter. The batter looks over her left shoulder
toward the pitcher.

Stride.   Just as the ball reaches the strike zone the batter slides her
left leg several inches toward the pitcher. The body moves forward as the
swing begins.

Swing.   The bat moves forward in a level plane as the hitter watches
the ball moving toward the plate. The hips pivot forward and the body
turns toward the pitcher with the bat moving rapidly forward. As the bat
meets the ball the arms extend, wrists snap and roll into the follow-through.
As the hands and wrists roll, the body weight shifts to the forward foot.
Near the completion of the follow-through the hands are completely over,
back of right hand uppermost; and the right foot, free of body weight,
strides toward first base.

Bunting.   A bunt is a well placed ball that is tapped onto the infield, usually along the first or third base line. It should be a deceptive hit,
therefore the batter should keep her regular batting stance as long as possible. As the pitched ball moves toward the plate the batter turns her body
toward the pitcher and pivots so that her feet come side by side and toes
point toward the pitcher. Simultaneously, she slides her right hand up and
behind the middle of the bat. (Some batters can bunt effectively with their

hands remaining in a "choked grip" position.) The bat is in front of the
player and parallel to the ground so that the incoming ball is blocked by the
bat. The head of the bat is turned in the direction of the bunt.

To execute a "drag" bunt along the first base line, the player begins
toward first base and *then* contacts the ball late with her bat extended behind her. She pulls the ball along as she runs for first.

Base Running.   A batter takes her first stride toward first base as
the ball is hit. Short strides and vigorous arm action lead her into a full
stride as she crosses first base. Once on base, the runner may stand with one
foot on base in a sprinter's start, ready to leave when the ball is pitched.
A player can observe the action of the game better if she places her left
foot on base and faces the infield. With her feet in side stride position she
is slightly crouched with her weight over the right foot. The runner's arms
hang freely down and away from the body to aid in balance and shift of
body weight. The runner takes two or three strides from the base in anticipation of a hit, wild pitch, or catcher's error. If none occurs she returns to
base and assumes the starting position. (For a more complete treatment see
section on *Offensive Strategy*.)

Base Stealing.   Stealing bases is a way a baserunner may advance
on weak defensive plays. Steals most often occur as the ball is missed by the
catcher, overthrown at a base, held too long by a fielder, or as a play is
made at another base. Stealing should be done in the interest of team play,
rather than as a spectacular individual feat.

Sliding.   This is a skill for advanced players who are properly
dressed in slacks or trousers. Sliding helps runners evade a tag at second
and third base and home, and serves as a method of stopping to avoid overrunning second and third base. The two most common slides are the straight
and the hook.

Straight Slide.   The straight slide begins from a full stride as the
runner tries to avoid a high tag or throw. The take-off leg bends, lowering
the body, as the top leg extends directly toward the base. Both legs come

Figure No. 18–12.   Bunting.

Figure No. 18–13.   The Hook Slide.

together and slide to the base. A quick recovery should be made if the player sees an opportunity to advance further.

Hook Slide.   The hook slide is used to avoid a low tag or to stop an overrun. The base runner goes wide, rather than directly to the base, and extends her right leg so she slides on the thigh. The left leg bends back and toward the base so the instep of the left foot hooks on the corner of the bag. Both slides should be started early so the body does not strike the bag at full power.

STRATEGY

The mental concentration and preplanning involved in softball strategy make the game more than a hitting-pitching contest between two teams.

Offensive Strategy.   This is built around batting and base running skills of individuals combined to make a team contribution.

1. The order of batting is one of the first strategic moves a team plans. Generally, the lead off batter is one who can get on base; the second, a fair hitter and bunter; third, a consistent hitter; fourth, the strongest and longest hitter who can advance baserunners. The weakest hitters hold the seventh, eighth, and last position.
2. Place hitting is more important to a team offensive than inconsistent, spasmodic hits. Generally, a low ball placed straight away through second base serves as a hit. This "spot" is not advised if a runner is on first base, as a weak hit is a perfect setup for a defensive double play.
3. Bunts and sacrifice flies serve to advance players to scoring position but both usually result in an out for the hitter. The sacrifice bunt is used when runners are on first, or first and second and there are no outs. The hitter places the bunt down the first or third base line and tried to "beat it out" to first.
4. Baserunners must be alert to the position of all other runners and to any plays called for runners. A few simple guides help the player anticipate her moves. She should run as fast as possible for first base, touching it and overrunning it along the right field line. If she can advance more than one base on her hit, she moves into foul territory before reaching first and turns toward second base.

The runner must not overrun second or third base. Some teachers suggest the slide for close plays; however, it should be avoided if players' legs are not protected. Players learn to "pull up short" from a rapid pace without abrupt muscle jerks.

Runners must not lead off bases until the pitcher releases the ball. On fly balls, other than with two outs, runners advance a safe distance toward the next base so they can return to their original bases if the ball is caught, or be ready to advance if the ball is dropped. When a fly is hit deep and the runner has time to advance after the ball is caught, she may hold near her base, touch, and then advance.

Runners should advance on wild pitches, overthrown bases, or a dropped ball by the catcher.

These additional plays are helpful for a basic team offensive:

1. *Double steal.*   Attempted with runners on first and third with one out. The runner on first starts a steal. If the ball moves to second base, the runner pulls up and acts as a decoy as the runner on third tries for home. If no play is made at second base the runner from first advances.

2. *Hit and run.*   A signal from the coach or batter indicates that an attempt will be made to hit the next pitched ball and the baserunner thus has additional seconds to run to the next base.

3. *Squeeze play.*   An attempt to score a runner from third by giving the runner a signal indicating a bunt down the first base line. The base runner moves toward home with the pitch.

Defensive Strategy.   A strong team defense depends upon individual skills and player cooperation. One of the best ways to teach defensive

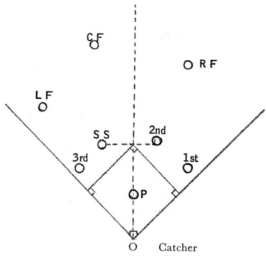

Figure No. 18–14.   Defensive Positions.

strategy is by actual situations which occur during a game. This encourages anticipation and preplanning by the fielding team. The situation of the offensive team dictates the defensive positioning. For example:

1. Normal playing position (Fig. 18–14) is assumed when there are no base runners and a straight away hitter is at bat. The fielders shift to the right for left-handed batters.
2. To combat a sacrifice bunt, the pitcher and first and third basemen move in to field the ball as the second baseman prepares to cover first base.
3. Double play positioning, with a runner on first, brings the first baseman closer to the first base line as second and third basemen move toward their bases and shortstop moves several steps toward the batter.

DUTIES AND SPECIFIC SKILLS OF EACH PLAYER

Catcher. Catching is one of the most important and demanding positions on the defending team. The catcher must be able to catch all varieties of pitches, foul tips and pop flies, move quickly and throw accurately and rapidly to all bases. The catcher is important if pitching signals are used. She evaluates the batter's ability and characteristics and signals for the pitch.

In preparation for the pitch the catcher assumes a semi-erect position directly behind the plate as close to the batter as is possible for safety. The body bends forward, feet parallel. The mitt hand is up as a target for the pitcher, and the right hand is closed and ready to close over the ball as it hits the glove. Like all basemen, when making a play at the plate she moves one foot to the corner and stretches to meet the ball so as not to interfere with the runner. The catcher should back up plays at first and third base as the situation demands.

Pitcher. The pitcher must master delivery of a well controlled ball. Her deliveries should include fast balls, curve balls, and slow balls which effectively cross the plate in an area approximately 3 feet high and 17 inches wide and two feet from the ground. Aside from fielding hits, she should cover home on a wild pitch or passed ball when runners are on base; cover first or third on hits to these basemen with a baserunner moving toward the base. Pitchers soon learn to throw fast balls to late swinging batters, inside curves to batters crowding the plate, outside curves to those standing away or stepping into the swing and balls above the waist to batters attempting a bunt.

First Basemen. A tall player with a good "reach" and ability to catch all types of throws is descriptive of a potential first baseman. She must play off base and field balls with general infield ability and then place a foot on first base and reach for throws. She must develop a quick pivot and throwing motion to all other bases for effective double plays.

Second Baseman.   She must move rapidly and throw accurately to all bases from many fielding positions. She is responsible for the area toward first base, as well as covering second base on attempted steals and most hits.

Shortstop.   The shortstop must be a versatile player of unusual speed. She is positioned between second and third base and receives many hits from right-handed batters. She backs up the pitcher on hits to the box, third base on throws from the outfield, and she covers second base when the baseman is fielding.

Third Baseman.   The third baseman plays slightly toward second base and is responsible for bunts, flies, fouls, and hits in that area. She must be able to throw accurately and fast to first base and recover her position quickly.

Outfielders.   An outfielder must be able to move rapidly to field balls and throw far and accurately. The centerfielder has more territory and should move faster than the left or right fielder. The fielders back up the bases when ground hits come in front of them. The centerfielder backs up both other outfielders; the leftfielder backs up the infield on hits to the left of the diamond; the rightfielder backs up the centerfielder and infielders to the right.

CLASS ORGANIZATION

Softball can be taught effectively to large groups with minimum organization. It is advisable to divide the class into teams of 11 or 12 players with the additional team members serving as coaches and officials during game play. Whenever possible, allow teams to play a game or a novelty game early in the unit to help maintain interest and give purpose to skill drills.

A certain amount of skill practice is basic to developing individual playing ability. The skills should be demonstrated and discussed before practice begins. One of the easiest formations for throwing and catching involves two teams. Teams face one another and each girl throws and receives from a partner on the other team. If gloves are not available for all players, the gloveless players should receive ground balls. If there is not an adequate supply of balls for each twosome, groups of four may practice together.

Batting practice is accomplished through the game of "pepper" as well as a game-like situation. In pepper, a semicircle of players faces the batter who is 35 to 40 feet away. The first player on the semicircle pitches to the batter who hits it to another player who tosses it back and so on.

Fielding is practiced by "fungo" hitting wherein the batter throws the ball and hits grounders or flies to the awaiting players in the field.

One of the best ways of teaching game play is by situations. The situation should first be explained and then enacted by the players. The following are examples of such set situations:

EXAMPLE I

Runner on first, one out, fly ball hit to centerfield.

1. The team in the field
   a. Fly caught by centerfielder and ball thrown immediately to first base to catch runner from first who started for second when ball was hit
   b. First baseman covers first, and tags base before runner returns
   c. Second baseman covers second base
   d. Shortstop backs up second baseman
2. Team at bat
   a. Batsman becomes baserunner immediately after hit and starts toward first
   b. Runner on first should wait until fly is caught or missed before advancing to second base

EXAMPLE II

Runners on first and second, two out, fly ball hit to centerfield.

1. The team in field
   a. Centerfielder catches the fly
   b. Leftfielder backs up centerfielder
   c. Second baseman covers second base
   d. Shortstop backs up second base
   e. First baseman covers first base
   f. Rightfielder backs up first baseman
   g. Pitcher backs up third baseman
2. The team at bat
   a. Batter becomes baserunner after ball is hit
   b. All baserunners advance as there are two outs

EXAMPLE III

Runner on first base, no outs, ball is hit toward shortstop.

1. The team in field
   a. Shortstop fields ball and throws to second to get runner who must advance from first
   b. Second baseman touches base and throws to first
   c. Centerfielder backs up shortstop

    d. Rightfielder backs up second baseman
    e. Catcher backs up first baseman
2. The team at bat
    a. Batter becomes baserunner on hit
    b. Runner on first advances to second

TEACHING PROGRESSION

The following lessons are suggested for beginning players with basic skills of catching and throwing:

LESSON I

1. Nature and value of softball
2. Brief history of the game
3. Review basic skills of:
   Throwing: underhand and overhand
   Catching: flies, grounders (thrown)
   Batting
4. Novelty game—One Old Cat

LESSON II

1. Throwing relays
2. Review batting
3. Pitching
4. Novelty game (Work Up or Scrub)

LESSON III

1. Review pitching
2. Fielding practice—batted grounders and flies using selected students who hit fungo style
3. Scrub

LESSON IV

1. Filmstrip or chalk talk stressing positions on field, safety precautions, brief rules discussion
2. Three inning game covering rules in game situation

LESSON V

1. Base running
2. Infield practice

3. Discussion and demonstration of:
    Relaying throws
    Backing up
    Covering
4. Game situation

Lesson VI

1. Review
2. Bunt
3. Scrub, stressing use of the bunt

Lesson VII

1. Review bunt
2. Batting practice, stressing placement of hits
3. Game situation

Lesson VIII

1. Brief explanation of officiating techniques and scoring
2. Class round robin tournament using student officials

Lesson IX

1. Complete round robin tournament
2. Class discussion of effectiveness of team play of previous day's game

Lesson X

1. Evaluation
    Brief written examination
    Begin skill tests

Lesson XI

1. Complete skill tests

Lesson XII

1. Review written examination
2. Class discussion and evaluation of the unit

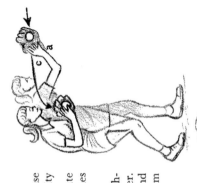

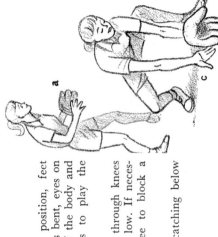

SKILL DIFFICULTIES AND THEIR CORRECTION

Difficulty	*Correction*

1. Catching

a. Tense hands and fingers resulting in loss of control of the ball

b. Failure to "give" with the body as the ball is caught

c. Incorrect positioning of the hands—thumbs up below the waist and little fingers down above the waist result in inability to hold ball

1.

a. Teacher stresses relaxation. The use of gloves gives players more security

b. Practice mimetically and demonstrate the relaxed "give" as the ball comes to the hands

c. Demonstrate proper catching technique, exaggerate improper manner. Student should practice throwing and catching at close range to stress form without concern for hard delivery

2. Fielding Ground and Fly Balls
(see above section)

a. Awaiting a ground ball in an erect position with arms at side resulting in delay and miss in stopping the ball

b. Bending at waist, knees stiff to field grounder as ball passes through legs

c. Incorrect hand position. Slapping at the ball, fingers spread toward the ball, or palms facing

2.

a. Demonstrate "ready" position, feet spread, hips and knees bent, eyes on ball, hands in front of the body and relaxed. Player moves to play the ball as soon as it is hit

b. Move the body down through knees and hips so weight is low. If necessary drop to one knee to block a hard rolling ball

c. Review technique of catching below the waist

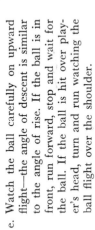

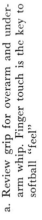

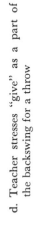

d. Failure to "give" as a preparation for a throw

e. Inability to judge descent of fly ball resulting in overrunning or underrunning the ball

d. Teacher stresses "give" as a part of the backswing for a throw

e. Watch the ball carefully on upward flight—the angle of descent is similar to the angle of rise. If the ball is in front, run forward, stop and wait for the ball. If the ball is hit over player's head, turn and run watching the ball flight over the shoulder.

3.

a. Review grip for overarm and underarm whip. Finger touch is the key to softball "feel"

3. *Throwing*

a. Holding the ball in the palm of the hand so a throw becomes an uncontrolled push

SKILL DIFFICULTIES AND THEIR CORRECTION (*Continued*)

Difficulty	*Correction*
b. Throwing off of wrong foot	b. Review principle of opposition—right arm moves forward with left leg
c. Throwing stiff arm with no wrist or finger snap, resulting in loss of power and accuracy	c. Relax the arm, keeping the elbow out from the body. Wrists cock and then flex on delivery. Stress wrist flexibility by "waving the hand"
d. Failure to use the body. Standing with the shoulders and hips facing the target—feet in side stride position	d. Practice throwing mimetically. In slow motion teacher may say, "body rotates, arm back, throw through, and follow-through." Check for body rotation
e. Releasing ball too early (a high, looping throw) or too late (throwing it into the ground)	e. Review grip. Ball is probably palmed or clutched in fingers on a late delivery. Correcting a stiff arm throw often remedies early release

4. *Pitching*
(see throwing above)

a. Illegal pitching motion or balks	a. Review rules and give an accurate demonstration of the stance, back-swing, delivery, and follow-through
b. Throwing wildly so ball goes into the dirt, over the catcher, or hits the batter	b. The pitcher should review her delivery motion and be certain her forward step is consistently timed and spaced. Check grip to avoid causes of early or late release

5. Batting

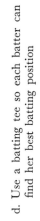
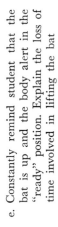
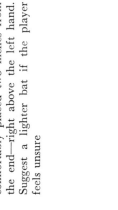
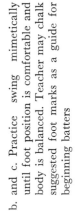
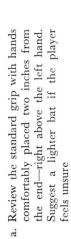
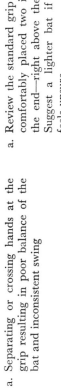

Difficulty	Correction
5. Batting	**5.**
a. Separating or crossing hands at the grip resulting in poor balance of the bat and inconsistent swing	a. Review the standard grip with hands comfortably placed two inches from the end—right above the left hand. Suggest a lighter bat if the player feels unsure
b. and c. Placing feet too close together resulting in poor balance and a leg slide or lift as the swing is made	b. and c. Practice swing mimetically until foot position is comfortable and body is balanced. Teacher may chalk suggested foot marks as a guide for beginning batters
d. Crowding or pulling away from the plate resulting in balls hit off the handle or tip	d. Use a batting tee so each batter can find her best batting position
e. Resting bat on shoulder in preparation for delivery resulting in late swing	e. Constantly remind student that the bat is up and the body alert in the "ready" position. Explain the loss of time involved in lifting the bat

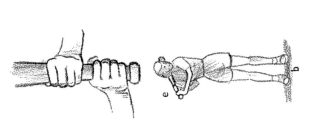

SKILL DIFFICULTIES AND THEIR CORRECTION (*Continued*)

Difficulty	*Correction*
f. Failure to swing the bat in an arc parallel to the ground. The ball is chopped downward or batted skyward	f. Player should set a swing pattern by working on the batting tee; analyzing why balls follow the flight path
g. Failure to use wrist snap resulting in no follow-through and power, or in a body whirl	g. Stress relaxation and suggest that student pretend she is driving nails into a board three feet from the ground with a bat
h. Throwing the bat	h. Stress the safety factor involved and insist player *puts* the bat on the ground or carries it to first base

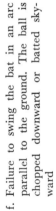

6. *Base running*

a. Overrunning second and third base	a. and b. Review rules and demonstrate running form
b. Slowing down before crossing first base	
c. Forcing a teammate because of inattention to other baserunner's position	c. and d. Stress the importance of *team awareness* (See section on Offensive Strategy, p. 467)
d. Failure to watch batter or coach for play signals	
e. Incorrect slides resulting in outs and minor injuries	e. Discourage sliding by inexperienced player. When sliding is taught, stress relaxation and proper execution. Practice slides slowly, increasing speed as skill is gained

NOVELTY EVENTS*

Many events serve as softball novelty games and have an important place as part of the instructional unit. There are numerous baseball and softball type games which are easily adapted for indoor situations and rainy day programs. The number and variety of games make selection easy when specific skills of batting, throwing, running, or game strategy should be stressed. The following games are suggested as novelty and "change of pace" events:

Punch Softball. Played under official softball rules, but the pitcher delivers a volleyball and the batter uses her hand (fist) as the bat.

Beatball. The batter throws the ball instead of batting it. She runs the bases as in an official softball game trying to make a home run. The fielder throws to first and then to each of the bases in order. The runner is out if the ball arrives home and is caught and held before the runner crosses the plate.

Wrong-handed Softball. Official softball rules apply except that the batter must use the opposite hand to which she is accustomed.

Variation: Fielders must throw with "wrong-hand", too.

Barbara's Batting Contest. The umpire stands behind the catcher and tells the batter what she is to do on the next pitch, that is, bunt, hit a grounder, a long fly, etc. If the batter fulfills the command, she scores a point; if she does not, she scores nothing. Each batter has five trials and does not have to strike at poorly pitched balls.

Soccer Softball. Played by regulation softball rules except the pitcher rolls a soccer ball to the batter who kicks the ball for a "hit."

One Old Cat. There is only one batter and two bases (home and first). The batter must reach first base and return home before the ball reaches the catcher. The batter may run only on fair balls and is out on caught flies.

Variation: **Two Old Cat.** Play as above with two batters so one may remain at first base.

Bunt Ball. Played as official softball except all balls must be bunted. If a bunt goes foul on the third strike the batter is out. If the ball is hit to the outfield the batter is out.

Tennis Softball. Played as softball except the pitcher delivers a tennis ball so it bounces in front of home plate and crosses the plate between the knees and shoulders of the batter. The batter attempts to hit the ball with her hand and to reach first base or beyond before the ball is fielded and thrown to the baseman.

* A complete chapter is devoted to "Games of the Baseball Type" in Mitchell, Elmer D., Helms, W. G., and Donnelly, Richard J.: *Active Games and Contests*, ed. 2, New York, The Ronald Press.

OFFICIATING TECHNIQUES*

No other team sport is so dependent upon skilled officiating to assure an enjoyable, spirited game. Every ball delivered and every play demands the attention of the umpire. Occasionally class games must be conducted with only one umpire, but a minimum of two umpires, a base umpire and a plate umpire, should officiate intramural, league, and interscholastic games. Some leagues recommend three umpires—one behind the plate and two covering the bases.

Costume.   An umpire should appear in the costume adopted by the local board of officials. If none is recommended she should wear a full skirt, blouse, blazer and low heeled shoes. Her dress must be distinct from that of either team. She should make certain her personal equipment is furnished, or bring her own mask, chest protector, sun visor, wisk broom, ball and strike indicator, and Official Softball Guide.

Pre-game Preparation.   Umpires should arrive at least 20 minutes before game time to meet coaches and officials, inspect the field, and clarify ground rules. Prior to the game she checks score books for the lineups and anounces the battery.

A Single Official.   This official has jurisdiction over the entire game and moves and places herself anywhere on or off the field to do her duty effectively. Usually her basic position is behind the catcher where she carefully watches pitching. She may move out toward the pitcher or third base, rarely more than 25 feet, to call plays at the bases, between bases, or in the outfield. She rarely "calls" pitches from behind the pitcher—perhaps only when there is a runner on first base.

The Double Umpiring System uses a plate umpire and a base umpire as field officials. Among other duties, the *plate umpire* is responsible for:

1. Beginning the game
2. Calling balls, strikes, illegal pitches
3. Determining whether the batted ball is fair or foul
4. Determining whether a fly is infield or outfield
5. Determining if a batter bunts
6. Determining whether a ball touches the person or clothing of the batter or umpire
7. Making decisions at the plate and at third base if other bases are occupied
8. Giving decisions, on appeal, whether or not the baserunner on third leaves the base before a fly ball is caught
9. Determining forfeited games

---

* For an excellent review of the responsibilities and duties in single, double and triple umpiring systems see Donnelly, Richard J., and French, Esther. Techniques for Officiating Girls Softball, *Selected Softball Articles,* N.S.G.W.S., 1201 16th Street, N.W., Washington 6, D.C.

To carry out her duties the plate umpire stations herself back of the catcher and slightly to the side in a semi-crouched position to observe the pitcher and the balls crossing the plate. When a ball is hit she moves to the right down the baseline (home to first or home to third) to determine foul or fair balls, or she moves down the third baseline to watch possible play at third.

The *base umpire* places herself for the best view of the pitcher and baserunner. She must avoid interference with the players as she makes:

1. All decisions at first and second
2. Decisions at third not made by the plate umpire

Both umpires use the standard signals to record the decisions during the game.

EVALUATING THE RESULTS*

Measuring individual skill in softball is difficult and there is some question that isolated skill is a true measure of playing ability as a team member. The following suggestions are helpful in planning a program for measuring total class progress.

Skill Tests.   There are test batteries for softball and selected baseball tests which are adaptable for measuring individual skill. When using skill tests for accuracy in pitching, throwing, or batting some allowance must be made for the style and type of delivery as well as speed. Below are given several measuring techniques.

Pitching Targets.   A rectangular area representing the strike zone may be painted, chalked, or taped on the gymnasium wall or tennis backboard. A wooden or rope frame, further divided by colored ribbon, is helpful in judging pitching ability to the "corner" areas.

For general throwing, players should be encouraged to throw 60 or more feet to a target area of three concentric circles, with the center of the circle 5 feet from the ground and circles of 1½ feet, 2 feet 3 inches, 3 feet, and 4½ feet in diameter inscribed to show the reach of a teammate.

Baserunning for Speed.   Time each player from her take-off from the batter's box while she runs all bases and touches home.

Batting Tests.   Although tests for accuracy have been devised for use with a batting tee, a situational test is advisable for most classes. If possible, the same pitcher should be used for all students tested. With the batter using good form she attempts to hit the first five balls into leftfield and the next five into rightfield. Called strikes should count as trials. The student is evaluated on the number of fair and foul hits made.

Throw for Distance.   This is one of the most valuable skill measures. With ten foot intervals marked from home to first, and 40 feet beyond;

* See Scott, M. Gladys, and French, Esther. *Evaluation in Physical Education: Better Teaching Through Testing,* St. Louis, C. V. Mosby Co., 1950, pp. 111–119.

and from third to second base and 40 feet beyond; each student takes three trials with her best distance recorded.

Pepper.   An informal measure of fielding ability is the game of "Pepper" or "Flies and Grounders." The ball is batted to the fielders who are lined up in the infield or outfield awaiting a turn to play the ball and return it to the batter.

Rating Scales.   Use of rating scales by the teacher and pupils is a means of evaluating an individual's ability and understanding of offensive and defensive strategy.

Incident Chart.   Use of an incident chart during a game to record errors, assists, hits, put outs, etc.

Written Examinations.   Use of written examinations to evaluate knowledge of the rules, officiating, and strategy. "Situational" examinations are very valuable as the student must solve the problem by strategy which would apply during the actual game.

TERMINOLOGY

Assist—A credit awarded each player who handles the ball in a series of plays which results in a baserunner being put out

Base on Balls—A walk. The batter is allowed to take a position as a baserunner on first base when four balls are called before she hits, strikes out, or is put out

Battery—The pitcher and the catcher

Batting Average—A percentage which indicates a batter's effectiveness at hitting. It is determined by dividing the number of hits by the number of turns at bat

Double—A two base hit

Double Play—A defensive play that results in two outs

Earned Run—A run scored by a player who reaches first base in any legal manner other than an error made by the defending team

Error—A misplay on a ball which the scorer rules as avoidable, resulting in advancement of baserunner or prolonged life of the batter

Fielder's Choice—An option which a fielder makes in playing a ball—to retire the baserunner rather than the hitter

Fungo Hitting—Batter tosses the ball and hits it to fielders for practice

Hot Corner—Third base

Keystone Sack—Second Base

No Hitter—A game in which one team was unable to make a safe hit

Pass—A walk or a base given by delivering four balls

Single—A one base hit

Sacrifice—A bunt, fly, or hit intended to advance the baserunner resulting in an out for the hitter

Squeeze Play—Bringing a player home from third base on a bunt

Stolen Base—A surprise advance to a base closer to scoring position made by a baserunner unaided by a hit, error or putout

Texas Leaguer—A fly ball that drops between the infielders which cannot be successfully fielded by either

Triple—A three base hit

Discussion Questions

1. Discuss the way in which softball developed. What are its major contributions as a team sport for women?
2. As manager of an intramural team, how would you determine who would be the first four batters?
3. Plan a "chalk talk" on strategy using game situations to explain the use of (a) a bunt, (b) a double steal, (c) hit and run.
4. Safety is extremely important in softball. Explain safety precautions that apply to (a) dress and equipment of players, (b) batting, (c) baserunning, and (d) fielding.
5. Plan a sports clinic using novelty events to demonstrate techniques for skill development.
6. What fundamental skills are necessary for each player? Demonstrate and explain how each skill should be executed.

Selected Audio-Visual Aids

Beginning Softball 1954. (8 Filmstrips, color). The Athletic Institute, 209 South State Street, Chicago 4, Illinois. (Purchase)

Fundamentals of Softball. (10 min., 16 mm., sound, b & w). Audio Film Center, 203 North Wabash Avenue, Chicago 1, Illinois. (Rental)

Fundamentals of Softball Pitching. (12 min., 16 mm., silent, b & w). United World Films, Inc., 1445 Park Avenue, New York 29, New York. (Rental and Purchase)

How to Play Better Softball 1952. (10 min., 16 mm., sound, b & w and filmstrip). View Productions, 1060 West Avenue 37, Los Angeles 65, California. (Purchase)

Softball for Girls 1948. (10 min., 16 mm., sound, b & w or color). Coronet Instructional Films, Inc., 65 East South Water Street, Chicago 1, Illinois. (Purchase)

Softball Rules for Girls 1956. (Six unit filmstrips with captions, color). National Section for Girls and Women's Sports, DGWS, 1201 16th Street, N.W., Washington 6, D.C. (Purchase)

Softball Fundamentals. (10 min., 16 mm., sound, b & w). Young America Films, Inc., 18 East 41st Street, New York 17, New York. (Purchase and Rental)

Charts and Boards

Illustrated Sports Charts 1951. Eight 11" × 17" wall charts. University of Colorado Book Store, Boulder, Colorado. Produced by Katherine Ley and Donna Mae Miller.

Softball Coaching Kit. Steel board with magnetic "players" and play indicators. The Program Aids Company, Inc., 550 Fifth Avenue, New York, New York.

Suggested Readings

Andrews, Emily *et al.: Physical Education for Girls and Women,* Englewood Cliffs, New Jersey, Prentice-Hall Book Company, Inc., 1955.

Dexter, Genevie: *Teachers Guide to Physical Education for Girls in High School,* Sacramento, California State Department of Education, 1957.

Division for Girls and Women's Sports, *Official Softball-Track and Field Guides,* current edition. American Association for Health, Physical Education, and Recreation, 1201 16th Street, N.W., Washington 6, D.C.

Fait, Hollis *et al.: A Manual of Physical Education Activities,* Philadelphia, W. B. Saunders Company, 1956.

Kneer, Marian, editor: *Selected Softball Articles,* Washington, D.C., Division for Girls and Women's Sports, 1955.

Meyer, Margaret, and Schwartz, Marguerite: *Team Sports for Girls and Women,* ed. 3, Philadelphia, W. B. Saunders Company, 1957.

Miller, Donna Mae, and Ley, Katherine: *Individual and Team Sports for Women.* Englewood Cliffs, New Jersey, Prentice-Hall Book Company, Inc., 1955.

Mitchell, Viola, *Softball for Girls,* revised edition, New York, The Ronald Press. 1952.

Paterson, Ann, editor: *Team Sports for Girls,* New York, The Ronald Press, 1958.

PERIODICALS

Journal of American Association for Health, Physical Education, and Recreation, 1201 16th Street, N.W., Washington 6, D.C.

Scholastic Coach, Scholastic Magazines, Inc., 33 W. 42nd Street, New York 36, N.Y.

Recreation Magazine, National Recreation Association, 8 W. 8th Avenue, New York 11, N.Y.

19

Speedball

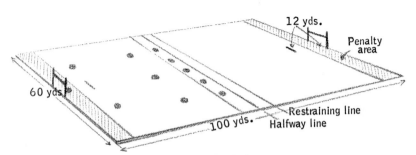

12 yds.

Penalty
area

60 yds.

Restraining line

100 yds.   Halfway line

Figure No. 19–1.

Speedball, one of our few nationally played games originating in America, was created by Elmer D. Mitchell in 1921 at the University of Michigan for the men's intramural program. Although girls and women started playing the game shortly afterwards, it was not until 1930 that the National Section on Women's Athletics (now DGWS) made the necessary rule changes which popularized the game and tailored it to the specific needs of women instructors and their students.

This sport, which combines basketball passing skills with the drop kick of football, and the dribble of soccer, is a good all-around conditioner that is great fun to play. It is especially ideal for younger, less skilled persons, and since the game calls for a wide variety of techniques which require top mental and physical coordination it is also suited for older, highly skilled players. Financially, it is a life saver for the many instructors faced with large classes and a small budget; here is a game in which 22 students playing with one ball can share a wonderfully rich educational experience. Since speedball is closely related to several other sports, the popular appeal of the game is high, especially to most girls who enjoy playing a game resembling the ever popular male sport of football. Today speedball is played enthusiastically by both sexes on all educational levels in the majority of our schools,

485

and is especially popular as a recreational sport in camps and on play-grounds.

The maximum length of the field is 100 yards with a width of 60 yards, but junior and senior high school girls should use an area 80 yards long and 40 yards wide. If the field dimensions are changed to fit particular situations however, the goal, penalty kick mark, end zone, penalty area, and restraining lines should be drawn to standard playing regulations. Goals posts are 6 yards apart with a cross bar between them, 8 feet from the ground. The posts are 20 feet high.

THE NATURE AND PURPOSE OF THE GAME

Speedball is a running, kicking, and passing field game played by two teams of 11 players each: the center forward, right and left inners, right and left wings, a center, right and left halfbacks, the right and left fullbacks, and a goalkeeper. The first five players compose the forward line whose main job is to score, and the duty of the halfbacks is to guard their op-ponents, to get and pass the ball up to their forwards, and to be ready to make touchdown passes or drop kicks for goals. The fullbacks have duties similar to those of the halfbacks except that they must play a more vitally defensive role. The goalkeeper's main, but tremendous, task is to prevent the opposing team from scoring.

A game comprises four, eight minute quarters with a two minute rest period between them, and a ten minute rest period between halves. The game is started with a place kick by the center forward and thereafter the team scored against puts the ball in play in the middle of the field, except that at the beginning of each quarter teams alternate kicking-off. Goals are changed at halftime.

When the ball is on the ground it can only be played as a ground ball with the feet, but all aerial balls may be played with the hands or blocked with the body. The *kick-up* is done by using one or both feet or rolling the ball into the air on the leg so it can be caught, and is but one of many methods of changing a ground ball into an aerial one. A player may not use a bounce or dribble, for as soon as the ball touches the ground it must be played with the feet or body until it again becomes an aerial ball.

Although no ground ball may be touched with the hands or arms, play-ers may block the ball with their bodies, as in soccer. Impeding the progress of any player by a personal contact, or a block of anyone who does not have the ball, is against the rules. *Boxing-up* (two players guarding an opponent between them so she cannot make a pass) is also illegal, as in basketball. Likewise, no person may hold the ball more than three seconds, take more than five seconds on a free kick or an out of bounds play, or use more than 10 seconds for a penalty kick. One may not take more than two steps while in possession of the ball after running, or more than one step while holding it.

A *free kick* is given for any foul which occurs on the field. This is a *place kick* and when taken, all opponents must be five yards away. A *toss-up* (like the basketball jump) is awarded when two players foul each other, or when the ball goes out of bounds off two opponents. For this, all other players must be stationed five yards away. When the ball goes out over the sidelines, it is thrown back in by an opposing team player (usually a half-back) using any type of pass. When it is sent out of bounds over the end lines by the attacking or defending team, it is put back in play by a punt, place kick, drop kick, or throw-in from a spot on the goal line opposite where the ball went out. A goal cannot be scored directly from a kick-off, throw-in, free kick awarded for offsides, a goalkeeper carry, or from a faulty taken kick-off, free kick, kick, or throw-in.

Fouls include:

Blocking—Impeding the progress, without personal contact, of an opponent who does not have the ball

Boxing-up—Two players who guard an opponent between them so closely that she cannot successfully pass the ball

Charging—Contacting an opponent either with the body or ball in an attempt to advance the ball

Handling—Touching a ground ball with the arms or hands

Holding—Grasping or impeding an opponent's progress by holding onto or tagging her often

Holding the Ball—Keeping the ball in one's possession for more than three seconds on the field, more than five seconds on an out of bounds play or free kick, or taking more than ten seconds for a penalty kick

Obstruction—Impeding (by personal contact) the progress of an opponent who has the ball

Pushing—Moving forcefully into an opponent by using the body, arms, or hands

Traveling—Taking more than two steps with the ball following a run, or more than one step after having caught the ball while standing still

SCORING

The methods and point values given for scoring are:

Field goal— 2 points
Touchdown— 2 points
Drop kick— 3 points
Penalty kick—1 point

D.K.=3   T.D.=2   F.G.=2   Pen.=1

Figure No. 19–2.   Methods of Scoring.

NEEDED FACILITIES AND EQUIPMENT

Needed equipment includes one regulation soccer ball (leather covered, 27 to 28 inches in circumference) for at least each six to eight players, shin guards for all, and additional padded equipment, if desired, for the goal-keeper. Teammates should be easily distinguished by their dress. As in all sports, where contact is possible those needing to wear eyeglasses while playing should wear protective guards. A first aid kit should be kept handy at all times. Pinnies, clip boards, and other similar equipment used in teaching sports classes are also necessary.

TEACHING UNITS

Suggested topics for a unit in speedball include:

Unit for Beginners	*Unit for Advanced Players*
Brief history, nature, and purpose of the game	Review of the nature and purpose of the game
Safety rules	Review of all fundamental skills
Soccer skills	Advanced soccer skills
Dribbling	Advanced basketball skills
Instep kick	Advanced speedball skills
Kicking with the inside and outside of the foot	Variations of body traps and blocks
Punting	Variations of the leg trap
Body traps and blocks	Position play
Sole of foot, one leg, two leg trap	Advanced strategy
Evading an opponent	Officiating
Kicking for a goal	Evaluation
Basketball skills	
Catching and passing	
Overhead juggle	
Pivoting	
Soccer skills	
Drop kick	
Passing	
Tackling	
Speedball skills	
Pick up with one foot on a moving ball, on a stationary ball, with two feet, with one foot over a moving ball	
Lifting the ball up to pass	
Guarding	
Rules	
Strategy	
Evaluation	

BASIC SKILLS

See the chapters on soccer and basketball for specific skills used in speedball from each sport. Those other skills of the game which are peculiar to this game are:

The Kick-up with Both Feet.   The kick-up with one or both feet is a method of converting a ball on the ground into an aerial ball by kicking and catching it before it touches the ground. When done with both feet, the ball is cradled between the inner part of the feet with the body weight equally distributed on the outer portions, knees slightly bent. As one jumps into the air, she pulls the ball up and catches it with the hands.

The Kick-up with One Foot.   The ball, placed on top of the foot, is pulled up for catching by flexing the leg sharply, turning the toes upward, slightly bending the knee outward and flipping the ball up quickly with an upward thrust of the ankle. The body should bend forward to receive the ball.

The Kick-up of a Rolling Ball.   Face the ball, stand with knees flexed in a stride position with the lifting foot forward. Quickly insert the toes of that foot under the ball and lift it up for catching. Bend forward to receive the catch.

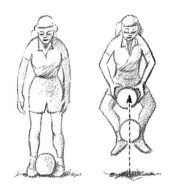

Figure No. 19–3.   The Kick-up with Both Feet.

Figure No. 19–4.   The Kick-up with One Foot.

Figure No. 19–5.   The Kick-up of a Rolling Ball.

Figure No. 19–6.   The Lift-up.

A Lift-up to Another Player.   Face the ball about one foot away and slightly to the right of the body. Slightly flex the right leg. With body weight quickly shifted to the left, insert the toes of the right foot and lift the ball with a foot and leg follow-through in the direction of the other player.

GAME STRATEGY

Offense.   Since most goals are scored by the forwards, the attacking team must be made up of fast, skillful ball handlers, passers, and receivers who can work as a unit taking the ball up and downfield. Ideally, there should be at least two tall girls in the line who are adept at ball passing and tall enough to catch the ball thrown over the end line players' heads for a touchdown. "Only the team with the ball can score" is a true concept to get across to any competing player, for it will instill in the forwards a desire to keep control of the ball once it is in their possession, and help their defensive team members to grasp the necessity of getting it up to them as speedily and accurately as possible.

Players should know the game score at all times and, if they are behind, work toward making a type of goal which will give them the most points.

When scoring attempts are made, the inners should draw the fullbacks away from the goal.

Usually, an aerial passing game will move the ball downfield more quickly. However, beginning players, when almost within scoring range often become overconfident and careless, causing them to lose the ball by having it snatched up by an opponent who boots it far down into the opposite end of the field. Wind and other environmental playing conditions, as well as a careful analysis of the weaknesses of the opposing team, should be studied and advantage taken of them.

The attackers should develop a variety of offensive skills and be able to seize upon opportunities for a surprise play. Since the ability to drop kick for goals and punt for distance are the two weakest skills of many female players, the wise instructor should drill her team thoroughly in both of them.

Other suggested pointers include:

1. Keep moving the ball downfield and take advantage of all chances to score.

2. Advance the ball down the sidelines instead of the middle of the field, then center it for a goal.

3. Advance the ball down the center of the field, pass out to the sidelines to score a touchdown.

4. Use short, accurate passes.

5. When dribbling, pass off on the opponent's left side.

The Defense. Speedball defensive players should use mainly soccer and basketball tactics to prevent goals from being scored. Since these back players must be skilled in the techniques of playing both an aerial and ground ball type of game, they should all be alert, possess the ability to anticipate opponent's movements, be physically strong, and possess much endurance. Likewise, each player should understand and be able to do well the defensive team tactics of interchanging, marking, backing-up, covering as used in soccer, as well as be able to utilize effectively the zone, man to man, and shifting zone defense as used in basketball.

It is imperative that the halfbacks and fullbacks work as a unit, rushing in at the right time to give needed assistance. Closely guarding the person each is marking, and possessing the ability to shift from one type of defense to another during an aerial attack, are the basic defensive techniques each player must master.

Other suggested pointers include:

1. Play the ball and not the player.

2. Keep moving the ball up and out of the scoring areas.

3. Anticipate plays and moves before they are made.

4. Study the weaknesses of the opponents and capitalize upon them. Force them to play an aerial game if they seemingly are better at a ground game.

5. Keep on your toes, ready for any type of an attack.

DUTIES AND SPECIFIC SKILLS OF PLAYERS

The Goalkeeper.   Since her main task is to prevent the opponents from scoring, this player should clear to the outside or to the fullbacks. She should stand 4 feet in front of the end line and quickly shift her position from there in relation to the approaching ball. Courage, ability, judgment, and skill are the qualities she should possess.

The Fullbacks.   As defensive team members, those playing this position should be strong, accurate kickers, fast on their feet, and be able to pass the ball in the air quickly. They should never crowd or obstruct the view of the goalkeeper, or pass across or in front of their own goal, but, instead, always place themselves between the ball and the goal. When on the offense, they should move with the faster fullbacks going downfield just over the 50 yard line while the slower ones should remain just back of it.

The Halfbacks.   As offensive players, the halfbacks can either score themselves, or pass the ball up to the forward line players so that they can. Each should play in her own respective one-third width area of the field, "backing up" the forwards. When on the defense, these players must assist the fullbacks by guarding three forwards or by dropping back in fullback position to cover for one who has moved out of place. While it is the job of the fullbacks to guard those of the opposing team's forwards nearest the goal, the halfbacks should mark the next three in that line. In clearing, the ball should be kicked toward the sidelines and never across the goal.

The Forward Line.   These five speedy players must be skilled in all of the offensive techniques of the game. The wings should play two yards in from the sidelines, but should move in when there is a chance to score. The inners and centers should avoid bunching. All should be ready to receive passes, pass off, shoot for goals, initiate a surprise attack, or be quick to change an aerial game to a ground one. The main task of the wings is to advance the ball and close the goal; of the inners, it is to advance the ball and score; the center forward to set up plays and shoot for goals. On the defense, the wings should move near the middle line and prevent the opponents from passing the ball up to their forward line. The inners should cover the right and left halfbacks and prevent them from passing while the center should cover the opposing center at field center. All of the forward line should be between the opponent's forward line and halfbacks.

CLASS ORGANIZATION

Many of the suggestions previously given for organizing a soccer or basketball class can be used when teaching speedball. However, it is wise to have the whole group drill at the same time on any technique taken from soccer, football, or basketball, rather than have one squad work on

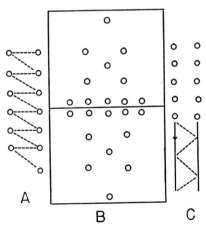

Figure No. 19–7.   Class organization for 45 students, with 22 playing, and the rest practicing skills on the sidelines. A. dribbling; B. team play; C. pass and body trap drill.

drop kicking, another on the throw-in, while a third group does the soccer dribble. Squads assigned for drilling purposes should never exceed ten in number, and be smaller, if possible. Here again, student leaders, selected for their leadership ability and playing skill, can be of great assistance.

The class should begin playing as soon as they have gained a basic concept of what the game is all about, and have learned enough playing skills to enjoy the thrill of team play in this exciting game. If class enrollment is large and only 22 can play at one time, squad leaders may drill their groups in certain skills along the sidelines while the game is in progress, as is shown above.

Since bunching is a big problem for both inexperienced players and teachers, it is suggested that the field be divided, either actually or imaginatively, into five lengthwise alleys, and players be taught to stay to their own areas. Another suggestion is to remove and replace all who consistently are out of position. Calling to players by their positions of play, instead of by their own names, sometimes works, as does using someone not playing in a game to chart one player's movements and report them to her.

Chalk talks and the use of magnetized boards are highly recommended when the class, seated on the floor around the instructor, can see as well as hear as she explains player position and game strategy.

A suggested unit of ten lessons may include the following:

Lesson I

1. Brief history, nature, and purpose of the game
2. Safety rules
3. Warm up exercises

4. Soccer skills
   Dribbling
   Instep kick
   Kicking with the inside and outside of the foot
5. Watch a short, one quarter game played, or in a film

Lesson II

1. Warm up exercises
2. Review of soccer skills learned in the previous lesson
3. Learn kicking with the inside and outside of the foot
4. Punting
5. Evading an opponent
6. Kicking for a goal
7. A simple novelty game or short pre-test of skills (See p. 501 for a suggested test made up of 10 separate items)

Lesson III

1. Warm up exercises
2. Review of the five soccer skills taught in the previous lesson
3. Basketball skills
   Pivoting
   Catching and passing
   The overhead juggle
4. Play a speedball novelty game or continue with pre-test items

Lesson IV

1. Warm up exercises
2. Review of the four basketball skills learned in the previous lesson
3. Speedball skills
   Drop kick
   Sole of foot, one leg, two leg trap
   Tackling
4. Practice time given for pre-test improvement

Lesson V

1. Warm up exercises
2. Review of the five speedball skills taught in the previous lesson
3. Additional speedball skills
   Pick up with one foot on a moving ball, on a stationary ball, with two feet, with one foot over a moving ball
   Lifting the ball up to pass
4. Chalk or magnetized board talk on player positions

5. Brief review of the nature and purpose of the game
6. Brief rule discussion

Lesson VI

1. Warm up exercises
2. Drill review of the most difficult skills of soccer, basketball, speedball
3. Play one quarter, stopping the game at teachable moments to learn rules

Lesson VII

1. Warm up exercises
2. Drill review of the most difficult skills of speedball
3. Play two quarters, stressing rules

Lesson VIII

1. Warm up exercises
2. Play the whole period
3. Evaluation of the game played by means of a class discussion with suggestions given for improved team play
4. Game strategy briefly discussed

Lesson IX

1. Warm up exercises
2. Play the whole period
3. Discussion of game strategy

Lesson X

1. Evaluation, paper-pencil knowledge test, skill test

Novelty games are recommended for beginners on the junior and senior high school level. Although squad drills are important means of gaining skill mastery, not too much time should be devoted to them unless the element of competition is introduced by contests between groups. The class should begin by playing modified or short speedball games just as soon as they are able, and have mastered enough of the basic skills that they may play safely and enjoyably. If possible, each class team should be given the opportunity to play against each other in an after school intra-class tournament. Individual coaching should also be given to as many players as possible. Youngsters just learning the game should have chances to play every team position, before starting to become a specialized wing or goalkeeper. Advanced players may be furnished ample opportunities to compete on teams playing other schools in play or sports day programs.

SKILL DIFFICULTIES AND THEIR CORRECTION

Difficulty	*Correction*

1. The Kick-up with Both Feet

1.

a. Holding the ball too close or out too far from the body

a. Too close—be sure the arms are fully extended; too far out—show how the body should bend only slightly forward before action is started, and that one need not strain too far forward

b. Letting the ball bounce too high before catching it

b. Bend to catch the ball before starting the foot action; watch the ball and practice to gain the correct timing

c. Failing to catch the ball as it rises from the feet

c. Watch the ball closely. Practice several times doing it with eyes closed in order to get the "feel" of the body movement and the place in space where the ball is usually caught

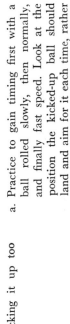

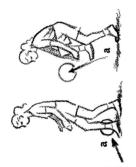

Difficulty

Correction

2. The One Foot Kick-up

2.

a. Failing to get the foot securely enough under the ball

a. Move so that the body is directly lined up with the ball, extend toes and whole foot until the ball feels securely balanced, then flip the foot up sharply

b. Losing control of the ball on the lift

b. Be sure the ball is controlled before the movement starts. Practice by using a heavier flat object placed on the foot long enough to get the "feel" of the movement, then use the ball. Practice to develop proper timing

3. Kicking Up of a Rolling Ball

3.

a. Missing the ball; kicking it up too high or too low

a. Practice to gain timing first with a ball rolled slowly, then normally, and finally fast speed. Look at the position the kicked-up ball should land and aim for it each time, rather than just kicking the ball

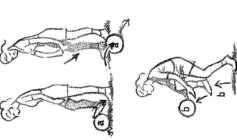

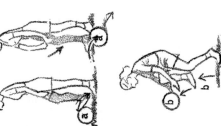

Difficulty	*Correction*
4. *Kicking Up a Stationary Ball With One Foot*	
a. Not letting the ball roll far enough up the toes	a. Turn the toes slightly up and flip the ankle up quickly. Be sure that the toes are completely under the ball before the motion begins
5. *A Lift-up to Another Player*	
a. Kicking the ball up too far instead of lifting it	a. Get the feel of the movement by doing it several times, first mimetically, then with the ball. Aim for the place the ball should land
b. Lack of ball control	b. Work on timing and control by using a heavier flat object several times, then using the ball

NOVELTY GAMES

Kick-up Contest (Beginners and Intermediates). Using a variety of kick-ups, players work first singly and then in pairs to see who can do the most kick-ups accurately in one minute. Repeat, each using different type of kick-ups each minute.

Relays (Beginners and Intermediates). Use double lines facing, unless otherwise shown, for the following:

1. Dribble and trap.
2. Dribble, pass, and trap.
3. Dribble, pass, and lift a moving ball to self.
4. Dribble, pass, and kick up to self with both legs.
5. Lift a stationary ball to player in the opposite line, or to a teammate on the right with two lines competing against time.
6. Pick up to self with one foot on a stationary ball, pass, and trap.
7. Volley and block.
8. Drop kick, catch, and punt back, reverse roles.
9. Tackling, front, and hook (two lines each in shuttle formation).
10. Passing with heel (regular relay line with first player going to designated spot, returning, and then going to the end of the line).
11. Passing, using the outside and inside of the foot (double column, side-by-side with number one in each line advancing to a designated spot passing ball diagonally forward and returning to the back of the line).
12. Passing with hands.
13. Juggling (players in line one juggle over heads of those advancing from line two). Reverse roles.

Seven Player Speedball (Intermediates and Advanced). Use a field 60 yards long and 35 yards wide. Play regular rules as much as possible using only seven players—three forwards, (center, right, and left), three backs (center, right and left), and a goalkeeper.

Tag Speedball (Beginners and Advanced). Running with the ball is permitted. However, no player may interfere with another's progress while running, and rules against personal contact and blocking are observed. If tagged while holding the ball, one must give the ball to the tagger at the spot, and the tagging side puts the ball in play from out of bounds at the nearest boundary line. A touchdown, the only method for scoring, can be made by running over the goal line while carrying the ball, and by the use of the overhead dribble. It counts two points.

Indoor Speedball (Beginners and Intermediates). Played on a basketball court, many of the regular speedball rules are used except that the court end lines are goal lines and the space beyond the end lines to the wall, or a line not exceeding five yards, is the end zone. Goal posts, or jumping standards, are placed 9 feet apart underneath the basketball backboard, and the penalty area is the free throw line. An old basketball or volleyball is used. A team is made up of seven players. The game starts with a toss-up at center, also used at the start of each quarter, and after each goal is made. A field goal counts three points, a touchdown two, and a penalty kick one point. The speedball rules for touchdowns, field goals, and penalty kicks are used. A field goal is scored when the ball is kicked through the goal markers. Instead of a free kick, the ball is taken out of bounds. Fouls and penalties, except for the free kick, are as in speedball.

Variations: 1. The ball is thrown into the basketball hoop instead of into the end zone for a touchdown.

2. Called Pin Speedball, in this game an Indian club is placed in the center of a 10 foot circle. To score, it must be knocked down by players who remain outside of the circle.

Rotate Kick Ball (Beginners). Used to practice kicking skills, all players are lined up along a straight line, except one. "It" stands 30 to 40 feet away. She calls one player's name and kicks the ball toward this person who must catch, and kick it from the line back to "it." Repeat until the ball has been kicked to each player. Then "it" shouts "free ball" and kicks the ball toward the whole line opposite her. The one who catches or successfully stops the ball becomes "it."

OFFICIATING TECHNIQUES

Many of the techniques used in officiating soccer are applicable in speedball also. There should be two officials, or one assisted by two linesmen, a timer, and two scorers. The official should check all players' feet before the game begins, for it is against the rules for them to wear shoes with metal cleats or projecting heavy soles.

When the ball crosses or goes out of bounds over a sideline, the umpire should stand behind the thrower at the place it left the field and carefully check to see that a legal throw-in is used. Likewise, when it goes out of the playing area over the goal line and no score is made, she should know the exact spot it crossed the line and give the ball to an opposing player, who may then put it back in play with a punt, throw, drop kick, or place kick.

Some players deliberately stand closer than the required five yards away on a free kick or for other penalities in order to stop the game long enough for them to reorganize or change their style of defense, the officials therefore, should not always call this rule violation, realizing that to do so would not be the real advantage to the team awarded the privilege of kicking that it *seems* to be.

The whistle should be used at the beginning of each quarter, after a score is made, and for fouls and violations. Otherwise, with the exception of the penalty kick, it is not blown throughout the game. Time outs may be called after a double foul, after each goal, following the penalty kick, and at any other time as called by the official. When a penalty kick is awarded, and there is no follow-up play, time out may also be taken until the ball is again put in play. Neither team should be charged with taking this time out, however.

The ball is in play as long as it is in the field and no foul or violation is called. Since speedball is a fast game, umpires on each side of the field should be able to move quickly and often up and down their whole area. All players should be watched carefully throughout the game, with additional attention given to each member of the defensive team when there is an attempted goal.

EVALUATING THE RESULTS

Achievement Practice Tests for Beginners. This is an ideal test for players of varying skill for it is a good motivator for learning. Each student should be given two tries and may keep an improved score, if made, after practicing over a period of time to do so.[1]

1. Dribble the ball 30 yards in six or less seconds. (Record the exact time taken.)
2. A two-legged kick-up to one's self at least five times in 30 seconds. (Only lifts done correctly count. One-half of the group counts and records while the other takes the test; reverse roles.)
3. Kick up to one's self a ball rolled from 10 yards for at least five times without missing. (Score only the greatest number done correctly.)
4. Lift a moving ball to a receiver five yards away at least five times without missing. (Score only the greatest number done correctly.)
5. Kick a ground ball 20 yards with either foot at least five consecutive times. (Use an instep kick with either foot, and score only those correctly done.)
6. Punt a soccer ball 20 yards at least five consecutive times. (Score only those correctly done and going 20 yards.)
7. Kick a rolling ball on the ground under the crossbar and between the goal posts at least five times without missing. (Score the greatest number correctly done.)
8. Catch five basketball-type passes in succession thrown by a passer 10 yards away. (Score the greatest number correctly caught.)
9. Drop kick a ball from a distance of 12 yards over a crossbar between the goal posts five times without missing. (Score the greatest number correctly kicked.)
10. Volley the ball five times consecutively with the foot or knee when tossed five yards away, back to the thrower so she can catch it with-

---

[1] This suggested test is one condensed and modified from that presented by Dr. Mary Buice in the article, Selected Achievement Standards as Practice Tests for Beginners, *Official Soccer-Speedball Guide,* 1956–1958, AAHPER, National Section of Girls and Women's Sports, Washington 6, D.C., pp. 84–86.

out moving more than one step. (Score the greatest number of volleys done correctly.)

For other speedball tests, see those suggested for soccer and basketball skills which are used in this game.

Knowledge tests covering rules, strategy, and player responsibilities should also be given.* The results of this examination coupled with those of a skill test should be considered if a final grade is to be recorded for each player at the end of a speedball unit.

TERMINOLOGY

Attackers—The team having possession of the ball, in contrast to the defenders who seek possession of it

End Goal—A ball that crosses the end line not between the goal posts. It does not count for a score in girls' rules

Fly Ball—A ball raised into the air from a kick

Foul—A rule infraction for which a free, or penalty, kick is given

Intercept—Catching a pass, a drop kick, or dribble, or getting a passed ball intended for a player on the opposing team

Kick-off—The way the game is started at its beginning, at each quarter, and after each scored goal. It is done with one foot and is a pass to another player

Passing—Advancing the ball downfield as in basketball

Trapping—Stopping a moving ball with the body, or one or both feet

Volley—Playing the ball with the head or any part of the body except the hands, forearms, and feet before it touches the ground

DISCUSSION QUESTIONS

1. Make a chart with three headings to show the qualifications, specific duties, and areas of the field each should cover for all players on a speedball team.
2. Devise five points you can use in a class discussion to show how speedball can bring increased student interest and enthusiasm for the physical education program.
3. Make a list of 10 helpful coaching and playing hints to pass along to a group of beginning speedball players.
4. Sketch on paper five defensive plays, and five offensive plays. Teach one of each type to any group. Evaluate your experience.
5. Officiate a speedball intramural game. Write a brief report of the strong and weak points (a) of your officiating ability, and (b) both teams' playing style and weaknesses.

SELECTED AUDIO-VISUAL AIDS

Speedball for Girls, 1948. (10 min., sound, b & w). Coronet Instructional Films, Inc., 65 East South Water Street, Chicago 1, Illinois. (Rental)

Speedball for Girls, Speed-A-Way, Marjorie Larson, 1754 Middlefield, Stockton, California.

Powell, Billie Jean: Portable Speedball Field, N.S.W.A., *Soccer-Speedball Guide* 1950–1952, p. 94.

* A suggested speedball examination is, *A Written Knowledge Examination for Speedball,* Phyllis Roney, Soccer-Speedball Guide, 1958–1960, pp. 91–94.

Griedrich, John A.: Magnetic Model Board, *Journal of Health, Physical Education, and Recreation,* April, 1933, p. 56.

SUGGESTED READINGS

Barton, Helen: *Speedball for Girls and Women,* Ann Arbor, Edwards Brothers, Inc., 1937.

Donnelly, Richard, Helms, William, and Mitchell, Elmer: *Active Games and Contests,* Ed. 2, New York, The Ronald Press, 1958.

Mitchell, Elmer: *Sports for Recreation,* Revised Edition, New York, A. S. Barnes, 1952.

Fielding, John: *Official Soccer-Speedball Guide (Including Fieldball),* Current Edition, Division for Girls and Women's Sports, AAHPER, 1201 16th Street, N.W., Washington 6, D.C.

Seaton, Don, Clayton, Irene, Leibee, Howard, and Messersmith, Lloyd: *Physical Education Handbook,* Ed. 3, New York, Prentice-Hall Book Company, Inc., 1958.

20

Volleyball

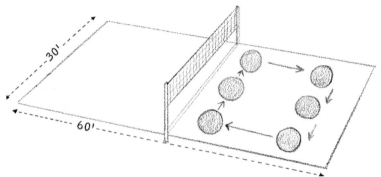

Figure No. 20-1.   Player Positions, Rotation Pattern, and Court Dimensions.

Volleyball is another increasingly popular team game which originated in America. It was devised by William C. Morgan, a Y.M.C.A. physical director in 1895 at Holyoke, Massachusetts, for a group of senior men looking for a less strenuous team activity than basketball or football, to play for fun after business hours. Originally, a rope was stretched across the gymnasium floor and a basketball bladder was batted slowly back and forth across it with the fists. Later, a tennis net replaced the rope and finally a regulation volleyball net, similar to the one used today, was manufactured by the Spalding Sporting Goods Company. The volleyball replaced the bladder, and the hands, the fists for hitting it across the court in a greatly speeded up game.

The sport has always had the enthusiastic endorsement of the Y.M.C.A. and it is largely through the efforts of leaders in this organization that volleyball has spread throughout the entire world. It is an ideal team game, for it can be modified and played with as many as 10 to 15 on a side in a relatively small area. It can be as mild or strenuous an activity as desired,

504

and is played with equal enjoyment by youngsters as well as oldsters. The game is well suited for teams made up of members of the same sex as well as co-recreational groups in schools, community centers, playgrounds, camps, institutions, and industrial plants. Volleyball has become tremendously popular in all branches of the armed services since it was first introduced during World War I.

The first Official Volleyball Rules for Women, published in 1924, were adopted by the National Section of Women's Athletics in 1937. Today the game is a major team sport for girls and women, and they are now playing it with such skill that it has become as exciting to watch as to play. It has few equals as an intramural activity because of its popularity among the lesser as well as the highly skilled. It is inexpensive for inclusion in the program in contrast to hockey or lacrosse, and can be easily modified so that those with physical defects, who usually are barred from participating, can and do play it with great gusto and much enjoyment.

THE NATURE AND PURPOSE OF THE GAME

The object of the game is to hit a regulation volleyball with the hands or forearms back and forth across the net and into the opponent's court using skilled placement so it cannot be returned easily. The playing area is a rectangular court 60 by 30 feet, equally divided by a net seven feet six inches from the floor. Each of the two competing teams consists of six players who rotate positions for all except the first serve, as is shown below.

The server on each side is given one try to put the ball in play by hitting it across the net with her opened or closed hand. She must stand behind the end line of her own court side when serving and cannot step over this line before the ball leaves her hands. Each server continues serving until a loss of service or "side out" is called. Only the serving team can score points. If a player serves out of turn "side out" is called, and no scored points are counted.

The ball may be batted in any direction with the forearms or with one, or both, open and closed hands, but it is called "dead" if it touches any part of the body. It may be hit three times on each side of the net, once by each player except when played by another teammate between times. Likewise, it can be played as soon as any part of it crosses the net and can be recovered from the net. A net ball is played except on a serve. A "replay"

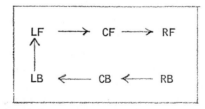

Figure No. 20–2.   Player Positions and Rotation Path.

is called if spectators interfere with the play, or when each team fouls simultaneously or on the same play.

"Side out" is called and the ball is awarded to the opposing team if one: serves out of turn or illegally; commits a foot fault on the serve; holds, throws, or lifts the ball; hits it twice in succession, or plays it with any body part except the forearms and hands; touches the net except when the ball is dead; plays out of position too often or too long as judged by the referee; touches floor in opponent's court when ball is in play; enters the game illegally after being disqualified, or leaves it without official permission. A "side out," or point is called against a team for taking more than two time out rest periods.

A game is completed when:

1. One team scores 15 points and has a two point advantage over its opponent;
2. A team leads by at least two points at the end of an 8 minute playing time.
3. At the end of 8 minutes if the game is tied or there is only a one point difference between opponents, the play continues until one team has a two point lead.

A point is won each time the receivers fail to return the ball legally.

The team captain who wins the coin toss has option of first service or choice of courts in the first game. In subsequent games the losing team of the previous game has first service.

NEEDED FACILITIES AND EQUIPMENT

Court.   A rectangular playing court should be provided that is 60 by 30 feet, bounded by 2 inch lines, with at least 6 feet of unobstructed area extending from the boundary lines. A minimum of 20 feet of overhead clearance should be allowed. A two inch center line divides the court into two playing areas.

Serving Areas.   If room permits, the serving area should be in back of the end lines between the extension of the sidelines and be 6 feet in depth. In a smaller gymnasium, the serving area may extend into the court.

Net.   A regulation net should be 32 feet in length and 3 feet wide, bound at the top and bottom with one-quarter inch manila rope. The net should be tightly stretched and the height should measure 7 feet, 6 inches from the top to the ground at the center of the court.

Ball.   A rubber ball may be used which carries 6 pounds of pressure, although a ball with a rubber bladder covered with a leather case is preferred. The latter should be 26 to 27 inches in circumference, weigh a minimum of 7 ounces and a maximum of 9, and be inflated to a pressure of between 7 and 8 pounds.

For a regulation game numbered pinnies, an official rule book, scorebook, and whistle should be provided.

TEACHING UNITS

The topics suggested for units for beginners and advanced students in volleyball include:

Unit for Beginners	*Unit for Advanced Students*
Brief history, nature and purpose of the game	Review of rules
	Review of basic techniques
Volleying the ball	Advanced techniques of serving
The serve	Incurve
Setup	Outcurve
Net recovery	Drop curve
The spike	Overhead
Block	Blocking
Returning the spike	Spike placement
Rules and regulations	Advanced strategy
Strategy	Officiating
Evaluation	Evaluation

BASIC SKILLS

The Underhand and Chest Volley. This is used for hitting a ball up from below the waist or at chest height. It is done by pushing the ball up sharply with a wrist snap and using the tips of the fingers. Keep knees slightly flexed, feet in stride position, extend arms and body as the ball is contacted and lifted upward in the follow-through.

Figure No. 20–3.   The Underhand and Chest Volley.

The Overhead Volley. The overhead volley is used for hitting a ball that is above the head. It is similar to that mentioned above. The body should be flexed and extended more as the ball is contacted in a "give, then push up" movement.

Figure No. 20–4.   The Overhead Volley.

Passing. This is used for hitting the ball to a teammate. The body position varies according to the height and direction of the ball. The forearms should be relaxed and force applied by a sharp wrist flexion to hit the ball well up, as the body is turned forward on contact toward the receiver.

Figure No. 20–5.   Passing.

Net Recovery. The net recovery is used to hit the ball out of the net. This skill is similar to the underhand volley. Bend knees sharply as the ball strikes the net, rise to meet it as it falls out, and then pass it high into the air to a waiting teammate.

Figure No. 20–6. Net Recovery.

The Setup. The setup is used for a high pass to a teammate who will spike it. Turn the body in the direction the ball is to be passed, hit it up approximately five feet above spiker's shoulder, flex knees, and extend the body as it is contacted.

Figure No. 20–7. The Setup.

The Spike. Crouch slightly to spring up as the ball is contacted above the net. Leap high, hit with the firm fingers of one hand of a flexed, then sharply extended arm. Snap wrist down and hit the ball on the top, driving it to the floor on the opposite side of the net.

Figure No. 20–8. The Spike.

The Block. The block is used by a defensive player to stop a spike at the net. The jump must be perfectly timed with the opposing spiker's movement, and is made by springing up high from both feet, fully extending the arms, and contacting the ball without touching the net.

Figure No. 20–9. The Block.

The Serve.   The three types of serve used to put the ball in play are the underhand, overhand, and sidearm. The three hand positions which may be used to do this are the open, curled, and the clenched fist.

Figure No. 20–10.   The Serve.

The Underhand Serve.   Hold the ball in the left hand across the body in line with the right hip. Swing the right arm back, then diagonally across to contact it as it drops from the supporting hand. Slightly flex knees and transfer weight from the rear to the forward foot. Hit the ball with the heel of the hand.

Figure No. 20–11.   The Underhand Serve.

The Overhand Serve.   Similar to the tennis serve and overhand baseball throw, this skill is done by holding the ball in the palm of the left hand. Toss it three to four feet above the right shoulder. At the same time, bend the right arm, and in an overhand throwing motion, contact the ball above the forehead with the fist or heel of the hand.

Figure No. 20–12.   The Overhand Serve.

Figure No. 20–13.   The Sidearm Serve.

The Sidearm Serve.   Similar in technique, body position, and timing to the underhand serve, the ball is hit off the hand with the body turned slightly and the extended arm swung horizontally to the floor.

GAME STRATEGY

Players often need help in gaining an understanding that the real fun of playing volleyball comes from team effort. Beginners, in their eagerness to score points all by themselves, will often hit the ball back over the net and into the hands of an opposing team member (who then can hit it into an unguarded court area), instead of using a pass and a spike setup on her own side of the net so that a play makes a sure point.

Official rules call for a rotation pattern of play whereby all players eventually play each court position and consequently must develop skill and strategy for such play. Modifications of the official rules allow, among other changes, for nonrotation play for younger or less skilled players. The following suggested strategy focuses on the skill needs of both types of play.

Since a team cannot win unless it scores more points than its opponent, offensive playing skills are far more important to master than those of defensive ones. The tallest person, assuming she is also a skilled player, should be the spiker. All forward line players, however, should be able to spike well, be agile, able to jump high into the air, and have quick reaction time. The backs, on the other hand, should realize that they rarely should send the ball over the net, but that their main job is to hit it up for their forwards.

The team should master the fundamental skills of the game and develop several set plays, so that each player knows and can carry out her responsibilities. If rotation is used, every player must be able to play all positions skillfully. Non-rotation play, wherein each individual has many opportunities to develop skills through repeated practice, is recommended if a group really is earnest in developing the techniques of good team play.

General playing strategy should incorporate playing the ball to the opponent's weaknesses, which are usually their poorest players. It is also wise to serve and hit the ball to the left side of the receiver's body. Serves should be made quickly and be accurately placed, and all team members should develop skill in looking into one court area and hitting the ball into another.

Offensive players should develop a strong, fast, effective method of attack, using plays which will end up in a setup and spike into diagonal areas close to the net. Bunching should be avoided, and will be if players are taught to move back into their own positions quickly after shifting to cover an unguarded area. A fast overhand serve placed low over the net with plenty of spin on it, that lands into the far corners or boundary lines of the opposite court is usually the most difficult to return. The center must be skilled at both blocking and spiking. She should face the net, whereas the left forward should have her left shoulder turned toward it and the right forward with her right shoulder. All players should keep their eyes on the ball and anticipate where the returned ball will be sent.

The server must be able to vary types of serves and to apply many kinds of spin to the ball, develop accurate placement, and be a master at using deceptive body movements so her opponents will not be sure into which court area the ball will go. The spiker must be able to jump high, have quick reaction time, use her body adeptly in all space levels, hit on top of the ball, and be able to put a fast back, top, or lateral spin on it, as well as be skilled in changing the pace of the game. The setup player should stand with her right side to the net and to the right of a right-handed spiker, develop skill in hitting the ball up with one as well as both hands, master setting the ball up close to the net without touching it, and be an agile, calm, and reliable player.

Defensive players must develop set plays for blocking successfully. The use of a player of equal or superior height from her blocking opponent across the net is almost imperative. The blocker should watch both the ball and the spiker carefully in order to synchronize her own movements perfectly with those of the attacker, as well as to anticipate where the ball will land. All back players must keep their eyes on the ball at all times, and be alert and ready to move quickly in any direction or space level. The center back should stand nearer the net than the other two defensive players; all three must be watchful of crowding or playing too close to their forwards. All returned balls should be strategically placed on the opposite court and kept low while going over the net. These players must cover for, back up, and get the ball up to the front line quickly and accurately for a spike. All must be skilled in playing the ball above and below the waist. They must also be ready to seize upon and create scoring opportunities, or to return the ball on a skillfully made play so it will result in a "side out."

CLASS ORGANIZATION

Carefully planned class drills are essential for teaching the basic techniques of the game. Squads, led by a selected student assistant, should be made up of six to eight players. Competition between groups as they drill or play novelty games increases interest and motivates students to master isolated skills more quickly. Initial drills should give players an opportunity to handle the ball so that they will first learn how to control it. Since the rules allow only one instead of a double hit, each player must first learn how to control the ball before she tries passing it on to a teammate.

Pointers to stress in teaching ball handling include: (a) "give" with the ball; (b) hit it high into the air so your teammates can get under it; (c) advance the left foot slightly, flex knees, relax the body; (d) keep your eyes on the ball; (e) get under and play a high ball in front of your face; (f) keep hands in a waiting position at the chest height, thumbs in and pointed down with fingers spread; and (g) *aim,* then pass. Never just hit the ball at random, hoping someone will get it.

Practice Drills for Passing

1. Arrange squads in a circle. One starts by hitting the ball to the next player on her left, etc. Then, pass to the right. Next have squads compete in

passing continuously in either direction, each trying to get up to 25 counts first without missing, and having to go back to count 1 when they do miss.

2. Arrange squads in a circle with a leader in the center who passes the ball to each person, going first right, then left. Repeat, having all hit the ball higher into the air.

3. In a circle formation, number the players. Number one passes the ball over the head of number two for player number three, who hits a short pass back to number two. The ball then goes from two to four in a long pass, etc. (First skip every other one, then pass back, etc.)

4. Arrange players close to the net in groups of three opposite couples. Players 1, 2, and 3 are on the same side with 4, 5, and 6 across the net. Number 1 hits the ball up high over to 4, 4 to 2, 2 to 5, 5 to 3, 3 to 6, 6 back high to 1.

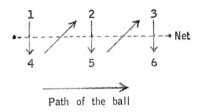

Path of the ball

5. Line two groups up on each side of the net. One hits to 2, 2 to 3, 3 to 4, and 4 back to 1.

6. Arrange players in a circle with one in the center. The ball always starts on the outside. Number 1 passes in to 2, and goes inside the circle. Number 2 passes the ball out to 3 and goes out of the circle to the place 2 stood, etc. Teach this by having the class say *"pass* the ball *in, go in,* pass the ball *out,* then *go out."* Have (a) circles compete against each other to

see which one can keep the ball in the air longest, (b) circles get to 25, 50, 100 times first without missing and returning to count 1 when doing so.

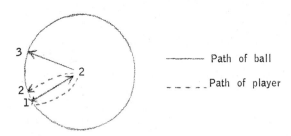

———————— Path of ball

_ _ _ _ _Path of player

7. Wall practice with six to eight players at each space hitting the ball up above a line drawn net height, playing it on a volley. Compete for numbers of times doing so correctly, or the greatest number landing above mark in a given time. Have two players working together alternate hitting volleys to each other. Compete for the greatest number of correct hits in a given time.

Net Recovery.   Pointers to stress include (a) get under the ball and time the recovery with the ball fall from the net, contact, and then use the whole body follow-through on the hit high into the air, and (b) watch the ball carefully.

Practice Drills for the Net Recovery

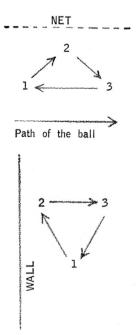

Path of the ball

1. Arrange players in three's, with 1 and 3 in a line, 2 forward as shown. Numbers 1 and 3 alternate throwing the ball into the net, 2 recovers and passes to either person. Players alternate roles.

2. Arrange beginning players at a wall in groups of three as shown, for work in gaining control of the ball before letting them practice this skill at the net. Mark the wall to show the correct net height. Number 1 throws the ball at the wall, 2 recovers it and makes an underhand pass to 3, who hits it back up to number 1 so she can catch it and repeat the drill. Give each player several tries in each role.

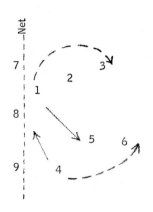

3. Arrange players in groups of six near the net as shown. Number 4 throws the ball into the net for 1 and goes to the rear of her own line. Number 1 recovers, and passes the ball up to 5 then goes to the end of her own line. Number 5 moves up to catch the ball and to throw it into the net for 2, who waits to get it as it falls from the net, etc. Player 7, 8, or 9 catches the ball and returns it under the net to the thrower. Each changes her role so that all have several practice tries.

Serving.   Pointers to stress in serving practice include: (a) *aim,* do not just hit the ball, (b) get your *whole body* into the hit, (c) put a *spin* on the ball, and (d) develop perfect *timing* and *control.*

Practice Drills for Serving.

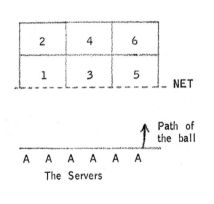

Mark off the court and arrange squads as shown. Have players in Column A take four turns, consecutively placing the ball in each area marked 1, 2, 3, 4, 5, and 6, while those across the net receive it and get it back across the net in three hits. Score one point each time a server hits into the right area for her team and give those on the opposite side one point each time they return the ball successfully using three passes.

The Pass Setup, Spike, and Block.   Pointers to stress in practice include: (a) develop a set play so the setup and spiker know what to do, (b) set the ball up so that the spiker can time her jump with the top of the ball hit, and (c) synchronize perfectly the block with the spike.

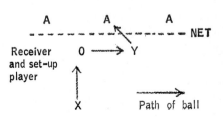

Practice Drills for the Pass, Set-up, and Spike.   Arrange groups of 6 players. X passes the ball up to O, who receives and sets it up for Y. As Y spikes it, any one or two A players block it. Repeat several times, change roles.

Large classes often present a problem to the inexperienced teacher who is unskilled in planning ways to take care of many students, but aware that all in the group should be as active as possible during the instructional period. The following plans showing how a class of 40 students can be arranged should prove helpful. In each, a skilled squad leader works with the group, and the teacher is free to give individual help to those most needing it.

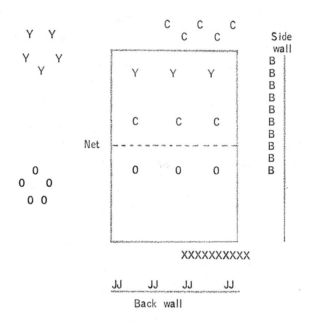

Plan for Drilling a Class of 40 Students.   Divide class into 5 squads made up of 8 players each, with each squad practicing a skill previously taught in class.

X's—Serve into backcourt

3 Y's—Receive in opposite backcourt and receiver passes the ball to any other back player who hits it to the third back player so she can catch and throw it back to the next X server

5 Y's—Work on circle passing with ball received below the waist

3 O's—Practice pass, setup, and spike

5 O's—work on circle passing with ball received above the waist

3 C's—Alternate turns on making a single and double block

5 C's—Sitting on the floor passing the ball high in the air to next player, then to any player

8 B's—At the side wall doing volley practice

8 J's—At back wall practicing in groups of 2, a low ball recovery and pass off

TEACHING PROGRESSION

A suggested unit composed of 12 lessons might include the following:

Lesson I

1. Brief history, nature, and purpose of the game
2. Individual volleys—underhand, overhead
3. Passing
4. Novelty games—"Keep It Up"

Lesson II

1. Review passing
2. Novelty game stressing passing for accuracy
3. Underhand serve
4. Serving rules

Lesson III

1. Review underhand serve
2. Illustrated chalk talk on player positioning, rotation
3. Brief demonstration game situation with explanation of rules
4. Game situation for all

Lesson IV

1. Ball passing drills
2. Net recovery
3. Game situation stressing positions, cooperative team play, and rules

Lesson V

1. Review net recovery
2. Sidearm serve
3. Brief explanation of officiating techniques
4. Game situation using student officials

Lesson VI

1. Brief drill of major game skills previously taught
2. Setup for the spike
3. Spike
4. Game situation stressing use of the spike

Lesson VII

1. Review setup for spike, and spike
2. Return of the spike (recovery)
3. Explanation of defense position for spike
4. Block
5. Game situation using student officials

Lesson VIII

1. Review block
2. Begin round robin tournament between squads, using student officials

Lesson IX

1. Continue round robin tournament

Lesson X

1. Brief written test
2. Begin skill testing

Lesson XI

1. Review written test
2. Complete skill tests

Lesson XII

1. Skill tests results posted and discussed
2. Class watches and demonstrates "all-star" game between two previously selected teams
3. Class discussion and evaluation of learning experiences of the volleyball unit

SKILL DIFFICULTIES AND THEIR CORRECTION

Difficulty   *Correction*

1. *Serving*   1.

a. Hitting the ball into the net

   a. Check to see if the ball is being held high enough before it is hit; hit with a higher follow-through; control the ball by hitting it more with the heel of the palm instead of the fingers

b. Hitting the ball too high over the net

   b. Bend more at the waist; check and improve the follow-through; lower the ball position before hitting

c. Hitting the ball out of bounds

   c. Pick a spot on the opposite court near the net and aim for it; develop a smoother, more controlled swing

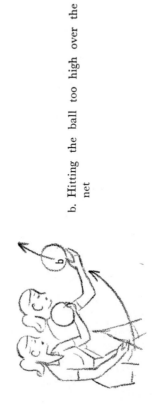

Difficulty	*Correction*

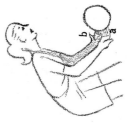

d. Missing the ball

d. Watch the ball as you hit it and know when it leaves your hand

2. *Receiving the Ball Below the Waist*

a. Incorrect position of the hands

b. Hitting with only one hand, losing control of the ball

2.

a. Keep arms below the waist, palms pointed out, little fingers close together

b. Stress hitting with two hands and demonstrate how doing so gives better ball control

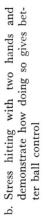

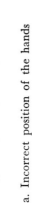

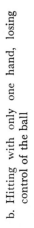

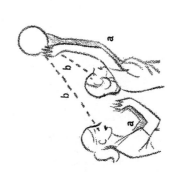

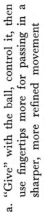

3. Receiving the Ball at Chest Height

3.

a. Striking at the ball instead of tapping it

a. "Give" with the ball, control it, then use fingertips more for passing in a sharper, more refined movement

b. Receiving the ball too low

b. Bend knees more deeply; get *under* the ball so it can be received at chest level

4. Receiving the Ball Above the Head

4.

a. Lack of body balance

a. Flex and relax body more, be *ready* to reach arms and extend body; keep feet evenly spaced

b. Missing the ball

b. Keep your eyes on the ball at all times

SKILL DIFFICULTIES AND THEIR CORRECTION (*Continued*)

Difficulty	*Correction*
5. *Passing the Ball*	**5.**
a. Hitting with the whole hand	a. Hit only with fingertips; listen for the soft "putt" sound a correct contact makes
b. Passing too low or high	b. Concentrate on aiming; know where you want the ball to meet a teammate's body; bend knees more if the ball is going too high; watch the follow-through if it is going too low
6. *Setting Up*	**6.**
a. Setting up too close to the net	a. Move closer to the net in order to make a more vertical pass
b. Setting the ball up too low for the spiker	b. Get the ball up 10 to 12 feet from the floor and more in front of the spiker
7. *Spiking*	**7.**
a. Hitting at the side or under the ball	a. Hit on top of the ball with great force, giving it a downward slap
b. Jumping too soon; incorrect timing	b. Start the leap just as the ball starts down; concentrate on, and practice, correct timing by analyzing all mistakes made, then avoid repeating them
c. Hitting the ball out of bounds	c. Hit the ball in a sharper downward motion; always making contact on top of it

Difficulty	Correction
8. *Recovery of the Ball from out of the Net*	8.
a. Missing the ball	a. Quick reaction time is necessary and must be developed for success; bend body more; anticipate where the ball will fall
b. Touching the net with the body	b. Stand back more; be ever cognizant of the rule and penalty for touching the net
9. *Playing the Game*	9.
a. Attempting to "star" by not passing off to a teammate	a. Remind player of her specific contribution as a team player
b. Playing out of position; bunching	b. Draw box for player and require her to stay in her own area until she understands the reason for doing so
c. Hitting the ball aimlessly, hoping it will go over the net	c. Play to opponent's weakness; aim *before* hitting; use your mind *and* body

OFFICIATING TECHNIQUES

Officials are not necessary, except for tournament competition which requires a referee, umpire, two timers, two scorekeepers and two linesmen. During any called game, the referee should not use her whistle except for fouls, points, and side out. She should be stationed at the net and be in a position on a stand where she can get a plain view of both courts. Throughout the contest, the following hand and arm positions should be used when refereeing:

SIGNALS FOR USE BY OFFICIALS

By JEAN PUTNAM

Smith College, Northampton, Massachusetts

Figure No. 20–14.   Signals used by the Referee. (A.A.H.P.E.R., DGWS, Volleyball Guide, reprinted by permission.)

The referee and her assistants should each perform the following duties:

Referee—Person in charge of the game who makes all decisions on all plays, and is responsible for seeing that all details of the contest are properly carried out.

Umpire—Stationed directly across the net from the referee, her main duties are concerned with rule infractions which cannot be seen clearly by the referee.

Scorers—Located at a table on the same side of the court as the umpire, their jobs are to keep the records on each player, and a running account of the score.

Timekeepers—Seated near the scorers, they keep the official time of each game, signal when to resume play again after a time out, and the end of the game.

NOVELTY GAMES

Giant Volleyball (Beginners and Intermediates). Play volleyball rules. Use a cageball or giant balloon at least 36 inches in diameter. The net is lowered to 6 feet. Give assistance on the serve, if needed. Have from 10 to 20 on a side; allow as many hits as necessary to get the ball across to the opposing side. Play for 15 points or a designated time.

Newcomb (Beginners). Use as many of the regulation volleyball rules as possible. The ball is caught and thrown across the net, with only one throw given per side. Only the person who catches the ball may throw it back, and is allowed to take only one step while throwing or after catching the ball. Play for time or points.

Volleyball Skill Game (Intermediates and Advanced). Play regular volleyball rules except score as follows:

Successful spike	3 points
Successful block	6 points
Successful pass	1 point
A serve no one on the opposing team can touch	3 points
Hitting a serve which falls on boundary line in opposing court	2 points
Successful net recovery	2 points
Successful net recovery and pass	3 points
Receiving a low ball and passing it correctly	1 point

Play for 21 points or the greatest number made in 10 minutes.

Curtain Volleyball. Players are seated on a tennis court or a court of approximate size. Only outside boundary lines are necessary. Hang a blanket or curtain over the net or use a rope strung between two trees, which makes it impossible for all players on either side to see each other. Play regular volleyball rules. Use a regular volleyball or softer playground ball of the same size.

Bounce Volleyball (Beginners).   Play as regular volleyball except that after service, and until a point or side out is called, all must let the ball bounce once before hitting it back.

Volley-Tennis (Beginners and Intermediates).   Played as regular volleyball using a net at the height for tennis on a court 36 by 50 feet, with a volleyball. There are 6 to 15 on each team and they rotate as in volleyball. Each server has 2 chances, using a permitted assist, when needed. The receiver may hit it in the air using two hits or only one hit if getting it from the bounce. Play for 15 points.

Keep It Up (Intermediates and Advanced).   Arrange two teams of six players and use all volleyball rules except that covering the number of hits. The object of the game is to pass a received ball to five teammates before it is hit across the net. Score one point for doing so. Next, the opposing team serves to their opponents who must make five different passes before hitting it back across the net. Play for 15 points.

EVALUATING THE RESULTS

Numerous and excellent skill tests are available in this sport. The better ones measure ball placement accuracy in serving. A suggested floor marking plan for testing this skill is shown below:

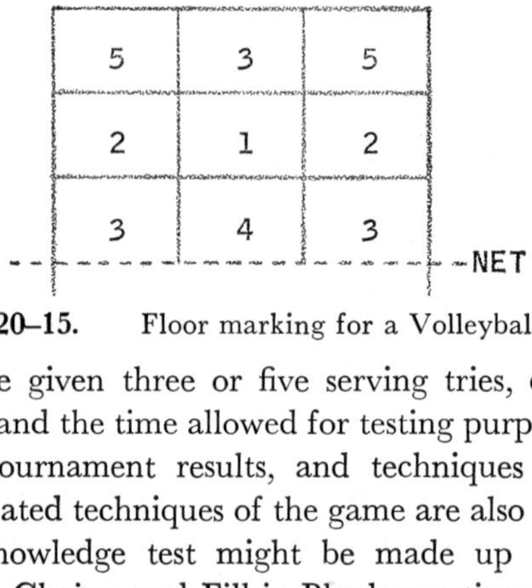

5	3	5
2	1	2
3	4	3

‒NET

Figure No. 20–15.   Floor marking for a Volleyball Serve Test.

Students may be given three or five serving tries, depending upon the number in the class and the time allowed for testing purposes.

Rating scales, tournament results, and techniques for measuring skill mastery in other isolated techniques of the game are also recommended.

An objective knowledge test might be made up of True and False, Matching, Multiple Choice, and Fill-in-Blank questions on playing strategy. To be of greatest value, test papers should be returned to their owners and discussed in class so that students who did poorly on the examination will gain an understanding of their errors.

TERMINOLOGY

Attack—A kill or a spike; changing the game pace
Block—One player jumps to stop a spike of an opposing player with both close to the net. A multiple block is done by two players on a side
Match—Usually two out of three games
Rotation—Players changing positions at the beginning of a serve

Service—A skill used for starting the game and putting the ball back into play

Setup—Setting the ball up into the air in the right position for a spike

Side Out—Loss of serve

Spike—A hard driven ball hit from the net sharply down at the feet of an opposing player

Volley—Hitting the ball in the air

DISCUSSION QUESTIONS

1. Compare the values of volleyball to those of hockey, tennis, and speedball.
2. Observe one student in a beginning class in volleyball for five or more minutes as she plays in a game. (a) Make a list of the mistakes she makes. (b) State in three sentences how she could correct each one.
3. Make up an objective volleyball test of 20 items for advanced players using: (a) 5 True-False, (b) 5 Matching, (c) 5 Multiple Choice, (d) 5 Fill-in-Blank questions. Go over each test item carefully, checking that you have avoided duplication, were obvious in your statements by making them too simple, and eliminated, as far as possible, the guessing of the correct answers.
4. Make a chart showing the names and duties of each team player.
5. Form a group of four with your teammates. Have each group select, describe, and demonstrate any of the following skills: (a) the net ball recovery, (b) the spike, (c) the block, or (d) the overhand serve. Discuss and choose which group was the most successful. Analyze the reasons.

SELECTED AUDIO-VISUAL AIDS

Beginning Volleyball. (A filmstrip of 208 frames. Four units, 10 minutes each.) Athletic Institute, 209 South State Street, Chicago, Illinois. (Rental)

Illustrated Sports Charts. (Volleyball, Basketball, and Softball wall charts.) Produced by Katherine Ley and Donna May Miller, University of Colorado Book Store, Boulder, Colorado. (Purchase)

How to Officiate Girls and Women's Volleyball. (Slides and Record). Audrey Kleinhandler, 150 Brighton Street, Brooklyn 15, New York.

Play Volleyball. (20 min., sound, b & w). Associated Films, 347 Madison Avenue, New York, N.Y. Branch offices in Chicago, San Francisco, and Dallas. (Rental)

Sports Teaching Aids (3 × 5 card file bibliography of films, filmstrips, and slides). Division for Girls and Women's Sports, AAHPER, 1201 16th Street, N.W., Washington 6, D.C.

Volleyball Strategy for Girls, 1957. (12 min., 16 mm., sound, b & w). McGraw-Hill Book Company, Text-Film Department, 330 W. 42nd Street, New York 36, N.Y. (Purchase)

Volleyball Techniques for Girls, 1957. (9 min., 16 mm., sound, b & w). McGraw-Hill Book Company, Text-Film Department, 330 W. 42nd Street, New York 36, N.Y. (Purchase)

SUGGESTED READINGS

Armbruster, David: *Basic Skills in Sports for Men and Women,* St. Louis, C. V. Mosby Company, 1953.

Friermood, Harold: Improving Your Volleyball, *Journal of AAHPER,* December, 1945.

Laveaga, Robert E.: *Volleyball,* New York, A. S. Barnes, 1942.

Division for Girls and Women's Sports, *Selected Volleyball Articles,* 1955, *Volleyball Guide* (Current Edition), 1201 16th Street, N.W., Washington 6, D.C.

Teacher's Guide to Physical Education for Girls in High School, California State Department of Education, Sacramento, 1957.

Vannier, Maryhelen, and Fait, Hollis: *Teaching Physical Education in Secondary Schools,* Philadelphia, W. B. Saunders Company, 1957.

IV

Extending the Program

"IF EDUCATION IS A MEANS OF DEVELOPING PERSONALITY, EQUIPPING THE MIND, STRENGTHENING THE BODY, LEARNING SKILLS, BUILDING CHARACTER, AND CREATING AN APPRECIATION FOR BEAUTY, THEN RECREATION HAS ENORMOUS EDUCATIONAL VALUES".....CHARLES BRIGHTBILL AND HAROLD MEYER

21

Standards in Sports for Girls and Women

Standards in the conduct of sports for girls and women as devised, endorsed, and promoted by the many outstanding leaders in the Division for Girls and Women's Sports of the AAHPER have given both great impetus and strong guidance to the rapidly growing sports programs for females throughout the nation. At first there was no such guiding group; highly organized competitive games for girls and women were introduced cautiously and slowly in a few of the better eastern women's colleges. The first women's game of basketball was played at Smith College in 1899, followed shortly afterwards by hockey as introduced by Constance Applebee in 1901, then by swimming, and track and field events.

The first attempt to guide women's sports on the national level was in 1907, when the Women's Basketball Guide of that year announced that a Women's Rules Committee had been formed. From this group developed the Women's Athletic Committee which later became the National Section for Women's Athletics, and now, since 1957, is the Division for Girls and Women's Sports of the AAHPER, a department of the National Education Association. The task of those working in this large division is to set the pattern for the conduct of games and sports for girls and women in this country, draw up and revise game rules, publish official guides, as well as offer many services to the many leaders of girls and women's activities. Dr. Rachael Bryant, National Consultant in Girls and Women's Sports for the AAHPER and NEA, is now doing much to further the development of good practices, strong and effective leadership, and more meaningful programs, not only to those in schools but also in the Y. W. and Y.M.C.A., community centers, and other youth and adult service agencies.

Found below are the specific standards for guiding competition for girls and women in the various team and individual sports which the Division for Girls and Women's Sports uphold.[1]

Leadership.   Administrators, teachers or coaches, and players should be primarily concerned with the outcomes of the program.

1. The Administrator is directly responsible for:
   a. Selecting qualified women to direct the program
   b. Providing facilities, equipment, and finances to carry on the program
   c. Providing equal use of facilities and equipment for boys and girls
   d. Providing health safeguards
   e. Guiding publicity to emphasize the educational and recreational values of the program

2. The teacher or coach is responsible for:
   a. Having a thorough knowledge of the games and their rules and strategy
   b. Providing opportunity for all girls to play
   c. Encouraging skillful play for full enjoyment of the game
   d. Emphasizing the importance of health examinations
   e. Developing intelligent leadership and wise following among the players
   f. Conducting activities on a sound competitive basis
   g. Exemplifying those traits which she tries to develop in others

3. The player is responsible for her own conduct as shown through:
   a. Intelligent health practices
   b. Courtesy, fair play, and good sportsmanship
   c. High quality leadership within her own group
   d. Emotional control in all game situations
   e. Playing to the best of her ability

Health.   Provision must be made for careful supervision of the health of all players.

1. Participants must have periodic health examinations
2. After serious illness or injury, written permission from a physician should be required to resume participation
3. First aid supplies should be available at practices and games
4. Participation during the menstrual period should be determined on the basis of individual differences
5. Equipment and facilities should be hygienic and safe

---

[1] Reprinted by permission of Division for Girls and Women's Sports and the American Association of Health, Physical Education, and Recreation from *Desirable Practices in Sports for Girls and Women.*

6. Players should be removed from activity if they are injured or over-fatigued, or show evidence of emotional instability

Publicity.   A planned program of publicity should present interesting information on the program, its standards, aims, and outcomes. The publicity should be carefully interpreted to newswriters, parents, community leaders, the players, and their associates. Publicity should stress:

a. The recreational and social values of sports rather than the winning of championships.
b. Achievements of the groups and teams rather than those of individuals.

THE PARTICIPANTS

The following age classification in grouping girls and women, and suggested activities for each group as endorsed by the Division for Girls and Women's Sports include:[2]

10 to 12—*Pre-adolescent.* (Formative stage, seeking peer status and approval, interest increasing in simple team games such as dodgeball and informal grouping such as hiking. Suggest sex segregation as little as possible for team play except where there are marked differences in strength and endurance.)

13 to 15—*Early Adolescent;* 15 to 18—*Late Adolescent.* (Making up the junior and senior high school, this group increases in height and weight rapidly, inaccuracy of movement decreasing, becoming sexually mature, seeking freedom and adventure yet needing surrounding cluster of gang friends. Awkwardness decreases with age, as does insecurity with successful experience, greatly needs approval, understanding, likes team and individual games requiring increasing skill, needs many coeducational game experiences.)

19 to 24—*Young Adult.* (Slower, more refined development, period of high physical efficiency, begins to participate more in community life and feels personally more responsibility to society, takes part in more service projects, has multiplicity of interests, prefers coeducational activities.)

24 and Over—*Mature Adult.* (Increasingly aware of responsibilities to self and others, now matured with fairly definite motor patterns well fixed, vigorous activity is satisfying. Prefers to learn new skills, needs diversified activities in many areas, wants to keep fit, plays mostly for exercise and fun, will seek out places to play and help others have improved areas for recreation.)

[2] Materials reprinted by permission of DGWS from *Standards in Sports for Girls and Women.*

PLAY FACILITIES

I. Public
   a. Schools
   b. Community centers
      1. national
      2. state
      3. local
   c. Parks
II. Semi-Private
   a. Churches
   b. YWCA-YWHA
   c. Denominational Community Centers
   d. Girl Scouts, Girl Reserves, Camp Fire Girls

III. Private
   a. Clubs
   b. Industrial play spaces
   c. Individual play spaces

OUTDOOR FACILITIES

I. Archery ranges
II. Beaches and swimming facilities (including outdoor pools)
III. Bicycle paths
IV. Bowling greens
V. Bridle paths
VI. Camps
VII. Courts
   a. Badminton
   b. Handball
   c. Shuffleboard
   d. Squash
   e. Tennis
   f. Volleyball
VIII. Field houses
IX. Fishing streams
X. Golf links
XI. Horseshoe pitching space
XII. Ice skating rinks
XIII. Jumping pits
XIV. Parks
XV. Playfields
   a. Softball
   b. Basketball
   c. Football (used for other games by girls)
   d. Hockey
   e. Soccer
   f. Speedball
   g. Lacrosse
   h. Volleyball
XVI. Playgrounds (including swings, slides, trapeze, and other playground equipment)
XVII. Roller skating rinks
XVIII. Running tracks
XIX. Ski slides
XX. Trails

INDOOR FACILITIES

I. Archery ranges
II. Softball diamonds
III. Bowling Alleys
IV. Courts
   a. Badminton
   b. Basketball
   c. Handball
   d. Shuffleboard
   e. Squash
   f. Tennis
   g. Volleyball
V. Ice skating rinks
VI. Rifle ranges
VII. Roller skating rinks
VIII. Swimming pools

THE PROGRAM

Types of Activities
(10 to 12 years)

I. Ball Games
   A. Softball Types
      1. Liberty Bat Ball
      2. Schlag Ball
      3. Long Ball
      4. Tap Baseball
      5. Softball
      6. Talley Ball
   B. Basketball Types
      1. Dodgeball
      2. Endball
      3. Captain Ball
   C. Field Types
      1. Line Soccer
      2. Corner Kickball
   D. Net Games (without rackets)
      1. Newcomb
      2. Bounceball
      3. Ring or Deck Tennis
      4. Cageball
   E. Net Games (with rackets)
      1. Paddle Tennis
      2. Table Tennis

II. Track Events
   A. Running
      1. Short Dashes (up to 40 yds)
      2. Relays
   B. Standard Broad Jump
   C. Throwing
      1. Baseball — Distance
      2. Soccer Ball—Distance
III. Swimming
   A. Short Distance (20 to 40 yds)
   B. Strokes for Form
   C. Water Games
   D. Simple Diving
IV. Miscellaneous
   A. Rope Jumping
   B. Hiking
   C. Bicycle Riding
   D. Roller Skating
   E. Coasting
   F. Ice Skating

(13 to 18 years)

I. Ball Games
  A. Softball Types
      1. Schlag Ball
      2. Hit Pin Baseball
      3. Soccer Baseball
      4. Softball
  B. Basketball Types
      1. Dodgeball
      2. Endball
      3. Captain Ball
      4. Pinball
      5. Nine Court Basket-
         ball
      6. Basketball
  C. Field Types
      1. Corner Kickball
      2. Fieldball
      3. Soccer
      4. Speedball
      5. Field Hockey
      6. Lacrosse
  D. Net Games (without
     rackets)
      1. Newcomb
      2. Giant Volleyball
      3. Ring or Deck Ten-
         nis
      4. Volleyball
  E. Net Games (with
     rackets)
      1. Paddle Tennis
      2. Table Tennis
      3. Badminton
      4. Tennis
  F. Wall Games
      1. Handball
      2. Squash

II. Track Events
  A. Running
      1. Dashes (up to 75
         yds)
      2. Low Hurdle Relays
  B. Jumping
      1. Standing   Hop,
         Step
      2. Standing   Broad
         Jump
  C. Throwing
      1. Basketball — Dis-
         tance
      2. Baseball — Dis-
         tance
      3. Shot Put (6 to 8
         lbs)*
      4. Discus Throw*
      5. Javelin Throw*
III. Swimming
  A. For Speed (up to 50
     yds)
  B. Strokes for Form
  C. Types of Diving (high
     dive   not   recom-
     mended)
  D. Water Games
  E. Lifesaving Events
IV. Miscellaneous
  A. Hiking
  B. Skating (Roller, Ice)
  C. Coasting
  D. Horseshoe Pitching
  E. Bowling
  F. Shuffleboard
  G. Horseback Riding
  H. Archery
  I. Golf
  J. Bicycle Riding
  K. Fencing

* Not recommended for junior high school girls.

(19 to 24 years)

I. Ball Games
   A. Softball Types
      1. Hit Pin Baseball
      2. Softball
   B. Basketball
   C. Field Types
      1. Soccer
      2. Fieldball
      3. Speedball
      4. Field Hockey
      5. Lacrosse
   D. Net Ball Games (without rackets)
      1. Ring or Deck Tennis
      2. Giant Volleyball
      3. Volleyball
   E. Net Ball Games (with rackets)
      1. Paddle Tennis
      2. Table Tennis
      3. Badminton
      4. Tennis
   F. Wall Games
      1. Handball
      2. Squash
II. Track Events
   A. Dashes
   B. Relays
   C. Hurdling (2 ft.)
   D. Jumping
      1. Broad Jump
      2. High Jump
      3. Running Hop, Step and Jump

   E. Throwing
      1. Baseball — Distance
      2. Shot Put
      3. Discus Throw
      4. Javelin Throw
III. Swimming
   A. For Speed—up to 100 yds
   B. Water Games
   C. Diving
   D. Lifesaving Events
IV. Miscellaneous
   A. Hiking
   B. Skating (Roller, Ice)
   C. Coasting
   D. Horseshoe Pitching
   E. Bowling
   F. Shuffleboard
   G. Horseback Riding
   H. Archery
   I. Golf
   J. Fencing
   K. Bicycle Riding
   L. Boating
      1. Sail
      2. Ice
      3. Canoeing
   M. Skiing

Although, ideally, a sports and games program should be offered to all participants at regularly scheduled times and be held outdoors whenever possible when vital energy is at a high level, there are also great values to be found in opening up facilities at odd hours so that any spontaneously-formed group—such as two would-be badminton players, or a single, lonesome individual looking for companionship and an opportunity to exercise for fun—can be served. Fortunately, today more and more schools are opening their facilities and furnishing or renting equipment, and providing supervisors or teachers for after work or after school fun.

Leadership is the real key to the success and value of any physical education or recreation program, whether it be furnished by a school, or any other organization. The real test of the program is in the enjoyment and benefit the participant receives from taking part in it. Any well rounded and conducted program planned to include the previously recommended activities for girls and women, and conducted according to standards devised by the Division for Girls and Women's Sports will have great value, not only to those engaging in it, but to society as well.

DISCUSSION QUESTIONS

1. Why should teams composed of girls or women players be coached by women? Support your answer by giving five, well-thought-through answers you would endorse as an educator.
2. It has been said that the social values inherent in play are more important for each one to discover today than ever before. Discuss this statement in light of a summary of any five articles you read in the current issue of *TIME* magazine or your daily newspaper. In view of your conclusions, would you agree or disagree with this statement, recalling from history the many problems our ancestors found in our own development as a nation.
3. Give a brief, oral report based upon any of the suggested readings.
4. Look through any official DGWS Sports Guide. Analyze it from the standpoint of a publication designed primarily to help instructors better understand the sport they are teaching and how to do a fine job of coaching it.
5. List the personal and professional qualifications a teacher of girls and women's sports should possess. How many of these do you have? How can you obtain those you do not possess or develop those in which you are the weakest?

SUGGESTED READINGS

AAHPER, *Report of the Joint Committee on Athletic Competition for Children of Elementary and Junior High School Age; Desirable Competition for Children*, Washington, D.C., 1952.

Cassidy, Rosalind, and Kozman, Hilda: *Counseling Girls in a Changing Society*, New York, McGraw-Hill Book Company, Inc., 1947.

Cozen, Frederick, and Stumpf, Florence: *Sports in American Life*, Chicago, University of Chicago Press, 1953.

Davis, Charles: Education for Sportsmanship, *Journal of AAHPER*, 26:36, June 1955.

Duncan, Margaret, and Johnson, Ralph: *Introduction to Physical Education*, New York, Prentice-Hall Book Company, Inc., 1954.

Fahr, Samuel: Legal Liability for Athletic Injury, *Journal of AAHPER*, 29:12, February, 1958.

Fitzgerald, Gerald: *Leadership in Recreation*, New York, The Ronald Press, 1951.

Foehrenback, Leonore: Why Girls Choose After School Sports, *Journal of AAHPER*, 24:34, June, 1953.

Gallagher, J. Roswell: Athletic Injuries Among Adolescents: Their Incidence and Types in Various Sports, *Research Quarterly*, 19:198, October 1948.

Lawther, John: *Psychology of Coaching*, New York, Prentice-Hall Book Company, Inc., 1952.

Mitchell, Elmer: *Sports for Recreation—How to Play Them*, New York, The Ronald Press, 1949.

Suggested Code of Ethics for Teachers of Physical Education, *Journal of AAHPER*, 21:10, June, 1950.

Murray, Ruth L., and Hussey, Delia P.: *From Student to Teacher in Physical Education*, New York, Prentice-Hall Book Company, Inc., 1959.

22

Competition

Under wholesome conditions, competition for girls and women *can* be a rich, educational experience. However, all who wish to take part in the program should be given an opportunity to do so, instead of limiting competition to only a few, highly skilled players. The intramural program should reach the majority of students who desire to play with and compete against others, either as an individual or a team member. The extramural program according to the recommendations of the Division for Girls and Women's Sports of the AAHPER, should provide for competition among teams from local schools, community centers, institutions, clubs, or other such organizations in the form of a *Sports Day* (each school or other team competes as a unit) ; *Play Day* (team members are made up from all invited units) ; *Telegraphic Meets* (results are compared by mail or wire), and other invitational events (such as a symposium, jamboree, game, or match).

The following list of standards of desirable practices governing athletic activities for girls is adapted from the DGWS recommendations. The program of athletic activities should:

1. Be based upon the recognition of individual differences (age, physique, interests, ability, experience, health) and the stage of maturity (physiological, emotional, social) of the participants.
2. Be determined by:
   a. The evaluation of the activity in its present and future use.
   b. The classification of individuals in ability from beginner to expert.
   c. The development from simple to complex activity.
3. Provide opportunity for each player to lead according to her merit and to follow according to her willingness and ability to adapt herself to others and to a common end.

4. Promote the acquisition of skill by using sound and varied methods.
5. Schedule regular play periods of limited length, at frequent intervals, at a time of day when energy is at a high level.
6. Provide for the selection of members of all teams so that they play against those of approximately the same ability and maturity.
7. Be taught, coached, and officiated by qualified women *whenever* and *wherever* possible.
8. Provide officials whose decisions are sound, consistent, and impartial.
9. Include the use of official rules authorized by the Division of Girls and Women's Sports of the American Association for Health, Physical Education, and Recreation.
10. Stimulate the participants to play for the enjoyment of playing and not for tangible rewards or artificial incentives.
11. Include a variety of sports, both team and individual, and provide opportunity, for all girls wishing to participate, to become a member of a team in those sports for which teams are organized.
12. Promote informal social events in connection with competition.
13. Secure written parental permission for minors engaging in any extramural competition.
14. Educate girls and women concerning appropriate costumes for sports.
15. Limit extramural competition to a small geographic area.
16. Provide safe transportation in bonded carriers.
17. Provide a program of competition for girls separate from that arranged for boys (eliminating such events as double header games or "curtains-raisers"), except in those activities in which boys and girls are encouraged to play together on mixed teams.
18. Limit the total length of sports seasons. The maximum number of recommendations pertaining to the above factors may be obtained in the "Specific Standards" referred to in each sport guide.

It is recommended that the junior high school intramurals be a natural outgrowth of the total physical education program, conducted largely on a round robin basis, and that all students be encouraged to take part in them. Class tournaments played during after school hours usually can draw most of the students. In the senior high school the program should likewise be a natural outgrowth of the physical education class, and be led by qualified instructors in an environment beneficial to all. The school may arrange interscholastic competition, as previously defined, if the rest of the program will not suffer from having done so, and the following conditions are met:[1]

1. The health of the players is carefully supervised.
2. Girls and women are not exploited for the purpose of promotion.

[1] *Standards in Sports for Girls and Women,* Division for Girls and Women's Sports. AAHPER, Washington 6, D.C., pp. 51–52.

3. The salary, retention, or promotion of the instructor is not dependent upon the outcome of the game.
4. Qualified women teach, coach, and officiate wherever and whenever possible, and, in any case, the professional training and experience of the leader meets established standards.
5. Approved, published DGWS rules are used.
6. Schedules are limited so as not to exceed maximums set in DGWS Standards for Specific Sports as defined in DGWS Sports Guides.
7. Games, where possible, are scheduled separately from the boys' games.
8. The program, including insurance for players, is financed by school funds and allocations of the budget rather than gate receipts.
9. Provision is made by the school for safe transportation by bonded carriers, with a chaperone responsible to the school, accompanying each group.

Competition for women students in colleges and universities should largely be of the intramural type and cover a wide range of offerings, and include many opportunities for individuals or groups to take part in co-educational activities. However, if the schools wish to take part in inter-collegiate competition, the following standards should be adhered to:[2]

1. Competition should be conducted in conformance with the DGWS standards of health, participation, leadership, and publicity.
2. They should not curtail the intramural and informal extramural programs of the sponsoring institution or the institution entering participants.
3. They should not include events in which women participate:
   a. As members of men's intercollegiate athletic teams.
   b. In touch football exhibition games, or any other activities of similar type.
   c. Either with or against men in activities not suitable to competition between men and women, such as basketball, touch football, speed-ball, soccer, hockey, or lacrosse.

TYPES OF TOURNAMENTS

Elimination Tournaments. Single and winner-loser tournaments are easily drawn up by using the perfect power of two if the number of contestants is 4, 8, 16, 32, etc. However, when there are more than the perfect power of two, byes are added until this is reached. The number of byes should equal the difference between the number of competitors and the next higher power of two. When fifteen are entered, there will be one bye $(16 - 15 = 1)$, etc.

[2] *Ibid.*, p. 52.

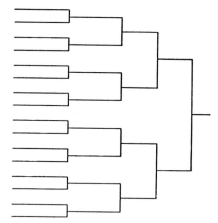

Figure No. 22–1.   Elimination Tournament.

If more than 25 players are entered, two tournaments are recommended rather than one. The best players should be seeded, and if there are four players on teams who are almost equally matched, numbers 1 and 4 should be in the first and eighth positions of the upper bracket, and 2 and 4 in the ninth and sixteenth positions.

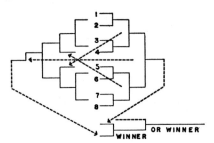

Figure 22–2.   Double Elimination Tournament.

In the double elimination tournament, no team is eliminated until it loses twice. The winners move to the right in the first elimination, and to the left in the second elimination. If the winner of the first elimination, however, loses to the winner of the second elimination, she has lost but once, and still another game must be played by the two before a winner is declared.

Round Robin Tournament.   Each team plays every other team once, with the final standing determined on a percentage basis.

The following formula will apply to any number of teams, whether the total is odd or even. With an odd number of teams there is the same number of rounds; with an even number of teams there is one less number of games than teams.

For an Uneven Number of Teams.   Assign to each team a number and then use only the figures in drawing the schedule. For example, in a league with 7 teams start with 1, putting down figures in the following order:

7	6	5	4	3	2	1
6–1	5–7	4–6	3–5	2–4	1–3	7–2
5–2	4–1	3–7	2–6	1–5	7–4	6–3
4–3	3–2	2–1	1–7	7–6	6–5	5–4

Note that the figures go down on the right side and up on the left. Number 7 draws a bye in the first round and the others play as indicated. With an odd number of teams, all numbers revolve and the last number each time draws a bye.

For an Even Number of Teams. With an even number of teams the plan is the same except the position of No. 1 remains stationary and the other numbers revolve about it until the original combination is reached. For example, with 8 teams:

1–2	1–8	1–7	1–6	1–5	1–4	1–3
8–3	7–2	6–8	5–7	4–6	3–5	2–4
7–4	6–3	5–2	4–8	3–7	2–6	8–5
6–5	5–4	4–3	3–2	2–8	8–7	7–6

Two things only must be remembered: (1) With an even number of teams, No. 1 remains stationary and the other numbers revolve. (2) With an odd number of teams, all numbers revolve and the last number each time draws a bye.

TEAM 1
TEAM 2
TEAM 3
TEAM 4
etc.

Ladder Tournament. Teams or players are arranged in ladder formation. Any player may challenge another person directly above. If she defeats her opponent, her name is moved up. The final winner stays in the first position longest.

Figure No. 22–3. Ladder Tournament.

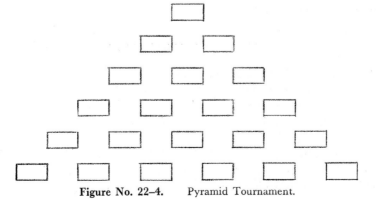

Figure No. 22–4. Pyramid Tournament.

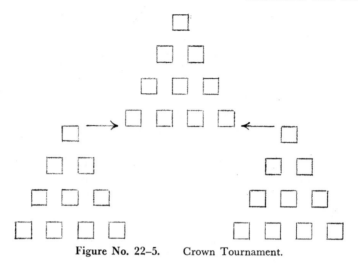

Figure No. 22–5.   Crown Tournament.

The Pyramid.   The number of spaces on the bottom line should be equal to one-half the number of contestants. In the beginning, no contestant has a position on the pyramid, but gains this by challenging another to a match. The winner then takes a place on the lowest pyramid. The loser must challenge another contestant and win before she can gain a position on the pyramid. Contestants advance to the next highest level by winning a match from someone on the same level. Losers change places with the winners. Advancement can be made only when there is a vacant spot on the next higher level (or, if there are no vacant spots on that level, by challenging to the next higher level). The winner arrives at the top first, or can be the one who stays there longest.

The Crown Tournament.   Made up of several pyramids, each of ten spaces at different levels, challenging is vertical within each pyramid and horizontal among pyramids. The winner advances first to the top of the highest pyramid. Players may gain their needed first position at the bottom of the horizontal pyramids by lot, challenging another, or by assignment with the better players placed there.

PLAYER CLASSIFICATION

Contestants may be classified according to age, height, weight, skill, physical examinations, or skill tests for competititve purpose. Care must be taken to assure that players are as equally matched as possible, and that every safety precaution has been taken in assigning groups to compete against each other in specific areas. The teams should elect their own captains by secret ballot, after listening to a brief talk from their teacher on the duties and qualifications of a good leader, followed by a short student discussion of the main points stressed. Throughout the entire competitive program, emphasis should be placed upon having fun, as well as winning and good sportsmanship.

POINT SYSTEM

A simple system should be devised for keeping points that is not time consuming, yet is an accurate one. Winners should receive the greatest number of points with runners-up the second most, and each participant given entry points for playing in one or more tournament games. The system should be kept on a yearly basis, and will, when used accumulatively over a longer period of time, increase participation. All records might well be kept by elected student intramural managers under close teacher guidance and supervision.

ELIGIBILITY RULES

Although each organization should draw up its own eligibility rules, such a group working on this project should be aware that rules (1) are primarily for the protection of the players, and (2) cover not only participation eligibility but also health requirements, forfeits, penalties for rule infractions, and player conduct. All who take part in the program should have permission to do so by a physician, after having had a physical examination. Those with physical or other types of defects must not be allowed to compete in strenuous sports against more capable and vigorous opponents, but, rather, they should have their own intramural program geared to their limitations. Such a program might include table tennis, shuffleboard, archery, or other similar types of non-combative sports.

AWARDS

If awards are given at the completion of a season semester, or school year they should be simple and inexpensive, for the major portion of any intramural budget should be spent on equipment rather than on costly cups, charm bracelets, or other awards. In granting the awards, it should be remembered that every student should have an equal opportunity to earn one. Rotating trophies with winners' names printed on them or on a plate have value, and their use is one way to keep the cost of awards down. A Sportsmanship Trophy should be given yearly and be as valued, or even more so, among the players as the first place trophy. An awards banquet is especially attractive to girls and women. It is suggested that the occasion become a most special one to which distinguished guests are invited, and that all who attend it be more dressed up than they are when attending most school functions. Colored slides or action films taken during the season when shown at such a banquet add greatly to a program interest, and do much to acquaint the school president, deans, the principal, or fellow teachers with the importance, scope, and value of the program. A student committee under the guidance of a selected representative (usually the G.A.A. or

W.R.A. president) and the instructor should plan the awards banquet around a unique theme yearly, and the occasion should become a highlighted, eagerly looked-forward-to occasion by every player. Such a dinner can be the "bright red cherry on the vanilla sundae."

it the best one?

DISCUSSION QUESTIONS

1. Discuss the place of intramurals in the total physical education program, and in the total educational program of the school.
2. Why should all who participate have a physical examination? Obtain several copies of such examination blanks and choose the best one. Why do you consider
3. Plan on paper an intramural program for a group of 30 girls on the senior high school level who have physical or other defects which prohibit them from taking part in the regular program.
4. A play day is built around a specific theme and all activities are re-named in light of it. Plan on paper a play day in detail for eight senior high schools in your city or community.
5. What reasons would you, as an educator, give for allowing (or not allowing) college women to compete on teams against those of neighboring schools.
6. Draw up a double elimination tournament for 28 players.
7. Plan in detail on paper an awards banquet for a high school or college group.

SUGGESTED READINGS

AAHPER, *Physical Education for High School Students,* Washington, D.C., 1955.

AAHPER, Intramural Conference, Washington, D.C., 1957.

Bunn, John: *The Art of Officiating Sports,* New York, Prentice-Hall Book Company, Inc., 1950.

Boyden, Douglas, and Burton, Roger: *Staging Successful Tournaments,* New York, Association Press, 1957.

Forsythe, Charles: *The Administration of High School Athletics,* New York, Prentice-Hall Book Company, Inc., 1948.

Loken, Newton, and Dypuick, Otis: *Cheerleading and Marching Bands,* New York, A. S. Barnes, 1945.

National Section on Women's Athletics, *Standards in Athletics for Girls and Women,* Washington, D.C., AAHPER.

Vannier, Maryhelen, and Fait, Hollis: *Teaching Physical Education in Secondary Schools,* Philadelphia, W. B. Saunders Company, 1957.

23

Co-recreational Activities

Co-recreational activities play an important role in any well rounded sports program for girls and women. Since many splendid resources for games, leadership tips, and party ideas can be found in the Suggested Readings at the end of this chapter, we shall be concerned mainly with those newer co-recreational sports which have great appeal to youth.[1] Certainly all young-sters, teenagers, and college students need many opportunities provided for finding fellowship and good clean fun with the opposite sex. Likewise, youth seeks assistance in developing democratic leadership, skills, techniques for getting approval for positive instead of negative actions, and the know-how for fitting into, as well as contributing to, groups. Consequently, the wise teen leader will help each person accept and carry out responsibilities in planning for her own fun and that of her increasing circle of friends. In co-recreational sports, girls as well as boys can, and do, learn the vital life lessons of give and take. They broaden and deepen their values of right and wrong, good and bad, as well as develop insight into personal strengths and weaknesses.

AGE CHARACTERISTICS

Junior high schoolers crave much activity, yet fatigue easily. Boys are not as keen to play either with or against girls as they are later, although the latter are more than eager for a chance to do so. This age group, especially, needs much individual help and encouragement from an admired leader with great patience, skill, and understanding. These youngsters should be given increased responsibilities—in situations set up for them around their limitations, as well as strengths—as young would-be democratic leaders or as longing-to-be-popular group members. Skill and equipment games are of special interest to high schoolers, but since their interest span is not as long as it will be later, they bore easily and "burn out" fast. Outdoor activities

[1] Most of the novelty games found in each chapter can also be played by co-recreational groups. If mixed teams are used, boys should guard boys.

such as hiking, camping, tennis, and water sports are especially popular with them.

Senor high students are "live wires" looking for fun, adventure fringed by danger, and are anxious to get a taste of forbidden fruit. Although all too often they are lumped together as "teen age delinquents" or "the wild ones," most individuals in this age group often are desperately in need of adult leaders they can admire, respect, go to for advice, and whose behavior they can copy. Even though they desire wholesome fun in their relationships with the opposite sex, they often seek activities of the opposite nature in order not to be different, or stand up against their gang in order to defend their own fast-developing concept of what is right and wrong. Since many of them "go steady" at this age, individual sports have a strong appeal, yet team games can be great fun too, especially when each competing unit is made up of players of both sexes. Many of the girls still prefer to compete in sports with girls only, and do develop great and often lasting loyalty for their friends and teammates during this period. These eager teenagers especially like to show-off skills and stand out as the best in any activity.

College-age fun is more sophisticated, often less strenuous, and more skilled. Yet ironically enough, these students often get a "charge" out of playing that "kid stuff" again. Since loyalty to the sub-group, such as the sorority, fraternity, or club, is intense, co-recreational sports should be played among brother and sister social groups with teams composed of girls and their "steadies" or socially accepted friends. A well equipped lounge with easy-to-play games such as table tennis, or tossing contests usually becomes a favorite, especially if refreshments can be obtained there at little cost. Work service projects, such as building a tennis court in the slum area, retreats, and weekend camps are all popular with student groups. Increased couple activity is a must at the college level.

Some strenuous co-recreational sports which appeal to youth from junior high school through college include:

Box Hockey	Volleyball	Cycling
Hiking	Skating	Hosteling
Boating	Skiing	Paddle Tennis
Water Skiing	Tobogganing	Gymnastics
Skin and Scuba Diving	Softball	Ping Pong
Swimming	Tether Ball	Rowing
Tennis	Badminton	Water Polo

Less strenuous girl and boy activities popular with these age groups are:

Fishing	Curling	Fencing
Skill Games	Bowling	Fly and Bait Casting
Outdoor Cooking	Croquet	Golf
Darts	Horseshoes	Riflery
Archery	Picnics	Sailing
Archery Golf	Dancing	Trap and Skeet Shooting

ACTIVITIES

Croquet.   Played with a wooden ball and mallet, the object of this game is to be the first to hit the ball through all the arches up and back the court. Simplified rules include:

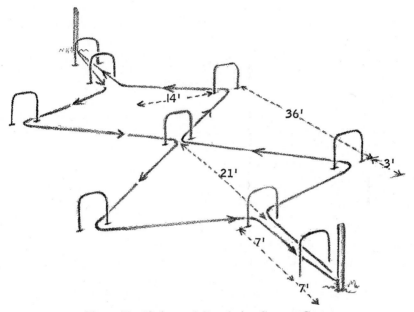

Figure No. 23–1.   A Regulation Croquet Court.

1. Each player alternates turns hitting the ball, starting a mallet's distance in front of the starting stake and attempting to drive the ball through the first two wickets.
2. Each player is given another hit for going through an arch, hitting another's ball, or the turning stake at the opposite end of the court. Two more hits are earned if the ball goes through both two first arches, but if through any other two arches, the player has the right of a mallet's length ahead in any direction, plus one stroke.
3. One loses a hit for playing out of turn.
4. Each ball must go through each numbered arch in proper progression.
5. A ball driven out of bounds may be put back on the boundary line where it went off.
6. One missing the ball entirely with the mallet may have a second turn.
7. If one's ball hits another, the owner may put it next to the one struck, step on it while she hits her own ball hard enough to send the other's far down the court or out of position, or she may measure a mallet's distance in any direction and hit her ball from there.

Shuffleboard.   Played by two or four, the game object is to propel discs, using a cue, onto scoring diagrams at the opposite end of the court

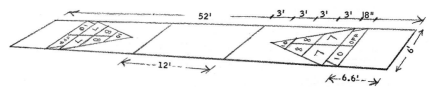

Figure No. 23–2.   A Regulation Shuffleboard Court.

in order to score, or prevent one's opponent from scoring. Simplified rules are:

1. The red disc is shot first and then the two players alternate shooting black and red discs until all are shot from one end of the court, then the other.
2. In doubles after all discs are played at the head of the court, play starts at the foot with red leading. Red player and a black one stand at each end of the court, alternating turns, each shooting 2 discs.
3. A game consists of 50, 75, or 100 points.
4. After players have shot all four discs, score all within the court area but do not count those on any line.

Scoop Throw

Equipment.   Plastic Scoop and Fun Ball.[2]

Game Object.   Using in turn an overhand throw, underhand throw, sidearm throw, snap throw, overhead catch, underhand catch, cover retrieve, and the sidearm retrieve as shown, arrange couples in competing units with each trying to score 10, 15, 25, or 30 successful throws and catches first. Have players return to count 1 when missing.

Scoop Goalball

Equipment.   One scoop for each player and one Fun Ball. The goal tender may use a Scoop, Safe-T-Bat[3] or both.

Playing Area.   Marked as shown, with dimensions changed according to available space and age of players.

Number of Players.   Five to ten on a team, with boys guarding and playing only against opposite boys on the team, all girls against each other.

Rules
1. Line up teams on each side of the field as in soccer, speedball, or hockey.
2. Play starts by the offensive center's flip of the ball to a teammate.
3. Players move the ball back and forth downfield by passing or intercepting passes.

---

[2] Available from the Cosom Industries, Minneapolis, Minnesota along with a booklet, *26 New Games for Safe Indoor and Outdoor Play.*
[3] Available from the Cosom Industries, Minneapolis, Minnesota, or most leading sporting goods companies.

Figure No. 23–3. Scoop Throw Techniques.

4. One may take only three steps while carrying the ball in the scoop.
5. Body contact is prohibited.
6. Players cannot hold or trap the ball on the ground, play it when they are not on their feet, touch it with their hands, dribble or juggle it to themselves, or play it in their own or opponent's goal crease (except the goal tender).
7. On the offensive, the goal tender may advance as far as midfield. When tending goal, she may deflect a shot with the scoop or hand, but only when in her own zone.
8. An out of bounds ball is put into play by the opposing team using a scoop throw. If the ball goes out of bounds through the goal crease, the goal tender puts it back in play.
9. On a penalty shot all except the player fouled and the goal tender stand outside the neutral area.

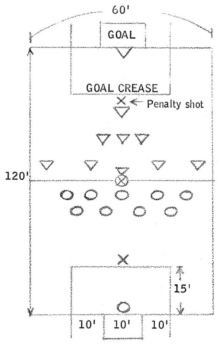

Figure No. 23–4.

10. Fouls which allow the fouled team to take a penalty shot are:
    a. Slashing or hitting an opponent's scoop
    b. Excessive, wild scoop swinging
    c. Hitting an opponent with a scoop
    d. Playing the ball in own or opponent's goal crease
    e. The goal tender leaving the penalty crease when a penalty shot is attempted at her goal
    f. Having more players on the field than the other team
    g. Interfering with an opponent's play by holding her scoop or her, running or falling in front of her to prevent her moving
11. If a penalty shot is unsuccessful, the fouled team puts the ball in play at midfield at either side.
12. The ball is given to the opposing team when:
    a. it goes out of bounds
    b. anyone holds it in her scoop over five seconds
    c. anyone touches it
    d. anyone takes more than three steps with it.
    e. anyone holds it on the ground or plays it while she is on the ground
    f. it is kicked, dribbled, or juggled
    g. the goal tender catches it in her hand

    h. anyone enters the goal crease of the opposing team

    i. the goal tender goes over the midfield line

13. An official game is four quarters of 10 minutes each with a three minute rest period between each one and a 10 minute rest between halves.

14. Each goal scores one point.

In-line Fun Ball

Equipment.   One scoop for each outfield or defensive player, one Fun Ball, one Safe-T-Bat.

Number of Players.   Seven to ten on each team. 1st, 2nd, 3rd basemen, fielders, and a catcher.

Playing Area.   As shown, a softball diamond with foul lines out from home plate. On a regular ball diamond, the In-Line baseline should run through the pitcher's box, second base, and out into center field. 1st, 2nd, and 3rd bases (or goal area) should be 35 feet apart.

Rules

1. Players must catch and throw the Fun Ball with a scoop at all times.
2. The batter places the Fun Ball on the top end of a Safe-T-Bat, shoves it upward, hits it as it comes down, and then runs toward 1st base. She does not have to swing at every ball, but she may never bunt one. Three swings put her out, or if she hits two foul balls, or if her pop foul is caught.
3. Baserunners are forced or tagged out.
4. No runner can overrun 1st or 2nd base, but if she does, must continue to the next base taking a chance on being put out. Once she leaves a base, she cannot return to it. There is no leading off or stealing of bases.
5. Scoring is as in softball; nine or less innings may be played.

Ball

Figure No. 23–5.   Batting Procedure for In-line Fun Ball.

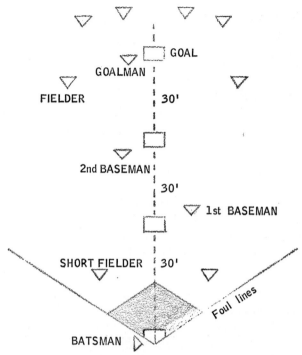

Figure No. 23–6.   Court Dimensions—In-line Fun Ball.

Bocce.   Bocce is played like the game of Bowling on the Green and is Italy's most popular outdoor recreation. The object is for the first player to roll her large Bocce ball as close to the Jack (Palino) as possible. Her opponent then tries to get her ball closer to the Jack than the first player and they continue in turn until all the balls have been played.

A point is scored for each ball of the same player or team that is closest to the Jack of all of the opponents' balls. Winning score in singles is 15 points and 18 points for doubles or team play. In case of a tie, an additional frame is played until the tie is broken.

Rules
  1. The game is played with eight large Bocce balls and one small ball, called the "Jack" or "Palino" which is the "Target" of the game.
  2. It is played by two teams and each team may consist of one to four players, with both teams having an equal number of players. When played as singles, each player plays with two large Bocce balls.
  3. The game starts with any member of a team (chosen by lot) rolling the Jack as follows: player must stand between line A and B and should release the Jack (rolled) before line B, but she may advance after releasing the ball not farther than line C (to step on a line is considered as passing it). The Jack must stop beyond line F, but not after line B, of the finishing half of the court. It must also not go out of bounds or stop closer than one foot to the borders. Any

violation of the above rules is a foul and a member of the opposing team rolls the Jack. If she also violates the rules, the Jack is placed at the center of line F of the finishing half.

4. If, during the game, the Jack is knocked before line F of the finishing half, or out of bounds, then the frame is considered invalid and must be started again.

5. The team which rolled the Jack for the first time should start the game and the winner of each frame starts the following frame. Players must follow their proper turn throughout the game. A player must use all her balls at each turn, except in a game of singles, then each player uses two balls at each turn.

6. There are three kinds of shots permitted in Bocce as follows:

   (1) *Standard Shot.* The player must stand between lines A and B of the starting half and roll the ball toward the Jack. She must release the ball before line B, but she may advance not further than line C, after she releases the ball. The ball must stop at least on or beyond line F, of the finishing half, must not run out of bounds, and must

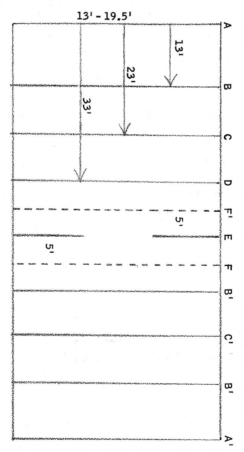

Figure No. 23–7.   Court Dimensions—Bocce.

not hit or move any other ball or the Jack on the court. The object of this shot is merely to get as close as possible to the Jack.

If the ball thrown fails to comply with the above regulations, it is disqualified and removed from the court. All balls moved by such a foul shot must be returned to their original positions.

(2) *Call Shot.* The player must stand between lines A and C and release her ball before line C, but she may advance not further than line D after she releases the ball. The ball must stop on or beyond line F of the finishing half, and must not run out of bounds.

In this case, however, the player specifies her target beforehand and her ball must hit that target, or at least another ball or the Jack, if they happen to be within one foot of the target named. In the absence of any object within one foot of the target, the player must hit the target itself. The ball must hit the target (or another within one foot) first, before hitting or moving any other ball on the court.

All measurements are made from the outer dimensions of the balls and not the distance between the balls. The ball is disqualified and removed from the court if it does not meet any of the foregoing regulations. All balls (or the Jack) moved by such a foul shot should be returned to their original position and the game resumed. If the shot was good, however, then the balls (or the Jack) moved, shall stand where they lay. All balls knocked out of bounds are disqualified. Also any ball knocked back before line F, of the finishing half is disqualified; and of course, if the Jack is knocked out of bounds, or before line F of the finishing half, the whole frame is invalid and must be repeated.

(3) *Aerial Call Shot.* This is similar to the Call Shot in all respects except that in it the ball is hurled through the air and must land either directly on, or within one foot of, the target named and immediately proceed to hit the target or an object (ball or Jack) within one foot thereof (the original target). The ball must, as in the case of the Call Shot hit the target (or another object within one foot thereof) before hitting or moving any other ball in the court.

Scoring

1. When all the players have used up their balls, measurement is made of the distance of the balls from the Jack, measuring from the outer dimensions.
2. Each ball that beats all the other balls of the opposing team, scores one point. In case of a tie between two balls of opposing teams, the balls can cancel each other's score or may be played again by the same players. (An agreement on this point can be reached before the game is started.)
3. In case of a tie between two balls of the same team, then both balls shall score.

4. All balls must be marked in a way so that they can be identified with the player using them. A player may not change her set of balls during the entire game.

5. After the scores are recorded, another frame is started, until one team scores the necessary points to win a game.

6. When there are one or two players on each team, the winning score is 15 points. When there are two or three players on each team, the winning score is 18 points.

7. If at the end of a given frame, both teams score more than the points required to win the game, then the team with the most points is the winner.

8. In case of a tie in such a score, an additional frame is played until the score is broken.

Deck Tennis

Number of Players.   Two or four.

Equipment.   Official deck tennis ring or one improvised out of a heavy rubber hose or rope.

Rules

Singles

1. The players shall stand on opposite sides of the net and the player who is delivering the ring shall be called "The Server" and her opponent "The Receiver."

2. A score is gained only from the service. If the ring is correctly caught and returned by the receiver, but missed by her opponent, no point is scored by either player, but the service changes hands. Thus points can only be scored from the service, and the server continues to serve until she fails to catch the ring in the proper manner, when the service passes to her opponent.

3. The server shall stand on or behind the baseline in delivering her ring, shall not serve until her opponent is ready, and immediately after serving shall move forward into the court to accept the return.

4. The server must not feint or hesitate in delivering her service, or play the ring flat overhand, but must direct the ring with a minimum upward flight of six inches.

5. Only one hand may be used in catching the ring, but the ring may be caught between the hand and the body. On no account may both hands be used, otherwise the player at fault loses the point of service

6. If in delivering the ring the server throws it into the net, no point is scored or lost, but the service passes to her opponent.

7. If in the service the ring shall touch the top of the net and pass over, falling into "dead ground" or outside the boundaries of the court, no point is scored or lost but the service changes hands.

8. The receiver shall have the option of accepting any ring which touches the net in the service and passes over, if she is of the opinion

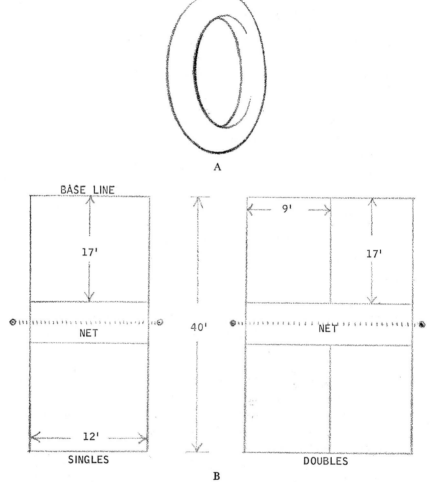

Figure No. 23–8.   A. Deck Tennis Ring; B. Court Markings.

it is likely to fall in her own court. If she does not wish to do so and the ring falls within the boundaries of the court, the service shall be played again. After the service, a ring which passes over after touching the net is playable.

9. The ring must be promptly returned by the player from approximately the receiving position until one side does not make the return, or plays it in "dead ground," or outside the boundaries of the court.

10. The ring must not touch the surface of the court in play and the players' feet must not step into the "dead ground" running alongside the net or outside the boundaries of the court, but their feet may touch the boundary lines, but not cross them.

11. Any ring falling in "dead ground" or outside the boundaries of the court is reckoned against the player by whom it was delivered, but

a ring alighting on any of the boundary lines is regarded as being in play even though it may roll out of court.

12. Each point shall count one and the first player to score 15 points is the winner, unless prior to the commencement of the game it shall have been decided to play Long Sets in which case, when the game has reached 14-all, it is necessary for one to secure an advantage of two points over her opponent, e.g., 17-15, or 18-16, etc.

13. The players shall play the best of three games, changing ends at the close of each game, and if in the third game one player shall score eight points before her opponent scores, (i.e., 8-0), the players shall change ends for the remainder of the game.

Doubles Rules

1. The game of Doubles is played on similar principles to the Singles game except that two persons shall stand on each side of the net and the service alternately passes diagonally to an opponent.

2. The first service shall be from the right hand court, and if the service be won the server then delivers her next ring from the lefthand court, i.e., she shall serve alternately from each court as in Lawn Tennis, her partner standing in the other court.

3. After losing her service the player takes up her position in the right-hand court and thus becomes the first receiver. When the service again changes hands it is taken by the player who has been occupying the lefthand side of the court, and in this way rings are served and received alternately by each player.

4. A ring may be caught by one hand of each partner, but must be returned by one player only, and a ring may be caught and returned by a player even though it may have touched her partner's hand or body, providing, of course, that the ring does not touch the surface of the court before the catch is effected.

Rope Quoits. Played by two or four or any number, with either purchased or improvised equipment.

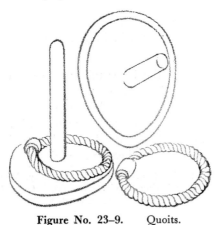

Figure No. 23-9. Quoits.

Rules

1. Each player shoots four quoits per frame, when it is her time to shoot.
2. Opponents then shoot four quoits in the same manner.
3. "Ringers" count five points each. All other quoits remaining on the base count one point each. Quoits that go off the board are lost, and do not score any points.
4. A game consists of 10 frames for each player in the game.
5. The player having the highest score wins.
6. Players' feet must be behind the foul line or designated shooting point, when the quoits is thrown; otherwise the shot is a foul and does not score.
7. The distance from foul line or shooting line to the rope quoit base should be as near 15 feet as possible.
8. Any number of partners may play in a game as in shuffleboard or bowling. Partners having the highest score win.

Sacket

Number of Players.   Nine or more on each team.

Equipment.   One Sacket semi-flat tapered handle bat, a 10 inch rubber covered ball and net backstop.[4]

This game is a form of baseball, cricket, and hockey. It is played like baseball with three bases instead of four. The net serves as automatic catcher and umpire. The ball "breathes" or compresses when hit, but regains its regular shape while in the air. A batter is retired by throwing to the base ahead of a runner, or if the ball is thrown into the net, from behind a field line 30 to 35 feet away, as she attempts to score.

IMPROVISED EQUIPMENT

Creative teachers have learned to improvise and use things in their environment for their program. Unfortunately, few have been trained to build or make equipment which could be used as a substitute for a desired or needed article. In almost every phase of the physical education program, however, certain pieces of inexpensive equipment can be made either by the school mechanical arts or home economics department, by the teacher, or by an interested and carefully supervised group of students. The following items are some that can be improvised for class use; each can be made from scrap or inexpensive materials.

Archery. Finger tabs from tire inner tubes; arm guards from heavy cardboard and rubber bands; quivers from mailing tubes.

Baseball. Home plate, a pitcher's box, backstops from discarded lumber and heavy wire; batting tees made with a heavy wooden base and a hard rubber tube; bases from flattened heavy fire hose held together in base form by nuts and bolts and covered with a heavy material.

---

[4] Available from the Sacket Sporting Goods Company, Beverly Hills, California, The Y.M.C.A. National Purchasing Service, New York City, The House of Harter, Goshen, Indiana, or from most leading sporting goods stores.

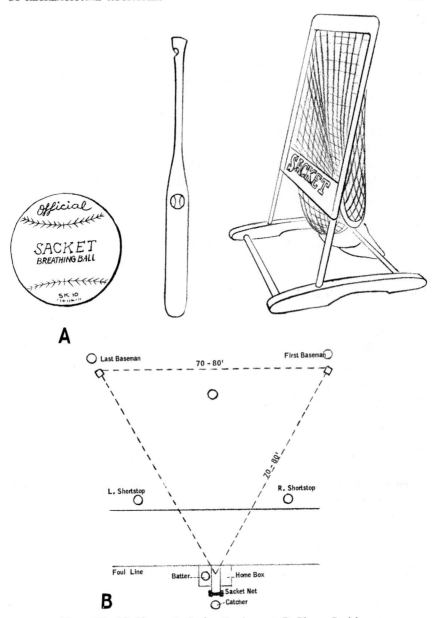

Figure No. 23–10.   A. Sacket Equipment; B. Player Positions.

Basketball. Goals made from heavy metal rings and heavy string nets.
Dance. Music for accompaniment from barrel kegs covered with leather; shakers from rock filled cans; tambourines from tin plates and metal bottle tops; wind and string instruments.
Golf. A miniature course, with tin cans driven into the ground for holes and the game played with hockey or broomsticks with balls of various size.

Gymnastics. A balance beam and Swedish box made from discarded lumber; broomsticks for the stick stunts and balancing; chinning bar, ladder walk, rope climbs.

Recreational Activities. Barrel stave skis, box hockey, dart boards and darts, ring toss equipment, tilting spears, tire quoits, toss boards and rings, checker board and discs.

Shuffleboard. Cue sticks and discs from discarded lumber.

Soccer, Hockey, Speedball. Goal posts from discarded lumber and heavy chicken wire.

Swimming. Buoys made from rope and unsinkable wood.

Tennis, Badminton, Volleyball. Net posts made of wood or iron pipes driven into the ground; a rope used for a net; tennis backboards from discarded lumber.

Tether Ball. Paddles, poles.

Track. Starting blocks, jump standards, broad jump take-off board, indicators of broad and high jumps, pole vault standard, shot put toe circle and toe board.

Tumbling. Mats from discarded bed mattresses or secured from army surplus stores.

Imaginative teachers will add greatly to this suggested list. No physical education program need be limited because of lack of equipment or supplies. The continued growth in the number of different activities to be included in the curriculum, as well as needed materials with which to learn to do them safely and skillfully, depends solely upon each professional worker's ability to obtain or create them.

CLUB ACTIVITIES

Club activities are especially popular and valuable for teenagers. Each activity included in the physical education program can be used as a club basis. The chief values of these group gatherings are to learn new skills or perfect old ones, to make new friends; to learn more about others, a sport, or life; to be of service, and to have fun.

Types of recommended clubs include:

Archery	Hobby
Bicycling	Hosteling
Bowling	Leaders
Checker	Nature
Chess	Recreational games
Dance (square, folk, social, acro-	Riding
batic, tap, or ballet)	Rifle
First aid	Service
Fly and bait casting	Swimming
Health	Teen

Officers. All club officers should be elected, including the sponsor. Each officer should be energetic, popular, respected, and capable of positively influencing others, as well as possess the ability to delegate responsibility and work democratically with others. The sponsor should regard herself as leader behind a younger developing leader and avoid superimposing her ideas or dominating tendencies upon the group. Since all clubs are miniature democratic societies, it is here that youth can learn the vital lessons and skills necessary to perpetuate our chosen way of life.

Each club should have a written constitution containing all governing rules, the club name, purpose, membership qualifications, officers, meetings, and procedures for amendments. Meetings should be conducted according to Robert's Rules of Order. An agenda should be planned for each meeting. It should include the call to order, reading of the minutes of the last meeting, old business, new business, announcements, and adjournment. Subcommittee groups, to which as many members may be appointed as possible, will both stimulate interest and increase group identification.

The Girls' Athletic Association (G.A.A.), a Leaders' Club, or Service Club can be an invaluable help to every physical educator; each is a rich source for recruiting youngsters into the profession. A Gym Leaders Club at the Wichita Falls High School in Texas has gained the attention of many physical educators. Students of both sexes are selected for membership by their teachers. Club meetings are held during the last class period of the day, and these highly skilled students receive additional instruction in physical education activities and leadership techniques. Each serves as a student assistant in the regular physical education classes. All wear special uniforms with a leader's seal on the breast pocket. The group gives a public demonstration yearly. Since membership into this select group is sought by other students, the club has been found to be a great motivator for increasing the effort, interest, and attitude of all other students in the physical education program. Many of these selected club members later enter into the physical education profession.

SOCIAL RECREATION

The purpose of social recreation is to provide for better use of leisure time, increase social contacts, release tensions, satisfy basic needs to "belong," gain recognition, and to provide self-expression, the development of leadership, and experiences in democratic group participation.

Activities, which may be held in after school or night programs, include:

Games—Active, quiet, musical, table, cards, low organization, relays
Informal Drama—Skits, stunts, charades, guessing games, amateur nights, radio shows
Music—Community singing, mixers, guessing games, dance bands, uke clubs, orchestras
Dance—Social, folk, square, barn dances, folk festivals, social dance contests
Co-recreational Sports—Individual and team

Arts and Crafts—Paper, junk, pipe cleaners, table decorations, costume design, metal and woodcrafts, painting and sketching
Parties—Seasonal, special
Banquets—Informal, formal, suppers
Snow and Ice Sports—Skating and sleigh parties
Teas, coke and coffee hours

All social recreation should give each person pleasure and feelings of group worth or acceptance. School parties are often highlight experiences in the lives of many students. These special events should be largely student planned, conducted, and evaluated with the assistance of teacher guidance. Naturally, the students will make many mistakes while learning the necessary skills for success. The wise adult who is patient enough to let them "muddle through" experiences and learn from their mistakes is indeed a valued educator. However, many needless errors can be avoided by having students capitalize upon the following leadership techniques for conducting social recreation activities successfully:

1. Plan well in advance.
2. Assign or elect students to needed committees. Compose with each group a list of their responsibilities and the completion dates set for each one.
3. Anticipate emergencies by drawing up alternate plans. (For example, plan for sunny as well as rainy weather.)
4. First select a theme, then games, decorations, invitations, entertainment and refreshments to blend with it.
5. Draw up a check list of all needed supplies and equipment such as a record player, microphone, etc., and be sure they are ready *before* the event begins.
6. Delegate authority and give each selected person a feeling of confidence and responsibility. Have students direct the games and serve as hosts and hostesses, for it is *their* party.
7. Plan a well balanced program, spacing active and less active games properly.
8. Include numerous mixers and easy-to-do games.
9. Begin with pre-party activities which enable all to feel welcome and that a big event is about to happen.
10. Plan a climactic ending. Do not drag out the event; make it short enough to be remembered.
11. Evaluate the results and help groups capitalize upon what they have learned from their experiences.

DISCUSSION QUESTIONS

1. Draw up and discuss four objectives you would endorse for a co-recreational program.

2. Visit any local teenage center in your community. Write a short, one page paper giving your suggestions of how its program, facilities, and leadership can be improved.
3. Interview 10 of your fellow students, five of them girls, five boys, in order to learn (a) what school co-recreational activities they take part in, and (b) what activities they would like to take part in but which are not offered by the school. Summarize your findings and present them to your classmates.
4. Play any of the new games mentioned in this chapter. Evaluate the game and your experience playing it.
5. Using any of the suggested readings, plan, on paper, a teenage party for 20 of your friends.
6. Bring to class any improvised game and equipment to play it. What have you learned from this experience?

Selected Audio-Visual Aids

Horse Shoes. (10 min., sound, b & w). Teaching Films Custodians, 25 West 43rd Street, New York, N.Y. (Rental)

How to Ski. (11 min., sound, b & w). Association Films, New York, Dallas, San Francisco. (Rental)

Table Tennis. (10 min., sound, b & w). Teaching Films Custodians, 25 West 43rd Street, New York, N.Y. (Rental)

Youth Hosteling. United World Films, New York City. (Rental)

Suggested Readings

AAHPER, *Official Recreational Games and Volleyball Guide,* Division of Girls and Women's Sports, Current Edition, Washington, D.C.

DeMarche, Edythe, and DeMarche, David: *Handbook of Co-Ed Teen Activities,* New York, Association Press, 1958.

Eisenberg, Helen, and Eisenberg, Larry: *Omnibus of Fun,* New York, Association Press, 1958.

Harbin, E. O.: *Fun Encyclopedia,* Nashville, Abington-Cokesbury Press, 1934.

Hindman, Darwin: *Handbook of Active Games,* Revised Edition, New York, Prentice-Hall Book Company, Inc., 1957.

Marran, Roy: *Table Games, How to Make and Play Them,* New York, A. S. Barnes, 1939.

McKay, Daird: *Betty White's Teen Age Dance Book,* New York, Daird McKay Company, 1952.

National Recreation Association, *Clubs in the Recreation Program; Teen Age Centers,* New York, 1947.

Vannier, Maryhelen: *Methods and Materials in Recreation Leadership,* Philadelphia, W. B. Saunders Company, 1956.

Wood, Marni: *Parties on a Shoestring,* New York, George W. Stewart, 1941.

Index